Mary Slessor—Everybody's Mother

Mary Slessor—Everybody's Mother

The Era and Impact of a Victorian Missionary

Jeanette Hardage

WIPF & STOCK • Eugene, Oregon

MARY SLESSOR—EVERYBODY'S MOTHER
The Era and Impact of a Victorian Missionary

www.wipfandstock.com

ISBN 13: 978-1-55635-601-8

All Scripture quotations are from the King James Version of the Holy Bible.

Manufactured in the U.S.A.

To The Presbyterian Church of Nigeria

past—present—future

Soli Deo gloria!

Contents

Introduction

She had been dead eighty years when I met Mary Slessor. Vacationing in Canada, I picked up a three-inch by four-inch, 237-page book called *Famous Scots*. I read, "David Livingstone's is the name that immediately comes to mind when one thinks of Scots missionaries, but in bringing practical benefits to humanity he was far outstripped by Mary Slessor."[1]

As I would learn later, they have statues of her in Nigeria and her face is on a ten-pound note in Scotland. Why hadn't I heard of her? The first biography about her was written the year she died, and many others followed. Legend sometimes replaces reality in the telling of a life story, and that appeared to be the case in some stories told about this remarkable woman and continues to this day.

I read everything I could find by and about Mary Slessor. I accumulated books, documents, papers, articles, and letters in Scotland. Those I met in Calabar repeated stories passed down through the years in Nigeria. My search took me on alluring sidetracks. I learned about slavery and malaria, about hippos and termites, about Nigeria and the British Empire and colonization. I met fascinating people, in person and in the materials I read.

Many events known about Slessor can be verified:

- She went where few Europeans went, sometimes over the objection of fellow missionaries and her mission board.
- She was criticized when she climbed trees, marched barefoot and bareheaded through the forest, ignored pleas to filter drinking water, shed her Victorian petticoats, and cut her hair short.
- The British government appointed her a magistrate, the first woman to hold that position, because of her understanding of and rapport with tribal peoples, and later honored her by nam-

1. Shaw, *Famous Scots*, 198–99.

ing her an Honorary Associate of the Order of the Hospital of St. John of Jerusalem.

- Her name appears on a plaque at Millennium Park in Calabar, Nigeria, where she is one of one hundred honorees of the last millennium in Cross River State.

But there was more to this woman than eccentricities and exploits, more than audacity in remote areas of Nigeria contrasted with dread and timidity in public meetings in Scotland. She could be obstinate and headstrong. Fellow missionaries sometimes felt her biting criticism. Some British officials found her hard to work with. Nigerians in trouble with the law felt her censure.

I was drawn to Mary Slessor because of her faith, her certainty that she was where God wanted her to be, her desire to go and teach and be a witness of the good news a people had not yet heard. Her love for the people among whom she lived and for her adopted children appealed to me.

I determined to write a biography that showed Slessor's interaction with the people, one that showed her relationship with colonizers, traders, and Nigerians; one that included information gleaned from her own writings and those who knew her; one in which dialogue was not invented, in which unwarranted assumptions were not made, and where documentation would back up the writing. Here, then, is *Mary Slessor—Everybody's Mother.*

—Jeanette Hardage
Charleston, South Carolina
February 2008

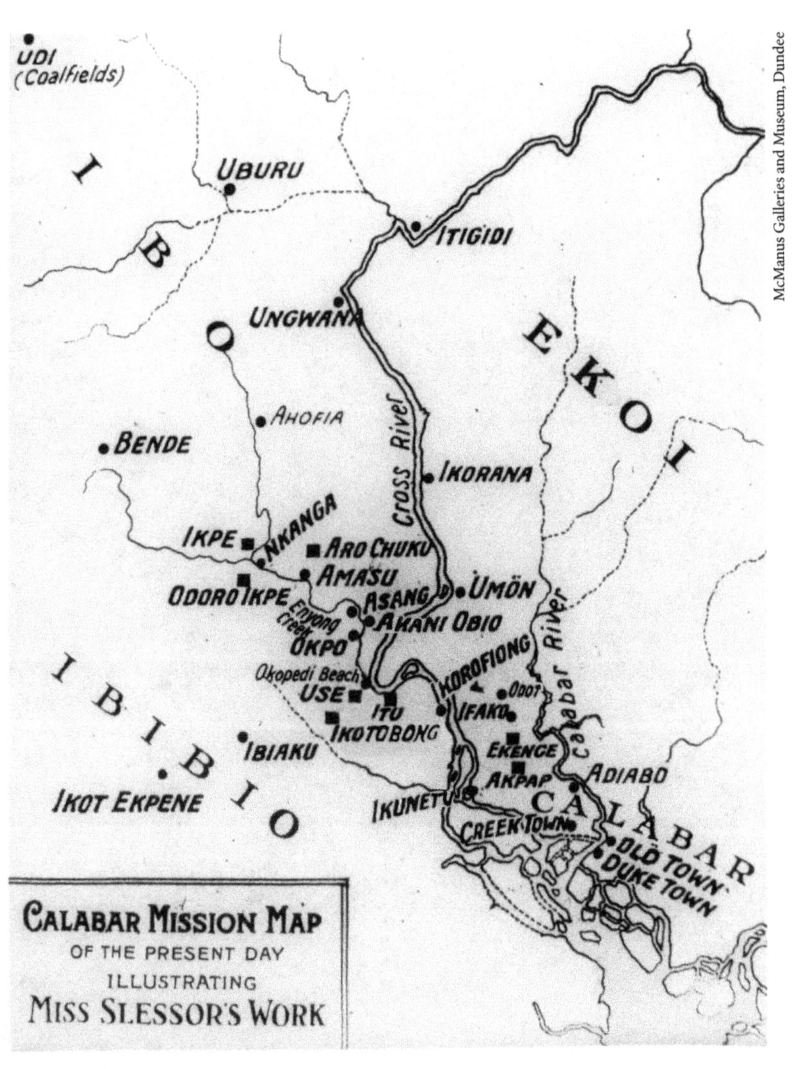

Calabar Mission map (1915)

Prologue

IN 1841, HOPE MASTERTON Waddell, an Irish clergyman serving in Jamaica with the Scottish Presbyterians, received a copy of T. Fowell Buxton's book, *The Slave Trade and Its Remedy*. The author insisted that God would inspire some from the West Indies to return to their African homeland with the gospel of Jesus Christ. The Scottish Mission had a strong ministry among former slaves in Jamaica. Waddell, his colleagues and Jamaican congregations were already praying about the need for a work in Africa when Buxton's book arrived. It confirmed their sense of urgency.

When the Jamaica Mission Presbytery sought permission from the Missionary Society in Edinburgh to establish a work in Africa, their request was denied. The committee declared the plan "premature, displaying more zeal than judgment" and "highly presumptuous" in view of earlier disastrous trailblazing efforts.[1] They knew the tales of expeditions where many or all of the parties died. They worried about hostile encounters. They feared missionaries could not survive the tropical climate, thought to be a major cause of disease and death. Even Charles Dickens echoed a belief that "religion should spread slowly and temperately." He wrote about the Niger Expedition of 1841, "The useful lives of scholars, students, mariners and officers—more precious than a wilderness of Africans—were thrown away!"[2]

After lengthy delays and with invitations in hand from "King Eyamba and the chiefs of Old Calabar,"[3] opposition in Scotland faded. Enthusiasm grew for the mission among church leaders and their congregations. Robert Jamieson of Liverpool loaned his 150-ton brigantine *Warree* "for so long as it shall be required" plus a hundred pounds per year toward

1. Christie, "Annals," September 14, 1841; McFarlan, *Calabar*, 9.

2. Powers, "Converting a Savage Mind" (Dickens, 56).

3. Christie, "Annals," January 19, 1843. The name Old Calabar was officially changed to Calabar, August 12, 1904.

sailing expenses.[4] The Missionary Society sent its emissaries out with their blessing:

> The *Warree* . . . is wholly a Mission Ship . . . rigged, painted, provisioned, and manned for the noblest ends. It conveys the servants of Christ, bent on deeds of mercy and love. . . . It is freighted with the blessings of a full salvation. . . . Go, little bark, on thy peaceful and noble errand . . . and may the children of Africa not merely welcome thy approach, but commemorate through succeeding generations the day of thy arrival, as the season when the jubilee trumpet was sounded on their shores, proclaiming the reign of Satan at an end, and the freedom of the Sons of God to all their sable tribes.[5]

Waddell and five others arrived in Calabar, on the Cross River delta of Africa's west coast, in April 1846. The party included Waddell, Mr. & Mrs. Samuel Edgerley, Jamaicans Andrew Chisholm and Edward Miller, and George Waddell, a rescued slave boy. The determined group set up mission stations at the settlements of Duke Town and Creek Town almost immediately and began to preach and to teach reading. They were the vanguard of many who followed for the next century. Among those who soon joined the mission were Waddell's wife, Jessie; Hugh and Jane Goldie; and William and Louisa Anderson. All came to Calabar from mission service in Jamaica.

Hope Waddell is recognized as the founder of the Calabar Mission. He was adept at garnering support for the mission and often acted as spokesman to Presbyterians in Scotland. After seventeen years in Jamaica, he remained another twelve in Calabar. Although he looked forward to expansion of the mission, as evidenced by more than a dozen visits with colleagues to other villages along the Cross River and elsewhere, he is described as being cautious and austere. He wanted to have a firm base before proceeding too far or fast. He tended to be domineering with colleagues and sometimes sent hostile letters to them.[6] He was, however, an excellent observer, who faithfully recorded each day's events and sights.

4. Ibid., May 7, 1845.

5. *Record*, 1846, 9. Secession and Relief churches joined as United Presbyterian Church in 1847; United Presbyterian and Free Church of Scotland became United Free Church in 1900. Each published magazines that included the wording *Missionary Record*.

6. Ajayi, *Christian Missions*, 279; E. U. Aye, "Foundations," 7; Johnston, *Maxim Guns*, 15; Nair, *Politics and Society*, 59; Waddell, "Journal," Letters to William Anderson, 10–15.

He bartered with Efik traders, dealt with British merchants and government representatives, and deliberated with kings and chiefs.[7] King Eyo VII wrote to Waddell after his retirement: "We of Creek Town are still having much interest in you as the one that had been first sent to open the way for the rest to walk thereby. . . . May we all meet in Heaven to part no more from each other."[8]

Hugh Goldie is remembered not only for many years of ministry at Creek Town but also as a scholar. Besides his New Testament and catechism translations, he produced a two-volume dictionary, an Efik grammar, many hymns, and a history of the mission's first forty years. William Anderson was the fighter of the mission, at least in his early service in Calabar. He often disagreed with fellow missionaries and with chiefs during his many years as pastor at Duke Town, though he mellowed with age.[9]

All three of these pioneers died in 1895. Waddell had retired to Ireland in 1858 for health reasons. Mary Slessor would have occasion to work with both Goldie and Anderson for nearly twenty years of her own missionary service.

Eyo Honesty II, king of Creek Town, was one of the most important men during the foundation era of the mission. Mission historian Geoffrey Johnston describes Eyo as "a typical Victorian businessman—honest, shrewd, and industrious."[10] Historian Kannan K. Nair states that the motive for Calabar's kings to invite missionaries was "the hope that they would in some way strengthen their respective economies," primarily because of the social changes caused by the change from slave trade to a palm oil economy.[11] Eyo did not become a Christian, but he did aid the mission's endeavors. He invited missionaries to hold meetings in his yard and translated at their preaching services. He provided canoes and often escorted missionaries on trips to other communities. Nair declares, though, that Eyo sanctioned reforms only in instances where tradition was already changing.[12].

7. See Nair, *Politics and Society*, Chapter 1, for a thorough discussion of Calabar society, including kings and lineage, the house system and Ekpe.

8. Goldie, *Memoir*, 36.

9. Buchan, *Expendable Mary Slessor*, 52; Johnston, *Maxim Guns*, 16.

10. Johnston, ibid., 14–15; See also Aye, *Efik People*, 165.

11. Nair, *Politics and Society*, 36, 85.

12. Ibid., 59.

The missionaries continued the work—preaching, education, translation and basic medical assistance—among the Efik people. They added outstations from time to time and made occasional exploratory visits and contacts in more distant places. By the 1860s some of the work was undertaken by Efik converts. The number of mission stations remained small for years, not only because of staff shortages, illnesses, furloughs and deaths but also because missionaries were sometimes not welcomed in other villages. By 1856, ten years after the founding of the mission, there were two dozen staff members at Calabar. They included ordained missionaries; teachers and evangelists; industrial missionaries (printers and carpenters); women missionaries; wives of missionaries; and "assistants and domestics," both Jamaicans and Scots.[13] Their number had shrunk to a dozen by the time of Mary Slessor's arrival in 1876, but nearly doubled by 1900 and stood at more than fifty by the time of Slessor's death in 1915.

SOCIETY IN CALABAR

When the missionaries arrived in Calabar, they came with the great commission of Jesus on their minds—go into all the world and preach the gospel. But they also came with preconceived ideas about the status of society in Calabar. They held prevalent Victorian views: They considered Africa a "dark continent," partly because it was a great unknown to Western Europeans, but also because Christianity had not reached it. They believed Africans were not only unchristian but were uncivilized heathen who were unable to govern themselves. They decried unacceptable cultural practices, the most notable of which were human sacrifice, twin murder, and trial by ordeal.

There were many more Ibibio in the Calabar area than Efik,[14] as well as a number of other tribes who did not speak Efik,[15] but the first missionary (and British trader) contacts were with the Efik community. They were the middlemen between the coast and inland markets. They spoke some Pidgin English, the trade language of the time, and had done so for years.[16] With their domination of the area's commerce and politics, Efik

13. Christie, "Roll of Missionaries" in "Annals."

14. Essien, *Grammar*, x–xi.

15. Goldie, in *Conference of West African*, 5–7.

16. Aye, *Old Calabar*, 108; Forde, *Efik Traders*, ix–x, 79.

became "the *lingua franca* of the lower Cross River area."[17] Thus, Efik was the first language selected for translation by the missionaries.

In Efik-speaking and neighboring communities, two powerful systems exercised authority: the "house" (*ufok*), and a secret society, Ekpe.[18] The *ufok* represented a patriarchal system that adapted to meet changing economic and social conditions.[19] Composed of a group of related families, it dealt mainly with lineage and property, while the powerful Ekpe made and enforced laws governing the social, political, and religious life of the people. Waddell wrote, "The towns of Calabar, are, in fact, a number of small republics, each with its own chief and council, united only by the Egbo confraternity."[20]

When writers refer to kings and chiefs, they have in mind the leaders of various houses,[21] though such leaders were also in positions of authority within Ekpe. An *ufok* included everything a chief owned—not only land and personal property but also family, servants and slaves, and some who simply chose to align themselves with a particular house leader. Lineage determined leadership to a large extent, but the chiefs and village councils of a house selected an individual as their king by vote. Chosen rulers tended to be among the wealthiest members of the community.

Ekpe was originally for religious purposes,[22] but like the house system, it changed to meet other needs, especially as Europeans became an increasing force to be reckoned with. Hope Waddell wrote, "The want of a bond of union among the different families, and of supreme authority to enforce peace and order between equals and rivals, became apparent, and the Egbo institution was adopted."[23] Every free male[24] became a member of the fraternity, paying an initiation fee. Each grade within the organiza-

17. Ibid., 3.

18. The society was called *Ekpo* in the Ibibio language, *Ekpe* in Efik, and written *Egbo* by Europeans.

19. Aye, *Efik People*, 86.

20. Dike, *Trade and Politics*, 33; Nair, *Politics and Society*, calls them a "conglomeration of loosely-knit towns," 6.

21. See Oku, *Kings & Chiefs* for biographies and genealogical charts.

22 Aye, *Efik People*, 70.

23. Waddell, *Twenty-nine Years*, 313.

24. European traders and slaves could sometimes purchase membership. Some historians say membership was open to women, but eligibility seems to have varied with different years and localities.

tion[25] had its duties. Entrance fees escalated with each succeeding grade and were distributed to those in higher grades.

Each village had a clearing for community gatherings. Here Ekpe staged colorful ceremonial masquerades, with dancing, plays and beating of drums. But "Egbo runners," enforcers of Ekpe laws, were feared when they ran through villages with whips, assaulting those who had the audacity to remain outside of their homes. Hugh Goldie wrote, concluding that Ekpe was given "all scope . . . for the oppression of the weak."

> Ekpe, the native [Efik] name for a leopard . . . is represented to be a supernatural being that inhabits the forest, and is brought into the town only on great occasions, concealed in a small tent borne along to suit his progress. . . . His voice is heard . . . resembling the growl of an angry animal; on hearing which the town is hushed, the street door of every house is shut, and all business is suspended while he remains. Though himself never seen, he has his *idems* or representatives, who mask themselves in fantastic dresses, a bell being hung at the back of those of the higher grades, who run about the town armed with formidable whips, which they lay mercilessly on the back of any one out of doors. . . . A grand display is, however sometimes made as part of the funeral rites of a great man, or on some other special occasion, to which all are free to witness. . . . It is a capital crime for any one not initiated to look upon any secret observance, or take part in any ceremony. Mr. Waddell mentions the case of a young man who intruded on the mysteries at Creek Town. . . . He was denounced by his own father . . . [and] was captured and publicly executed.[26]

Ekpe could arrest, fine or execute those judged guilty of wrongdoing. Boycott of an offending person or group (called "blowing Egbo") was another punishment imposed by the group. This action prevented trade or other contacts with the offender. In fact, it was used at times against the Calabar Mission during its early years, when chiefs were incensed at the harboring of slaves or rescue of twins.

Missionaries put pressure on both Africans and British officials to change or eliminate some cultural practices and excesses of Ekpe, especially the seeming disregard for the sanctity of human life. However, they

25. The number of grades named varies from five to twenty-three. See Aye, *Efik People*, 81; Ema, "The Ekpe Society," 314; Forde, *Efik Traders*, 137–38; Nair, *Politics and Society*, 16; Offiong, "Functions," 80.

26. Goldie, *Calabar*, 30–34.

often failed to recognize that there was some value in the systems that were already in place and that had governed the indigenous society for many years. Nair states, "Because they were horrified by some cruel customs, [they] tended to condemn everything."[27]

A modern Nigerian writer states, "Despite the fact that women and male non-members know quite well that the masquerades are not ancestral spirits, Ekpo [Ekpe] members, even to this day [1984] still want people to believe that they are." He says that despite attempts of the colonial administration to eliminate Ekpe/Ekpo, it continues to exert its influence in modern Nigeria.[28]

Charles Partridge, a District Commissioner during Mary Slessor's era, believed that secret societies were an outgrowth of change. "They play an important part in the progress of civilisation," he wrote, "but, in course of time, their power tends to become tyrannical and antagonistic to progress." He expressed the hope that someone would one day explain the organization completely.[29] Explanations continue to be varied and at times confusing. Missionary letters and reports detailed encounters with Calabar's kings, chiefs and Ekpe for years.

An Infamous Trade

Thousands of slaves were exported from Calabar. Britain encouraged and participated in that infamous period of history, as did France, Portugal, Holland, and independent traders from America, the West Indies, and elsewhere. James I issued the first royal charter to establish slave trading in Africa in 1618. Charles I did the same in 1631. In 1662 a new company was formed, headed by the Duke of York. That charter stipulated that the company would supply 3,000 slaves annually to Jamaica.[30] With the development of the Americas, more and more workers were required to meet the needs of expanding markets. Sugar, gold, coffee, rice, and cotton were important products shipped from the new to the old world. Estimates are that a half-million slaves were shipped to the United States, as many as ten million to all the Americas. Brazil imported more than four million,

27. Nair, *Politics and Society*, 69.
28. Offiong, "Functions," 87.
29. Partridge, *Cross River*, 35.
30. Hutchinson, *Impressions*, 33.

and the West Indies, two million.[31] At least thirty percent of the total were shipped from the Gulf of Guinea—the Bights of Benin and Biafra.[32]

Slavery was nothing new in the land that is now Nigeria. European slave-traders simply created (or expanded) a market, and Africans met the market demand. When the slave trade was abolished, it did not mark the end of slavery in Africa. Palm oil became the top export, and slaves became a surplus commodity. Waddell wrote in 1847 that slavery seemed to be "normal" in West Africa. He contrasted it with the slavery that resulted from the slave trade, when campaigns tracked down people to sell and send across the sea. For domestic slaves in Calabar, "Absolute authority on the one part, entire subjection on the other, is the theory; but in practice both the authority and subjection are checked and limited in many ways." He did not approve of slavery but disclosed the frequent family-like relationships that existed in Calabar between slaves and their masters. The Efik had no word for "master" or "mistress," so "the sweet and precious names, father and mother, alone are used to express the relation," he wrote.[33] That does not mean that to be a slave was desirable. The powerful secret Ekpe organization managed to keep slaves in subjection. Sometimes masters inflicted punishments such as flogging, chaining, drowning, or death (especially when a man of importance died).[34] One punishment was to free an unwanted slave, which left him incapable of protecting or providing for himself. Waddell listed the ways in which a person could become enslaved:

> *First*, [free men may become slaves] by selling themselves, either in time of famine, or for protection, or to better their circumstances; as a rich, head slave may be better off than a poor despised freeman. . . .
>
> *Second*, Men may be sold for debt. . . . Egbo [Ekpe] is powerful in enforcing such claims. . . .
>
> *Third*, Men may be sold as prisoners of war, or as criminals. . . . It is a matter of choice whether to kill them or sell them. . . .[35]

31. Klein, *Atlantic Slave*, 208–11.

32. The Bight of Biafra is also known as Bight of Bonny since 1970.

33. Waddell, *Twenty-nine Years*, 315.

34. Aye, *Old Calabar*, 96; Ayandele, *Missionary Impact*, 83; Waddell, *Twenty-Nine Years*, 320.

35. Waddell, ibid., 316.

Domestic slavery existed well beyond Mary Slessor's years of service.

Victorian Dundee

The beautiful city of Dundee, fourth largest in Scotland, bears little resemblance today to the Dundee of the Victorian era. It was then a part of the Scottish wellspring for much missionary effort that arose from the evangelical movement.

A typical city of the Industrial Revolution, it grew at such a pace during the nineteenth century that proper housing and sanitation could not be provided. Wealth increased, but so did poverty. Although the city was a leading whaling port, it was the proliferation of textile mills—especially after the introduction of jute—and the need for workers that drew immigrants in droves.

As in other industrial cities in the mid-nineteenth century, Dundee's factories spewed smoke, and slum living was the norm for many people. Workers spent long hours in mills, and women and children formed a large part of the work force. Unemployment for men was extremely high because working women and children received lower pay.[36] Alcoholism became a severe social problem, even among women.

Some historians compare Victorian Dundee to Charles Dickens' depressing, mythical Coketown.[37] The population of the city doubled to over 90,00 between 1841 and 1861 (the Slessor family was among the newcomers), but fewer than six hundred new houses were built.[38] By 1871, another 30,000 people had moved into the overcrowded city. Some mill owners built a few tenements for their employees. Baxter's,[39] where Mary Slessor worked, was among them. They built a tenement block of two- or three-room dwellings in the 1860s for eighty families, an improvement over some "houses" being built in the city that were said to be just ten feet square.[40]

36. Dundee was known as a woman's city. See N. Watson, "Emerging from Obscurity," 199–213.

37. Whatley, *Remaking of Juteopolis*, 12.

38. Whatley, *Life and Times*, 103, 106.

39. Baxter's produced linen, canvas, tarpaulins, and gun covers to meet the needs of the Crimean War and the American Civil War. They were the largest firm in town in 1864, with 4,000 workers. See Cooke, ed. *Baxter's of Dundee*, 55.

40. Wilkinson, "Housing and Health," 55.

Tenements clustered around the mills. The majority of people survived in one- and two-room dwellings with no running water or toilets. Disease and crime flourished. Because of the high incidence of alcoholism, concerned Dundee citizens reacted by forming temperance societies and temperance hotels, but even long after Mary Slessor's working days in Dundee "Winston Churchill, who represented Dundee from 1908–1922, dubbed it the most drunken city in the British Empire."[41] Dundee's citizens eventually organized the Prohibition Party, and one of their own became the only Prohibitionist ever elected to Parliament.[42]

Life in Dundee, as in other growing industrialized cities, was hard enough for adults working twelve to fourteen hours a day. For children, conditions would be unthinkable today. By 1844, all the mills worked children on a half-time system, after laws were enacted to limit child labor. Children (including Mary Slessor fifteen years later) worked six hours and attended school six hours while they were half-timers. At age thirteen or fourteen they went to full-time work and could attend school at night. Few of those who worked twelve-hour days, however, had the incentive to spend the evening at school. Since families often depended on the earnings of their children to keep them above the starvation level, there was a thriving business in falsified birth certificates, especially after 1872, with enactment of stricter laws regarding the employment of children.[43] Factories were required to provide basic education by Mary Slessor's time. In 1858, a year before her employment, Baxter's opened a new school with "washing up facilities" that boasted hot and cold water, and even combs and mirrors.[44] Some people insisted that children were better off working in the mills than they were at home, where conditions could be worse.

Hunger was common among the poor of Dundee. A poem by Robert Mullen of Dundee published in 1849 bears witness to the problem of hunger, as well as to the resistance of some in society to sending missionaries to foreign lands. A portion of it follows:

41. Ogilvy, "Most Drunken City," in *Scotsman*, 2000.

42. Peterkin, "Spirits Above and Spirits Below," 181.

43. Lenman. *Dundee*, 59.

44. Blackburn, "Baxter's Half-Time," 65.

STARVED TO DEATH

"The Jury returned a verdict of—'Death from Starvation.'"
"Starved to death!" "Starved to death!"
Think on it, Christian women and men;
This is no idle sentence I pen;
'Twas the verdict of "twelve good men and true"
On the corpse of one whom gaunt hunger slew;
Who sank beneath want's pitiless wave,
With none to help her—no hand to save;
This is the epitaph over her grave—
"Starved to death!"
. . . .
"Starved to death!" "Starved to death!"
Think on it, Christians! think, is it right,
While want and darkness around we slight,
To spend so much money, and toil, and thought,
That the savage afar may be fed and taught?
Let's look at home, and do all we can
To help our struggling, weak fellow man,
That no more those fearful words we may scan—
"Starved to death!"[45]

The Slessor family was one of many that struggled with hunger, as Mary herself would do years later in Africa.

45. Mullen, in *Poems by the People*, 5–6.

PART ONE

Preparing and Going

1848–1879

1

Early Influences

> I have a note from Miss Crawford asking me to send you the exact date of my birth: that's rather a large order isn't it! To a gentleman I do not have the honour of knowing personally either. But as I am settled in a large family, having 13 of my own rearing in hand, I need not blush, need I? Well, I don't know whether I was born in 1848 or 49, & the old Family Bible is given away, & the "Act & Testimony" in which also our births were registered was eaten by the ants here [*in Africa*] years ago, so I don't know when I can get it. But it was the 2nd day of December of one of those years, that had the doubtful honour of my entrance into this world.
>
> —Mary Slessor, 1901[1]

SHOEMAKER ROBERT SLESSOR AND teenaged weaver Mary Mitchell, both born in Aberdeen, Scotland, were married there on May 16, 1840. Their daughter Mary is listed as second of seven children by other biographers, though two of the children's names are not known, and birth and death records are scanty. Mary Mitchell Slessor was born December 2, 1848 at her maternal grandmother's house in Gilcomston, a suburb of Aberdeen.

Mary's brother, Robert, was born in Aberdeen two years later, then sister Susan in 1855. John and Jane were born in Dundee, John in 1857 and Jane in 1862.[2] No available records mention the other two Slessor children, who probably died in infancy.

1. Mary Slessor [MS] to Stevenson, GD/X260/1, December 16, 1901.

2. Mary's first brother's name was William Robert. There is no mention in other biographies of her having a brother named William, but he is listed as William both in the Dundee census of 1861 and on his death certificate. I will refer to him as Robert, the name he was obviously called at home. Susan Slessor was born March 3, 1855; John

Mrs. Slessor took her children to services at Belmont Street United Presbyterian Church in Aberdeen. She, like hundreds of other Scottish Presbyterians, eagerly read each issue of *The Missionary Record.* Churches circulated the monthly magazine to inform members of mission comings and goings, progress, problems and needs. The chronicled exploits of David Livingstone, as well as stories of those serving in Calabar and elsewhere, enthralled Mrs. Slessor. She communicated her enthusiasm to her young children, telling them missionary stories.

The mission work at Calabar became a part of Mary's earliest memories. She often played "church" and "missionaries" with her siblings. With a fiery temper to match her red hair—Mary wrote years later about her brothers and sisters calling her "Carrots" and "Fire"—she was upset when Robert insisted that women couldn't be preachers or missionaries. She didn't intend to let him have all the glory she imagined went with being a missionary. When he relented and told her he would take her with him into the pulpit, Mary was satisfied.

Mary's childhood had a dark side. The skeleton in the closet was her father. Mrs. Slessor tried to keep her husband's drinking and its dismal results hidden from those around them. He lost his job in Aberdeen in 1857 because of his increasing dependence on alcohol, and the family moved to Dundee. They hoped Mr. Slessor could get a fresh start and that the family's financial situation would improve. He worked briefly at his old occupation as a shoemaker, then in one of the city's textile mills. Soon, though, he joined the ranks of the many unemployed men in Dundee and reverted to his old lifestyle. His alcoholism, which one biographer attempts to blame on Mrs. Slessor,[3] played its part in molding Mary's character.

W. P. Livingstone, Mary Slessor's first biographer wrote: "She was usually reticent regarding her father, but once she wrote and published under her own name what is known to be the story of this painful period of her girlhood. There is no need to reproduce it."[4]

Later biographers would wish he had reproduced this manuscript. It is nowhere to be found today, as Livingstone's papers were destroyed during World War II. His biography first appeared the year Mary Slessor

Paterson Slessor, November 18, 1857; Jane Ann Slessor, February 24, 1862.

3. Young-O'Brian, *She Had a Magic*, 16–18. Neither Mary's writings nor any others support this portrayal of Mrs. Slessor as a puritanical nag.

4. Livingstone, *Mary Slessor*, 6.

died and went through many reprints. It presents many details of her life that are not available elsewhere. Mary's report apparently expressed the dread that came with a father who arrived home drunk late on Saturday nights and threw food saved for him into the fire. She told of being locked out at night in tears and waiting until her mother could let her sneak back inside. She told of the embarrassment of often carrying a parcel to the pawnbroker for enough funds for the week's needs, then rushing off to pay the most urgent bills. All the while, she and her mother tried to keep the facts hidden from the family's younger children, the neighbors and, more especially, church members.

Mrs. Slessor, already a skilled weaver, began work in one of the mills to help support the family. Mary went to work in the mill, too, probably before she was eleven. Dundee's 1861 census shows Mary working as a power loom weaver at age twelve, her brother Robert employed as a power loom worker at age ten. Both children were listed as "partly at school," and both contributed to family sustenance.[5]

The conversion of the young "wild lassie," as she called herself later in life, came through the frightening counsel of an old widow who lived nearby. She invited several girls into her warm room from their play. Once they were inside, she began to tell them of their need for a savior. With her strong Calvinist beliefs, she compared the fire in her hearth to the horrors of hell. Their souls would burn in hellfire "for ever and ever" if they did not repent, she told them.[6] Mary was appalled. She decided that "repent and believe" was her only option, and once she made that decision she never looked back. Hellfire-and-damnation was never a part of her own mode of operation. In her years of ministry she emphasized a loving God and freedom from fear to a people who already had too many fears.

When she was eighteen Mrs. Slessor took Mary and John (nine years younger) to hear Calabar missionary William Anderson speak in Dundee. She hoped that one of her sons would go as a missionary to Calabar, but Robert died of tuberculosis in 1870. (Mr. Slessor also died a few months later.) That left only thirteen-year-old John as a possible missionary candidate, but John, too, developed tuberculosis—one of the diseases that plagued slums everywhere. Advisors thought a warmer climate might

5. Both Mary and her mother worked as linen power-loom weavers in Baxter's Lower Dens factory, an occupation a step up socially from some other jobs. To be a weaver was more desirable than to be a "mill girl."

6. Livingstone, *Mary Slessor*, 3.

help. He emigrated to New Zealand in 1873 but died a week after arriving there, leaving behind only Mary, her mother and two younger sisters.[7]

EDUCATION AND WORK

In 1550, Scotland's Protestant reformers produced their *Book of Discipline*, which served as a guide for three centuries. Parishes were admonished to provide education. "Elementary schooling for all, girls and boys alike, was the means to salvation: no longer to be gained through the intercession of priests or saints, but by a justification of faith achieved by an individual and personal reading of the Scriptures."[8]

Government became involved in education in the 1800s, partly at the behest of church leaders requesting financial aid. The Argyll Commission and others made enquiries and wrote reports, but the major changes came with Scotland's Education Act of 1872. It outlined strict regulations and required annual inspections of schools, but this came after Mary Slessor's school days.

It is possible that Mary obtained some schooling at Belmont Street United Presbyterian Church in Aberdeen in her early childhood. As a half-timer at Baxter's Lower Dens Factory in Dundee, Mary attended Baxter's new school after work: six hours a day for two or three years. When she went to work full-time at age fourteen, she attended evening school, where she continued to study the required subjects: reading, writing, arithmetic, Bible and Scottish history. Her teens and twenties show an intermingling of education with work and the church. More and more, she began to read independently, often under the direction and encouragement of an older church friend, but she also enjoyed the popular fiction of the day.[9] Widespread stories tell of Mary following the lead of David Livingstone by propping a book on her loom at work and snatching moments to read surrounded by the clamor of the factory's machines. She was also known to read while walking to and from work at the mill. It is obvious, from "lessons" she wrote, that she depended on the Bible as a textbook and for devotional study.

7. Ibid., 13.

8. Withrington, *Going to School*, 7.

9. Slessor referred to (and sometimes critiqued) novels in later correspondence.

When Mary read Philip Doddridge's *The Rise and Progress of Religion in the Soul*, she was dismayed.[10] She complained to a friend that she couldn't meditate, "and Doddridge says it is necessary for the soul." Her friend advised her not to worry about her wandering mind but to "Go and work, for that's what God means us to do."[11]

When someone gave her *Sartor Resartus*, though, she stayed up all night reading. She, like many Victorians, appreciated Thomas Carlyle's best-selling portrayal of his moral and spiritual crisis and his admonition, "Love not Pleasure; love God."[12]

CHRISTIAN COMMITMENT

Besides work and reading, Mary Slessor's life was filled with church meetings—worship, Sunday school, youth work and prayer meetings. The family (except for Mr. Slessor) attended Wishart Church, in the Cowgate district of Dundee. The area was one of tenements and slums. The church met in the upstairs of a large brick building. John O' Groats pub and other shops were downstairs.[13] Mary wrote to a friend in later years of being washed with Brown Windsor soap before church, having a drop of Bergamot perfume on gloves and handkerchiefs, "and each [child] a peppermint for the sermon time, when mother had babies and could not be there to give us the lozenge herself."[14] Shortly before she died, she wrote, "We would as soon have thought of going to the moon as of being absent from a service. And we throve very well on it too. How often, when lying awake at night, my time for thinking, do I go back to those wonderful days!"[15]

As a teenager, Mary volunteered to teach children when the church began a mission work around the corner. "I had the impudence of ignorance then in special degree surely," she admitted years later.[16] She also

10. Doddridge was a stern Calvinist minister of the eighteenth century, whose works were translated and greatly admired in Scotland.

11. Livingstone, *Mary Slessor*, 11.

12. Ibid., 12. See also Robertson, "Carlyle."

13. Wishart Church and John O'Groats pub (also known as "Heaven and Hell") can be viewed at http://tinyurl.com/2fg7k2.

14. MS to Mrs. Jaime, August 24, 1912.

15. Livingstone, *Mary Slessor*, 8.

16. Ibid., 7.

began to distribute the YMCA paper, *Monthly Visitor*.[17] (It is difficult to imagine how she added this project, which required house-to-house visitation. Her hours were already filled with work, study and church.) At the mission she was first confronted by the bullying of young ruffians. Boys who had nothing to do and no supervision took delight in harassing those who worked at the mission, as well as those who attended the meetings. Rude taunts were easier to ignore than the mudslinging that often accompanied them. Sometimes unemployed men joined in the torment, too. Mission workers were admonished to travel in pairs for their own safety. Mary didn't always abide by that advice. She learned to dodge trouble, just as she had learned to dodge her father when he was drunk, but she also wasn't afraid to stand up to the gangs. Growing up in their midst and with an alcoholic father, she learned to be tough and resourceful.

A story Mary often told, after years as a missionary, was of her encounter with a gang of boys whose leader had a lead weight tied to a cord. As he began to threaten her, swinging the weight around his head, she carefully removed her new hat (decorated with cherries) and stood facing him. He swung the weight closer and closer to her head until it nearly grazed her forehead. Finally, the boy threw the weight down and declared, "She's game, boys!" whereupon the group sheepishly followed her in to a prayer meeting.[18] One frame of the memorial stained glass windows erected in her honor depicts this episode. The leader of the gang sent Mary a picture of himself and his family when she lived in Africa. He told her that day was a turning point in his life.

Another tough youth cracked a whip at those coming to meetings. Mary confronted him one day, saying, "If we changed places what would happen?" When he said he would get the whip across his back, she proposed a deal: "I'll bear it for you if you'll go in." The astonished boy deserted his whip and followed her. He also decided to become a follower of Jesus.[19]

Mary's mission work and her commitment to the gospel continued to bear fruit. She cajoled youths and kidded with them and preached to

17. The *Monthly Visitor* was published as an evangelistic tool by the YMCA. By the time Mary Slessor left for Calabar, it had a circulation of more than a quarter million with some 500 distributors.

18. *Record*, 1913, 372.

19. Livingstone, *Mary Slessor*, 10.

them. Her sense of humor, her honesty and her down-to-earth temperament attracted them.

Minister James Logie, under the auspices of Victoria Street United Presbyterian Church, opened another mission for the young people of Dundee. By this time, Mary was in her early twenties and no longer attending school. She offered to help with meetings. Logie soon came to appreciate her devotion and her influence. He saw that those from the slums confided in her in a way they would not do to those of a so-called higher class. She had earned their respect; she was one of them. She knew the hardships they faced: the hand-to-mouth existence, poor housing, hunger, problems at home and at work (when there was work) and sometimes despair.

Logie became Mary's mentor. He and his wife introduced the shy but tough, petite redhead to the niceties of Victorian society in their own home. Even though the minister's home was not luxurious, its possessions and the social conduct there differed from what Mary was accustomed to in the slums. She learned how to behave "in polite society." Once, when she and her sister Susan were cleaning one of the mission rooms, an elder suggested they shouldn't be doing a charwoman's job. The famous temper surfaced again, and Mary snapped back that *they* were not ladies.[20] Victorian class-consciousness extended to all levels of society.

Mary not only taught the youths on Sunday, she took them on Saturday country hikes and picnics. She hiked up her skirts, ran races with them, and climbed trees. This unacceptable behavior drew criticism from stern church elders. They complained to Logie. When he suggested that Mary be more discreet, biographer James Buchan reports that "[Logie's] normally respectful assistant flared up and told him what she thought of elderly hypocrites."[21]

When Logie asked Mary to read aloud a paper she wrote for a church discussion group, she refused. Her reason? She feared they would laugh at her "rough accent."[22] As Slessor's popularity grew, church groups in other parts of Dundee asked her to address meetings. At first, she balked. She was too shy to consider such audacity. Finally convinced it was her duty, she began to fulfill requests. She insisted that she speak seated in the

20. Buchan, *Expendable Mary Slessor*, 16, 20.

21. Ibid., 18.

22. Ibid., 21.

center of such groups, would not go up on the platform, and sometimes asked men in the audience to hide themselves behind a pillar or leave the meeting.[23] Her talks and papers always included a plea for commitment to Jesus Christ.

DAVID LIVINGSTONE AND MISSION

In 1874 the world received news of the death of David Livingstone, Scotland's famous missionary-explorer of Africa. Newspapers were full of the story of his life and of the remarkable undertaking of two native men carrying his body hundreds of miles across Africa so that it could be returned to England. Full honors were accorded Livingstone, with burial in Westminster Abbey. A wave of missionary enthusiasm swept through Scotland. For Mary Slessor, now twenty-five years old, it was the final prod she needed to fully consider missionary service herself. Her brothers were gone. The family had moved to better living quarters.[24] Both Susan and Janie were working. Her mother consented without hesitation when Mary suggested she apply to go to Calabar. James Logie and a few other church friends encouraged her, too.[25]

Mary applied to go to Calabar in May 1875, though she agreed to go where she was most needed. Most single women missionaries were the educated daughters of churchmen or other professional men. Mary didn't fit the mold. Nevertheless, the Foreign Mission Board[26] was impressed by her character references and reports of her Christian activities.

Most folks were aware of some version of the ditty, "Beware, beware of the Bight of Benin. There's few come out, though many go in." Some asked why Mary would want to go to "the white man's grave." Surely, they reasoned, she could serve God in a better place. She was not swayed.

23. Christian and Plummer, *Redhead*, 20; Livingstone, *Mary Slessor*, 12.

24. The family moved frequently throughout Mary's years in Dundee, but moves were within about a mile of each other. The 1861 census shows them on Dura Street; in 1862 they were on Stobbswell Road; in 1870 at 6 Eliza Street. The 1871 census lists Mrs. Slessor as a grocer at 2 Catherine Street; in 1874 they were at 17 Harriet Street.

25. W. P. Livingstone reported that James Logie was interested in missionary work and later became a member of the Foreign Mission Committee. J. H. Smith was another of Slessor's older friends and mission co-workers in Dundee who encouraged her to apply for missionary status.

26. There are frequent mentions of both a Foreign Mission Committee and a Foreign Mission Board in writings of the time.

In December she won approval to go to Calabar as a "female agent." She would continue her unofficial education in Dundee until she received word to travel to Edinburgh for a brief training course. Hamilton MacGill, Foreign Mission Secretary, wrote, "The branches of education which it is most desirable for a female teacher in Old Calabar to possess are those which would enable her to teach the art of reading in Efik as well as English and this with the view of giving Bible lessons to the women and girls. Attendance at a Normal Seminary would be an immense advantage as the way of acquiring practically the art of teaching."[27]

Fear and uncertainty finally overwhelmed Mary Slessor on the eve of her departure for Edinburgh in March 1876. A friend found her crying in the narrow alleyway by her home. "Pray for me," she begged.[28]

EDINBURGH

Mary's first stop in Edinburgh was Darling's Temperance Hotel. The Darling family participated in the Moody and Sankey evangelistic meetings. Slessor may have attended with them; at least, we know that she took part in evening worship meetings held at the hotel. She then found a room in the home of city missionary Robert Martin and became friends with his daughter, Mary. Another Mary entered the picture when Slessor met and moved in with the Doig family.[29] The three young women became known in local circles as the three Marys. They participated in various mission activities in the city together. At one mission meeting, Slessor met John Bishop, a missionary-printer from Calabar. He would later accompany her on at least one trip in Africa. The other two Marys also became missionaries. Both went to China.[30]

Whatever the course at Moray House in Edinburgh entailed, Mary later complained that it was not practical enough.[31] Building or roofing houses, mixing and spreading cement— projects Slessor found herself occupied with in Africa—were obviously not included in the studies. In Africa, she would come to exemplify the truth missions historian Andrew

27. Foreign Mission Board [FMB] to MS, MS7654, 735, December 9, 1874.

28. Livingstone, *Mary Slessor*, 17.

29. Slessor also became friends with the Doig's married daughter, Mrs. McCrindle, who welcomed and housed her during furloughs from Africa.

30. Livingstone, *Mary Slessor*, 18–20.

31. Buchan, *Expendable Mary Slessor*, 25.

Walls propounds, that missionaries "set themselves to intellectual effort and acquired learning skills far beyond anything which would have been required of them in their ordinary run of life."[32]

By July 1876, the Board decided Mary Slessor was ready to go to Calabar. She packed her high-necked white blouses and long dark skirts, looked forward to her sixty pounds annual salary plus the twenty-five pounds allowed for outfitting, and went home to Dundee for a farewell visit. On August 5, two friends accompanied her on the train to Liverpool to see her board the steamship *Ethiopia*. There, as she watched the ship's cargo of rum being loaded, she complained, "Scores of casks, and only one missionary!"[33]

32. Walls, *Missionary Movement*, 172.

33. Buchan, *Expendable Mary Slessor*, 25; Livingstone, *Mary Slessor*, 20. The casks probably carried rum. Missionaries and others often referred only to gin, but gin was the term commonly used for all alcoholic beverages. Slessor may not have known it before the voyage began, but according to Christie's "Annals," Mr. and Mrs. George Thomson and two craftsmen reached Calabar on the same steamer, en route to erect a sanatorium in Cameroon. Mary Kingsley reported (*Travels in West Africa*, 619): "A very noble and devoted Scotch gentleman named Thomson, possessed of considerable wealth and anxious to do what he could to aid the mission work of the United Presbyterians in Calabar, came out and did his best to establish a sanatorium where fever-stricken missionaries could come and recruit their health without having to make the voyage home to England." Thomson died in Cameroon two years later.

2

Duke Town

> When you have made up your mind to go to West Africa, the very best thing you can do is to get it unmade again and go to Scotland instead; but if your intelligence is not strong enough to do so, abstain from exposing yourself to the direct rays of the sun, take 4 grains of quinine every day for a fortnight before you reach the Rivers, and get some introduction to the Wesleyans; they are the only people on the Coast who have got a hearse with feathers.
>
> —Mary Kingsley, 1893[1]

DID THE NEW MISSIONARY have misgivings about what lay ahead? Others certainly did. Christian and Plummer quote Hope Waddell as saying that men went "as though condemned, taking their coffins with them."[2] Waddell also wrote in 1846 that some of his countrymen "talked of Death coming with his scythe when the smokes began [the harmattan that blows from Sahara during the dry months]; and others dreaded the rivers then 'more than loaded cannon.'"[3] (The season of "the smokes" was feared as a time of much sickness.) Mary Kingsley, whose 1897 book *Travels in West Africa* made her famous, noted that steamboat agents would not issue return trip tickets for West Africa. Her physician friends advised, "I wouldn't go there if I were you. You'll catch something."[4]

Nobody traveled to West Africa on holiday. Most passengers were either traders, government employees or missionaries; they went "for the

1. Kingsley, Travels, 4.
2. Christian and Plummer, Redhead, 25.
3. Waddell, Twenty-Nine Years, 290.
4. Kingsley, Travels, 3.

sake of gain, glory, or God."[5] Mary, firmly in the third category and having made up her mind, revealed no hint of fear in her letters.

Vessels en route from Liverpool to Calabar headed south for Africa with trade goods and passengers. The first land sighted was often the peak of Teneriffe in the Grand Canary Islands. After passing Sierra Leone, at the big bend on the west coast of the continent, ships began to sail nearer the coast in the Gulf of Guinea. They passed or stopped at various ports along the grain coast, ivory coast, gold coast, and slave coast, before reaching Lagos, then "the Rivers"—from the Niger delta to the Cross River. Ships anchored offshore near port cities, while small boats ferried materials and people. African passengers embarked and disembarked along the way, camping out on open decks.

There are reports of a storm while Mary's ship, *Ethiopia*, made her way to Calabar and of Mary's insistence that God wouldn't send her all that way just to drown in a ship.[6] But Mary herself wrote of her trip, "We had a very pleasant voyage; everyone was kind and pleasant, and the weather was all that could be desired." She admitted to being lonely and wrote of her hunger "for a Scotch Sabbath," which was not satisfied until her first Sunday in Calabar, as none were observed during the voyage. "But the upholding, the freedom from all anxiety, the sense of His presence I have had since I left home," she said, "have been above all I could have asked or expected."[7]

On the five-week voyage, Slessor had time to ponder the letter Foreign Mission Secretary Hamilton Macgill sent her just a few weeks earlier. He congratulated her on her appointment and suggested she seek the assistance of "the two sisters who have been so long in the field, Mrs. Sutherland & Miss Edgerley,"[8] as she began her new life's work. He instructed her to study Goldie's Efik dictionary and grammar and, of course, the Bible. He reminded her that she did not go in her own strength. Macgill wrote:

5. Christian and Plummer, Redhead, 25.

6. Buchan, Expendable Mary Slessor, 26; Young-O'Brien, She Had a Magic, 43. He also states Slessor was seasick and "well purged," but this is not recorded by Slessor or other biographers, 39.

7. Record, 1877, 376–77. MS letter to unnamed woman in Scotland, October 11, 1876.

8. During Slessor's years with the Calabar Mission, missionaries and others were not on a first-name basis with each other, always addressing or referring to each other as Miss Slessor, Miss Crawford, Mr. Hart, etc. This practice persisted even in W. P. Livingstone's biography of Mary Slessor.

> Your first great work is to master the language. For the first year, though you do little else than set yourself to understand the talk of the natives, and make them understand you, you will have done a great work. To master the Efik tongue will indeed take much more than a year. But I have always said that if some good use of a foreign tongue is not commanded during the first twelve or eighteen months, it will never be satisfactorily acquired. . . . You will find it well to pronounce aloud in your own hearing, even when alone, portions of the Efik Scriptures. . . . Plunge into the company of native women and take your pronunciation not from Europeans.[9]

Mary would take his advice seriously in the days that followed.

REACHING THE PROMISED LAND

The chill of Scotland was far behind, and the memory of dark days in the slums of Dundee faded for Mary Slessor. She felt the hot glare of sun on a seemingly endless ocean. She watched the long, low coastline with its occasional palm trees and great mangrove forests and swamps that hid an unknown land and people. She saw flying fish and dolphin, and soft tropical air warmed her lungs. The appearance of the night sky and sea impressed her. Thomas Hutchinson, one-time Consul, wrote, "No spectacle is more imposing and magnificent than the luminous appearance of the sea at night in these latitudes. . . . Sometimes myriads of luminous stars and spots float and dance upon the surface."[10]

Entering the twelve-mile wide estuary of the Cross and Calabar rivers in the Bight of Biafra, the water changed to brown from the floods of mud carried downstream—mud that supported the growth of Nigeria's extensive mangrove swamps. Mary Kingsley wrote of West African rivers that they tend to reach the sea "with as much mystery as possible; lounging lazily along among its mangrove swamps in a what's-it-matter-when-one-comes-out and where's-the-hurry style, through quantities of channels . . . [and each is] as like the other as peas in a pod."[11] With the large island of Fernando Po[12] and its nearly 10,000-foot peak behind, and

9. FMB to MS, MS7655, July 29, 1876, 804–7.

10. Hutchinson, Impressions, 17. Hutchinson lived eight years in West Africa, serving first "in a medical capacity," then as Consul of the Bight of Biafra from 1855 to 1861.

11. Kingsley, Travels, 89.

12. Now known as Bioko, it is the largest of the islands of Equatorial Guinea. It lies about 100 miles south of Calabar, its most obvious feature Pico de Santa Isabel (known

Mount Cameroon, at over 13,000 feet, looming on the starboard side, both clearly visible, travelers knew their journey would soon end.

Calabar's anchorage at Duke Town, where the river is a thousand yards wide, lies about forty miles up the estuary—past a maze of winding, interconnecting tributaries, creeks and swamps; past James's Island, Parrot Island, Alligator Island, and other smaller islands. British traders, the so-called "gentlemen of the river," anchored their ships in the river for months at a time while they waited for enough palm oil to be delivered to make a full load. Old hulks were moored in the river, too, as permanent warehouses and living quarters for supercargoes—those responsible for bargaining trade goods for palm oil—and other "West Coasters." Mats like those used on native houses roofed the decks of the hulks to protect them from the blazing sun and tropical downpours.

Ethiopia rounded Seven Fathom Point, out of the Cross River and into the Calabar. After another five miles and another bend, Mary caught her first glimpse of her new home. Jessie Hogg, another Calabar missionary, wrote, "You could not see a prettier picture than Duke Town, on a fine day, set off with its tropical greenery . . . with a background of high cotton trees. Its mat-roofed mud huts are relieved by a few gaily-painted wooden houses belonging to the King and Chiefs."[13]

The steamer anchored in sight of the town and Mission Hill. A cluster of mission buildings, including a whitewashed church, school, dispensary and houses, looked inviting in a setting of tropical fruit trees. Canoes threaded their way among the ships, some to deliver goods, some to pick up passengers. The mission boat, with its white awning, manned by six Kru men (dependable hard workers hired on at Liberia for work) dressed in white tee shirts, red caps and dark loincloths, made an impressive sight. The one who would become known as everybody's mother climbed down the ship's ladder for the short boat-ride to Mission Beach. Alexander Ross, who had been in Calabar less than a year himself, greeted Mary in the small boat. He may have wondered at the petite, frail-looking recruit and recalled William Anderson's urging that the Foreign Mission Board send out more missionaries "with broad shoulders and expansive chest."[14]

during the British period as Clarence Peak).

13. Christian and Plummer, Redhead, 31, quoting Jessie Hogg, who served in Calabar from 1884 until invalided home twelve years later.

14. McFarlan, Calabar, 70.

A Calabar welcome had all the trappings of a country holiday. School children marched down the hill to the mission jetty. Missionaries came to greet newcomers or those returning from furlough and to retrieve much-desired mail from the steamer that came only every two weeks. Government officials and traders were often among the group. Mary Kingsley reported that, when she arrived in Calabar in 1895 with Sir Claude MacDonald[15] and his wife, there were fireworks "and what not" and that "the whole settlement, white and black" turned out to welcome Lady MacDonald.[16] Mary Slessor's coming didn't warrant fireworks when she arrived in Calabar on September 9, 1876.[17] Honor would come her way years later.

One of the first to welcome Mary Slessor on land was the famed Mrs. Sutherland, a veteran of twenty-seven years' mission service, one of the "sisters" the Foreign Mission Secretary had advised her to seek.[18] After the long climb up the hill, Mary knew for sure that living in the tropics would be a far cry from the life she left behind in Dundee. She wore Victorian skirts and petticoats, gloves and boots—proper attire for a Victorian lady. Sweat soaked her through, but it couldn't dampen her enthusiasm and elation at finally being where she was certain God wanted her.

WHAT MARY FIRST SAW

In Slessor's lengthy early letter to an unnamed woman friend in Scotland, dated a month after her arrival, she described the country in one word—lovely—and hoped Calabar's long time missionaries were correct when they said, "the unhealthiness for which it is proverbial is largely owing to want of proper care."[19] She had not yet experienced her first bout of malaria. She also spoke of the success of the Calabar Mission and applauded attendance at services, "the demeanour of the audience," the contrast between church members "and the heathen around," and "the respectful, deferential manner in which the people from highest to lowest receive

15. Claude Maxwell MacDonald was Commissioner of the Bight of Biafra from 1891 to 1896. He was knighted in 1892.

16. Kingsley, Travels, 42.

17. Christie, "Annals," reports the date was September 9. Livingstone and Buchan say it was September ll.

18. Euphemia Miller arrived in Calabar in 1849, married Alexander Sutherland in 1855, was widowed the next year and remained in Calabar until her death in 1881.

19. Record, 1877, MS letter, October 11, 1876, 377.

the missionaries." Here, and in later references in the same letter, Mary revealed the extent to which she harbored the cultural and racial prejudices common to most Victorians of the era: prejudices that would lessen in later years, after she learned to understand and appreciate the native peoples, after she came to love both the country and individuals in it. It is unlikely, though, that she ever lost completely those ingrained views of the superiority of European (especially British) civilization.

Mary declared that she hadn't been "of much use" at the mission, partly because she did not know much of the language yet. For the two weeks prior to the letter, she had been visiting the various mission stations, as Samuel Edgerley and other missionaries insisted, before starting her normal daily activities. At a worship service and communion at Creek Town she was pleased by "so many of Africa's sons and daughters sitting beside us . . . and to hear one of themselves from the pulpit address with eloquence and fervour the assembled crowd." This may have been Esien Esien Ukpabio, who was ordained by the Presbytery of Biafra on April 9, 1872. He was the first Calabar convert, baptized at Creek Town in 1853. Slessor was also impressed with King Eyo Honesty VII, who offered a "very nice speech" at a congregational meeting. She wrote, "He seems to be a sincere Christian man, quite a pattern to his people."

It is noteworthy that by this time that by Mary Slessor's time there were numerous African teachers and evangelists active in the work of the mission. Sixteen other European and Jamaican missionaries were assigned to Calabar in 1876, but five of those were on furlough. Calabar mission historian Donald McFarlan wrote, "Had it not been for the native agents who were carrying on fully half the work of the mission, the veterans who still remained would have been defeated."[20]

Mary described a visit with Samuel Edgerley to Adiabo and to another unnamed village, where "the women and children crowded round to see the white 'Ma.'" She confessed that their "gesticulations" frightened her until Edgerley said the people were just trying to be friendly.[21] She added her concern that the village had no teacher. "It was really painful to bid them goodbye," she wrote, "and not have a person to leave among them. Oh, what a work is to be done here, if the Church could *see* it!"

20. McFarlan, Calabar, 69.

21. Record, 1877, MS letter October 11, 1876, 377.

Slessor also went with Edgerley and his wife, Agnes, to Ikunetu, about twenty-five miles upriver from Creek Town, where Edgerley's sister was stationed.[22] She wrote:

> Miss Edgerley is staying there alone just now, but she is quite cheerful and happy. She, [like] Mr. Edgerley, has such an amount of *humour* and *tact* in dealing with the natives, that they are not only loved and respected, but they can administer any amount of rebuke, their manner of doing so disarming anything like retaliation. I have admired both of them very much. Their firmness is tempered so with prudence and pleasantry, that they seem to have been born for their present post, as of course they were.[23]

Mary not only expressed her esteem for the Edgerleys, but as the years passed, she adopted their methods in dealing with Africans.

The young novice lauded the beauty of Ikunetu. "You ought to have seen the sunsets we saw there. There was all the softness and beauty that were displayed in certain sunsets seen from a certain window in the metropolis of Scotland [Edinburgh], and in addition, the rich, gorgeous magnificence that belongs to the tropics."

There were three native teachers at Ikot Offiong,[24] another ten miles upriver from Ikunetu, where Mary and the Edgerleys spent two days. "There is much less work at hand there than at Ikunetu, the town being nearly demolished by [intertribal] war; but there are villages all round, which makes it a capital centre for work." She told of a "good walk" with missionary John Baillie on that trip, when they visited two villages for meetings—a walk that was more "pushing and climbing and jumping and wading" than walking. "Bush proper," she called it. She was grateful for the three Kru men Edgerley sent to assist her along the way when she needed help. She needed help "more than once," she admitted.

Baillie preached at the first "church" meeting under a tree. When he finished, he asked Mary if she would like to speak. Her preconceived notions revealed again, the newcomer wrote, "Looking at the groups of degraded, ignorant creatures, and looking at the outcome of that superstitious ignorance in the shape of a 'devil-house' at my right hand, I hardly knew where to begin." Not one to miss a chance to speak, though, she

22. Mary Willis Edgerley served in Calabar from 1854 until she retired in 1896.

23. Record, 1877, 377.

24. Ikot Offiong is the modern spelling of Ikorofiong.

asked Baillie to read the story from John 5 about the healing of the man by the pool at Bethesda. "Then," she said, "I tried in a few simple words to show them their need of healing . . . and told them that the same Lord put the same question to them to-day, 'Wilt thou be made whole?'"

Slessor's long letter continued with details of their meeting at the second village:

> We came to a palaver house; the blood of their latest sacrifice was still fresh on the altar. Some fierce-looking men were sitting beside it, but in less than five minutes they were sitting beside me in the house of the Chief, who received me with great kindness.
>
> Scarcely had we been seated, when a crowd of men, women and children almost smothered us. The Chief drove them off with a whip and made them stand at a respectful distance. After my appearance had been discussed, the result of which I am entirely, perhaps *luckily*, ignorant of, John began his work. They all followed him audibly in prayer, and repeated after him a portion of the first Catechism.
>
> I spoke a few simple words on the scene on Carmel between the priests of Baal and Elijah . . . while John interpreted, and at the close [the people] gave assent to all that was said, though it was not flattering to themselves. The chief thanked me for the visit, and offered me a drink of their native beverage—a token of hospitality and respect. We were followed by crowds, and many of the children ran screaming with fright. I learned then that Mrs. Sutherland is the only white lady who has visited the place, which visit was paid many years ago.[25]

Already, after only a month in the country, Mary felt she must speak out about the need for a ministry to women. She bemoaned the fact that not one woman belonged to the church yet. She insisted: "*Something more must be done* for the women here if we are to raise the men. The women are the great drawback to our success." She excused the men on the basis of what she saw the women doing (or not doing). Mary condemned the women's "habits and their deceit" and their "lolling about almost naked."

Slessor apologized for the mistakes in her letter. "The blots are caused by my onslaughts on cockroaches & c. . . . This is a very prolific land in every department of life,—oh I must except intellectual and spiritual," she wrote. Mary's "first impressions" were just that: wonder and excitement,

25. Record, 1877, 377–79, quoting MS letter of October 11, 1876.

misconceptions about the people and culture she found in Calabar, reflecting the notions prevalent in her homeland, impressions that changed during her years in Africa.

Almost as a postscript, she added a note about visiting the graves of those who had died in mission service in Calabar. She felt "solemnized," but also "stimulated and comforted," as she and Edgerley stood by Mrs. Baillie's grave. She thought Edgerley felt the same way, "for all that he said during all our walk," she wrote, was 'Ah! well, it matters little where they lay the poor body; it shall surely rise again.'"[26]

LIFE IN DUKE TOWN

New missionaries began their mission life and work at Duke Town. Mary was no exception. She was so excited about her trips to other villages and the walks she took with school children that she bragged she had climbed every tree worth climbing between Duke Town and Old Town.[27] This was not good news to her colleagues. They frowned upon it as unsuitable behavior for a Victorian woman, especially a missionary. It did not improve their opinion of her when they learned that she even discarded her skirt and ran in her petticoat.[28]

The Andersons, Duke Town pioneers, were on furlough in Scotland when Slessor appeared on the scene. William Anderson didn't return for another year, as he was holding evangelistic meetings in Jamaica for the Foreign Mission Board. Louisa returned, though, three months after Mary's arrival. She ruled the household sternly. Mary's first assigned task was to ring the five a.m. bell for morning prayers. When Mary overslept, she received a sharp reprimand. Not wanting to repeat the episode, one night she made matters worse by jumping from bed, when moonlight flooded her room, and ringing the bell hours early.[29]

Running races and climbing trees also sometimes made the adventurer late for meals. Louisa told her that if she came late, she would get no meal. It still happened. William brought food to her room, though, when he was there. Mary learned later that he did so with Louisa's help. The newcomer came to love and appreciate the Andersons during the years they

26. Ibid.
27. Livingstone, Mary Slessor, 28.
28. Buchan, Expendable Mary Slessor, 52.
29. Livingstone, Mary Slessor, 28.

spent together in Calabar. They were known affectionately as Daddy and Mammy. Even the chiefs of Duke Town were awed by Louisa. One chief declared, "I tell you true, them women be the best man for Mission!"[30]

Mary admired her assigned overseer, Euphemia Sutherland, whom she dutifully followed around as she learned the business of being a "female agent"—teaching, dispensing medications, and making the rounds of the women's yards surrounding Duke Town. Years before Mary's arrival Mrs. Sutherland had gone to places in the forest where no white person had been. Biographer James Buchan wrote, "In spite of warnings that she would be killed . . . [Sutherland] had more than once defied the officials of the ruling body, Egbo, and stopped them flogging a slave to death by intercepting the lash with her umbrella. She was one of the few white women honoured by the Africans with the title of *Ma Akamba*—Great Mother."[31]

As with the Edgerleys, Mary Slessor would emulate the example of Euphemia Sutherland throughout her own years in Africa.

Hope Waddell had been impressed by Calabar's well-built houses, and there had been little change in the thirty years since he wrote. He described a typical quadrangular courtyard with a number of apartments, each facing inside, their back walls forming a windowless appearance to outsiders. An entrance at one end kept each yard private. House walls stood six feet inside the long posts that supported the roof. They were wattle and daub construction—interlaced sticks plastered with clay and mud. The earthen floor inside the house and its perimeter was a foot above ground level, keeping occupants relatively clean and dry during rains.[32] Inside, a clay bench was formed along the walls. This added to the stability of the walls and also provided a place for sitting or sleeping. It was the kind of house Mary would call home when she moved to new African territory.

Slessor's concern about women was related to their houses and yards. Hugh Goldie wrote that in the early years of the mission head men "jealously secluded" their wives, concubines and daughters, who were unable to leave their yards without permission. He said that almost every house included a women's yard, "corresponding to the harem or zenana of the

30. Ibid., 37.

31. Buchan, Expendable Mary Slessor, 29.

32. Waddell, Twenty-Nine Years, 325–26.

East."[33] By 1890, he could report that wives had their own farms and slaves and could travel to tend to the farms some distance from town.

In Mary Slessor's time, the duties of a "female agent" still included visits to the women's yards. These served as schools for the young Scot. Here she learned the language well and also became aware of cultural practices, fears and superstitions. She deplored the low status accorded women and began to apply pressure on their behalf, both in Scotland and Calabar.

Six months after her "first impressions" letter, Mary wrote to "Maggie," another friend in Scotland, one of her long, sometimes indecipherable letters, a letter decrying "the surrounding heathenism" and its "depressing influence." She wrote, " Oh, for a heart *full* of love to Jesus and to these perishing ones for *His Sake*.... You may *read* and *hear*, but to *see* the state of society here is sickening.... The scenes, we cannot speak or write of, so that when one comes to *see* them there is something to learn.[34]

ALL IN A DAY'S WORK

Mary wrote an article for the *United Presbyterian Missionary Record* describing her Sunday rounds, a depiction she called "a common and uninteresting sketch." She told of visiting various houses and groups. In one, a man grieved for the death of his only son. Slessor wrote of the "tokens of mourning,... filth and squalor and drunkenness." She spoke to him of the resurrection, and he seemed somewhat comforted. "Well, if God took the child," he said, "I don't care so much, but to think that an enemy bewitched it, is strong, strong!" When Mary told the child's mother that her own mother had lost children and trusted them to God's care, the woman began to weep, and Mary wrote, "Tears show how much the mother-heart is the same all the world over."[35]

At another place, the master of the house was dead. Slessor considered his widow "the very embodiment of all that is repulsive," as the woman dealt harshly with "cowed-looking, half-starved women and dirty girls, covered with sores." Mary could hardly find her way "through bushes, skulls, sacrifices, charms, and all sorts of things," she wrote.

33. Goldie, Calabar, 17.

34. MS letter to "Maggie," April 17, 1877.

35. Record, 1879, 688.

She spoke briefly on a Scripture passage but thought it had little effect. "Nevertheless we must 'preach the gospel to every creature,'" she wrote, "according as He gave us commandment, and leave the results with Him."

Some women Mary visited on her rounds complained that she didn't give them enough attention, but they still showed little interest in her teaching. Mary bantered with them in Efik, showing her grasp of the language. "We say a few severe words, without sitting down, and answer their protestations of willingness to be 'god-man' with a bit of sharp sarcasm, which is given and taken in good part." Some she visited were "polished hypocrites as far as our work is concerned," Slessor reported. Others, she believed, "sincerely ask God's forgiveness, protection, and teaching, and are trying to live in accordance with what they know of His word."

Finally, Mary visited a group of men who were selling rum. They put the rum away and asked her to stay. "They are very quiet and all attention till we come to speak of that detestable stuff [rum] with which Christian Britain so successfully obstructs and cripples the progress of the gospel, and even of the civilization of which she professes to be the champion and the leader. Here the usual question is asked in the usually triumphant fashion, 'What for white man bring them rum, suppose them rum no be good? He be god-man he bring them rum, what for god-man talk so?'"[36]

At the close of Slessor's supposedly "common and uninteresting sketch," she remarked that is was nearly time for the afternoon service at Duke Town, and asked her readers to pray that the Lord would "send forth labourers into His harvest"

SICK AND HOMESICK

Hints that things were not going well for Mary began appearing early on. In her letter to "Maggie," she spoke of staying in, out of the rainstorm, on Efik meeting night.

"I am as tired as an old horse, and the pen is just flying over the paper," she wrote. "I don't know that you will manage to read it or make any sense of it. You must not expect to get *proper* letters for I am so busy, and here we cannot spend so much strength as at home."[37]

36. Ibid., 688–89.

37. MS letter to "Maggie," April 17, 1877.

Within two years, Slessor had experienced plenty of sickness. On December 10, 1878 she wrote to David Stewart, a friend from her mill-working days, who had been in contact with her mother:

> You are not thinking I have forgotten you are you? . . . Home: What a flood of feeling fills my heart at the sound. Aye, truly "there's no place like home." How are you? and your wife, and the bairns? How many of the latter now? Why you will be like an old man when I come home, and that reveals another fact, of which my Mammy [Anderson] has just been apprising me, that I am growing an *old woman*. Really, among my bairns, I am like to forget the facts, for I am as young in spirit yet as ever I was, and some of the Europeans were telling me lately that I was growing younger and better looking. This means that I am better in health for after an Africa fever one looks as if one had escaped from a lunatic asylum. But a truce to nonsense! Mother tells me of your kindness to them and butters you up as far as possible. So I suppose for the look of the thing I will have to thank you, and say that I am glad to hear it all, and *so I really am* Davie![38]

Not fond of playing the part of a Victorian hostess at tea parties, this woman of action intimated, "I am now, as you know, among quite a different class of people from that I was accustomed to at home. The European society, apart from the members of the mission, are merchants, the Government officials, the commanders, doctors, and pursers of the steamers. Travellers, Botanists, Explorers, etc., etc. But though I value the refinement, education, set, of such society, I love to be in fancy with the dear old friends at home. I am often in the factory, listening to the music of the shuttles and it is sweet."[39]

Mary told Stewart to tell his wife, a weaver, that natives of Calabar believed cloth was woven by ghosts, not men. She ended with comments on the climate and her physical status. The hot season had begun and many were sidelined with "fever." Writing made her back hurt and she was nervous, she said, and it was "not pleasant to be sick on strangers."

Six months after her letter to "Davie" and less than three years in Calabar, Mary was ill and homesick. Alexander Ross wrote to the Foreign Mission Board that Miss Slessor was teaching at the Duke Town school

38. MS to Davie Stewart, MS1986-396, December 10, 1878.

39. Ibid.

"when not indisposed."[40] Whether he intended criticism is not clear, but he may well have recalled his impression when he met the thin newcomer upon her arrival in Calabar. Frequent attacks of fever sidelined her; she disliked the harmattan that consumed her energy. She had grown to dislike Duke Town. "I want my home and my mother," she said—hardly words expected of one to become "everybody's mother." Mary Slessor sailed for home on June 22, 1879, more than a year short of the normal term before furlough. Some doubted she would return.

40. Buchan, Expendable Mary Slessor, 61.

PART TWO

Branching Out

1879–1890

3

Old Town—Too Busy

> To denounce evil customs or preach against the sins of the land is tolerated, because none . . . believe it as anything other than mere babbling; but dare to oppose their customs by anything stronger than words, and you incur all their hostility and malice. . . . We are just now in this position (from having preserved twin children), and I cannot describe the uneasiness, apprehension, and trouble we have undergone lest our premises should be burned, or our house broken into at night, and the mother and children butchered, or ourselves despatched from the bush by the gun of some unseen assassin.
>
> —Samuel Edgerley, May 1855[1]

MARY WENT STRAIGHT HOME to Dundee and her mother and sisters. She recovered quickly from her illness, as shown by a letter to her from the Foreign Mission Secretary's office welcoming her home. "I am glad that you are now quite well," it read, "although your experience in the first part of the voyage was unpleasant, and I trust your stay at home will be happy and pleasant all through, and beneficial to many of us here."[2]

She moved her mother and sisters to better housing in Downfield, on the outskirts of Dundee, then began the customary missionary furlough occupation of making the rounds of churches, women's groups, and youth meetings. The need to recruit volunteers and obtain funds for the church's missionary endeavors was ever present. Two schoolgirls who attended one of Slessor's youth meetings, Janet Wright and Martha Peacock, were

1. Goldie, Calabar, 152.
2. FMB to MS, MS7657/486, August 1, 1879.

convinced that they, too, should serve God in Calabar. Both followed up on their decisions after they grew up.[3]

Mary's old friend in Dundee, James Logie, advised her to write to the mission board to ask for a new assignment, since she disliked Duke Town. She did this, though she agreed to serve where she was needed. She also told friends that she was eager to move into uncharted territory as soon as possible but that missionary William Anderson was opposed to the idea.[4]

By September 1880 Slessor had been in Scotland fourteen months. Although the designated furlough length was one year, it was not unusual for missionaries to stay somewhat longer. Travel time that could take up to a month each way was not counted as part of the year. That month Mary met Hugh and Jane Goldie, who were also on furlough, and she decided on the spur of the moment to accompany them on the same ship back to Calabar. She made her own travel arrangements and later wrote to the mission board that she had made the decision herself. There wasn't time to confer about it, she argued, and said she accepted complete responsibility for her action.[5] This impulsive decision-making became a characteristic of Mary Slessor's practice—one that was all too familiar and sometimes disconcerting to colleagues. When she was convinced that God wanted her to do something, there was no holding her back.

The three missionaries reached Calabar on October 4, 1880. They joined a skeleton crew of European missionaries; more than half of the listed fifteen missionaries were on furlough. The arrival of Slessor and the Goldies swelled Calabar's on-site mission staff to nine.

OLD TOWN

The refreshed Mary was delighted to find she had been assigned to Old Town, where she would be the only missionary. The station had been unoccupied for nearly two years, since the death of Alexander Morton and the departure of his wife. Slessor knew she was theoretically under the supervision of her colleagues at Duke Town three miles away, but she was glad to be serving alone, where she could use her own discretion about

3. Buchan, Expendable Mary Slessor, 62; Christie, "Annals."

4. Livingstone, Mary Slessor, 33.

5. Buchan, Expendable Mary Slessor, 63.

how to minister to the people. She would be preacher, teacher, nurse, and social worker here and in the surrounding areas.

Old Town had a history of resistance to any changes to old-time customs and practices. In 1853 Chief Willy Tom Robins had a nephew and two nieces, whom he accused of causing his illness, put to death. Before he died the next year, Robins had a number of wives, sons and others chained together and held hostage for his health. They were all killed when he died. Missionaries expressed their dismay to British officials and traders at the massacre that followed Willy Tom Robins' death. In January 1855, the "gentlemen of the river" (European traders), and British officers held a meeting from which they excluded the missionaries and native representatives. They persuaded Acting Consul James Lynslager to raze Old Town, both as punishment and as an example of what could happen if anyone crossed the British or disobeyed new laws. The seven men known to be mainly responsible for the slaughter hid out. King Eyo Honesty II of Creek Town and other chiefs wanted to deal with the culprits themselves, and the missionaries favored this path. The Consul disagreed and ruled that unless the men were delivered to him within twenty-four hours the city would be destroyed. The time limit was an impossible goal for the chiefs, so bombardment by *HMS Antelope* proceeded. Men were sent into the town to burn everything and ruin every house. Fortunately, there was no loss of life, since the people had evacuated within the twenty-four hours. Hope Waddell wrote:

> The proceedings were quite illegal. . . . Strange to say, as if ashamed of their work, or afraid of the consequences, the instigators of the mischief tried to shift the responsibility. The missionaries, they said, were at the bottom of it. . . . Yea, similar misrepresentations were made to Her Majesty's Government, repeated in Parliament, and published in some of the newspapers. The imputation of such a crime to us was ridiculous, as well as injurious and untrue. . . . But we were all of one mind, that our gospel work could never be carried on in league with the embodiment of foreign power, and, in fact, would be ruined, if the natives should suspect that our endeavours at reformation were a snare to entangle them in promises, to be enforced by the thunder of war guns.[6]

Lynslager's decree that Old Town could not be rebuilt was rescinded a year later.

6. Waddell, Twenty-Nine Years, 553–55.

The Mission resumed its presence in the town and, except for the period just before Slessor's arrival, maintained it until she left there in 1883. After that year African teachers and Duke Town missionaries served Old Town.

Slessor found the mission's wattle-and-mud house in Old Town rundown and wrote to the Foreign Mission Board to complain, as well as to report on her work. The secretary responded, thanking her for her "long and interesting letter," expressing regret at the condition of her house and praising her work. The final word was a routine request for a report. "You have told me of the start you have made," it read, "but you can tell me more."[7]

In Old Town Mary began to live more simply. She could live on available local foods: yams, plantains, bananas, cassava, coco, maize, and sugar cane. She found she could do without the foods to which she was accustomed in Scotland, except for her precious tea. She could send more of her salary home to support her family. She was living like an African—a poor African. She would live this way for the rest of her life, and it opened the way for her work to be effective.

NO TIME TO WASTE

Mary soon opened schools and held meetings in the neighboring villages of Qua, Akim and Ikot Ansa. At the end of 1881 two deputies from Scotland visited Calabar and wrote of Mary Slessor's work, wondering how she could keep up the pace.

> One Sabbath morning, at six o-clock, we set out . . . for the purpose of meeting Miss Slessor . . . and accompanying her on her round of duty for the day. We first passed through a part of Duke Town, and we were not sorry when we emerged from the unsavoury place, and struck a footpath fringed with verdure wet with the dew of the morning, that skirted lands under cultivation, and brought us after a pleasant walk of forty minutes to Qua. . . . Soon a hundred people assembled, of whom about thirty were men, and the rest young persons from five to sixteen years of age. . . . The service was begun with prayer; next a hymn was sung, and the ten commandments recited, by the whole assembly; and then a verse of Scripture was taught them clause by clause until they were able to repeat it themselves. These exercises were conducted, in Efik of course, by

7. FMB to MS, MS7657/792, January 28, 1881.

> Miss Slessor, who, after giving with singular fluency a short address herself, acted as interpreter while we spoke at greater length.[8]

The writer concluded that Mary Slessor was "devoted, diligent, and energetic." In another report the visitor expressed his surprise at seeing a skull "roll out between his feet" as he preached.[9]

William Anderson's report in the June 1882 *United Presbyterian Record* said that she worked "nobly" and gave further details about Slessor's activities. "After an early Sunday morning service at Qua, Miss Slessor sets out for the next town or towns, as she feels able, visiting several of the 'farms' also, either on her way out or on her way back. About mid-day she returns to Old Town, where she conducts Sabbath school, and in the evening there is a regular church service held in the chief's yard, and attended by almost the entire community. This is *the* meeting of the week (says Miss Slessor)."[10]

The weekly meeting in the Old Town chief's yard always left her encouraged. Mary found the response "novel and impressive" and appreciated the fact that the people accompanied her home with lanterns. As to results, she said, "More than one of the big men have told me that they have been awakened to the fact that their laws and customs were at variance with God's Word. Then the young people have been brought directly under Christian influence; and so, as the chief here said to me the other day, 'When they grow up, God's fashions won't be too strong for them.'"[11]

Mary also reported happily that there had been no demonstration or sacrifice for "the god of the town" for nine months.

Six months later, Foreign Mission Secretary James Buchanan wrote:

> By this time you will have got our Annual Report, from which you will see that I made good use of what you sent me about your work. I wish to tell you how much pleased I was with your report, and . . . I have reason to know that the Church as a whole have been very much interested in your account. . . . I should like very much if you would send me from time to time a short sketch of anything connected with your work—any of your observations or your experiences—which would be interesting to the readers of the Record. Of course I expect to have from you at the close of the

8. Record, 1882, 150.
9. Buchan, Expendable Mary Slessor, 64.
10. Record, 1882, 194.
11. Ibid.

> year another report like the one you sent me: but you might send me any little thing that occurs to you even before that.[12]

He concluded with the good news that Slessor's annual salary had been increased from sixty to eighty pounds and advising her to take care of herself, as it sounded as if she were doing too much.

TWINS AND ORPHANS

Each move into new territory revealed more evidence that some of the old customs persisted. One of the most troubling practices was the killing of twins and orphans, and the banishment of twin-mothers. Slessor found herself taking in children, as missionaries had been doing for more than a quarter century. Mrs. Edgerley first rescued twins in May of 1852 in Old Town. Mrs. Waddell or Mrs. Sutherland did the same in Creek Town. As for orphans, they were abandoned simply because no one would take responsibility to raise them.

Consul David Hopkins had signed a treaty with the chiefs of Duke Town in 1878 that prohibited the murder of twins and treating their mothers as outcasts. Mary Slessor wrote of that event at the time, while she was stationed at Duke Town. She told of the excitement and celebration that the news inspired. The twin-mothers "laughed and clapped their hands and shouted '*Sosono*! *Sosono*! (Thank you! Thank you!)" Mary was tearful. "It was a glorious day for Calabar," she said.[13]

Things were slow to change, though. Calabar mission chronicler Donald McFarlan wrote, "In the country districts round about all the superstitious practices still continued. Even in the town they persisted in secret. The tiny bodies of twins were broken and crushed into clay pots or cast on to ant heaps in the bush to be eaten alive. Soon [Slessor's] dilapidated mud house was filled to overflowing with rescued babies."[14]

Percy Amaury Talbot, District Commissioner for a neighboring district to Calabar wrote as late as 1912: "The birth of twins was regarded as so great a misfortune that, in olden times, it was followed in many tribes by the death of both mother and babes. . . ." He remarked that the custom

12. FMB to MS, MS7657/908, July 7, 1882.

13. Christian and Plummer, Redhead, 43.

14. McFarlan, Calabar, 93.

had diminished to the point that after the babies were killed, twin mothers could flee to a twin-mothers' village.[15]

Amaury Talbot's wife, who wrote her own book, said that during her time in Calabar with her husband, native men insisted that they only hated and feared twin babies as "something monstrous." But the women believed that "one of the pair, at least, was no merely mortal offspring but that of some wandering demon." She wrote, "Except where the fear of the white man is too strong, twins are not allowed to live even now."[16]

Hugh Goldie confirmed that the custom of destroying twins was strongly approved by women when he wrote in 1890. The fact that women suffered most from the practice did not dissuade them. He also told of the twin-mother villages to which those mothers were banished. One native, befriended by a missionary, thought it strange to be rebuked for throwing his twins and their mother into the river to drown.

"Having succeeded in getting the people to abandon the practice of killing human victims for the dead," Goldie wrote, "we judged that it would be no difficult matter to induce them to abandon twin-murder." The missionaries, however, found that most chiefs "would not even discuss that possibility" in the early days of the mission. Only King Eyo II agreed. Goldie said Eyo, who died in 1858, "made infanticide a capital crime, but he had power to do so only among his own people."[17]

McFarlan, a missionary in Calabar at the time he wrote his history of the mission, said in 1946, "The end of twin-murder is not yet, though the work of the pioneers stamped it out long ago in Calabar itself."[18] In a brief autobiographical sketch in 1958, Nwachuku Eme poignantly reported that the rescue of twins continued for many years in outlying districts.

Born in 1919 in Umuahia Province, Eme's father, a "witch doctor and a juju priest," trained him to follow in his footsteps; but after attending a Scottish mission school "to learn the white man's language but not his religion," Eme became a Christian. He later wrote, "My father was furious for my disobedience. I tried to explain myself by saying that the power of the church people's message was beyond my control and did not know how it gripped my mind. . . . He resorted to methods that would make me come

15. P. Amaury Talbot, Life in Southern Nigeria, 205.

16. D. Amaury Talbot, Woman's Mysteries, 23–26.

17. Goldie, Calabar, 24–27.

18. McFarlan, Calabar, 38.

out of it. . . . Some of these methods included flogging, denial of food and clothing, etc. That was a very trying period for me at my age, when I had nothing of my own and could not earn anything."[19]

In 1943 Eme married a dreaded twin, one from his home village who was rescued in infancy and raised elsewhere by missionaries. One of the curses pronounced upon Eme at his marriage was that the couple would be childless. However, when normal, healthy children were born to them many villagers became Christians. "The people . . . had seen enough proof that the witch doctors and juju priests' statements were quite false and could not be relied on."[20]

African historian John Mbiti wrote in 1967 (and the information remains in the 1990 edition of his book): "Since this belief was so entrenched in some societies I doubt whether the practice of killing twins has been stopped completely by modern governments."[21] It is no wonder that the saving of twins is the most memorable accomplishment many Nigerians attribute to Mary Slessor. Statues of her always depict her holding a twin in each arm.

IBAKA

Was Mary doing too much? During her two and one-half years at Old Town, the ardent missionary, now in her early thirties, faced many challenges. She learned more of the customs and superstitions of the people and became more proficient in their language; she learned about their religion, their fears, their dependence on magic and witchcraft; she became more eager to find some means of raising the status of women; and she continued to rescue twins and orphans. In addition to her other duties, she refereed arguments.

Slessor was not happy sticking close to home and began to explore communities in rural "bush" settlements and along the Cross River. (Anything not urban was called bush. A bushman in modern parlance might be called a hick or a country bumpkin.) During this period, Slessor met Chief Okon from Ibaka. He urged her to visit his town (known later as James Town), thirty miles down the river on the west bank of the Cross River estuary. She finally agreed to go, and the residents of Old Town

19. Eme, "From Heathenism," March 1958.

20. Ibid.

21. Mbiti, African Religions, 189.

were appalled. Something might happen to her, they warned. When they saw that Mary was determined to go, her friend, Creek Town's King Eyo Honesty VII, insisted that she travel in his royal canoe.

When the day and time arrived for the trip, there was no canoe. Mary wasn't worried; she knew it would come eventually. When she finally received word at six p.m. that the craft was ready, she found it had been freshly painted to honor the white *Ma*. Workers had arranged rice bags, gifts to Okon, as a couch, and a shelter had been rigged up from matting. Mary herded four of her current children into the boat with her. With all the excitement and farewells, the voyage did not begin until after dark. Thirty-three oarsmen paddled ten hours to reach Ibaka at dawn. A drummer drummed, and the paddlers sang songs to honor Mary: "Ma, our beautiful, beloved mother, is on board, Ho! Ho! Ho!"[22]

Carried ashore in true chief's fashion, Slessor and the children found themselves deposited in Chief Okon's compound. They were given his own room for their use—a room that opened into the women's yard. The chief's wives were delighted with this new stranger and wanted to sit as close to the white woman as possible. Beautiful and fat according to custom, sweating profusely in the heat, the women pressed against her in the room, and with no ventilation Mary was very uncomfortable. Lizards in the roof and rats hopping about were disconcerting, too, especially at night. People came from miles around to see and touch this strange white woman with red hair and blue eyes. Some watched her eat and gave bite-by-bite descriptions to those outside. A circus atmosphere prevailed.

The pioneer settled into a routine of morning and evening preaching, daily nursing chores, and, according to biographer Livingstone, she "superintended washing, and initiated women into the secrets of starching and ironing." The people, on the other hand, oversaw Mary's safety, warning her that she must not venture from the village because of wild animals and elephants. (Elephants, with their destructive ways, were not found in the Calabar area.) She saw skulls and carved images all around, and noted that witchcraft and poisoning were prevalent.

One day a violent tornado struck. Roofs, canoes and trees sailed through the air. Lightning flashed, and thunder roared. Mary was used to the frequent tornadoes that struck Calabar, but this one was especially fierce. She was afraid. The roof of the house she was in blew away, and rain

22. Livingstone, Mary Slessor, details of the Ibaka episode, 38–44.

beat down on her. She began to sing with the children: "Oh, come let us sing to the Lord." When it was all over, Mary suffered a bout of fever.

On another morning, when people seemed somber, Mary knew something was wrong. She learned that two of Chief Okon's young wives had left his compound and gone to another, where a boy slept. This crime had to be punished under Efik law. They, along with two other girls who knew what happened, were called before the chief and other village men. The punishment decreed was a hundred lashes for each girl. Mary tried to influence the chief. He said, "If you say we must not flog, we must listen to you as our mother and our guest. But they will say that God's word be no good if it destroy the power of the law to punish evildoers."[23]

Mary talked Okon into calling another council meeting later in the day. When they gathered, she spoke first to the girls. She told them they had brought punishment on themselves by disobeying their laws. "Ask God to keep you in the future," she warned, "so that your conduct may not be a reproach to yourselves and the word of God which you know."

The girls looked defiant, and the men looked pleased. But then she turned to the men and told them this problem was really their fault. She denounced their polygamy, calling it "a disgrace to you and a cruel injustice to these helpless women." These were mere girls, she reminded them, and "to confine them as you do is a shame and a blot on your manhood."

Now the men were disgruntled. Who did this white woman think she was? After much discussion, though, the punishment was reduced to ten lashes. Mary knew she could not hope for more. She went back to Okon's hut, got out her supply of laudanum and bandages and treated the girls' bleeding backs after their whippings.

After two weeks in Ibaka, the trip home was in Chief Okon's own canoe with him at the helm. This was not a repeat of the smooth trip down. A storm came up suddenly shortly after their late departure from Ibaka. Everyone was terrified, and the chief's paddlers would not follow his commands. Mary reacted in a way that was typical of her when she was angry. She shouted at the drummer to resume his duty and the paddlers to paddle, and they complied. Their fear of Mary Slessor was apparently greater than their fear of either the chief or the likelihood of impending death from the storm. They brought the canoe near a mangrove tree overhanging the water and struggled against the storm until it abated, clinging

23. Ibid., 41.

to the tree while the water in the canoe rose to their knees. Mary shivered so badly that Okon and his wife nestled against her to try to warm her. When they reached Old Town before sunrise, the weak and feverish Ma was carried to her house, where she was confined to bed for a week.

SICK AGAIN

Mary had been saddened by the death of her mentor, Euphemia Sutherland in October 1881, and of Louisa Anderson—the early taskmaster she had come to love—in January 1882. Seldom did a year pass without at least one missionary dying or being sent home ill.

Later that year Foreign Mission Secretary Buchanan applauded a letter Slessor had sent. Mission Board correspondence is preserved, but that from missionaries to the Board was not, so one must look at one-sided conversations. The letter he praised probably told of her experiences at Ibaka. Buchanan reported that she had been "the means of awakening to new interest in Calabar in the minds of many of our people." People back home were hungry for exciting news from all Scottish Presbyterian foreign mission fields. Missionaries were prodded to provide such news, so that mission offerings would be maintained at a high level. Recitations of mundane day-to-day life were unlikely to fill this need. The secretary closed by issuing the request familiar to every missionary: Submit a report. He reminded Slessor that he needed it for his own year-end report.[24]

At the end of February 1883, Mary was saddened by the accidental death of Samuel Howell Edgerley, (whose parents were with the first missionary group to arrive in Calabar in 1846). Mary recalled her first weeks in Calabar, getting acquainted with mission work in the company of Edgerley and his wife. About the same time another tornado struck Old Town. Mary's house lost its roof, and she went to bed with a high fever again.

On March 30, Buchanan wrote again to Mary. He had given up on receiving another report from her soon.

> I had your interesting letter containing an account of your illness and also for the storm that damaged your house. I shall try to gather out a few particulars to form something like a report. I trust you are now keeping well, and that you have got over the effects of your exposure and excitement. You seem to have your hands

24. FMB to MS, MS7659/152, November 10, 1882.

> full with various kinds of work, and I hope you will be careful of yourself and not do too much. . . . I hope to have a letter from you occasionally, with a note of some of your observations and experiences.[25]

When Slessor didn't rally, colleagues sent her to Duke Town to recuperate. She was so ill that they decided to send her home. She seemed near death. Two weeks after Buchanan's letter was written, most likely before Slessor received it, Mary was carried aboard a ship bound for Liverpool. She was not alone. She had saved a pair of twins not long before, but the boy had been kidnapped and killed, and she absolutely refused to leave without the baby girl. That child, Janie—or as she came to be called by Slessor, "wonderful Jean"—would become her companion, helper, and nurse as the child grew to adulthood. Once again, as she left, colleagues and other Europeans suspected that was the last they would see of Mary Slessor.

25. FMB to MS, MS7659/351, March 30, 1883.

4

A Long Pause—Creek Town

> While Miss Slessor addressed many public meetings during her furloughs . . . she never told what she had done—she was too modest for that—but what the Lord had done; she always reckoned herself a feeble instrument in His hands.
>
> —John McCrindle, 1915[1]

After a reunion with her mother and sisters in Dundee and recovering from her illness, Mary had baby Janie baptized at Wishart Church. Then she began her round of deputation assignments. Various church and ladies' meetings and youth groups fell under her spell as she challenged them, not only for money but also for missionary volunteers. Janie was a big hit wherever Mary took her. This child was living proof of the worth of mission work in Calabar. Her presence was a better fund-raiser than the usual drums, masks or other items missionaries brought home. One young woman, Jessie Hogg, met Mary personally early in her furlough, and Mary asked what was keeping her from serving God as a missionary. Jessie decided immediately that she should go to Calabar, too. She applied to the Foreign Mission Board, was accepted, and reached Calabar June 27,1884, long before Mary and Janie returned from what ended up being a very long furlough.[2]

Mary also kept busy corresponding with the Foreign Mission Secretary, voicing suggestions, requests and complaints. She asked the Board to consider sending someone to Calabar to care for the large number of twins, since that occupied so much of her time there—time she

1. WMM, February, 1915, 58.
2. Livingstone, Mary Slessor, 45; Christie, "Annals," 1884.

needed to teach and do other work. Secretary James Buchanan wrote back, "I laid your letter of the 6th August [1883] before the Board on Tuesday, and the various matters you speak of were carefully considered. Your suggestion about some one to take charge of Twin Children the Board agreed to keep before them for future consideration."[3]

There is no evidence the Foreign Mission Board ever approved this suggestion. Slessor had also included a request that the missionary term before furlough be reduced from four years to three. Buchanan's letter said the Board agreed to consider that recommendation "when arrangements are being made for your going out again to Calabar."

At no time in Mary's future did a change in the rules affect her. In fact, the few furloughs she took were farther apart as time went on. Not until 1902, nearly twenty years after Slessor's request, did a new furlough rule go into effect: the first two terms of service would be just twenty months before furloughs were granted. A survey of William Christie's "Annals" reveals that few took advantage of the ruling allowing them to return home early. Furloughs were individualized affairs. Some missionaries stayed just a few months away from their stations; others remained at their post for several years before taking a furlough.

Slessor's letters sometimes puzzled and frustrated the Foreign Mission Board. In November 1883 Buchanan wrote, "I am sorry you have been annoyed about the photograph but after the steps you have now taken, perhaps it may be as well just to let the matter drop. I trust you will not have any more annoyance with reference to it."

What was Mary's annoyance about the photo? We are left to guess. In the same letter she asked the Board to consider sending a friend of hers—a Baptist—as a missionary to Calabar. "As to the young lady you speak of," Buchanan wrote, "perhaps I had better mention this fact. It seems that on one or two occasions some little difficulty has arisen in our mission work in connection with parties holding Baptist views."

> From this experience in the past, the Board some little time ago declined . . . the services of a Baptist Missionary who offered himself to our mission, though we all had a high opinion of his character and qualifications. I rather think that the Board would not be inclined to look favourably on any application coming from a member of the Baptist Church: they feel indeed that our own

3. FMB to MS, MS7660/169, September 28, 1883.

> Church should provide the men and women, as well as the funds, for our mission work.[4]

"Of course if you wish it," he concluded, "I can mention the matter to the Board but I am quite sure they would just say to you officially what I have said above in a less official way."

It is an interesting aside to note that the mission had appointed a Miss Diboll "from the Baptist Mission, Cameroons, for one year" in 1870. Her one year in Calabar with the Presbyterian Mission stretched to thirteen years. After seven years serving at Creek Town, she married missionary teacher James D. Swan. They resigned from the mission in 1883, shortly before Mary Slessor left on this furlough. Whether their resignation was part of the "some little difficulty with parties holding Baptist views" is unknown. It may be assumed that the couple remained in the Calabar district, since Christie's "Annals" tells us that Swan died at Creek Town fifteen years after his resignation.

In the spring of 1884, when Mary's furlough should have ended, the Secretary wrote:

> The question of your remaining a little longer in Scotland so as to have the opportunity of telling your story to Bible Classes, Mother's meetings and other quiet gatherings of the female members of the Church, was before the Board yesterday. . . . The Board are quite willing that your stay here should be prolonged for a short time, say three months, to admit of your doing the work intreated. . . . Kindly write to me and let me know what you think of this proposal. I myself think well of it, and that you should at once agree to remain for the time spoken of. This would also allow the repairs on the Old Town house to be completed.[5]

Mary agreed to stay.

PROBLEMS

Slessor had notified the Foreign Mission Board early in 1884 that she was ready to return to Calabar, eager to get back to her repaired house in Old Town and the people she had come to consider her own. Her extension of leave continued for another year and involved a number of letters back and forth between Mary and Secretary Buchanan. In December it looked

4. FMB to MS, MS 7660/296, November 19, 1883.

5. FMB to MS, MS7660/561, April 23, 1884.

as if things were on track for her to return to Creek Town, since the Board had already decided to have Old Town served by native agents and missionaries from Duke Town. However, her home situation began to cause her worry. Younger sister Janie developed tuberculosis. Mary recalled how her brother John had died just after emigrating to New Zealand hoping to regain his health. She came up with a desperate plan for Janie's recovery in a warm climate. Slessor's letter startled Secretary Buchanan. She told him she could not return to Calabar unless Janie could accompany her and unless permission was granted for her to build a small mud house with her own money for their use, rather than boarding with other missionaries.[6]

Buchanan responded,

> In regard to a house, I don't think the Board would like to see you in a house that is not of a kind with the other houses of the mission (unless of course in some emergency,) nor do I think they would care that you had a house of your own when the rule is for the Board to provide houses for our agents. In regard to your sister going out . . . do you think that Calabar is the place where one should go who has a weak chest? If the climate were telling unfavourably on her, as I fear it would, would she not require more attention than you with your duties could give her, and if she was obliged to come home, would you not have a strong desire to come with her rather than allow her to come alone?
>
> I have just hinted these things as they occur to myself and for your consideration. But our Western Committee meet on the 20th, and I shall lay the matter before them. Meantime I think it better not to fix the time of your leaving until after the meeting.[7]

Mary was displeased with Buchanan's letter. He wrote four days later,

> I am very sorry that you seem to be vexed at the contents of my last letter. When your letter of Dec. 1st was laid before the Board the question of your sister going with you was not entered upon. I did not understand till I had your next letter (of 5th January) that you made it an absolute condition of your returning to Calabar that your sister should go with you. . . . I trust you will not do me the injustice to think that I was keeping anything back or taking you at any disadvantage. You know well that I would do anything

6. Livingstone, Mary Slessor, 47.

7. FMB to MS, MS7661/394, January 13, 1885.

> in my power to promote your comfort and encourage you in your work.[8]

Of course, the Board did not approve of her sister going to Calabar with Slessor. Nor did they approve of her idea regarding housing. Buchanan notified Mary of the decision, saying, "I trust you will not fail to see the reasonableness of the conclusion to which the Board have come."[9]

Within a month, Mary moved her mother and sister to the warmer climate of Devon, in the south of England. A woman had mentioned to her that Janie might get better there, and she grasped at this possible solution to her problem. A deacon of the Congregational Church in Topsham (now part of Exeter) helped find a place for them to live. They moved into a Georgian house on The Strand, the ground behind leading down to the River Exe. Mary soon became involved in the life of the local church, giving talks on her work in Calabar. She had not been in Devon long, though, before it dawned on her that she might not, at least for a long time, be able to return to Calabar. The Foreign Mission Board proposed paying her salary through May of 1885, but Mary felt uncomfortable about the offer. She accepted her pay only through February. Her mother and sister transferred their membership from Wishart Presbyterian Church in Dundee to Topsham's Congregational Church April 27, 1885.[10]

At about this time the women received the shocking news that Susan Slessor had gone to visit a mutual friend in Edinburgh and dropped dead upon arrival. Mary returned to Dundee to see to her other sister's burial and close up the house. Now the family had no income: Although Janie's health improved, she was unable to work. Supporting the family fell entirely on Mary. She laid the problem before her mother and expressed her longing to go "up-country" in Calabar. "You are my child, given to me by God, and I have given you back to Him," Mrs. Slessor said.[11] Neither of them had any doubt that Calabar was where Mary belonged.

In May, Mary applied to return to Calabar. The Foreign Mission Board quickly reinstated her. She could go as soon as everything could be arranged. The first of July, Secretary Buchanan wrote that her "suggestion

8. FMB to MS7661/399, January 17, 1885.

9. FMB to MS, MS7661/412, January 28, 1885.

10. Topsham, "Mary Slessor."

11. Livingstone, Mary Slessor, 49.

of going to the Exeter Infirmary" was a good one.[12] It is not clear how she spent her time at the Infirmary; there seems to be no mention of her presence in modern Exeter's archives. Caroline Oliver writes in *Western Women in Colonial Africa*, "Mary regularly attended Exeter Hospital to widen her medical knowledge for when she could go abroad again."[13] Biographer James Buchan said she worked there as a nurse, since she had no income.[14] Slessor does not mention this period in existing letters.

As time drew nearer for Mary's return to Africa, her mother came down with bronchitis and Janie had a relapse. In her distress, she wrote to a friend in Dundee to ask if she would come to act as caretaker, so that her return to Calabar would not be further jeopardized. The friend packed up at once and moved from Dundee to Topsham. By October, Buchanan asked Slessor if she could leave on November 11. She did. She and young Janie arrived in Calabar on December 5, 1885, ending what was one of the longest furloughs for any agent of the mission—a hiatus of two and a half years.

CHANGES IN AFRICA

While Mary was busy facing family problems, raising money for the church's foreign mission work, and urging volunteers to serve as missionaries, the world was changing in a way that would impact her life, the lives of many missionaries, and the lives of countless Africans. European nations, excluding Africa from any voice in the matter, carved out empires for themselves in a comity arrangement, in order to protect their own commercial interests.

Back in Calabar, mission work went on as usual. The children of Scotland sent a New Year's gift to the mission in 1884: the river steamer *David Williamson*—a "smoking canoe." Goldie, several others of the Creek Town and Duke Town mission staff, and native teacher Asuquo Ekanem explored up the Cross River in the new vessel.

Alexander Cruickshank, who arrived in Calabar three years after Slessor, continued mission work at Ikot Offiong, about twenty miles up the Cross River from Creek Town. Jamaican missionaries Ezekiel Jarrett

12. FMB to MS, MS7662/12, July 2, 1885.

13. Oliver, Western Women, 105.

14. Buchan, Expendable Mary Slessor, 78.

and his wife[15] left Ikot Offiong to open a new station at Ikotana, even further up the Cross River.

The staff at the Calabar Mission continued to grow during Slessor's absence. Besides Jessie Hogg, James Luke and his wife arrived. The Lukes were stationed at Creek Town when Mary returned in December 1885. They had heard of the feisty redhead before their arrival in Calabar; there they would also be able to watch her work close up. Luke spoke highly of Slessor in his writings.

HOME TO CREEK TOWN

Creek Town, called Obio Oko by the Efik, lies about five miles from Duke Town, on the north side of a creek that connects the Cross and Calabar Rivers. According to Chief E. U. Aye, Creek Town was settled by Efik "as early as the fourteenth century," and it was and still is, "to all intents and purposes, the center of Efik life, culture and traditions."[16]

When Mary and Janie were welcomed back to Creek Town, they were housed in the mission compound where veteran missionaries Hugh and Jane Goldie lived. The Goldies had left on furlough, but the Lukes and Jamaicans Hopetoun Clerk and his wife were there, along with carpenter John Morison, and two other Marys—Mary Edgerley and Mary Johnstone.

Slessor soon fell into the routine she had left behind nearly three years before: teaching, dispensing medicines, taking in children and visiting African women in their yards. She kept busy, but concern about the welfare of her mother and sister worried her. The first mail of 1886 brought good news in a letter from her mother: both mother and sister were better. Mary was relieved and emotional. She wrote, "I rushed to my room and behaved like a silly body, as if it had been bad news. It brought you all so clearly before me. At church I sat beside the King [Eyo] and cried quietly into my wrap all the evening."[17] The good news, however, did not last.

By the time Mary received the "good news" letter, her mother had already died. She died on the eve of the new year, when Mary had been

15. Missionary wives who were not designated as missionaries themselves were usually identified only as Mrs. (first name not recorded).

16. Aye, Old Calabar, 31, 3.

17. Livingstone, Mary Slessor, 50.

at Creek Town hardly a month. Three months later her sister Janie, just twenty-four years old, died, too. Mary was overcome with grief. She was alone in the world, she declared. "Heaven is now nearer to me than Britain, and no one will be anxious about me if I go up-country."[18] She knew many in the mission opposed her going further afield, especially alone, but she had been more concerned about her mother's opinion and about following God's leading.

Mary Edgerley and Mary Johnstone both left Creek Town for furlough six months after Slessor returned. After they sailed, Mary and Janie were able to live separately after all. They most likely lived in the new house that had been built for Edgerley just before Slessor's return.

Three and a half-year-old Janie was spoiled. She was Mary's family. She ate and slept with her, and Janie learned to pray for their friends in Scotland. One day a man appeared who claimed he was Janie's father. He didn't want to get too close, he said, remembering the twin taboo. He just wanted to see her from a distance. Slessor laughed and said, "Hoots, what harm can a wee girlie do you!"[19] Mary insisted he receive a hug, and he was won over. From then until his death a short time later, he visited often and brought gifts of food. Janie was not the only child in Slessor's household. She continued to take them in. A girl of six, boys eight and ten, and a thirteen-year-old girl, Inyang, rounded out her list of more or less permanent residents at Creek Town. Other babies and children came and went. Inyang acted as babysitter much of the time that Mary nursed, taught, and counseled.

Slessor valued her friendship with King Eyo at Creek Town and also wrote of a blind Christian woman there. "Blind Mary is our one living, bright, clear light. . . . The other day I heard the King say that she was the only visible witness among the Church members in the town, but he added, 'She is a proper one.'" Slessor concluded that Blind Mary's house was "like a heaven here to more than me."[20]

18. Ibid., 51.

19. Christian and Plummer, Redhead, 51.

20. Livingstone, Mary Slessor, 55.

WHERE TO GO NEXT

There had been discussion both in Scotland and in Calabar of the need to expand the mission's work. There were only four permanent stations, although there were a number of smaller teaching stations served by European or Jamaican missionaries and by African teachers and evangelists. The opening of the fourth station at Ikotana extended mission presence eighty miles up the Cross River, but the work still hugged the river for the most part. A number of visits had been made to groups up the Cross River in earlier years. Hugh Goldie visited them in1851 and 1862 but was not encouraged to return. Not until the end of the 1870s did missionaries visit Okoyong territory again. African pastor Esien Ukpabio pushed for a mission station there, inland from Creek Town between the Cross and Calabar Rivers. African teachers took on the challenge but had to give up the work when the Okoyong and Creek Town peoples had one of their "periodic quarrels."[21]

Mary Slessor was determined to move into Okoyong territory. She grew impatient. She apparently hounded William Anderson and Hugh Goldie into finally saying she could go. Goldie made it clear to the Foreign Mission Board the move was Mary's own choice. Anderson wrote that they would meet with the tribe before she went.[22] They passed the decision along to Scotland in mid-1886. Mary thought the Board was too slow, so she harassed them about the matter herself. Secretary Buchanan wrote a year after the Calabar Committee had agreed she could go, chronicling the Board's actions—approving her move "in accordance with your own request" as soon as Edgerley and Johnstone returned from furlough; granting fifty pounds to build her a house; and keeping in touch with the Calabar Committee. "All these decisions of the Board were duly sent out to the Calabar Committee to be communicated to you," he wrote, "so that I cannot understand what you mean by saying that you have had no answer to your communications to the Board regarding your work or your accommodation."[23]

Slessor enjoyed visiting Okoyong territory with other missionaries to see the lay of the land and to negotiate terms for her to make her home among them. According to Nora Adam of the Foreign Mission staff, the

21. Johnston, Maxim Guns, 23.

22. Buchan, Expendable Mary Slessor, 83.

23. FMB to MS, MS7664/209–13, May 29, 1888.

Okoyong were already eager to have a teacher.[24] Since Efik teachers were reluctant to go and the Mission Board had no one else to send, Slessor's insistence that she go was opportune. She wrote, "Our first visits were not particularly cheering. Everybody seemed afraid to meet us, and when we did get them gathered, they and their followers were armed to the teeth. They offered to give a piece of land, and took us about that we might choose it; but they promised little else of a definite character. . . . Though each visit found [the chiefs] less reserved and more friendly, the Chiefs as a *body* did not appear very enthusiastic."[25]

For her fourth visit to the Okoyong, Mary decided to take matters into her own hands. King Eyo loaned his canoe for the trip, as he had done for her Ibaka adventure. He provided a carpet and cushions for Mary's comfort, and a kerosene stove so she could have her tea. Her cup was left behind, though. She drank her tea from a saucer.

A reluctant crew paddled her up the river, worried that they might lose their heads to their traditional enemies. Trade between Creek Town and Okoyong people consisted of guns, gin and chains, besides the occasional taking of heads. Okoyong hated Calabar and were jealous of the Efik trade monopoly.

Eyo's canoe landed Mary in a creek off the Calabar River, and she was led to the village of Ekenge by Okoyong sentries. There she met Chief Edem and his influential sister, Ma Eme Ete. The Ekpe council of chiefs were divided about Slessor's request at first, but they finally decided she could come to live in Ekenge. Edem and most of his chiefs spoke Efik, the trade language, so Mary did not need an interpreter as she haggled with them over the conditions of her coming.

As soon as Okoyong leaders approved her move, she told them she needed land for a house and school. They agreed that mission property would be a safe haven for anyone who came there and that no firearms would be allowed there, an agreement like that in the Calabar districts. The question remains: why did they decide to allow Mary Slessor become a part of their community? It is likely she was seen as a source of protection from their Efik enemies. And a woman would be unlikely to attempt a takeover of Okoyong. With her God and her Book she might help them deal with the presence of the British. The tribe was shrinking numerically

24. WMM, March, 1915, 50.

25. Christian and Plummer, Redhead, 53–54.

(which many thought was due to their warring lifestyle and their habit of drunken revelry), and they were finding it difficult to cope with the new economic and social upheaval they faced.

Slessor, in spite of her fears of this people with the unsavory reputation, described the Okoyong as brave and good-looking, with "eyes fearless and piercing," and "as reckless of their own lives as they are of others.'" She asked to visit the nearby village of Ifako while she was there, but Chief Edem said that Ifako was holding a celebration and all the chiefs would be drunk, that she should wait another day to visit that people. Since she had to spend the night, she called her boatmen from the river to come to the village for a worship service, one that was watched with curiosity.[26]

"I often had a lump in my throat," Slessor confessed, "and my courage threatened to take wings and fly away."[27] She wrote to a friend, "I am not very particular about my bed nowadays but as I lay on a few dirty sticks laid across and across and covered with a litter of dirty cornshells, with plenty of rats and insects, three women and an infant three days old alongside, and over a dozen goats and sheep and cows and countless dogs outside, you won't wonder that I slept little!"[28]

Gunshots awakened her in the morning. Someone had shot at two women who were walking to a spring for water. A search failed to turn up the guilty party. If she had ignored the possibility in the past, Mary was now highly aware that no woman could safely wander outside her own village. One of Mary's colleagues, J. K. McGregor, wrote: "Every village had a feud with its neighbour . . . [and] besides the spirits that were supposed to dwell in the bush and molest people, any tree might have behind it a foe of flesh and blood."[29]

In spite of the little sleep and the rude morning awakening, Mary claimed she had "a comfortable quiet night in my own heart." After twelve years with the Calabar Mission, she knew she would soon say farewell to Creek Town. She believed she could make a difference in the lives of another group of people who needed to know God's love, a knowledge that could change their lives. Mission historian Geoffrey Johnston writes

26. Buchan, Expendable Mary Slessor, 86.

27. Ibid., 84.

28. Christian and Plummer, Redhead, 54.

29. Buchan, Expendable Mary Slessor, 87.

that Slessor's move into Okoyong territory would become "the most celebrated advance of the period" for the mission.[30]

30. Johnston, Maxim Guns, 22.

5

Marsh Fever and Other Afflictions[1]

> When you ask your white friends how they can be so reckless about the water, which, as they know, is a decoction of the malarious earth . . . they all up and say . . . they have "got an awfully good filter. . . ." The safest way of dealing with water I know is to boil it hard for ten minutes at least. . . . Before boiling the water you can carefully filter it if you like. A good filter is a very fine thing for clearing drinking water of hippopotami, crocodiles, water snakes, catfish, &c., and I daresay it will stop back sixty per cent. of the live or dead African natives that may be in it; but if you think it is going to stop back the microbe of marsh fever—my good sir, you are mistaken.
>
> —Mary Kingsley, 1897[2]

FEVER! THE WORD ITSELF could unnerve those who ventured to West Africa, especially in the tropical coastal areas. An African fever, whether malaria or something else, was simply called "fever" most of the time.

David Livingstone believed that living a sedentary life and remaining in one spot for an extended period was likely to bring on fever. "The best preventive against fever," he said, "is plenty of interesting work to do, and abundance of wholesome food to eat." He did note, however, that mosquitoes "appear so commonly at malarious spots that their presence may be taken as a hint to man to be off to more healthy localities."[3]

1. A variation of this chapter appeared *in Journal of Medical Biography*, Vol. 14, November, 2006.

2. Kingsley, *Travels*, 688.

3. D. Livingstone, *Popular Account.*

Thomas Wells Campbell, a missionary to Calabar from 1873 to 1878 wrote, "The last three months of the year are the worst, bringing pestilential fogs and vapours which are perilous if not fatal to the white. . . . Europeans are liable to a peculiar deadly fever, similar, probably to typhoid or gastric of an intensified type."[4]

In 1881 an American recited the woes of "fever" thus: "The poison of the undrained swamps has made us all to shiver and shake with ague. . . . [When the doctor arrived,] Oh, what doses of medicine he gave us —calomel, jalap, ipecac, Dovers powders, with Peruvian bark and pills as big as peas, with pink and senna and snakeroot. Oh, how they vomited, and purged, and bled us, and how, after weeks of fever and shakes, we pulled through, mere skeletons."[5]

Mary Kingsley, Victorian African explorer, declared that "everyone" was bound to get malaria eventually, no matter how careful they were.

> You will find lots of people ready to give advice on fever, particularly how to avoid getting it. . . . They tell you, truly enough no doubt, that the malaria is in the air, in the exhalations from the ground, which are greatest about sunrise and sunset . . . and in the drinking water, and that you must avoid chill, excessive mental and bodily exertion, that you must never get anxious, or excited, or lose your temper. . . . May I ask how you are to do without air from 6.30 P.M. to 6.30 A.M.? or what other air there is but night air, heavy with malarious exhalations, available then?

Kingsley's personal recommendations included eating an early dinner, sleeping under a mosquito net, and having a meal in the morning with "a good hot cup of tea or coffee and bread and butter, if you can get it." Her advice also included alcohol "of a proper sort, taken at proper times, and in proper quantities." She pointed out that most missionaries were teetotalers and that they had a high mortality rate.[6] "Remember always," she said, "your life hangs on quinine." Kingsley's instructions:

> By taking it when in a malarious district, say, in a dose of five grains a day, you keep down the malaria. . . . When you have got very chilled or over-tired, take an extra five grains with a little wine or spirit. . . . If, as generally happens, there is no doctor near to send for, take a compound calomel and colocynth pill, fifteen grains of

4. Stewart, *Old Calabar*, 9.

5. Barber, "An Address," 231.

6. Kingsley, *Travels*, 684–85.

> quinine and a grain of opium and go to bed wrapped up in the best blanket available. When safely there take lashings of hot tea or, what is better, a hot drink made from fresh lime-juice, strong and without sugar."[7]

And she took to heart the concern of a friend who told her, "Nothing hinders a man, Miss Kingsley, half so much as dying."[8]

A late twentieth century report on health in Africa during the colonial period claims that more people probably died from tropical fevers than all who died "at sea or on land by accidents, violence, or wars."[9] The World Health Organization states that malaria still claims a million victims a year. Diagnosis continues to be difficult in its early stages, its symptoms mimicking other more common ailments.[10]

ATTACKING MALARIA

David Livingstone developed his own cure, which came to be known as "Livingstone's Rousers" and was in widespread use.

> A remedy composed of from six to eight grains of resin of jalap, the same of rhubarb, and three each of calomel and quinine, made up into four pills, with tincture of cardamoms, usually relieved all the symptoms in five or six hours. Four pills are a full dose for a man—one will suffice for a woman. . . . When their operation is delayed, a dessert-spoonful of Epsom salts should be given. Quinine after or during the operation of the pills, in large doses every two or three hours, until deafness or cinchonism ensued, completed the cure. The only cases in which we found ourselves completely helpless were those in which obstinate vomiting ensued. . . . A missionary must never forget that, in the tropics, he is an exotic plant.[11]

In 1880 Charles-Louis-Alphonse Laveran discovered the parasite that causes malaria, but it wasn't until 1897 that Ronald Ross found and proved that the disease was spread by the Anopheles mosquito and was unconnected to "miasms." His discovery was corroborated by the research

7. Ibid., 689.
8. Ibid., 681.
9. Bruce-Chwatt and Bruce-Chwatt, "Malaria and yellow fever," 49.
10. World Health Organization, "Global Malaria."
11. D. Livingstone, *Popular Account.*

of Battista Grassi in Italy at about the same time. Later research indicated that many indigenous people carried the disease without showing symptoms. Ross proved that malaria was spread by the mosquito biting a carrier, then biting an uninfected person.

"No wild deserts, no savage races, no geographical difficulties have proved so inimical to civilization as this disease," wrote Dr. Rubert Boyce. "What we call the Dark Continent should be called the Malarious Continent."[12] The immediate result of Ross's findings resulted in a plan to reduce infection, especially in the European population: First, avoid living near those already infected—segregation. Second, screen verandas and windows and sleep under a mosquito net. Third, get rid of mosquitoes by eliminating breeding places, using oil or natural enemies of the mosquito. Finally, penalties for failure to follow these procedures were announced, and education was given high priority.[13]

News of Ross's discoveries was slow to be acknowledged throughout the world. In 1907 a physician reported "synonyms" for malaria as "ague; chills and fever; intermittent fever; swamp fever; marsh fever; paludal fever." He repeated the common belief that "miasms" from the soil caused these fevers and stated that heat, moisture, the seasons and winds influenced their spread as well. "That the poison may be transferred some distance by strong winds," he said, "has been clearly proven by sailors contracting the disease while anchored three to five miles off malarial shores." He went on to describe the three theories of how the parasites entered the body: the water theory, the air theory, and the inoculation theory. He did concede that the inoculation theory (by mosquito) "is the only one which has, to date, been demonstrated experimentally."[14]

In a cheerful letter to a group of girls back home, feisty Mary Slessor told of flies biting, seeing birds, monkeys, and snakes, and watching for alligators and hippos. She added, "I wish the mosquitoes were just half as tired as I am."[15]

12. Boyce, *Mosquito or Man?*, 46–48.

13. Ibid., 48–53.

14. Thomas, "Malarial Fever."

15. Christian and Plummer, *Redhead*, 158.

DOCTORS COME TO CALABAR

Hope Waddell wanted to take a physician along when the missionaries started for Calabar in 1846, but he couldn't find a qualified person willing to go. Archibald Hewan, a Jamaican, became the first medical missionary to Scotland's Presbyterian Mission ten years later. By 1890 a steady supply of physicians began to come to the mission, many serving only a couple of years; most either died or went home ill. Ten doctors served in Calabar during Mary Slessor's years there. She spoke highly of Drs. David Robertson and John William Hitchcock, who cared for her as her health waned toward the end of her life.

Some European Christians were reluctant to send medical missionaries to Africa. "Why trouble so about the heathen?" people asked. But at least two physicians began, near the end of the nineteenth century, to urge competent men to follow Christ's great commission. Dr. George Dowkontt believed "countless people" were being murdered by the neglect of their physical needs. "From thirty to forty millions of these people die every year without the knowledge of the gospel . . . lost for lack of the knowledge we possess," he wrote, "and who is responsible for these lives if not those who could help them, but do not? Surely such are the murderers of these millions."[16]

Dr. John Lowe, Secretary of the Edinburgh Missionary Society, wrote, "What, indeed, is the book of the Acts of the Apostles, but the first report of the first Medical Missionary Society?"[17] He insisted that medical training alone was not enough for a medical missionary candidate. "The function *par excellence* of the medical missionary," he wrote, "is that of the evangelist. . . . He must be a devout believer, holding with a firm and intelligent grasp of the saving truths of the Gospel, a thoughtful student of the Bible, and possessed of evangelistic gifts."[18]

Lowe also made an appeal for funds. "We do not want your money only," he wrote. "'Your money or your life' is the startling demand of the highwayman; ours is more startling still, 'Your money *and* your life.'"[19]

While appeals were being made for evangelistic doctors, missionaries often sent pleas home for more missionaries. James Luke, who served

16. Dowkontt, *Murdered Millions*, 17–18.

17. Lowe, *Medical Missions*, 17.

18. Ibid., 29, 42.

19. Ibid., 282.

in Calabar with Mary Slessor, emphasized the need for good health. He wrote, "Do urge upon the Church to send us more men. We want men with heads, hearts, hands, and stomachs—especially stomachs. No man with either a bad stomach or a bad set of teeth need come out here except to see the country and be sent back. It is time our medical men knew this."[20]

AMATEUR DOCTORING

Medical doctors declared that ordinary missionaries should not practice medicine. But whether or not physicians were available, many missionaries found themselves in the position of having to tend the sick and injured around them.

The testimony of three Presbyterian missionaries in Congo during Mary Slessor's era, describes the odd position in which they found themselves. The first black American Presbyterian missionary, William Sheppard, was once appointed a ship's doctor simply because he was a missionary; the captain supposed missionaries knew more about medicine than anyone else available. Sheppard, who was only in his early twenties—as was his colleague—described caring for fellow missionary Samuel Lapsley: "I nursed him carefully and tenderly through it and he was much improved in color from the purges and quinine." (Sheppard's biographer, William Phipps, says the young missionary used "Livingstone's Rousers" to good effect.)[21]

Lapsley wrote home, "You will be a bit surprised to learn that I have become something of a doctor. How, I don't know, unless by having first to take a good deal of physic from others, and then learning to dose myself and Sheppard." He told of taking medicine to town, "and now I have many cases a day, and they have all got well. . . . It is always a good means of interesting them in the "Balm of Gilead."[22]

Congo missionary William Morrison wrote, "I unfortunately belong to that large class of missionaries who have had no special medical training, yet necessity compelled me, during the greater part of my sojourn in Africa, to be the physician at Luebo both for the missionaries and for the native people, to say nothing of the white traders and government

20. *Record*, 1890, 238.

21. Phipps, *William Sheppard*, 61.

22. Ibid., 63.

officials. . . . I had, however, several good medical books and plenty of patients of practice on."[23]

Mary Slessor needed a physician many times herself. She also found herself in the position of having to doctor the people around her. Excerpts from her 1911 diary give some idea of the variety of complaints she faced. She gave no indication whether or not she imparted the 1850s advice of Hope Waddell, whose rules for patients were: "Use no native medicine; employ no country doctor; drink no rum; pray to Jesus for a blessing; and praise him for recovery."[24]

She wrote of a schoolboy who "had the bone laid bare" in a tree-splitting accident; of sending to Bende for serum for vaccination against smallpox during an outbreak; of snake bites and rat bites and dysentery and hydrophobia. In addition to the poultices, castor oil, and lymph Mary mentions in her diary, she refers to the necessary quinine and "powders." She also wrote of too many patients and little or no medicines on hand.[25]

The medicine chest of non-doctors was likely limited to those items found in many British homes during Slessor's era. Reputable drug companies provided laudanum in Victorian over-the-counter medicine kits. This mixture of alcohol, sugar and opium was widely used for pain. Looked upon as something of a cure-all, it was prescribed for insomnia and many other complaints. Isabella Beeton's *The Book of Household Management*, published in the mid-nineteenth century, included opium and laudanum in a list of "Drugs, &c." the householder was advised to have on hand.[26] Many became addicted to laudanum or opium—sometimes beginning with a prescription for a specific illness and progressing to addiction, sometimes taking it as a recreational drug, such as heroin or cocaine might be abused in a later era. Hope Waddell wrote in 1850 that Africans "called opium pills 'the little doctor,' and having got them once, had a great desire for them again."[27]

Mary's adopted son, Dan, wrote of his mother, "What an excellent nurse she was. Every child had a dose of quinine every other day, and that habit has gone through life with me and to-day I take paludrine every

23. Morrison, "Medical Work," 178–80.

24. Waddell, *Twenty-nine Years*, 453.

25. MS Diary, 1911, *e.g.*, February 16, March 16, 20, 23, 27.

26. Beeton, *Book of Household Management*.

27. Waddell, *Twenty-nine Years*, 453.

other day, and insist that my children do the same. When I am laid up with malaria, the whole house is in a stir. She would lay me gently on her bed, tuck me up, and with her work basket, papers etc. she would mount watch over me day and night till I get well again."[28]

PERSONAL ILLNESS

Slessor's earliest recorded reference to her own illness was in the 1878 letter that told of looking like an escapee from a lunatic asylum after an episode of fever.[29] Malaria would be an intermittent unwelcome affliction for the rest of her life, and it was responsible for her first two furloughs to Scotland. She suffered various other illnesses through the years, sometimes writing to friends about them, sometimes confiding only in her diaries.

"I do not think you had any idea of how queer I felt for six weeks before I left," Mary wrote to a friend while she was in Scotland for her final furlough in 1907. "I was sure it was paralysis. I could not walk a dozen steps, and if I did so, I nearly fainted after it." People were shocked at her appearance when she first arrived home, but by the time of the letter she wrote, "Here I am now only waiting for the rain to go off to get on my cycle and go anywhere."[30]

To another friend she later reported that she wasn't sure if her heart trouble was gone, but she was being careful. Her main problem then, she said, was "Billious Diarrhea, which brings me to my last gasp." She went on to express her conviction that it was only the prayers of those at home that kept her going.[31]

When asked how she managed a certain trip while she was sick, Slessor responded, "Oh, I just had to take as big a dose of laudanum as I dared, and wrap myself up in a blanket, and lie in the bottom of the canoe all the time, and managed fine."[32] A curious statement in a letter to a friend is typical of Slessor's "keep going" attitude: "I have not been *ill* but I have been unwell."[33]

28. D. Slessor, "Reminiscences."
29. MS to Davie Stewart, MS1986/396, December 10, 1878.
30. MS to Charles Partridge [CP], June 27, 1907.
31. MS to "My Dear Friend," ACC 6825/15, September 2, 1910.
32. Livingstone, *Mary Slessor*, 270.
33. MS to CP February 17, 1909.

Daniel Slessor wrote that his Ma "had all sorts of sicknesses peculiar to the local area"[34] She wore glasses in those later years, too, which were lost or broken from time to time.

Corresponding frequently with British officer Charles Partridge, Mary kept him informed about her problems with boils, which recurred from about 1905 until 1910 and caused her to lose her hair. As usual, after the fact she brought some levity to her situation. In 1907, she wrote:

> Out of your dreams has come the best Joke of the season. 'You have very pretty hair,' 'It looks best uncovered' & etc, etc. O my heart!! A good many have shared the joke, and it isnt finished yet. I was 'Carrots' and 'Fire' to my brothers and sisters, and my poor hair was the bane of my girlhood . . . and now in my old age it has 'Gold Glints' in the sun. . . . The poor half dozen white threads that barely covered the scalp during the last two or three years, have multiplied exceedingly from my trip to Bonnie Scotland, but alas! that the 'Carrots' should have developed into a baser metal than gold, with which even the sun cannot conjure!! So my dear boy, prepare for disillusionments, and if I take your advice—as I did last Sunday after reading your epistle—know for a truth, that it is not for health reasons that I wear a hat, but because there is nothing now on my pate to 'Glint.'[35]

The following year, she announced herself "rudely well" with only a "couple of boils" that were "humbugging" her. She was disappointed Partridge couldn't see her "rejuvenated, and with teeth [which she obtained during her 1907 furlough], i.e. when I don't forget to put them in—and with my 'Pretty Hair' as thick, tho' more silvern, than ever it was."[36] In June 1908 Mary reported one huge boil that kept her from sitting up or raising her arm to write.[37] In November she said, "I've had a bit of fever, but so has everyone else as the smokes [harmattan] are heavy."[38] Her worst episode of boils came in 1909, so severe that she lost her hair again.

> [I was] very ill, with at least 100 boils over my head! . . . For a whole month I was in one prolonged agony of pain. Then the boils came in shoals, over my face, till you wd. not have recognized me, all over

34. D. Slessor to Thomas Hart, November 30, 1948.
35. MS to CP, April 17, 1907.
36. Ibid., July 14 and August 14, 1908.
37. Ibid., June 20, 1908.
38. Ibid., November 28, 1908.

> my neck and ears, and whenever I got rested long enough from one operation of having the cores pressed out, another began and I cried like a child. When I was not shrieking all the long weeks, no sleeping draught could keep out the pain, and I am a very shakey bundle of nerves down to this hour. . . . I have often written to and joked with you . . . about the "Pretty Hair" and the halo. Poor hair!! Poor head!! It is as bald as a sixpence now all over the back, and . . . the few hairs left on the front are like those of a doll's head put on with bad glue. Every time I put in the brush, it comes off in heaps. I don't think it can last many days more, and it is so very painful still to brush my hair that I dread the process. The Dr. never saw anything like it, and said it was blood poisoning, which I believe is right, as one day three weeks or so before it came on, while teaching, a fly got on my hair, and a girl said "sit still Ma" and clapped the thing which was so full of blood that it splashed all over us, and the cloth I was sewing was soiled. Next day it itched, and I scraped it with my comb . . . and I scraped it so very fiercely every day after that, when the itch came back, till three small boils came, which was the awful beginning.[39]

When boils recurred in March of 1910, Mary wrote of "a miracle of healing" by a British military doctor. "He said one of the oldest doctors on the Coast had the same thing last year, and I was to take his drastic measures, and when I think of how he has healed me in such a short time, and quite killed the hundreds of things, and made life quite bearable again, I feel mad at the month of agony I suffered last year."[40]

Slessor gave no hint as to what the drastic measures were, but this was the last time she mentioned a severe outbreak. She reported a year later that her "halo" was getting grayer, and that she was "renewing my youth [and] working like a navvy."[41] Not long after that optimistic note, though, a severe vomiting episode sent her to Dr, and Mrs. Robertson's house at Itu for three weeks of treatment and recuperation.[42]

Mary wrote of personal frailties to only a few friends. She confided more fully in her diaries. Her 1911 diary tells of delirium, of bleeding hands after working on her storm-damaged roof; of "an overstrain of the

39. Ibid., July 7, 1909.

40. Ibid., March 3, 1910.

41. Ibid., April 12, 1911.

42. Ibid., April 27, 1910.

heart" that spurred her doctor to restrict her activities, and often of bouts of fever and weakness.[43]

In 1912 Slessor complained of "terrible pain in side and loins, cannot breathe."[44] The next year she suffered a painful infection after being struck in the eye with mud.[45]

By 1914, Mary was ill more often than not. A month of diary entries before she died reveals her ongoing struggle to live and serve the God she loved. The ailing missionary wrote at various times of back pain, swollen joints ("this gouty Calabar swelling"), hemorrhage and blood poisoning. Vomiting and diarrhea were not unusual, along with fever. She often attributed her fever episodes to the harmattan and said quinine was useless. She wrote of crawling to church for a women's meeting at ten A.M. one day and finding that daughter Annie had told everyone the meeting would be at four P.M. instead. Slessor wrote of losing a day, of being "distressingly weak" or that "neither head nor body will work." A month before she died, it was a very sick woman who wrote, "Children very bothersome. Myself perhaps irritable."[46]

A remark typical of Mary was one she made to Charles Partridge five years earlier: "You would be the first to cry shame if I turned tail for a bit of fever, or even a bald head."[47] In spite of any physical setback, the faithful servant would honor her commitment to God until the very end.

43. Ibid., September 4, 1911.

44. MS Diary, August 30, 1912.

45. Livingstone, *Mary Slessor*, 286; MS to CP Sr., June 7, 1913.

46. MS Diary, December 14, 1914..

47. MS to CP, October 15, 1909.

6

Opening a Territory

> They are the princes of drunkards, and smash and hash at each other, and at all and sundry as none of the other tribes do. Calabar people are so frightened for them, that to ask any one to come to see us is to bring a volley of isungi (abuse) or imam (laughter) down on your head. They would as soon think of going to the moon as of going to Okoyong.
>
> —Mary Slessor, 1890[1]

An excited Mary Slessor returned to Creek Town after her excursion to Ekenge. She reported to Goldie and Anderson that she was ready to go—the sooner the better—and she would take her children with her. Consternation reigned in Calabar's towns. Traders arrived from Duke Town to try to convince her not to go.[2] As it turned out, the move was three months in coming.

In May 1888 Foreign Mission Secretary Buchanan addressed a letter to Slessor at Okoyong, though she didn't get there until August. He reminded her of her failure to meet her obligations to the Foreign Mission Board. "According to the standing rule of the Board," he wrote, "all the missionaries of the Church (both male and female) are to send communications about their work to the Board from time to time, and specially a report at the close of the year." He reiterated that letters to the Ladies Committee or other correspondence could not substitute for reports to the Board.

Buchanan also wrote, "I hope you will not contemplate having the little girl [Janie] brought to this country for her education. The Board are

1. *Record*, 1890, 304–5.
2. Buchan, *Expendable Mary Slessor*, 87.

not disposed to look upon such an arrangement with any favour." He worried about the notions Slessor might advocate. In addition, he showed the sexist discrimination common in Victorian culture. Promising African men students were welcomed when recommended by mission presbyteries. Women were neither recommended nor welcomed. No matter that Janie was still a child. In effect, the secretary said: Don't get any wild ideas.

Buchanan did manage a compliment, saying, "We have heard of the large amount of work which fell to you in Creek Town on account of illness in the Mission Staff [and were told] how much your services were appreciated."[3]

August 4, 1888 was set for Mary and her bairns to leave Creek Town. King Eyo was not happy about it, but when he saw Mary's determination he again provided his canoe. Hugh Goldie was so uneasy about her going off alone that missionary printer John Bishop volunteered at the last moment to see her safely to Ekenge. Paddlers argued about loading the boat until Eyo came to give directions. Rain poured down. People were as gloomy as the weather, weeping and warning Mary for inviting peril.

The canoe landed three miles from the village with darkness about to fall. Mary went ahead with the children to get them fed and bedded down. Bishop and the paddlers would follow along. Hungry, tired and wet, Mary and the children slogged up the dark forest path. An eleven-year-old boy led the way, carrying their "chop" box—with its treasured bread, tea and sugar—on his head. Two other boys, ages eight and three, wailed behind him. Then came Janie, also crying. Mary brought up the rear, carrying baby Annie. She distracted them from their dismay with silly songs.

The arrival of visitors in the village usually resulted in a noisy greeting. This evening there was silence. The place was deserted except for a few slaves. One showed Mary to abandoned quarters and brought water. Another hurried away to let Ekenge's Chief Edem know the missionary had arrived. Where was everyone? Gone to a funeral feast in the village of Ifako, two miles away, where the chief's mother had died. They were not expected back for several days.

Mary fed the children and got them to sleep, but they had no sleeping mats or dry clothes. She couldn't imagine why John Bishop didn't come. He finally showed up with news that the Calabar men were tired

3. FMB to MS, MS7664, 209, 213.

and refused to bring anything that night. While others might have fallen apart at the news, Mary was fuming. They were tired? Her "carrots and fire" temper took over. The next day was Sunday, a day when no loads would be carried.

She sent a boy with a lantern ahead but doubted (correctly) that he could succeed in urging the paddlers to action. Then leaving Bishop as babysitter, off she marched, alone and barefoot—since she couldn't get her swollen feet back into her boots—three miles back down the muddy path to the canoe. She was surprised and grateful when a young Okoyong boy offered to carry her lantern. At the beach she shook the men awake, then threatened and cajoled until she loaded boxes and baskets of essential items on their heads and started them toward the village.

Slessor's first Sunday in Okoyong territory was not a happy one. Rain still poured down. She had no audience for her preaching. She and the children suffered from scratches and insect bites after their nighttime forest walk. She was cooped up in a dirty place with no door or window, and the rest of her goods were still in the canoe. Yes, she was free to serve God alone here with no supervision, but what success could she hope for?

On Monday and Tuesday, Bishop and the crew brought the remaining gear from the boat. This was no take-along-a-few-suitcases trip. A small folding organ was even included with the supplies (a departing gift for her new ministry) and a door and window for her "house." Bishop oversaw the hanging of the door and window in the dilapidated lodging before he left Wednesday. Mary was miserable. Rain still fell; it came through the thatch roof onto boxes and bedding. Mud was everywhere. There were gaps around the door and window.[4]

People began to return from the funeral celebrations late in the week, but the men soon left again to fight some men they had quarreled with in Ifako. Chief Edem did move the weary missionary to better quarters in his compound before they left. Mary spent her time cutting brush and trees, fencing part of the yard for washing and cooking, moving packing crates around to make partitions for privacy and preparing "a few conveniences," which probably included digging a latrine for her household. She kept busy with the manual tasks that missionaries faced, tasks that had nothing to do with preaching the gospel.

4. Buchan, *Expendable Mary Slessor*, 91.

One day, after things returned to normal in Ekenge, Mary noticed the boy who had carried her lantern to the canoe surrounded by a circle of headmen. She did not realize what was happening until too late. A chief ladled boiling oil out of a pot and poured it over the boy's hands. Mary was not able to save him from this ordeal, but she hurried to doctor him with laudanum and ointment. The boy was accused of breaking tribal customs by not taking part in the funeral celebration at Ifako. Buchan writes, "It may have been that those among them who had opposed [Mary's] coming to the tribe intended the boy's punishment as a warning both to her and to the people as to what would happen to anybody who took up with her newfangled ideas."[5]

WITCHCRAFT AND MAGIC, ORDEALS, AND OATHS

The use of boiling oil was just one of several ordeals used to judge innocence or guilt in West Africa during Mary Slessor's lifetime. The defendant dipped his hands into water before the oil was poured over them. If blistering followed, he had obviously committed the offense and could be punished further with flogging or death. It is difficult to imagine that many escaped a guilty verdict with this kind of trial.

Those charged with witchcraft drank a mixture of water and pounded *esere*—a poisonous bean. The person undergoing this ordeal was said to "chop nut" or "drink doctor." Europeans called it "taking the bean." If the concoction was vomited up, the verdict was innocence. If not, death was likely and was presumed a fitting punishment for the guilty. Often the accused insisted on taking the bean, convinced they would be saved by their innocence.[6] Victorian traveler and writer Mary Kingsley said some tribes were decimated when entire villages took *esere* after being accused of witchcraft by another village. Kingsley wrote, "It is no uncommon thing for ten or more people to be destroyed for one man's sickness or death; and thus over immense tracts of country the death-rate exceeds the birth-rate."[7]

5. Ibid., 92.
6. Goldie, *Calabar*, 34.
7. Kingsley, *Travels*, 466.

One ethnologist stated in 1956, "Nigerian law forbids the *esere* ordeal, but occasional cases still occur when individuals desire to show their innocence of any imputation of witchcraft."[8]

Historian Kannan K. Nair attributes an increasing use of witchcraft charges to the breakdown of traditional relationships in society. The breakdown came as drastic economic changes occurred with growing British presence and changes in trade. "Witchcraft," he writes, "was no more than trickery by which men and women outwitted their neighbours, or a peg on which to hang notions that their neighbours were turning against them."[9] Nair and others also point out that the person who administered *esere* could determine the outcome by how it was given. "An excessive or a deficient dose merely produced vomiting."[10]

A milder form of judgment, but no less feared, came from *mbiam*, a solemn oath designed to destroy liars. Hope Waddell said King Eyo II admitted in 1855 that "they knew *mbiam* was nothing, but they had to use it as the form of oath the people feared."[11]

Waddell compared the liquid used for the oath to the "bitter waters" of the Israelites in the wilderness. Goldie described it as "a dirty-looking liquid kept in a bottle, ornamented with old feathers."[12] Missionary James Luke described watching a man take *mbiam*. He did not describe the liquid's ingredients but called it "a *ju-ju* mixture of awful and immediate power." He wrote, "He took the monkey-bone which stuck in the stuff like a forgotten spoon, dipped it afresh in the fateful contents, lifted it, and drew it across his lips. . . ."[13] This action was followed by recitation of the *mbiam* oath.

Apparently, the liquid and the accompanying oath varied from district to district. Mary Kingsley described it as being made of "filth and blood." It was not poisonous, she admitted, "but it is the most respected and dreaded of all oaths." She recounted one form of it:

8. Simmons, "Ethnographic Sketch," 22.

9. Nair, *Politics and Society*, 52–53.

10. Ibid., 52; Buchan, *Expendable Mary Slessor*, 69.

11. Waddell, *Twenty-Nine Years*, 174.

12. Goldie, *Calabar*, 41.

13. Luke, *Pioneering*, 152.

If I have been guilty of this crime,
If I have gone and sought the sick one's hurt,
If I have sent another to seek the sick one's hurt,
If I have employed any one to make charms or to cook bush,
Or to put anything in the road,
Or to touch his cloth,
Or to touch his yams,
Or to touch his goats,
Or to touch his fowl,
Or to touch his children,
If I have prayed for his hurt,
If I have thought to hurt him in my heart,
If I have any intention to hurt him,
If I ever, at any time, do any of these things (recite in full),
Or employed others to do these things (recite in full)
Then, Mbiam! *Thou* deal with me.[14]

Mary Slessor regarded *mbiam* as an acceptable alternative to other ordeals, especially *esere*. It was the lesser of other evils, she reasoned. But many of Slessor's colleagues condemned its use. Native Christians refused the oath as a "heathen" practice, no doubt taught this by missionaries. Though it did lead to death in some cases, certainly death was a less likely outcome from *mbiam* than from the *esere* bean and did not produce the pain or disfigurement caused by boiling oil. Slessor allowed the oath in her court in later years and even advised District Commissioner Charles Partridge to use it.[15]

Belief in witchcraft and magic was widespread in the African worldview. Anyone could be accused of *ifot*—witchcraft or magic—by anyone else, hardly different from the suit-happy culture in some western countries today, where anyone may sue another for anything. When a person became ill or died, the belief was that someone else (or numbers of others) caused the calamity. Chief E. U. Aye discusses the belief in *ifot* and its "very important role in the destruction of human lives in Old Calabar." He points to Old Testament references to witchcraft and later European beliefs about witches and declares that the belief in witchcraft "has been common to all humanity in the young days of their development." He writes, too, of the persistence of the belief, not only in Africa but also in other parts of the world. "In Africa today the belief in witchcraft is a great

14. Kingsley, *Travels*, 465.

15. MS to CP, January 17, 1905.

social drawback and spreads fear and panic and death among many. The result is that witchhunts are still common [in 1967], especially in many out-of-the-way villages, and the so-called witch doctors command a powerful influence in the social life of each community."[16]

Rosalind Hackett, in *Religion in Calabar*, points out, "The fear of witchcraft continues unabated, despite earlier predictions that it would disappear with education and social development."[17]

THE CHIEF'S YARD

The move to better housing in Edem's yard brought Mary Slessor into close and constant contact with the women of the community. It was customary for village guests to be housed in the king's compound, and she was still a guest after many months, unable to get her own house built. It was also the custom to stay as close as possible to an important guest. Mary was the center of attention, a curiosity, a source of entertainment. People crowded into the yard to watch her. She had no peace, no privacy.

Living in the rooms next to the king and his head wife, other wives' lodging nearby, Mary saw and heard much more of the king's intimate personal life than she wished. She was unsettled by frequent bickering, slaves being flogged, punishment of children by withholding food or branding, and nights of drinking, drumming, and dancing. She sometimes fled to the bush with a machete, not just to clear the land assigned to her, but also to be alone. There she could work (or pray) in peace.

Mary had been in Ekenge less than a month when Chief Edem bit one of his wives on the arm during a funeral feast. The bite festered. Evidence of blood poisoning appeared, red streaks along the woman's arm. A native doctor had no success in treating the wound, so the chief asked the missionary for help. Slessor applied what limited poultices and medications she had, and the arm gradually healed. Local chiefs were impressed. "From this my fame spread far and wide," Mary wrote, ". . . [and] after this I had many visitors from the interior towns some of whose names were familiar as the terror of Calabar, but everyone was gentlemanly and gracious, everyone laid aside his arms at the entrance to our yard, and everyone gave us an invitation to spend a week or two at his place."[18]

16. Aye, *Old Calabar*, 76–77.

17. Hackett, *Religion in Calabar*, 327.

18. Buchan, *Expendable Mary Slessor*, 96–97.

Chief Edem's problems multiplied with Mary living in his compound. As distant villagers heard of the lone white woman, people began to show up at his doorstep to see her. Once, a mob of drunken women arrived, expecting the white woman to provide them with rum and other gifts. These women had the reputation of appearing at villages and making demands until they were satisfied. They came to Ekenge shooting and shouting, waving guns and swords. The rich white woman would give them what they wanted. Chief Edem gave them a *dash*—a gift—of rum, then guarded Mary's door through the night to protect her. In the morning the women got a scolding from Mary, and they responded by threatening and cursing her before leaving empty-handed.[19]

Another time, a chief's young wife hired a slave to work. When the chief called for him unexpectedly, the slave demanded partial payment from the girl. She refused. It was against the law for her to do so in her husband's absence, but when the slave insisted she gave him a piece of yam. When others found out, the young wife was chained up and sentenced to the boiling oil ordeal. Mary begged for the girl's freedom, and she was finally taken to Slessor's house and kept in chains "until the dancing and rioting ended with the dawn."[20]

When Chief Edem became ill with an abscess in his back, Slessor nursed him. One morning she arrived to care for him and was dismayed to see that he had consulted a local *abia idiong*—commonly called a witch doctor by Europeans. In 1847 Hope Waddell defined another person—the *abia ebok*—as a native practitioner.[21] As opposed to the *abia idiong*, ministrations by the *abia ebok* used native remedies that were often effective. Some of these men willingly shared their knowledge with missionaries. An *abia idiong* (called by Waddell a sorcerer or magician) was more likely to name the source of *ifot* and to produce items he claimed he removed from the body.

When Mary arrived, charms lay around the patient, and a chicken was impaled on a stick nearby. Edem praised the white man's medicine but said white men could not possibly understand the evil of a black man's heart. "Ma," he said, "it has been made known to us that some one is to

19. Livingstone, *Mary Slessor*, 73; Christian and Plummer, *Redhead*, 62.

20. Ibid., 72.

21. Waddell, *Vocabulary*, 12.

blame for this sickness, and here is proof of it—all these have been taken out of my back."[22]

The chief displayed a container of "shot, powder, teeth, bones, seeds, egg-shells, and other odds and ends." Men and women were grabbed and chained for punishment. Slessor's pleadings were useless. When he tired of Mary's harangue, the chief ordered his men to carry him to one of his farms, along with his wives and the prisoners. He forbade Mary to follow. Later, some people came to see Mary from the farm and told her they heard that native pastor Esien Ukpabio could cure this disease. They asked Mary for a letter requesting his presence, which she gladly supplied. Unfortunately, when Ukpabio asked the letter-bearers what was wrong with Chief Edem, they said someone's "soul" was troubling him. Ukpabio refused to go, but his sister obtained permission to go in his place. Ukpabio's sister succeeded in treating the abscess and the chief fully recovered. All the prisoners were finally released except one. It was small comfort to Mary to learn that "only" one woman was killed.

GROWING RECOGNITION

A woman who went to visit relatives at a village eight hours away from Ekenge found the chief there very ill. People stood around waiting for him to die. She assured them that if they sent for the powerful white woman at Ekenge the chief would live. Her own granddaughter had been healed, and so had many others. The people agreed to try it. They sent a *dash* to get Slessor to come. "What's wrong with him?" Mary wanted to know. Nobody knew. Chief Edem and his influential sister, Ma Eme Ete, didn't want her to go. The trip was too long, too many deep streams to be crossed, the rains were too heavy.

Mary, impetuous as usual, decided to go. When the chief and his sister saw her determination, they sent a message back demanding "an escort of freewomen and armed men." It obviously wasn't merely concern about the weather and the length of the journey. The chief worried about Mary's safety in a violent area. He knew that if the patient died, Mary might be included among many others who would die as a result; and his own village could become implicated in the aftermath.

The women escorts arrived in the morning and said the men would meet them before they reached their village. "The rain was falling as they

22. Livingstone, *Mary Slessor*, 78–80.

set out and later came down in torrents, continuous, and pitiless. Her boots were soon abandoned; then her stockings; next her umbrella, broken in battle with the vegetation, was thrown aside. Bit by bit her clothes, too heavy to be endured, were transferred to the calabashes carried by the women on their heads, and in the lightest of garments [her knee-length chemise] she struggled on through the steaming bush."[23]

Mary found she needed more medicine than she had taken with her to treat the ailing chief. She asked for someone to go to Ikot Offiong, where Alexander Cruickshank lived, to get more. They couldn't go there, the people said, or they would be captured and killed. They told her of a Calabar man not far away who might go. He agreed to go on the mercy journey and returned with what the missionary needed. Along with medicine, Mr. and Mrs. Cruickshank sent tea and sugar to refresh Mary and revive her spirits.

As the "foreign" chief regained his strength, people were attentive to this strange white woman who seemed to have her own *ifot*. Mary held morning and evening worship services with no opposition. The people told her they would like to be at peace and trade with Calabar. When she left, she promised "always to be their mother, to try and secure a teacher, and to come again and see them."

Mary was concerned another time when she heard a certain chief was coming to visit—a chief known as a boisterous troublemaker. Often, the arrival of a visiting chief and his entourage meant that the men were invited to select a slave girl for their pleasure. On such nights, Mary didn't venture outside her house, as sounds of revelry and sexual encounters filled the air.

The chief brought a group of free men and slaves along with him, all armed with guns and machetes. Days of feasting and drinking and quarrels passed. Finally, Slessor thought he gave a hint of going home, so she rounded up all his men and headed the whole bunch toward their own village. She went along to keep peace as they passed other villages on their way.

The trip was uneventful until they came to a plantain sucker stuck in the ground on the path. The men were horrified at this sight. It was witchcraft, they were sure. They became enraged, turned and dashed past Mary, headed for the last village they passed. They would find those responsible

23. Ibid., 76–78.

for this terrible *juju* and punish them. Mary ran to get ahead of them. When she was at the head of the crowd, she stopped abruptly, faced them, and dared them to pass her. They shouted and argued with her, but finally calmed down. The resolute missionary somehow got them to turn around and resume their trek. When they came to the plantain, she pulled it up and threw it aside. The men detoured around the spot in the path, but continued on their journey. Mary picked up the plantain again and joked that she would take it home and plant it to prove it had no evil power.

Some of the men obtained more liquor along the way and began to fight. Mary got others to help her tie a few inebriated troublemakers to trees. Before dark, they went back to release "the delinquents," but "sent them homewards with their hands [still] fastened behind their backs."[24]

That was not the end of the plantain episode. The chief Mary escorted home called for her the next morning. He had a bad night, he said, and his native doctor had taken an assortment of teeth, hair, seeds, and other things out of his leg. He wanted the plantain. "That means the death of someone," he told her. No person was found responsible for this *juju* in spite of various ordeals, but a young man was seized anyway and chained up. Mary begged the chief to let the man go and complained that his action was "unjust and unlawful." He countered with, "It is due to your presence alone that I escaped; they murdered me in intention if not in fact." A few days later the young man was let go without any explanation. The whole matter came to nothing. It was forgotten as if it had never happened. Mary felt responsible for the penalty imposed on the youth; she was relieved and thankful for this answer to her prayers.

Often, just as Mary seemed convinced that the Okoyong really were "gentlemanly and gracious" and that they completely accepted her, she had to rethink her position. One of Ekenge's chiefs bought a beautiful young slave girl to add to his harem. This girl decided she loved a young slave, went to his quarters, and begged him to run away with her. He knew the dire consequences of such an action, so he refused her and hurried off to his assigned work. The frustrated girl went into the forest and hanged herself. However, someone had seen her going to the young man's apartment; he was accused of *ifot*.

The Ekpe council said the slave must be flogged and executed. Slessor argued that the sentence was unjust. After all, she argued, he refused the

24. Ibid., 80–83.

girl's advances and left the premises. What else could he do? The chiefs answered that he wasn't being killed for that; he would die because he must have used *ifot* against the girl. Mary grew agitated. They had no evidence, she said, that he bewitched the girl.

The men paused. What right did she, an outsider, a woman, have to intervene in their business? They did not need evidence. They could condemn a man without it. "Carrots and fire" took over. Shouts were traded. The five-foot redhead faced them with her anger. She wouldn't back down. She had learned from Mrs. Sutherland and Mrs. Anderson that to show fear was dangerous, so she stood glaring at the men.

The "court" calmed down a bit and the chiefs agreed to "discuss" the case with Mary. Maybe this wasn't "just a woman." Maybe she had the power of the white man's God. They finally agreed not to kill the slave; they would just flog him. Mary thanked the chiefs for their mercy.

To her dismay, a post behind Slessor's living space was chosen for the young man's punishment. He was chained there and flogged every day for three days, not allowed food or water. She could hear his screams through her mud wall. Sentries stood guard so Mary couldn't go to him. When he was almost dead, he was freed, and Mary tended his wounds and nursed him.[25]

WOMEN AND POLYGAMY

Girls were promised to men at a young age, and marriages were often arranged for economic or political reasons. E. U. Aye says a man's wealth depended on the number of wives he had. He discusses the preparation for marriage that girls underwent. Older women taught them "home management and etiquette, economics and cookery." He also writes, "[C]ircumcision was a serious pre-marital affair."[26] (Female circumsion seems to be one of those things Mary Slessor and other missionaries felt could not be talked about.) Along with circumcision went the custom of fattening the bride. As young teenagers, girls were secluded for some time (from a few weeks to two years), not allowed any exercise, and stuffed with food. "Corpulence," Aye writes, was a "sign of good health and an item of beauty."

25. Buchan, *Expendable Mary Slessor*, 97–99.

26. Aye, *Old Calabar*, 103.

Dorothy Amaury Talbot, whose husband was a British District Commissioner near Calabar in the early twentieth century, wrote regarding the fattening period. "The result is that [the girls] emerge, to the admiration of their adoring relatives, and of the townsfolk at large, perfect mountains of flesh—naked, in most parts of the district, save for a few strings of beads and bells, or else decked out with an extravagant array of native ornaments, but always with an air at once arrogant and querulous. . . . Of the kindly, gentle air and friendly greeting to be found at all other times, there is no trace in this their little hour of triumph."[27]

When the marriage ceremony took place, the girl was again the center of attention and received many gifts. Amaury Talbot points out that following this "triumph" a bride's status changed completely. She often became "the slighted, hard-worked drudge of her new lord."[28] She was expected not only to produce children but also to work at the farms to help provide sustenance for the entire family of husband, wives, and children. There were rules to follow. She was not allowed to leave the family compound without her husband's permission.

When her husband died, the wife was in danger. Even if she were found innocent of causing his death by witchcraft, her life was made miserable by old customs. Widows were confined to their quarters, given little to eat, and not allowed to wash themselves or comb their hair. One of the articles of the treaty Consul Hopkins signed with the king and chiefs of Duke Town in 1878 reads: "The custom of compelling widows to remain in their houses, in filth and in wretchedness, after the death of their husband, until his devil-making is over (they having been sometimes kept for even years in this state of misery), is abolished. The widows are to remain mourning for one month after the death of their husbands, and after that no further restraint will be put upon them."[29]

The custom continued, however, in distant districts, as did other practices missionaries and other Europeans condemned.

Hope Waddell wrote in 1846 that one got used to slavery.[30] But Victorian missionaries did not get used to polygamy. They accepted slavery as a necessary evil, one that would go away gradually once the expor-

27. D. Amaury Talbot, *Woman's Mysteries*, 84.

28. Ibid., 87.

29. McFarlan, *Calabar*, 66.

30. Waddell, *Twenty-Nine Years*, iv–v.

tation of slaves to other lands ceased. Mission historian Geoffrey Johnston states that polygamy produced a different emotional response. Polygamy was considered both unscriptural and pernicious. "So persistent has been the rejection of polygamy by the missions that one commentator called it almost a mark of the church: one, holy, catholic, and monogamous."[31]

The question of polygamy was a stickler for the missionaries. To completely reject it was to reject an entire social system.[32] Though they believed it was wrong, they recognized the dilemma of those who were required to put aside "extra" wives in order to become members of the church. This undoubtedly contributed to the fact that after twenty-five years in Calabar, the Church of Scotland Mission claimed only forty-seven communicant members, even though hundreds attended worship services and Bible teaching classes in some towns.

Hugh Goldie wrote in 1890 about the "prevailing practice" of polygamy:

> The headmen have their harems . . . and a chief may keep adding to his harem so long as he lives. . . . It is a question still under debate among Christians, whether a polygamist is admissible into the Christian Church. The practice of most missionaries is to exclude such. But it is argued that we have not scriptural authority for such action, and that it inflicts great wrong on the poor women who may be cast off. . . . The refusal to condone the custom of polygamy . . . restricts much the numbers of those who come forward to profess Christianity.[33]

The church did not formally require monogamy, though missionaries generally followed the decision the Presbytery of Biafra made in 1859. That decision recognized the legitimacy of Efik marriage and permitted divorce only for adultery.[34]

Mary Slessor agreed with the church's ban on polygamy, but in later years she addressed the problem of single women who had no "house" to provide for them. She wrote that she would ask the current District Commissioner "if these women may make 'friend' marriages . . . as women

31. Johnston, *Maxim Guns, 285*, referring to H. W. Turner in *International Review of Missions*, No. 219, 313–21.

32. Ibid., 286, referring to J. F. Ade Ajayi, *Christian Missions in Nigeria*, 107–8.

33. Goldie, *Calabar*, 20–23.

34. Johnston, *Maxim Guns*, 289.

here can't live single for years."[35] This is in character with Mary's concern about the status and treatment of women, which she expressed soon after her arrival in Calabar. Although it is unclear what Slessor meant by "friend marriages," she probably thought in terms of marriage in name only.

MA EME ETE

The chief's sister, Ma Eme Ete, whom Mary met on an early visit to Ekenge, became her friend, eventually "almost a sister." Her husband, an important chief in another village, died some time earlier, and she had undergone an ordeal with his other wives. A chicken was beheaded in the center of a circle of wives, and it flopped around on the ground until it died. The direction in which the neck pointed determined which woman was guilty of the witchcraft that caused her husband's death. Ma Eme, the chief's head wife, was so traumatized by this experience that she fainted when she was pronounced innocent. A few weeks later, through her brother's intervention, she returned to Ekenge—much sooner than most widows were allowed to be seen in public again.

Ma Eme's experience with the chicken ordeal convinced her that many of the old customs were not good. She became a secret ally of Mary Slessor and warned her not to try to interfere too soon in tribal affairs or she might be killed. When there was trouble brewing, Ma Eme sent Mary an empty bottle, asking for medicine. This was a signal to come. Mary went. She often found situations in which she did not hesitate to intervene, such as the need to rescue twins or to plead for someone's life.

One day when some women were chained in Edem's yard, condemned to "take the bean," they were left in the hot sun all day with no food or water, even though some of them had babies with them. Slessor recalled Ma Eme's advice to beware of intervening too soon in tribal affairs, but by the end of the day she had cooked something for the women. When she took it to them, the guards were temporarily gone, and Edem's wives were carrying water to the prisoners while others served as lookouts. Mary realized then that the women of Okoyong were kinder than their bad reputation indicated.[36] Her appreciation for the women grew, and she valued her connection with Ma Eme even more than before.

35. MS to CP, April 30, 1906.

36. Buchan, *Expendable Mary Slessor*, 93.

One day Mary noticed scars on Ma Eme's arms and asked about them. "Those are the marks of the teeth of my husband," she said.[37] A husband had full authority to do as he pleased with his wives—he could bite or beat or kill them, and no one dared complain. But Ma Eme worked as a peacemaker in a violent society. When her brother was irritable or drunk, she acted as intermediary between the chief and his wives. Mary called her "a noble woman, according to her lights and knowledge,"[38] a description that would shock some Europeans.

Missionary Elizabeth Hutton wrote in her diary, three years after Mary Slessor's arrival at Ekenge, "Have just been to Ma Eme's house. She owns this place, is very rich and has great power and influence. She is not Christian but is very kind to the missionary, and is an excellent, true, kind hearted woman . . . and, as she is friendly to us, then her people are also."[39]

Neither Ma Eme Ete nor her brother became Christians, but as Christian and Plummer point out, Ma Eme's secret support was a tremendous help in the struggle against abuse. Mary felt compelled to write home, "Faith cannot exist without knowledge, and they have hardly as yet got over the very first principles. . . . The harvest *will* be gathered, but as yet it is only the seed time."[40]

LIQUOR IS KING

The liquor trade appalled Mary. She blamed it for the drunkenness she witnessed. She had lived with its effects as she grew up in Dundee; in Okoyong, it seemed worse. "*Everybody* drinks," she complained. "I have lain down at night knowing that not a sober man and hardly a sober woman was within miles of me."[41] When a boatload of gin arrived from Calabar, women went to collect it as if they were going for their water supply.[42]

Most of the missionary establishment shared Slessor's concern. In 1869 Hugh Goldie had declared that "Scotland did more to ruin missions

37. Livingstone, *Mary Slessor*, 71.
38. Ibid., 72.
39. Elizabeth (Hutton) Marwick diary, April 23–24, 1891.
40. Christian and Plummer, *Redhead*, 65.
41. Buchan, *Expendable Mary Slessor*, 95.
42. Livingstone, *Mary Slessor*, 86.

by the [liquor] trade through its own merchants than it did to support the missions through the church."[43]

Ten years later, Alexander Ross—the missionary who met Mary when she arrived in Calabar—wrote of visiting a new area in Cameroon: "I spoke sharply of their dearest idol—strong drink. The headman rose up and said he would like very much to know who brought rum and gin into his country, and if my own countrymen were not responsible for the evil results of strong drink. I replied, 'Those who send drink into this country do not care for your soul's welfare, what they want is to make money.'"[44]

At the Conference on Protestant Missions of the World, held at London's Exeter Hall in June 1888, the Rev. W. Allan (Church Missionary Society) declared, "If the African be . . . the image of God carved in ebony, we may truly say of every white man engaged in this iniquitous and diabolical [liquor] traffic . . . that he is the image of the devil carved in ivory."[45]

The next year Alexander Cruickshank badgered the Foreign Mission Board to do something about the trade. For the most part, the Board treated the question as one that would be solved "by education in Nigeria and agitation in Europe." However, neither education nor European politics lessened the problems missionaries faced in West Africa.[46]

James Luke wrote of missionary concern about "the weekly arrival of seven-thousand ton ships loaded up with gin—nothing but gin." He added his grim conclusion that "men who are supplied with gin seldom rise to want aught else."[47]

Not everyone agreed with the missionary stance on alcohol. Mary Kingsley accused the missionaries of exaggerating "both the evil and the extent of the liquor traffic in West Africa." She charged them with "preying on emotional sympathy by misrepresentation," and blamed "the missionary public in England and Scotland" for a "perpetual thirst for thrilling details of the amount of Baptisms and Experiences."[48] She wrote, "I have no hesitation in saying that in the whole of West Africa, in one week, there

43. Johnston, *Maxim Guns*, 280 (referring to *Record*, August 1869).

44. *Record*, 1879, 691.

45. *Report of the Centenary Conference*, 124.

46. Ibid.

47. Luke, *Pioneering*, 264.

48. Kingsley, *Travels*, 662–65.

is not one-quarter the amount of drunkenness you can see any Saturday night you choose in a couple of hours in the Vauxhall Road; and you will not find in a whole year's investigation on the Coast, one seventieth part of the evil, degradation, and premature decay you can see any afternoon you choose to take a walk in the more densely-populated parts of any of our towns."[49]

Kingsley also disagreed with the prohibitionists in Scotland and England who proclaimed the alcohol shipped to West Africa was worse than that at home. "It is customary to refer to the spirit sent out to West Africa as 'poisonous' and as raw alcohol. It is neither," she wrote. She had a bottle of trade gin analyzed and reported that it was "neither more nor less deleterious to health than gin produced in London."[50] Kingsley allowed that the liquor trade required regulation, but said she could see no reason for more taxes on it than were already in place when she was in Calabar. She believed it required more regulation in Europe than in Africa.[51]

Slessor enjoyed Mary Kingsley's visits to Okoyong but disagreed with her stand on the issue: "When she lived with me my people were steeped in drink; it could not be exaggerated as an evil, a gigantic evil, but though I told her so she did not *see* it."[52]

British Consul Claude Macdonald echoed the belief that the situation was not as bad as missionaries and others portrayed it. He contended that the liquor trade was not only essential to the economic development of the area, but also that the protectorate needed the import duties the trade provided. Geoffrey Johnston quotes the editor of *The Record* as saying, "Macdonald was a fine fellow, but . . . in this case, he didn't know what he was talking about."[53] The missionaries argued that those who did not live with the people on a daily basis didn't really know what was going on.

TRADE

Not one missionary opposed the idea of enabling inland peoples to trade. They believed it would help in the process of "civilizing" the people and

49. Kingsley, "Development of Dodos," 75.
50. Ibid., 76.
51. Kingsley, *Travels*, 675.
52. Christian and Plummer, *Redhead*, 100.
53. Johnston, *Maxim Guns*, 281.

gain entrance for the gospel. Mary Slessor endorsed trade and sought to bring it about for the Okoyong people. Back in her days at Old Town, when the neighboring Qua and Efik people were warring, the only way the Qua could get to their goods to the trading stores (called "factories") by the river was by going through the grounds of her house at Old Town at night.[54]

When she first mentioned the possibility of the Okoyong trading with the Efik, Chief Edem told Mary with a grin that they already did—they traded heads.[55] She aroused the interest of the chiefs, though, with her stories of how Calabar's chiefs lived. They had nice houses and nice things, she told them. She found that all the people liked to see her belongings—things that were commonplace in Calabar and that they could acquire, too, through trade: mirrors, clocks, soap, china, tools, and other items. Christian and Plummer wrote, "[Mary] was not averse to stimulating the people's desire for shirts and curtains if this distracted them from their preoccupation with feuds and drink [and sex, Buchan adds to the list]."[56]

Slessor wrote to her friend King Eyo VII in Creek Town asking him to invite the Okoyong to send a delegation to hold a palaver about possible trade. He did so at once. Okoyong's chiefs worried. They needed time to discuss the proposition. They finally decided they would go if Mary came, too. Mary took her bairns to the beach for the trip on the appointed morning and found a crowd waiting to watch the departure. Wailing filled the air. Surely the men would be killed if they went to Calabar! They loaded a canoe haphazardly with farm produce—and the canoe sank. This was not a good sign.

They set another day for the trip, found another canoe, and loaded it more carefully. At the last minute, several chiefs decided they could not risk such a trip. Some others wouldn't go if Mary would not allow them to carry weapons. She refused. This was to be a peaceful trip, not a conquest. But the Okoyong never went anywhere unarmed. How could they defend themselves? "Ma, you make women of us! Did ever a man go to a strange place without his arms?"[57]

54. *Record*, February 1915; Livingstone, *Mary Slessor*, 37.

55. Christian and Plummer, *Redhead*, 72.

56. Ibid., 64; Buchan, *Expendable Mary Slessor*, 116.

57. Livingstone, *Mary Slessor*, 88.

Mary assured them that King Eyo was her friend, and they would not need to defend themselves. They were not convinced. The men argued for almost an hour. When Mary noticed more men were missing, she brought laughter by asking where the other "brave heroes" were. Then she spied weapons hidden under the trade items. She was furious. "They were old women—(and one sword whistled into the crowd)—they were cowards!—(another sword)—imbeciles!—(another sword)—babies! [She saw three chiefs,] yanked her skirt up above her knees, jumped out of the canoe, grabbed them, and pushed them forward ordering them to get in. So, five chiefs, and a missionary with a wet skirt, set out for Creek Town."[58]

King Eyo received his bush neighbors kindly. He took them around the town and showed them his house. He showed them his own cache of trade goods and bartered with them for the produce and palm oil they brought. The quality was good, he said. He thought others would want to trade with them, too. Eyo even preached at the evening worship service. The best thing to come of the palaver? He agreed to send Creek Town traders to the Ekenge beach regularly and to loan the Okoyong canoes until they got more of their own.

The Okoyong delegation were impressed. They promised not to raid Calabar farms or attack Efiks who passed by their villages. Mary made the rounds of the missionaries at Duke Town to assure them they could now come to visit her safely any time. Most were in no hurry to do so, though.[59]

When the Okoyong returned home, they regaled the people long into the night with stories of what they had seen in Calabar. Everyone admired the goods they brought back with them. Not only were the five chiefs of the delegation welcomed as heroes of sorts, but Mary's reputation also went up another notch. People began to call her *Ma Akamba*—Great Mother—a title of respect bestowed on women considered especially worthy of honor.

In the morning, Slessor heard commotion outside and arose to find chiefs and slaves clearing ground. One of the chiefs who had gone with her to Calabar reiterated to the crowd everything they saw in Creek Town and how everyone at Creek Town "treated their Mother as a person supe-

58. Buchan, *Expendable Mary Slessor*, 119.

59. Ibid., 120.

rior to them, and had given her all honour."[60] Now they must honor her, too. How? By building her a "proper house."

While Mary was promoting trade in Okoyong territory, other missionaries were having their own problems dealing with questions of trade. Peoples up the Cross River didn't like the intrusion of the British government or missionaries, but they knew it could provide education and hoped it would help overcome the jealously guarded Efik control of trade. E. U. Aye writes, "The economic explanation lies at the root of the crisis on the Cross River."[61]

One example of the trade crisis on the Cross River happened in the summer of 1889. James Luke took a trip to Duke Town from Emuramura, far up the Cross River, to pick up materials for a house, medicines, tools, and miscellaneous items. On the return trip, he and his eight paddlers were detained by a chief who accused him of "spoiling the market." By taking along men from Emuramura, the chief said Luke was "interfering with the profits of the middlemen who pass down the produce of the interior to the Efik tribe, and pass up the British goods to the interior. . . . [But] I assured this middleman that we were, as men of God, not mixed up in any way with trade."[62] While "matters looked rather serious," Luke reported, they were allowed to pass after about an hour.

Mary had advocated and facilitated trade. By the time she had been in Ekenge two years, she wrote home,

> I have taken Okoyong to see [the Efik], and they have begun to send their own produce to the river direct, which has had a good effect on them already. In all the neighbourhood the influence of our presence has been very marked in the saving of life, and in the laying aside of arms; and the drunken revelries which were perfectly dreadful have almost ceased entirely. The women specially have become more sober, and they are clothing themselves and becoming very respectful and quiet. It is almost a strange thing now to see one of them tipsy or having tipsy women with her. The men have begun to make oil and buy and sell kernels, and the almost weekly excursion to neighbouring villages with the drunken fight, almost more or less an attendant, has become a thing of the past.

60. Livingstone, *Mary Slessor*, 90.

61. Aye, "Foundations," 8.

62. *Record*, 1889, 335.

> Having work, they have fewer palavers, and such as they have, they have begun to settle by arbitration instead of by the sword.[63]

She said, too, that the fact that God had blessed her medical work, "in some instances marvelously," had made her welcome throughout the territory. "Every chief, more or less, has been under my care, or some of his people have been," she wrote, "and they have expressed in various ways their appreciation of my services." Made her welcome? Yes, but in the days ahead, Mary Slessor would have more showdowns with an unpredictable people. At least she had a foot in the door.

63. *Record*, 1890, 305.

PART THREE

New Possibilities

1890–1900

7

Escapades and Romance

> She was no soured spinster, searching for sin in every dark corner. Nor yet was she all lovingkindness, creepin' about the place forgiving everyone whether they wanted it or not. There's some so pious you're afraid to spit, and others so sickenin' meek and mild you want to do something bad just to shock them. Mary was none of those. . . . For four hundred years . . . we'd been sitting off Duke Town Beach, scared to break through the Efik middlemen. It took that little barefoot missionary to open the whole country to trade. . . . Man, if she'd been a trader she'd have made millions!
>
> —An "Old Coaster," ca. 1950[1]

MARY MAINTAINED THAT SHE must guard her strength for the day she could build her own house. That day always seemed just out of reach. Neither in Ekenge nor in Ifako did the promised building of house, church or school begin, in spite of Okoyong's early burst of enthusiasm, clearing ground for the project after their trip to Creek Town to discuss trade. For months she heard excuses.

When she could stand the delays no longer, Slessor began working the ground allotted to her and prepared to build. Finally, seeing her hard at work, the chief urged the people to help. Men cut thick, straight tree branches and the smaller branches needed to make the house frame. They planted four long, forked tree trunks in the ground and began to build. More poles were lashed to the corner posts with tie-tie—rope made from plant fibers—and the house began to take shape.

Mary decided the house would consist of two eleven-by-six-foot rooms, with extra rooms (for storage or to use as bedrooms for children

1. Young-O'Brien, *She Had a Magic*, 9–10.

or refugees) jutting out from the house at each end, forming a U-shaped compound. The house was constructed with typical wattle and daub: interlaced branches and twigs, with clay plaster. Women plastered the walls and made furnishings from the local clay (often called mud). They were also experts at weaving palm-frond mats for the roof. Slessor worked right alongside them.

Furnishings were simple and few. In the customary manner, "mud" benches were attached to walls, to provide seating and add stability. One room served as kitchen and living room. It had a clay fireplace and countertops with holes or indentations for dishes or bowls. A raised edge was added to keep items from sliding off the counter. A built-in seat near the fireplace was handy for kitchen work, and a clay "sofa" was added for Mary's comfort. The second room served as bedroom. It held books and boxes, Mary's rusty sewing machine, and the portable organ (which occupied her bed during the day). Pots, pans, jugs, ABC charts—anything that could hang—hung on posts or from bamboo rafters. All the clay items were rubbed to a shiny gloss.

Workers pounded the mud floor to harden it. An all-night fire inside the house to dry out the clay and wood and rid the house of insects finished the job. Doors and windows were the crowning touch, in the local people's opinion. They pronounced it a very good house. Mary would live there for months until a more impressive mission house was completed.[2]

SCHOOL AND CHURCH

Typical of missionaries at new stations, Mary's first project in 1899 was to start school classes at Ekenge and Ifako. She did this before her first month with the Okoyong ended. Christian worship with "Book" (the Bible) went along with learning to read and write Efik and basic arithmetic.

School attracted everybody at first, men and women, young and old, slave and free. When the novelty wore off, many drifted away, leaving about thirty pupils to study. Mary shared the attitude of other missionaries: "I think it best," she wrote, "to create readers and lay foundations as fast and as far-spread as we can, so that the Word may propagate itself."[3] She wrote that people wanted education but not a church: "I've told them that I shall

2. Buchan, *Expendable Mary Slessor*, 111–14; Christian and Plummer, *Redhead*, 63; Livingstone, *Mary Slessor*, 83–84.

3. *WMM*, January 1906, 19.

never give them a teacher without the gospel."[4] In the afternoon, Mary held class and worship at Ifako. At day's end, Chief Edem's yard served as the meeting place in Ekenge.

Since her house was in Ekenge, Mary decided the school and church should be "next door" in Ifako. Missionary Thomas Wells Campbell described a visit to Ifako ten years earlier. He wrote that when he and mission teacher James Swan denounced the beheading of a slave, the chiefs expressed "utter astonishment." They were also "horrified" at the news that twin children and their mothers were being accepted in Duke Town. Swan asked why everyone in Ifako kept loaded guns "on full cock." They replied, "Inside or outside, speaking, eating, or sleeping, we must have our guns always ready for use; we trust ourselves with no man, and know not the moment we may be attacked." They said that if the missionaries could make "our palaver with Calabar come to an end" they would put away their guns.[5]

Things had not changed much since Campbell's visit. Guns were still in evidence everywhere, and the old customs continued. Ifako's chiefs, just as in Ekenge before Mary's house was built, were in no hurry to build a church. However, one day a young man showed up at her doorstep saying the chief wanted to see her. She was in for a pleasant surprise. She arrived to find the spot for the church cleared and people ready to work. They told her that this would be a sacred place as she requested, so no slaves would work on it.

Mary asked them to make the building about thirty feet long and twenty-five feet wide, with two rooms attached at one end for times she might need to stay. At her request, King Eyo sent more than a thousand roof mats for the church from Creek Town. Ekenge and Ifako women walked the three miles to and from the beach for several days carrying the roof mats on their heads. After the floor was pounded, they built clay benches for the congregation. They stained and polished walls to make the church beautiful.

Excitement reigned at both villages as preparations were made for the first meeting in the church. Hugh Goldie sent up "mission boxes" of children's clothes, which Mary distributed before the dedication service. Mary wrote that most of the parents came to the service in "their

4. *MS* "Letters to Miss Findlay," ACC 6825/15, September 2, 1910.

5. Stewart, *Old Calabar*, 97–98.

own clean skin," but the children were decked out in their new clothes. Mothers had washed and cut hair and bandaged sores for the occasion. Chiefs promised the building would be dedicated to God, that even slaves could come for teaching, that it would be a safe haven for refugees, and that no weapons would be brought into it.[6]

CLOTHES OR NO CLOTHES

About the same time Mary was opening the new church at Ifako, Calabar's Acting Consul Harry Johnston was observing customs of dress (or no dress).

> The Efik people of Old Calabar . . . were on the verge of complete nudity, I think I may say, of innocence. . . . Efik men of importance were given to calling on the Consul or the merchants clad in little more than a yachting cap or a helmet or some other head-gear. . . . [The Consul] had to reprove King Duke for coming there on business with simply a tall hat on; otherwise in a state of nudity. After his attention had been called to the want of respect evidenced in this carelessness as to clothing, the costumes he next assumed at official meetings were disturbing to one's gravity of countenance. The last time I saw him, when he came to bid me good bye in May, 1888, he wore pink tights, a cabman's many caped coat, a red chimney-pot hat, and blue spectacles.[7]

Some traders pawned off outlandish costumes on chiefs, touting them as being stylish in Britain. At other times, chiefs appeared wearing what Johnston called "royal robes trimmed with real or imitation ermine."

Church historian Adrian Hastings wrote, "For most missionaries, in common with most other Europeans, the wearing of western-type clothes was decidedly important. . . . Civilizers like Robert Moffat simply could not understand how Africans could refuse 'to adopt our plain and simple modes of dress' in place of theirs."[8] Hastings acknowledged that not all missionaries were so insistent, and he included Mary Slessor among those he called "the eccentrics."

6. Buchan, *Expendable Mary Slessor*, 115; Christian and Plummer, *Redhead*, 64; Livingstone, Mary Slessor, 85.

7. H. Johnston, *Story of My Life*, 174, 192.

8. Hastings, *Church in Africa*, 204–5.

Biographer Livingstone wrote that the women of Okoyong not only wanted to obtain "things" like those Slessor had in her house, but they also wanted dresses like hers, "and she spent a large portion of her time cutting out and shaping the long simple garment that served to hide their nakedness."[9]

She did say "the wearing of a garment never fails to create self-respect,"[10] obviously mirroring the thinking of British culture (as the Consul did in reprimanding a chief for his "lack of respect" at appearing before him in only a hat). But Mary also spouted her indignation to a friend as late as 1910. "This morning I have just answered a very prudish epistle from a black clerk, asking me "to tell my Church member women to cover their nakedness when they pass here, else I shall make the boys *drive* them *away*." Rather a tall order, seeing Government has planted its shed at the ford where the women cross the Creek to their farms, and which takes a woman up to the arm pits. *I've answered him*."[11]

CONFRONTATIONS

When Mary Slessor had been in Okoyong just under a year, she met the first of three men named Charles who were to affect her life to a great extent and on whose lives she made a profound impact. Charles Ovens, missionary carpenter, arrived in May 1889. He was there at the urging of an aunt who showed him an article in *The Record* saying Mary Slessor needed someone to finish her house for her. He had planned to go to America but signed on for Calabar instead. Two months after he arrived at Duke Town, he went to Ekenge to help Mary with her house.

The two were a good team. They shared a sense of humor, as well as a strong homeland accent. Slessor moved her young boys to one of the side rooms, so the newcomer could have some space. They both worked, ate, and dressed with little regard for what was "proper," as each day or occasion demanded. Ovens shunned the European pith helmet, as Mary did, but he sported a flat-topped broad-brimmed hat. He sang old Scottish songs as he worked, and he and Mary enjoyed sitting by a fire at night singing such songs as "Loch Lomond" and "Auld Lang Syne." Ovens' African helper, Tom, told them he didn't like to hear these songs.

9. Livingstone, *Mary Slessor*, 87.

10. Ibid., 85.

11. MS to CP, December 23, 1910.

"They make my heart big and my eyes water," he said.[12] They sang anyway. Janie, seven years old by this time, sang along with them. She also acted as interpreter for Ovens during his Ekenge stay.

Charles Ovens was responsible for spreading the stories of Mary's escapades. He told how she worked with (and sometimes against) the natives. He could write without stretching the truth one bit, "We had troublous times while I was in Okoyong."[13] He saw the doughty redhead at work close-up, living under her roof two months. He later told people about how she angrily pushed men away from their gin or rum, sometimes throwing them to the ground. He related the story of the intoxicated man who showed up on her grounds with a gun. When he refused to put it down, she grabbed it away from him and wouldn't allow him to retrieve it for a week. When another man asked for medicine, she brought out her store of castor oil and told him to open his mouth. Afraid this was some sort of foreign witchcraft, he declined, whereupon she "gave him a smart box on the ear and repeated the order," and he accepted the "cure."[14]

Ovens had hardly settled in when he first saw his hostess intervene in a dangerous situation. A cry from the bush interrupted a morning of carpentry. Mary ran toward the cry, and Ovens followed. The chief's son, Etim, lay unconscious in a clearing where he was building a house in preparation for his marriage. A heavy log had fallen on him. When he came to, they found that he was paralyzed from the waist down. Ovens rigged up a stretcher from his shirt and some poles, and they managed to get the young man back to his mother's house, where he drifted in and out of consciousness.

Slessor told Ovens what was likely to happen. If Etim died, others would be accused of causing his death by *ifot*. Many people would lose their lives; people would die from "the bean;" wives and slaves would be strangled. Everyone would say that the death of a young man by accident was unnatural—an old man, perhaps, but not one so young; someone must have bewitched him. Mary nursed him for two weeks but knew he would probably die. Meanwhile, she tried to work out a plan to save lives. One morning she heard wailing from the chief's compound. She found the youth surrounded by people trying to call his spirit back. They rubbed

12. Buchan, *Expendable Mary Slessor*, 123; Christian and Plummer, *Redhead*, 75–76; Livingstone, *Mary Slessor*, 91.

13. *Record*, 1889, 358.

14. Livingstone, *Mary Slessor*, 105.

pepper into his eyes and blew smoke up his nose. They propped his mouth open with a stick. Everyone yelled, calling the boy back, to no avail.

Chief Edem was determined to find out who caused his son's death. The *abia idiong*—the so-called witch doctor—declared another village responsible. Armed men raided the other village, brought prisoners back and chained them up in the chief's yard. Mary began her work by dressing young Etim like a chief and ordered the carpenter to make an elaborate coffin. The corpse wore a European suit with lengths of silk cloth added. A mission box came in handy for finding items that would satisfy onlookers, such as strings of buttons, rings, and feathers. A large chief's umbrella was fastened over Etim's head, and a mirror placed in front of him so his ghost could see how impressive he looked.[15] On a table beside him were the skulls of enemies he had killed, along with his weapons and other prized possessions that would be buried with him.[16] Ovens wrote of the event and of Mary.

> Not many could or would do what I have seen her do these few days. The corpse is sitting in a chair all dressed up with a hat and feathers, rings on his fingers, and a whip in his hand, and more than two dozen women sitting singing him on his way to the other world. . . . Then there are about fifty men armed with swords and guns. There are twelve people in chains, three mothers with infants, and some young men brought from the next village. If Miss Slessor or I leave they will all be put to death.[17]

When Slessor saw beans being ground up, she insisted that the deadly concoction could not be used. "By this time they were nearly all drunk and running about with their guns loaded and swords in their hands," wrote Ovens. Chief Edem and the others were furious with her meddling in their affairs. No matter how angry they became, though, they hesitated to follow through with their threats in her presence. They argued with this insane white woman instead. If the prisoners were not guilty the bean would not kill them. It was also true, Mary countered, that prisoners could take the *mbiam* oath instead with the same result; they would die only if they were guilty. Men from other villages arrived daily, each crowd insistent that the prisoners "chop nut." Slessor and Ovens kept a twenty-four-

15. Buchan, *Expendable Mary Slessor*, 76–79; Christian and Plummer, *Redhead*, 124–26; Livingstone, *Mary Slessor*, 92–96.

16. Buchan, *Expendable Mary Slessor*, 125.

17. *WMM*, March 1915, 55.

hour watch over the prisoners for two weeks. Most of the prisoners were finally allowed to take the *mbiam* oath. None who took the oath died.

During the turmoil, some men came into Edem's yard, unchained one woman and took her away for the *esere* ordeal. Mary ran after them and found the woman ready to drink the liquid. Instead, Mary told the woman, "Run!" Together they ran to Slessor's compound. Ovens hid her inside the house and locked the door. Again, the chiefs were enraged, but they did not try to get into the house.[18]

One of the few prisoners still chained was a slave woman. Chief Edem announced that at least one slave must go with Etim to the other world. He threatened to burn Mary's house when she refused to let anyone come near the slave. The slave was beside herself with terror and asked Mary to let them behead her and be done with it. Mary said no. Ma Eme intervened and was able to have the slave removed from the chief's yard to Slessor's grounds. The woman was so loaded with chains that escape was impossible; there would be a palaver to decide what would become of her after the funeral.[19]

Another chained woman appeared at Slessor's during the night. She claimed she had somehow cut the chain, but Mary suspected Ma Eme had something to do with her escape.

Charles Ovens wrote, "It was a terrible time for us; we had two of the prisoners—the last two—for twenty-one days in our house. God has been with us, and kept our minds in perfect peace. The chief's son was buried, and not one life was sacrificed. Such a thing was never known in Okoyon before."[20]

At one point, when the tumult reached a point of frenzy, Mary had Ovens send a message to Duke Town asking someone to bring a "magic lantern show" to Ifako. She knew it had been effective in Hope Waddell's days in distracting the people long enough for tempers to simmer down. It would be another important element in making Etim's funeral something special. Two missionaries came and showed pictures of horses (white man's cows) and carriages, ships, and great cities—things the people had

18. Livingstone, *Mary Slessor*, 95.

19. Buchan, *Expendable Mary Slessor*, 126–27.

20. *Record*, 1889, 358.

never seen. The showing allowed time for things to settle down to some extent.[21]

In the aftermath of Etim's death, Chief Ekpenyong, his uncle, decided to "chop nut" when he was belatedly accused of witchcraft in his nephew's death. Mary thought she had talked him out of taking *esere*, but he fled, determined to follow through with his threat. A chief in another village detained him and sent for the missionary. Mary found him, and she and others finally convinced him that he should take the *mbiam* oath instead.

It is true that no lives (except that of a cow) were sacrificed to accompany the chief's son to the spirit world. It is true that Chief Ekpenyong's death was averted. Unfortunately, it is not true that no deaths followed. Some men on their way to the funeral celebrations met another party. One, remembering an old grudge, beheaded another, and his action led to a declaration of war. Mary talked the two factions into seeking arbitration by a Calabar chief. She wasn't pleased when the verdict was "blood for blood." The offer of slaves as a substitute for the murderer was refused, but the two parties agreed that the death of Ekpenyong's twenty-year-old brother would be acceptable.

Mary was glad when she heard the brother had escaped but angry that the murderer was free. She was sad and disgusted when she learned later that the brother had been captured, "filled with gin, and amidst discharge of guns, beating of drums, singing and dancing, had been strangled and hung in the presence of his mother and sister."[22]

After things quieted down, Chief Edem came to Slessor and confessed, "We are all weary of the old customs."[23] Neither one person nor his House could stop them, though, he told her, as the Ekpe system of law and custom still persisted.

Mary wrote to Scotland, "Will you please to pray regularly for me? My one great consolation and rest is in prayer."[24] The old violent customs would be a long time dying out in Okoyong, as in other places served by the Calabar Mission.

21. Buchan, *Expendable Mary Slessor*, 125, 127; Christian and Plummer, *Redhead*, 79; Livingstone, *Mary Slessor*, 97.

22. Livingstone, *Mary Slessor*, 101.

23. Ibid., 102.

24. *Record*, 1890, 305.

TWIN TROUBLES

The episode of the death of Chief Edem's son was only the first of the "troubles" Charles Ovens witnessed. He wrote,

> We had also trouble on account of twins. The children were murdered before Miss Slessor got to the house, and the mother was lying outside in a small hut on the bare ground. Miss Slessor sent a bed and pillow, and something to cover her; and when we were coming away, Miss Slessor spoke to the husband, and told him to be kind to his wife. The next news we heard was that he had taken her back to his home, and she was the same as she had been before. Such a thing was never heard of here.[25]

W. P. Livingstone called Slessor's house "the refuge of little children." She kept so many through the years that friends in Scotland couldn't keep up with who and how many were in her household. Some children were brought to her sick; others were outcasts she rescued. She pampered them, nursed them, and walked the miles to Creek Town when she was out of milk for the babies. "Those who died she dressed and placed among flowers in a box, held a service over them, and buried them in a little cemetery. . . . She mourned over them as if they had been blood of her blood. Mr. Ovens used to say to her, 'Never mind, lassie, you'll get plenty mair'—and indeed there were always plenty."[26] The promise of "plenty mair" was little comfort to Mary when she grieved over a dead child.

Ovens kept busy with building projects. Hugh Goldie gave Mary a canoe, and Ma Eme and her workers helped build a two-room boathouse. The people were willing workers in these projects because of their esteem for Mary. Ovens wrote, "She was at their beck and call day and night. . . . She was always ready for anything and equal to any emergency."[27] The carpenter marveled at her exhausting routine and her full house with its fluctuating flock of temporary and permanent children.

Ovens chuckled over Slessor's "lost Sabbath." She may have lost more than one in her years of isolation. In his travels to and from Ekenge and Duke Town, Ovens arrived one Monday morning to do some work and found Mary leading a worship service. When he informed her it was Monday, she said, "Well, we'll have to keep it as Sabbath now. . . . I was

25. Ibid., Dec. 2, 1889, 358.

26. Livingstone, *Mary Slessor*, 138.

27. Ibid., 103.

whitewashing the rooms yesterday."[28] He said he couldn't afford to have two Sabbaths in one week, but Mary won the hurried debate.

ANOTHER CHARLES

After two months with Slessor, Charles Ovens returned to Duke Town. Newly arrived missionary Rev. A. M. Porteous wrote that he had received a warm welcome and had met Ovens, who was "just recovering from a serious attack of fever, brought on by exposure in helping Miss Slessor in her work at Okoyon."[29] He could have added that the Okoyong house was completed and that Mary, too, was suffering from malaria.

Slessor endured a couple of malaria episodes in her first weeks at Ekenge in 1889 but said she was not sick enough to retreat to Creek Town or Duke Town. She wrote, "I am entering on the fourth year of my term, so am not so strong as I was three years ago, and am living in a single apartment with mud floor, and that not in the best condition. Moreover it is shared by three boys, and two girls, and we are crowded on every side by men, women, goats, dogs, fowls, cows, rats and cats, all coming and going indiscriminately, so there is no accommodation for being sick, and it is too far to go to Calabar to lie down."[30]

Malaria bouts continued, though, and Mary relented and retreated to Duke Town several times in 1890 to recuperate. During her convalescence, she met another man named Charles. Charles Watt Morrison was a new teacher at Duke Town, still struggling to learn Efik. He probably heard of Slessor's work before he left Scotland. He certainly heard about her after he reached Calabar on his twenty-ninth birthday: January 17, 1890. He listened to the stories told by Charles Ovens and visited Mary while she recovered. Someone who knew Mary said, "She had the power of attracting young men, and she had great influence with them. Whether they were in Mission work, or traders, or government men, they were sure to be attracted by her vigorous character and by the large-hearted, understanding way she would talk to them or listen to their talk of their work or other interests."[31]

28. Ibid., 133.

29. *Record*, 1889, 357.

30. Christian and Plummer, *Redhead*, 63.

31. Livingstone, *Mary Slessor*, 136.

Morrison, twelve years younger than Mary, was among those young men who were attracted to her. Maybe she was unorthodox in her lifestyle and methods, but the tales of her work in Okoyong fascinated him and made him thirsty for adventure. He found that they had common interests aside from mission work, too. Both were interested in world affairs, and both liked to read. (In fact, Morrison wrote some poetry and was attempting to write a novel.) He read to Mary as she convalesced and was impressed by her critical analysis. When Mary returned to Ekenge, they corresponded, and their friendship blossomed.[32]

Slessor's furlough had been due in December 1889. She wasn't able to leave until a year later. As 1890 wore on and spells of down time for malaria episodes increased, Mary knew she must take a furlough. She had been with the Okoyong nearly two years and had seen some good changes. Trade was expanding; there was less drunkenness; people hurried to her with the cry, "Run, Ma! Run!" when secret palavers were likely to lead to deaths;[33] chiefs asked her to settle their quarrels. Still, she was reluctant to leave without a missionary presence there. She pooh-poohed the idea that only she or a man could manage in Okoyong territory. "No person connected with me need fear to come to Okoyong, or suffer from lack of hospitality," she said.[34] As usual, there was no rush from missionary quarters to stand in the gap if she left.

Margaret Dunlop, a young missionary nurse who had been in Calabar just over a year and had cared for Mary in Duke Town, finally came forward to volunteer. She joined Mary in Ekenge in November 1890 to allow time for people to become accustomed to a new face. The chiefs agreed to "behave themselves" and to help the new missionary during Slessor's absence, a promise they managed to keep. Dunlop thought the people seemed friendly and peaceful. She apparently changed her opinion during her stay, as she later wrote, "[They are] a wild and lawless class, boasting of their wildness." Besides that, she said, they came to church drunk.[35]

Charles Morrison wrote of Okoyong, "For years [Okoyong and Efik] carried on a kind of guerilla warfare. At one time Efik won, at

32. Buchan, *Expendable Mary Slessor*, 121, 134; Christian and Plummer, *Redhead*, 81–86; Livingstone, *Mary Slessor*, 113–15.

33. Livingstone, *Mary Slessor*, 121.

34. Ibid., 106.

35. Ibid., 107.

another Okoyong. Through sheer weariness and the superior forces of Efik, Okoyong had at last to give way; and so the Calabar tribes have maintained and kept their position. So fearful, however, had been the slaughter, and so fierce their opponents, that until to-day [in 1893] Efik traders are very wary in all their approaches to the Okoyong country."[36]

Not only did Calabar-Okoyong rivalries persist, but flare-ups continued between various Houses or villages in Okoyong territory. Slessor had her bags packed for the trip to Scotland when word came that a distant chief had injured himself and died. His brother blamed the chief of another House, and war seemed imminent. A peacemaking trip would mean a six-hour walk for an already sick woman. Those close to her—Ma Eme, Chief Edem, Margaret Dunlop—all insisted she must not go. To no one's great surprise, Mary went. Edem provided an Ekpe escort for part of the way: a man and his drum.

At the next House boundary, a chief declared that no war was planned, and Mary couldn't stop it if there was one. She told him to remember her God's power. She went on down the jungle path with a few guides, minus her Ekpe escort, until warriors "stripped and painted for battle" suddenly appeared. When they wanted to know why she had come in the night, she told them she was there to keep peace. Their chiefs agreed to delay the battle and allow Slessor to attempt an accord. After a short sleep, she awakened to learn the warriors had left for the other village. Mary overtook the two groups and found that one of the chiefs was a man she had treated for a serious illness. He credited her with his cure and was receptive to her plea to settle the quarrel by negotiation.

One group admitted they were wrong and agreed to pay a fine—in gin. As the cases were piled up, biographer Buchan wrote, "Her knowledge of tribal custom came to the rescue. . . . If the clothes of an Egbo official were spread over any article, to touch it was held to be an attack on the official himself." Mary Slessor, it seems, had been given honorary membership in the Ekpe organization at some time.[37] She took off as many of her clothes as she dared and threw them over the gin cases. Nobody would touch them, angry as they were and despite their grumbling.

"It would have been an interesting scene: the sick, bedraggled, presbyterian female agent facing up, half-dressed, to a crowd of yelling,

36. *Record*, 1893, 286.

37. *WMM*, March 1915, 56.

painted, warriors who could so easily have killed her and taken their gin. . . . When eventually they calmed down a little one of the chiefs pointed out that it was customary to taste the gin to make sure that it had not been watered down."[38]

Mary agreed it was the custom. She doled out a taste to chiefs and headmen from one bottle in each case of gin. Then she watched as the cases were loaded onto heads and the warriors headed home. Slessor followed them to their village, slept a little, then headed back to Ekenge. Her baggage was already gone. The next day she and Janie left for Duke Town.

When Mary and Janie boarded the steamer for home, Mary carried a secret.

Charles Morrison had asked her to marry him. It is difficult to see how the two managed to keep their deepening relationship private in the mission setting. Mary told Charles they could be married only if the Foreign Mission Board would allow him to join her in the work at Okoyong. With this caveat, they decided to keep their engagement a secret for the time being. She would not consent to join him in his work at Duke Town, where she believed there were already plenty of workers. She was convinced that God had her where he wanted her. And she definitely needed help with the work there. They would wait for the Board's decision. The third Charles in Mary's life would come a few years later.

38. Buchan, *Expendable Mary Slessor*, 131–33; Christian and Plummer, *Redhead*, 83–84; Livingstone, *Mary Slessor*, 107–11.

8

Hopes and Disappointments

> I need scarcely [say] that I am much interested in the proposal which you and Mr. Morrison make, and the whole matter will have our best attention.
>
> —James Buchanan, 1891[1]

Mary and Janie landed in Plymouth, Devon in January 1891 and headed for Topsham to meet old friends and visit the graves of Mary's mother and sister. Staying at "Majorfield," a nearby house in the village, Mary rested much of the spring to regain her strength.[2]

In both March and April Slessor received letters from James Buchanan, Foreign Mission Secretary, which chided her for not sending in her required reports. In April he wrote,

> The report which I expected from you is of course the Annual report which each missionary is instructed to send home as prescribed in our *Rules & Methods of Procedure*. The rule prescribes that missionaries "transmit from time to time to the Foreign Mission Secretary such extracts as are fitted to show the progress of the work and promote the interest which the Church at home takes in the Missionary cause, and *to transmit, each year, before 31st January, full account of the income and expenditure of the congregations of the Membership and attendance, of the day School, the Prayer Meetings, the classes for religious instruction, and of the Spiritual State of the Stations.*"

1. FMB to MS, MS7666, August 8, 1891.
2. Christian and Plummer, *Redhead*, 85.

> In the month of May last I sent a circular letter to all the Missionaries, calling attention anew to this rule and asking that reports should be sent to me early.[3]

Slessor disregarded this rule more often than not. It did not appear to be a matter of importance to her, and the secretary frequently had to make up a report from various letters and columns Mary wrote.

REMEMBERING

In Topsham Mary would have had time to think of her fiancé, to recall the times they spent together and the promises they made. She and Charles both had concerns about the reception news of their engagement would receive from the Foreign Mission Board. She may have spent time rereading the only two books she left behind at her death besides her Bibles, books in which she and Charles had inscribed their initials: Charles Dickens's collection of essays of often comic characters, *Sketches by Boz: Illustrative of Every-Day Life and Every-Day People*, and a popular psychological crime thriller by Edward Bulwer-Lytton, *Eugene Aram*.

It is tempting to speculate on the question of the relationship between the couple and on the strength of their love for each other. Was Morrison simply infatuated with the popular, if eccentric, woman twelve years his senior? Was Slessor just hoping for the closeness she saw in some missionary couples around her, a closeness she never witnessed in childhood? Their feelings remained a private matter. Some time during the spring or summer, Mary let friends know about her engagement and posed for a photograph wearing an engagement ring.

Slessor did not even send the letters she carried from Calabar to the Mission Board—one from Morrison and one her own—until August, after she had been home more than six months. A letter from Secretary Buchanan in August acknowledged receiving the letters and informed Mary the Board would not meet again for another month.[4]

One wonders if eyebrows were raised on learning the popular forty-one-year-old missionary was engaged to a younger man. Some people may have been shocked; others may have thought this was simply one more example of eccentric, headstrong Mary Slessor, making another rash decision. The Board may have taken the age difference into account,

3. FMB to MS, MS7666/171, Mar. 31, and MS7666/173–4, Apr. 7, 1891.

4. FMB to MS, MS7666/338, Aug. 8, 1891.

but they expressed a legitimate concern when they finally got around to making their decision.

When Mary began the mandatory round of speaking engagements, she made her headquarters with her friend Mrs. McCrindle at Joppa for churches in the Edinburgh area. She stayed with Charles Morrison's parents in Kirkintilloch when she visited churches there. She stayed in Bowden in the Scottish Borders—the Bowden church had sent "missionary boxes" to Calabar. She also stayed in Annan with Mr. and Mrs. William Peebles, who had served in Calabar from 1881 to 1883. She wrote to Mrs. Peebles in September 1891 apologizing for taking so long to thank her for her hospitality. She had been ill with a severe cold, she said, but she had a fire to keep her warm and "plenty of over kind nurses" to take care of her. She was better by the time she wrote, had her hair cut, and planned to go for a walk and drive that day.[5]

From time to time, Buchanan sent Slessor a new list of speaking engagements. September and October were filled up, as May and June had been. Some weeks Mary had to speak several times to various groups. By mid-November she was ill in Dundee, and the secretary cancelled meetings for a time. (W. P. Livingstone said she had influenza and bronchitis.[6]) There was no letup in requests from churches and women's groups to meet and hear the famous missionary and see her daughter Janie, who was now nine years old.

Livingstone reported that Mary loved to sit at tea and tell stories of her adventures in "the bush." When it came time for a meeting, though, the people were apt to get a sermon. "It is a trial to speak," she said; "but He has asked me to, and it is an honour to be allowed to testify for Him in any way, and I wish to do it cheerfully." She intimated that God didn't really need any outside help in raising support for missions "if the heart was right and the life consecrated."[7] She wanted to see hearts made right and lives consecrated, both in Scotland and in Calabar.

THE BOARD DECIDES

The Foreign Mission Board didn't answer Slessor's or Morrison's letters about their engagement until November. To Charles Morrison, Secretary

5. MS to Mrs. Peebles, MS5239/1, Sept. 3, 1891.
6. Livingstone, *Mary Slessor*, 116.
7. Ibid, 112.

Buchanan wrote two letters on the same day. One communicated the Board's decision: "That it be intimated to Mr. Morrison that in view of the fact that he offered his services for Teaching work in Duke Town, that a school has been erected there under his superintendence, and that it is of the utmost importance to the mission that school work should be vigorously carried out in that populous centre, the Board cannot see their way to sanction his removal from Duke Town until full provision is made for carrying on the school work there to the satisfaction of the Calabar Committee and the Board." Buchanan added, "I may state that we are making every effort to secure one or even two additional teachers for Old Calabar, and we trust that we may be successful ere long."[8]

The second was a normal business letter thanking Charles for a report regarding his students, telling of correspondence with shipping company Elder Dempster & Co. regarding coal they failed to deliver, and making general comments and observations, including the hope that the mission's steamboat had been fixed.[9]

Buchanan wrote to Mary a week later asking her to meet with the Western Committee in Glasgow on December 1 to discuss her ideas about an industrial school in Calabar. The only other paragraph of the letter simply said, "I suppose you are quite aware of the decision of the Board regarding Mr. Morrison's proposal to go to Okoyong." Then he repeated the Board's written decision.[10] No word of sympathy or hope was added.

Mary accepted the Board's decision without question. "I lay it all in God's hands, and will take from Him whatever he sees best for His work in Okoyong." If God would let Charles join her work, she would be grateful, she wrote. "If not I will still try to be grateful, as He knows best. . . . What the Lord ordains is right." She had already told Charles she could not marry him unless the Mission Board sent him to serve in Ekenge. "If he does not come," she said, "I must ask the Committee to give me some one, for it is impossible for me to work the station alone."[11]

No correspondence between Mary and Charles survives to give an indication of their disappointment. Biographers Christian and Plummer report that Mary wrote to Charles's mother telling her the two missionar-

8. FMB to Morrison, MS7666/424–25, Nov. 3, 1891.

9. Ibid., 426.

10. Ibid., MS7666/438, Nov. 11, 1891.

11. Livingstone, *Mary Slessor*, 114–15.

ies could not marry for the present, but that if his health improved and he could come to Ekenge, their marriage would still be possible.[12]

INDUSTRIAL MISSIONARIES

The Calabar Mission had a missionary printer on staff from its inception. Printing was considered essential once translations were made of Bible portions, hymns, lessons and creeds, or other matter. Samuel Edgerley was among those who arrived in Calabar in 1846. He remained there until his death eleven years later. His son, Samuel Howell Edgerley, landed in Calabar the year before his father died and served twenty-six years, until he, too, died in Duke Town in 1883. Both father and son are listed in William Christie's "Annals," first as printers, then as teacher/evangelists, and finally as ordained missionaries.[13] Mary treasured her memories of working with the younger Edgerley and his sister.

When the mission acquired steamboats for river travel, a missionary engineer became a necessity. One of those engineers, James Lindsay, who stayed in Calabar just over a year, talked about one of Mary Slessor's eccentricities: not wearing shoes. "I walked many miles with her through the bush," he said, "and only once did I know her to be troubled with her feet. She had been to Duke Town, attending Presbytery, and made some small concession to the conventions by wearing a pair of knitted woollen slippers. On returning to Okoyong through the bush, small twigs and sticks penetrated the wool and pricked her feet. With an expression of disgust she took the slippers off and threw them into the bush. That was the only time I saw her other than barefoot."[14]

A succession of carpenters served the mission. Most of them remained for just a couple of years. But Charles Ovens, who brought Slessor to into the limelight of the church in Scotland, served almost fourteen years before he resigned.

Not long after reading the Foreign Mission Board's letter in which her hopes for marriage were dashed, Slessor picked up a new issue of *The Missionary Record of the United Presbyterian Church* and found an article from James Luke appealing for more industrial missionaries. Mary immediately wrote a very long letter to *The Record*, which she addressed to the

12. Christian and Plummer, *Redhead*, 89–90.

13. Christie, "Roll of Missionaries" in "Annals."

14. Livingstone, *Mary Slessor*, 131.

church at large. She applauded Luke's letter in the December 1891 issue and expressed her hope that people would respond. "Surely the call in that letter has already entered the hearts of many of our Christian artisans," she wrote, "and prompted the prayerful question, 'Lord, is it I'?"

Mary went on to address the need for a training institution for Calabar's people, "to provide legitimate employment for the young people being educated and brought up under Christian influence." She said missionaries couldn't do everything themselves and that the church should not expect the Foreign Mission Board to meet the need: the Board's function was to be administrative. "A question like this belongs to the Church at large," she insisted. "Too much is expected of the Mission Board, and too little of the Church." Her solution? "Let the science of the evangelisation of the nations occupy the attention of our sessions, our congregations, our conferences, and our Church literature, and we will soon have more workers, more wealth, and more life, as well as new methods." She made the challenge more explicit: "Surely there are half-a-score of leisured men in the United Presbyterian Church who could make this matter their special business." A practical step, she added would be to send a deputation of two men to Calabar to determine what could and should be done. Mary even outlined a plan of operation for when artisan missionaries came and how their work could be financed.

> Each worker could manage his own department, live in his own compound with his own men, influence them, educate them, have stated days on which he will accompany them, either by boat or on foot, to the villages and hamlets all round—he thus learning the language and the manners of the people, while he guides and encourages, and gives prestige to them as they deliver the message of God's salvation. . . . Why should not a private individual, or a dozen of individuals, send out and support each an artisan missionary, the Mission Board and local Presbytery guiding and controlling and superintending him?[15]

Mary's letter discounted a popular notion that Calabar's wood was not fit for good use. "Would it be like God's ordinary way of working to make hundreds of miles of fine forest of unworkable wood?" She told of the export of ebony, of how early missionary Samuel Edgerley sawed wood to floor his house, of how the natives "with a sixpenny matcheat, or an ordinary hatchet" made canoes, paddles, doors, tables, and other items.

15. *Record*, 1892, 11–12.

She also addressed the belief that Africans couldn't be trained. It had been proven otherwise, she claimed, not only in Africa but also in the West Indies and the Americas.

"The weak point in the race, with ourselves as elsewhere, is their want of staying power, their want of perseverance and persistency in the face of difficulties," Slessor wrote. She attributed this to their history and added, "This no more proves that they cannot be trained, than the fact that there are lapsed masses in Britain proves the European incapable of steady work."[16]

Mary did not sign her name to this lengthy letter, but simply ended with "One of the Zenana staff." (The Scottish Presbyterian women's work had come under the "Zenana Committee" in 1886.)[17]

Foreign Mission Board members were already aware of Slessor's views on a training school. She had not kept it a secret, and the Board had invited her to meet with them to discuss it, before her illness in Dundee. As the time drew near for her return to Calabar, Buchanan wrote to say that Board members "were much grieved" about her illness, then expressed displeasure that she continued to operate outside regular channels.

> We all have been much disappointed that you could not arrange for meeting our Committee or even for calling here before you went South. There are a number of matters that our Committee would like to confer with you about, especially some matters bearing upon industrial work in Old Calabar. We know something of your views from the letter which you have sent to the *Record*. . . . You cannot however but feel that this is not satisfactory as the Board would like to do full justice to any suggestions which you would like to make, and this can only be secured by having a personal conference with you.[18]

Perhaps the Board appreciated Mary's attempt to shift responsibility to the church at large, but they still thought proposals should first come through the Board. Ever the renegade, Slessor operated on the spur-of-the-moment when it suited her. Buchanan kept trying for a meeting. The

16. Ibid.

17. The interdenominational work with women in India's zenanas (harems) began in 1852 as Indian Female Normal School Society. By 1880, the mission added medical work and became Zenana Bible & Medical Mission under the Church of England. As time passed, Zenana became a generic term for women's missionary work.

18. FMB to MS, MS7666/485, December 31, 1891.

upshot was that the Western Committee would hold a special meeting in Glasgow on February 12. "Kindly note the place, day and hour," Buchanan stressed.[19] Slessor had already missed two meeting dates.

DURING MARY'S ABSENCE

While Mary was on furlough, newly arrived missionary Elizabeth Hutton (later Marwick) went to help Margaret Dunlop in Okoyong. The diary of her early days in mission territory sheds light on the time during Mary's furlough.

Hutton wrote in her diary of her first trip to Ekenge by canoe and commented on the "pretty little Creek" and the three-mile walk along the narrow path to the village. "On either side long grass, ferns, bush of all description. Foliage of trees so dense as to exclude the sky, but when we come to an open part, how pleasant is the bright blue sky." She remarked that she had slept well "in spite of the rats which abound here," and expressed her fear the house would fall completely down with a few more storms. Rain was coming in through the roof, and part of the house had already fallen.[20]

Hutton chronicled her approval of Ma Eme, always helpful to the missionaries, who had sent them "a large Calabar chop, and yams and vegetables, and jug of mimbo." But her high opinion of Eme was affected by an episode four months later.

The two women missionaries heard a commotion and learned that Chief Edem was about to administer the oil ordeal to some of his men. Hutton and Dunlop rushed to see what was going on and found a large crowd of people. Hutton wrote:

> In the middle was a pot sitting on a fire. This pot contained oil, not only boiling but also burning, flames coming out of it. One man standing with a long wooden spoon, ready to lift the oil and pour it on the hands of two men who were standing close by. We ran forward and stood between the men and the pot and told them to stop [just as Mary Slessor would have done]. Edim [*sic*] came forward then and said that the oil would not harm them unless they were guilty.[21]

19. FMB to MS, MS7666/506, January 22, 1892.
20. Marwick Diary, April 23, 1891.
21. Ibid., August 3, 1891.

Hutton could hardly believe that the men who were about to undergo the ordeal were angry that the women had interfered. Since they were innocent, the men were certain they would not be harmed. Edem reluctantly threw the oil out. The missionary was even more shocked to learn the reason for the ordeal. "Last week," she wrote, "Ma Eme had a quantity of yams devoured by wild beasts at her farm, and she declared that the souls of these men had entered into the beasts and caused them to do so. It is disappointing to find that Ma Eme, of whom we expected better things, should still cherish such superstition."[22]

Another time, Elizabeth wrote of seeing native dancing for the first time in Ekenge. "It is a weird performance," she wrote.

> The instruments are large pieces of trunk or thick branch of tree, hollow, and skin covering the ends. The musicians beat on this drum with their fingers and palms of their hands, and though not very musical, still there is a pleasing rhythm and all keep time. The dancing is not so much with feet as the body. The dancers slowly move round in a circle or ring and wiggle their body, keeping time to the music, and they either get giddy or are magnetised by their performance, for they get quite absorbed in it and pay little or no attention to what is going on around. At intervals one and another leave the ring and make obeisance to the players and to the onlookers. They also sing in a chanting strain, one sings a little alone, then the others reply in chorus.[23]

Charles Morrison visited Okoyong a few times during Mary's absence. Elizabeth Hutton recorded that he and physician William Rae preached at Ekenge and the people enjoyed some of "Sankey's Hymns." When Morrison preached again, she said he "spoke very earnestly and well." On another occasion she and Dunlop had a surprise visit from Charles. He promised to bring mails to them and to return to take them to Presbytery in Duke Town. He would take Ma Eme along to see the town, too, he said. Elizabeth also wrote of a steamboat trip with other missionaries, including Morrison.

The Congregational Church at Topsham gave Mary a big sendoff before she left for her return to Calabar. Even as she prepared to return to Okoyong, Charles Morrison's health waned. She arrived back in Calabar on March 19, 1892, along with fellow missionary Ebenezer Deas. She and

22. Ibid.

23. Ibid., June 23, 1891.

Charles had a brief reunion at Duke Town before she returned to Ekenge. She was saddened by the death of her friend, King Eyo, less than a week after her arrival.

Three weeks later she traveled from Okoyong back to Duke Town to see several of the mission staff off for home on the weekly steamer: Mary Edgerley, who had already been in Calabar thirty-eight years and would return to serve four more; Mary Johnstone, in Calabar twenty years; Charles Ovens, going home on furlough; and Morrison, his health failing. Hutton wrote of the visit, "They were all looking pretty well and all were very lively except Miss Johnstone. She seemed so sad and lonely."[24] Mary and Charles may have felt particularly lonely, too, at this parting. There is no record of their meeting and time together, but Mary surely was at the departure because of their relationship. He was among those mentioned by Hutton as "looking pretty well" and "very lively."

When she returned to Ekenge, Mary found herself as busy as ever. She wrote to a friend in Scotland about the problem of repairing her house. "Our mud and sand is very easily let out of order, and will not patch up," she wrote. She complained that she was fatigued but otherwise had not been ill.[25] Ebenezer Deas came from Duke Town to lend a hand before he went to Ikotana, another thirty or so miles up the Cross River, where he would serve until his death five years later. Slessor appreciated him as much as she appreciated Charles Ovens. She wrote of Deas,

> He came up and worked like a hatter to get my flitting done. . . . He said, as we sat at my beach one day, "What would some of the braw folk of Edinburgh think if they saw you just now?" referring to my bare feet and very unconventional dress. He sat on the ground as I did, so I just said, "And what would they think if they saw you?" A woolen under garment, and some unmentionables on his understandings. He looked as much a tinker as I did. . . . It is splendid to have people who know your people at home, and who can sympathise with your inclination to shout "Hallelujah!" sometimes.[26]

24. Ibid., April 16, 1892.

25. Christian and Plummer, *Redhead*, quoting May 27, 1892 MS letter to "Dundee friends," 92.

26. MS to "My dear brother & sister," 1984–259–2/1, 4.

A DISTANT CHARLES

Back in Scotland, Charles Morrison wrote "A Chapter of Old Calabar History," which appeared in *The Record* on October 13, 1893. The article told the story of the mission's expansion. "When the mission was firmly established in Calabar territories, the missionary began to turn his thoughts towards the interior," he wrote. Near the end of the article, Morrison paid tribute to several men who were instrumental in bringing about changes in those later years. "One man will long be remembered in this connection—Samuel Edgerley the younger. . . . Then a Jarett, a Porteous, a Ludwig, a Gartshore, a Luke sat down amongst these tribes, and gave the last blow to Efik's assumed power and dominion. . . . [Their influence is] bringing about a state of progress and prosperity."[27]

It seems odd that Morrison did not mention Mary Slessor in his article, while he extolled the virtues of the work of Edgerley, Jarrett, Porteous, Ludwig, Gartshore, and Luke. Gartshore did not even arrive in Calabar until the year Mary moved to Okoyong territory, and Luke not only mentioned Slessor's work but also named his own book after her.[28] Hugh Goldie wrote of Mary's entry "into this wild tribe" of Okoyong, "She was cordially received, and is treated with all respect, as she visits their various farm hamlets with the Divine word of light and love . . . giving herself to a labour which few would undertake. She is making an impression upon them, denouncing vehemently their customs of blood, and teaching more confidence in each other."[29]

Morrison's health did not improve greatly in Scotland. In April 1893, when it was time for his furlough to end, the Foreign Mission Board notified him they had continued his pay until the end of April and that they were granting a "parting gift" of twenty-five pounds.[30] Morrison kept in touch with the Mission Board, obviously hoping to return to Calabar. In December 1894, when he had already been home thirty-two months—matching Slessor's "long pause"—the Foreign Mission Secretary wrote to him, "Our medical adviser, Dr. Robertson . . . thinks it would be very unwise for you to return to Calabar and he seems strongly to recommend such a climate as South Africa, Australia or New Zealand as being

27. *Record*, 1893, 284–86.

28. Luke, *Pioneering.*

29. Goldie, *Memoir of King Eyo,* 19–20.

30. FMB to Morrison, , 7667/244, April 25, 1893.

favourable for your health. In these circumstances we should never think of exposing you to the risk of the West Africa climate, but if you think of looking towards any of the Colonies . . . we will do all in our power to give you a recommendation and to further your interests."[31]

Biographer Livingstone wrote that Morrison volunteered to serve in Kaffraria, South Africa, but no position was available for him there. "To the regret and disappointment of the Committee, who regarded him as an able and valued worker, he resigned."[32]

There is no evidence to indicate Charles was depressed or lovesick. He emigrated to America, probably in 1895, where his brother was helping build a railroad in the North Carolina mountains. Dates remain unclear, but it is known that Morrison's writings were destroyed by a fire in the forest cabin where he lived and that he died some time later. When Mary learned of his death, she wrote to Morrison's mother—a letter "that left his family in no doubt that the bond between them was heartfelt and strong."[33]

31. FMB to Morrison, , 7708/10, December 21, 1894.

32. Livingstone, *Mary Slessor*, 115.

33. Christian and Plummer, *Redhead*, 90; See also Buchan, *Expendable Mary Slessor*, 137.

9

British Imperial Agents

> European empires were a vast confidence trick, dependent as colonialism must be on the rule of the few over the many, that relied on the docility, cooperation or disunity of the colonized.... Patronizing superiority or benevolent indulgence underlay much colonial government, a belief that "primitive" peoples were like children who needed firm paternal guidance.
>
> —John Springhall, 2001[1]

The Charles Dickens character Dombey reflected a popular British attitude of the nineteenth century: Britain had the best culture in the world and deserved the best. "The earth was made for Dombey and Son to trade in, and the sun and moon were made to give them light. Rivers and seas were formed to float their ships; rainbows gave them promise of fair weather; winds blew for or against their enterprises; stars and planets circled in their orbits, to preserve inviolate a system of which they were the center."[2] It wasn't much of a jump to the notion that the queen's government had a duty to help other peoples become "civilized."

There had been a British presence in what is now Nigeria at least since the height of the slave trade in the eighteenth century. Early British traders were among those who participated in the transportation and sale of slaves. When that infamous trade was outlawed, British naval ships worked to intercept those who continued the practice. John Beecroft was appointed Consul to the Bights of Benin and Biafra in 1849 to protect British interests and to help enforce the ban. As the slave trade subsided, Efik traders provided palm oil as the main alternate product.

1. Springhall, *Decolonization*, 21.
2. Dickens, *Dombey and Son*, 2.

The office of consul became increasingly important in the years following Beecroft's appointment. The consul's power as an agent of Queen Victoria went largely unquestioned, whether or not it was gladly received. When Consul David Hopkins died in 1879, two dozen Efik signed a letter to the Marquis of Salisbury, then Foreign Secretary, praising Hopkins and lamenting his death. He did much "for the glory of God and the honour of the Queen of Great Britain and Ireland and for the benefit of Efik people," they wrote. They feared those who said the treaties were dead along with Hopkins. They reported instances of flogging and murder and worried that the offenses would not be punished.[3]

Not all consuls were as admired as Hopkins. Acting Consul Easton, by "injudicious intervention," crowned Duke Ephraim king of Duke Town in 1879, a year after Slessor's arrival in Calabar.[4] This angered many Africans, and internecine quarrels continued. Consul Edward Hyde Hewitt eventually called kings and chiefs together to elect a different king. Even then, dissension did not abate, and missionaries found themselves drawn into the dispute as it dragged on. The Foreign Office instructed Hewitt to return to Calabar from sick leave in 1885 to "concentrate on restoring order, good administration and judicial work in the Oil Rivers territory," even though his only government support would be "the occasional presence of one of Her Majesty's ships of war."[5]

THE SCRAMBLE FOR AFRICA

1885 marked the year that the "General Act of the Berlin Conference" was signed. Three months of talks—talks that came to be known as the Scramble for Africa—resulted in the parceling out of the continent between various European nations. Britain, France, and Germany were the major players in imperialism in Africa at the time, but representatives of fourteen nations attended the conference. Britain wanted to keep trade routes open, especially the Suez Canal. And it was thought that countless "heathens" and "savages" would be "civilized" and converted along the way in this "dark continent," so that foreign cultures would more nearly match Britain's. Protecting already-dominated areas from German or French invasion was also a high priority.

3. United Presbyterian Church, Calabar to Marquis of Salisbury, October 16, 1879.
4. Nair, *Politics and Society*, 198.
5. Oliver, *Harry Johnston*, 93, citing PRO/FO 84/1701.

The Act confirmed Britain's control of vast chunks of the great continent. It declared free trade for all nations, prohibited excessive taxes and duties, emphasized the ban on the slave trade, and encouraged "all the powers exercising sovereign rights or influence" in African territories to "watch over the preservation of the native tribes, and to care for the improvement of the conditions of their moral and material well-being." Any country occupying new territory was obliged to declare a protectorate and notify other "Signatory Powers."[6] A notice appeared in *The London Gazette* on June 5, 1885:

> "It is hereby notified for public information that, under and by virtue of certain Treaties concluded between the month of July last and the present date, and by other lawful means, the territories on the West Coast of Africa, herein after referred to as the Niger Districts, were placed under the Protection of Her Majesty the Queen."[7]

The British used "protection treaties" to expand their control in Calabar and elsewhere in West Africa, not only in Beecroft's days, but extending to Mary Slessor's time thirty years later and beyond. As professor Peter Ekeh points out, it is unlikely that the native leaders who signed such treaties realized they would lose their sovereignty. The "pro forma texts," he writes, "were printed in England, written in English, and 'interpreted' by British imperial agents."[8]

New treaties were handled the same way treaties had been handled since the earliest days of British presence in Calabar, with more insistence than persuasion. Historian Onwunka Dike reported that the "coercive element" of treaties was obvious.[9] Historian J. C. Anene called the practice "the farce of treaty-making."[10] Hugh Goldie wrote that gunboats came up the river with the Consul, treaties in hand, ready for signatures. "The signatures of those of Creek Town were at once given," he reported, and "the heads of Duke Town also gave their names, with the petty tribes in

6. "Berlin Conference."
7. Anene, *Southern Nigeria*, 67.
8. Ekeh, "Colonial Treaties."
9. Dike, *Trade and Politics*, 66.
10. Anene, *Southern Nigeria*, 63.

the neighborhood, on being assured that their normal relations would not be disturbed."[11]

The benefits of a protectorate to the people were questionable, and the native people's understanding of the import of the treaties even more questionable, but at least during this phase the treaties assumed that ownership of the lands lay in the hands of those who were to be protected. Anene points out that the term protectorate had various meanings, according to the circumstances and who was doing the talking.[12] Under The General Act millions fell under the rule of a supposedly benevolent foreign country. Having already claimed India as part of the British Empire, now an empire in Africa was being built.

Mary Slessor did not hint in her writings at whether or not she was aware of the Berlin Conference and the changes it foreshadowed. She was home during this period—a time that coincided with her "long pause" furlough. She was preoccupied with illnesses (her own and her family's), with speaking engagements, with urging the creation of training centers in Calabar, and with Foreign Mission Board matters.

During one of Consul Hewitt's sick leaves, Harry Johnston served as Acting Consul. He was considered something of a loose cannon in the Foreign Office, albeit one with connections and with some artistic and scientific accomplishments. His views left no doubt that Britain should obtain greater control of all of West Africa—the Empire must expand. He considered the middlemen who controlled trade, such as the Efik, the "curse of Western Africa."[13] A letter to Booker T. Washington warned that Johnston was coming to America and that he had "an unsavory reputation on the West Coast in his treatment of the Negro."[14]

Johnston (who had tasted human flesh[15]) had no qualms about espousing the pronouncement of Cecil Rhodes that "we are the first race in the world, and that the more of the world we inhabit the better it is for the human race."[16]

11. Goldie, *Calabar*, 254.

12. Anene, *Southern Nigeria*, 65–66.

13. Oliver, *Harry Johnston*, 94–125.

14 Harlan and Smock, eds. *Booker T. Washington*, 626, quoting Ernest Lyon letter to Washington, September 19, 1908.

15. A. Johnston, *Harry Johnston*, 106–7.

16. "Black and White in Britain."

Johnston had written an article that denigrated missionaries before he visited Calabar; as a result, they were suspicious of him. In spite of this negative information, some missionaries held him in high esteem after they met him. When he visited Mission Hill and was served tea and scones, Johnston seemed impressed, despite his written opinions. A missionary wife asked, "But you did not really mean, in that article of yours, Mr. Johnston, to caricature us missionaries?" His equivocal reply was, "Believe me . . . that when I wrote that article I had not the remotest idea of ever meeting the ladies and gentlemen of your mission!"[17]

MISSIONARIES AND EMPIRE

Much has been written of the three Cs of British imperialism—civilization, commerce and Christianity—a catch phrase that some attribute to David Livingstone. Livingstone did espouse the basic concept (though not imperialism with all its "baggage") but insisted that his real work was as a missionary. Before he returned to Africa in 1858, he spoke at Cambridge and urged men to become missionaries. He said of his own plan, "I intend to go out as a missionary, and hope boldly, but with civility, to state the truth of Christianity and my belief that those who do not possess it are in error. My object in Africa is not only the elevation of man, but that the country might be so opened, that man might see the need of his soul's salvation."[18]

When his motives were questioned, Livingstone's response was one that could well have served as a model for Mary Slessor at a later date:

> My views of what is missionary duty are not so contracted as those whose ideal is a dumpy sort of man with a Bible under his arm. I have laboured in bricks and mortar, at the forge and at the carpenter's bench, as well as in preaching and in medical practice. . . . I am serving Christ when shooting a buffalo for my men, or taking an astronomical observation, or writing to one of His children. . . . Am I to hide the light under a bushel, merely because some will consider it not sufficiently, or even at all, *missionary*?[19]

17. Luke, *Pioneering*, 80–81.

18. D. Livingstone, "Lecture II," 46.

19. Ross, *David Livingstone*, 123, quoting Livingstone letter to D. G. Watt, January 17, 1847.

David Livingstone's biographer, Andrew Ross, writes, "The relationship of civilisation and Christianity had been debated hotly in missionary circles from the 1790s onwards." In 1828 John Philip, a director of London Missionary Society in South Africa, argued that while Christianity would bring about civilization, civilization did not necessarily guarantee converts to Christianity. Philip's vision of civilization, Ross says, included the importance of both education and commerce.[20]

Anthropologist Paul Hiebert remarks on the extent to which missionaries agreed with their contemporaries back home. "They were convinced of the superiority of their culture, and they did not always differentiate this from their faith in the superiority of Christianity. . . . At times [they] were funded by colonial monies, and they were not above using their relationships with colonial rulers to bring about changes in native cultures."[21]

E. U. Aye points out the difficulty the relationship caused: "When the church had recourse to British gunboats . . . [it] created the theological problem over the use of force in the Christian cause and the blurred perception of the missionary as an imperialist writ large."[22] E. M. Uka, professor of theology at the University of Calabar, maintains that although the Great Commission to go into all the world and make disciples motivated nineteenth century missions, missionaries sometimes forgot the importance of the command to love. "This motive of love" he writes, "was not always free from feelings of cultural superiority."[23]

Mary Slessor demonstrated the motive of love, especially shown in her adoption of the children she considered her own family. But she also shared her compatriots' belief that Britain's culture should be emulated. She spoke of the intelligence and caring of native individuals (and denounced the stupidity of some Britons in Calabar), but she also spoke of many Africans as savages. She wrote, "Okoyon and its people are very very dear to me. No place on earth now is quite as dear, but to leave these hordes of untamed, unwashed, unlovely savages, and withdraw the little rushlight begun to flicker out over its darkness!! I dare not think of it!"[24]

20. Ibid., 25.
21. Hiebert, "Missions and Anthropology," 166–67.
22. Aye, "Foundations," 6.
23. Uka, *Missionaries*, 99.
24. MS to. Stevenson, GD.X.260.02, Feb. 28, 1906.

A NEW ERA

Consul Claude Macdonald arrived in Calabar in August 1891. "What the new task in the Oil Rivers required was not a rabid imperialist but a diplomat," writes J. C. Anene.[25] Macdonald (who said he believed "that British rule had but one justification—the improvement of the social and material conditions of the ruled"[26]) seemed to fit the need. The Scottish missionaries thought so highly of Macdonald that they asked him to join their mission committee. He apparently considered the invitation an honorary one, as he did not attend meetings.[27]

Macdonald soon heard stories of that radical Presbyterian missionary, Mary Slessor. As he began to set up a system of courts, he asked for her opinion. Okoyong's people were not ready for a European to step in and settle their disputes, she argued. If he proceeded with his plan, disaster would surely follow. Consequently, he asked Mary to serve as his Vice-Consul to Okoyong. The official document read:

> Whereas Her Majesty has been pleased to direct that [Mary Slessor] shall be appointed a Judicial Officer to perform, in and for all that district or region which is comprised within the limits of the local jurisdiction styled the Niger Coast Protectorate all or any of the powers and authorities vested in a Consular Court by "The African Order in Council, 1889."
>
> Now, Therefore [Mary Slessor] is hereby appointed to perform all such powers aforesaid, and to hold and form a Court, at such place or places, within the said district or region as may hereafter, with the authority of a Secretary of State, be appointed in writing by Her Majesty's Consul-General or Acting Consul-General.[28]

Mary would continue to do what she had been doing informally for some time. She was clearly already acting as judge at the request of the people. From then on, her position would have the endorsement of the British government—and it would involve paper work for a woman who despised paper work. Some missionaries opposed Slessor taking on this responsibility, claiming it would distract from her missionary duties. In fact, the Presbytery declared "that acting in an official or semi-official

25. Anene, *Nigeria in Transition*, 135.

26. Ibid., citing FO 2/85, September 12, 1895, 177.

27. Johnston, *Maxim Guns*, 256.

28. Jeffreys, "Magistrate," 628.

capacity in court is calculated to compromise her position and interfere with her usefulness."[29] She, of course, did as she pleased. Her reasoning? It would be best for the people, and God would want her to serve this way.

The increased British presence posed a new dilemma for missionaries. They risked losing their independence if they aligned themselves too closely with governmental forces. And, in the eyes of Africans, they were likely to be seen as instruments of the British government. Yet there were times when missionaries, even Mary Slessor, called on the government to come to their aid. The Mission Council asked Dr. Rattray, missionary physician, to "be careful not to compromise the Mission in connection with war in any way that would be injurious to the work," when he arranged to lease mission boats to the government. When Rattray went along as medical officer on an "expedition" against the Aro people, he was supposedly serving as a Red Cross agent, though the Aro may have had no idea what that meant.[30]

Calabar mission historian Geoffrey Johnston states that as the British government gained more and more control over places and peoples, "a new [and younger] generation of missionaries succumbed to a kind of colonial mentality." In the early days of the Calabar mission, the church "was governed without discrimination based on race . . . black and white sat as equals."[31] Africans were trusted and authority was delegated to them. When new missionaries arrived at the end of the nineteenth century, the British were already ensconced in the territory. Britain theoretically allowed native kings and chiefs to rule in a sort of benign paternalism, but when they were not happy with the results, the British dictated what was to be. In the same way, younger missionaries acted as if they knew best how to run things, telling the natives how the church must operate. They were less likely to empower Africans. Some of the younger men did tend to look more favorably on Mary Slessor as an independent operator than older colleagues; they recognized that her methods were often more effective than the mission's had been historically.

Missionary James Luke, one the "new generation of missionaries," wrote, "To us missionaries the presence or absence of a Consul was usually a matter of indifference. From him we required no assistance nor

29. Johnston, *Maxim Guns*, 257–58.

30. Ibid., 257.

31. Ibid.

looked for any kind of sympathy; we seldom gave him a thought, and the attitude was mutual."[32]

Nevertheless, there was a peculiar interdependency of British rulers, traders and missionaries. Government officials and traders applauded the changes in unacceptable practices and appreciated missionary efforts in this area, but they did not always go along with missionary beliefs or their insistence on certain policies. Missionaries depended on traders for transportation or called on the government to come to their aid, though they often also butted heads with traders or government representatives for their activities or demands on the people. Traders and government officers had disagreements, too. Traders were accustomed to making their own trading deals. Government presence added one more level of interference.

ORDER IN THE COURTS

Consul General Macdonald aimed to maintain order and justice through a new system of courts. Native councils and outlying minor courts, staffed by natives and appointed by the Consul, dealt with minor offenses according to customary law. The Native Council of Old Calabar and Consular Courts served as appeals courts. Local peoples soon learned that their power was limited. Macdonald's successor, Ralph Moor, used native authorities "only in subordinate capacities and always subject to management and veto by British administration."[33]

When Calabar was subdivided into districts, each district came under the authority of a District Commissioner and his assistant. These men, good and bad, had a lot of territory to worry about. Districts covered up to two thousand square miles, usually two days' march in every direction from the district station. The fact that districts "bore little relation to the unity of the people within them" was a major problem.[34] They were simply large areas marked out on a map that some bureaucrat assumed would work for their officers. A district often had people from different ethnic and language groups, and their traditions and practices varied.

British agents, Anene states, had "preconceptions which were both prejudiced and ignorant . . . [and] the complexity and subtlety which char-

32. Luke, *Pioneering*, 79.

33. Gailey, *Road to Aba*, 55.

34. Ibid.

acterized the social and political institutions of the indigenous peoples were not appreciated . . . . British intervention inevitably unleashed disintegrating forces. . . ."[35] The British added other Cs to the three original: control and conquest became an increasing part of Empire. (N. S. S. Iwe wrote of other Cs during "the initial stages" of contact with Western civilization—clashes, chaos, confusion and consternation—but he includes a discussion of positive influences of the West as well.)[36]

Thomas Pakenham writes, "Soon the Maxim gun—not trade or the cross—became the symbol of the age in Africa."[37] Even Geoffrey Johnston's mission history ties the cross to the Maxim gun—the machine gun Hiram Maxim invented when he was challenged to "invent something that will enable these Europeans to cut each other's throats with greater facility."[38]

What did Empire mean to Mary Slessor? Her life was mostly "business as usual," caring for her large household of children, acting as nurse, teaching, preaching, and settling disputes. At times, malaria or other illness laid her low and she retreated to Duke Town to recuperate. She knew she had the support of Claude Macdonald if help was needed. He wrote, "There comes a time when their [missionary] efforts need backing up by the strong arm of the law of civilisation and right."[39]

35. Anene, *Nigeria in Transition*, 2.

36. Iwe, *Christianity*, 69–72.

37. Pakenham, *Scramble for Africa*, xxiii.

38. Johnston, *Maxim Guns*; "Hiram Maxim."

39. Livingstone, *Mary Slessor*, 150.

10

Visitors and Empire

> I made a point on this visit to Calabar of going up river to see Miss Slessor at Okyon, and she allowed me to stay with her, giving me invaluable help in the matter of fetish and some of the pleasantest days in my life. This very wonderful lady has been eighteen years in Calabar; for the last six or seven living entirely alone, as far as white folks go, in a clearing in the forest near to one of the principal villages of the Okyon district, and ruling as a veritable white chief over the entire Okyon district.
>
> —Mary Kingsley, 1895[1]

Mary Slessor and Chief Edem walked to Creek Town through heavy rain. They were "drenched to the skin," according to Elizabeth Hutton, but she and Mary went visiting that afternoon, as Mary did not seem to suffer from this particular soaking.[2] She often had an attack of malaria after such incidents, but Elizabeth would not necessarily have known whether fever laid Mary low when she got back to Okoyong afterward.

This was not the only time Slessor walked the more than ten miles from Ekenge to Creek Town. At least once, she walked the distance at night. She needed milk for one of "her babies" during a crisis. A group of angry men planned to murder some women, but with her usual show of bravado, Mary held them off. She was only able to get away to Creek Town without detection because a storm struck suddenly; King Eyo sent her back by canoe before her absence was discovered.[3]

1. Kingsley, *Travels*, 74.
2. Elizabeth Marwick, Diary, June 30, 1892.
3. Livingstone, *Mary Slessor*, 144.

On July 31, 1893 Dr. Robert Laws, founder of the Livingstonia Mission, and Rev. William Risk Thomson arrived in Calabar. The Foreign Mission Board was following Mary Slessor's advice to send men to assess the need for a training institution. The visitors stayed in Calabar four months, and on the basis of their appraisal the Board "resolved to proceed at once with the building of the Training Institution. A site was granted, rent-free, by the Consul-General (Sir Claude Macdonald)."[4] The Hope Waddell Training Institution was on its way to becoming an actuality, and William Risk Thomson would become its first principal.

In August, Dr. Laws heard Slessor was ill and agreed to go see her. News passed ahead of him that he was coming, so Mary stood, holding on to a table for support, to welcome him. He ordered her back to bed. His missionary guide was amused when she complied. Had she not been in the midst of one of her attacks of fever, Mary might have ignored Laws' demand. Instead, "Laws . . . found that he was famous in mission circles as 'the man who made Miss Slessor do as she was told.'"[5]

Dr. Laws wrote to a friend: "She is a bit of a character. What a Salvation Army lass is to the Church at home, Miss Slessor is to the mission. . . . I could not commend her as a pattern to others but she has saved lives as no other man or woman would have dared to do. Had a man attempted to do what she has done in [a] recent riot, he would have had his throat cut.[6]

Mary's dream of a vocational training school began to be fulfilled in mid-1894, when the first students registered as apprentices to mission carpenters, printers and engineers. The boys received a uniform and a small cash allowance. The curriculum included English and general education classes along with apprenticeship training.[7] Classes met at the Duke Town church until a building was finished at the end of the year.

Hope Waddell Training Institution officially opened March 8, 1895 in a two-story prefabricated building that had been shipped from Scotland. It was reassembled on the ridge behind Calabar's riverside trading sheds, overlooking the river 200 feet below. Boys came from many areas, some from as far away as Sierra Leone and Liberia. British officials applauded the Calabar Mission's teaching at the Institution and enrolled African

4. Christie, "Annals," 1893–94.

5. Buchan, *Expendable Mary Slessor*, 151. The entire episode with Dr. Laws is found in Buchan's biography.

6. Buchan, *Expendable Mary Slessor*, 151–52.

7. Macrae, *First Sixty Years*, 16.

pupils themselves. Within a short time, Britain would help finance the school to the tune of 500 pounds a year.[8] E. U. Aye reports that some missionaries, including Mary Slessor, also paid for pupils to attend school. Aye also states that the aim of the school was to produce students "of high moral principle and with no foreign ingredients in their patriotism."[9] One might say that as a result of this strategy (and with perhaps unintended consequences), missionaries were the first to plant seeds of African nationalism.[10]

A wing was opened for training girls at the Hope Waddell school in 1896, but boys were the primary target of training. When the boys needed more space, the girls were moved to Creek Town for the formation of a Girls' Institute. Martha Chalmers, who arrived in Duke Town in 1899 (and spent a brief time with Mary Slessor in Akpap), was instrumental in expanding a second school for girls in Duke Town.[11]

MARY KINGSLEY VISITS

The year after both of Mary Kingsley's parents died, she embarked on a journey to West Africa. She planned to study native peoples and to collect zoological specimens for the British Museum—primarily fresh-water fish and insects. Kingsley's father had been a physician who often wandered the world as an amateur naturalist and ethnologist, and Mary's home education came from studying his books and helping him with his papers. Her 1893 trip included a brief visit to Calabar; then she returned to England, where her reputation grew because of the specimens she brought back from her trip and her writings. In December 1894 she set sail for Africa again in the *Batanga*, along with the wife of the Consul-General.

Once settled in Calabar, Kingsley found, like Mary Slessor, that she did not relish the confined consular life. The stylishly-dressed traveler decided to escape to Okoyong, to meet the celebrated missionary. She described her approach to Ekenge during a tornado in April 1895:

8. Ibid., 17.

9. Aye, *Hope Waddell*, 3, 25.

10. See Peterson, "Rhetoric of the Word," for a discussion of the relationship between literacy and nationalism. He refers to Adrian Hastings' emphasis on "how the vernacular Bible fixed words and ideas, inviting readers to imagine themselves . . . as sharers of a national identity," 166.

11. Johnston, *Maxim Guns*, 224–26.

> The whole air was a rushing swishing water sheet. . . . The uproar was sublime, the demoniacal squeal of the wind, the groans of the strong creaking crashing enormous trees. . . . The roar, roll, and sharp whiplike crack of the continuous thunder. . . . I thought—being nervous at the best of times, and all alone and by myself . . . it was the last scene I was ever to see in the flesh.[12]

Kingsley survived the tornado and stayed with Slessor, fourteen years her senior, for two weeks. She found a kindred spirit in the other Mary, who shunned the niceties of polite society and lived as one of the people she served. They held long night discussions and arguments. They enjoyed each other's company and, in spite of difference in beliefs, became good friends. Kingsley was opposed to missionaries in general, but expressed admiration for a few individuals among them. She admitted that she held to "a form of pantheism."[13] She saw nothing wrong with the liquor trade. She had no objection to polygamy. Kingsley would later write of "roustabouts like Mary Slessor and me." She wrote of her new friend:

> Her great abilities, both physical and intellectual, have given her among that savage tribe an unique position, and won her, from white and black who know her, a profound esteem. Her knowledge of the native, his language, his ways of thought, his disease, his difficulties, and all that is his, is extraordinary, and the amount of good she has done, no man can fully estimate. . . . This instance of what one white can do would give many important lessons in West Coast administration and development. Only the sort of man Miss Slessor represents is rare.[14]

And though Kingsley thought highly of her new friend, she wrote in a letter that Slessor had "lost most of her missionary ideas . . . and is regarded by the other missionaries as mad and dangerous."[15]

Slessor would have disagreed with Kingsley about her loss of "missionary ideas," arguing that only her methods that were different. She may also have been surprised to learn that she was considered "mad and dangerous."

12. Birkett, *Mary Kingsley*, quoting a letter from Kingsley to Albert Gunther, April 15, 1895, 33.

13. Ibid., 35.

14. Kingsley, 74.

15. Birkett, *Mary Kingsley*, 34.

Jessie Hogg wrote of the two Marys, "These two unconventional people . . . sat up far on in the morning arguing on the immortality of the soul, and afterwards Miss Kingsley said she would give anything to possess [Slessor's] beliefs.[16]

SAVING TWINS

Kingsley's arrival coincided with a twin-saving episode. She witnessed Slessor's actions and remarked on her "unbounded courage and energy." She wrote about the slave mother of the twins, a slave named Iye.

> [She was] an Eboe [Ibo], the most expensive and valuable of slaves. She was the property of a big woman who had always treated her—as indeed most slaves are treated in Calabar—with great kindness and consideration, but when [twins] arrived all was changed; immediately she was subjected to torrents of virulent abuse, her things were torn from her, her English china basins, possessions she valued most highly, were smashed, her clothes were torn, and she was driven out as . . . unclean.
>
> Miss Slessor had heard of the twins' arrival and had started off, barefooted and bareheaded, at that pace she can go down a bush path. By the time she had gone four miles she met the procession, the woman coming to her and all the rest of the village yelling and howling behind her. On the top of her head was the gin-case, into which the children had been stuffed, on the top of them the woman's big brass skillet, and on the top of that her two market calabashcs.[17]

Mary Kingsley had her first lesson in Slessor's working within the confines of native culture, seeing the missionary lead the woman to her own house by way of a special path cut through the forest. She explained that to take the normal path would "pollute" an important market road and make it unusable. Kingsley wrote:

> I arrived in the middle of this affair for my first meeting with Miss Slessor, and things at Okyon were rather crowded, one way and another, that afternoon. All the attention one of the children wanted . . . was burying, for the people who had crammed them into the box had utterly smashed the child's head. The other child was

16. *WMM*, March 1915, 67.
17. Kingsley, *Travels*, 473–74.

> alive, and is still a member of that household of rescued children all of whom owe their lives to Miss Slessor.[18]

The other twin became Mary's cherished Susie. People would later come near the baby only if Slessor or Kingsley held her. "If either of us wanted to do or get something, and we handed over the bundle to one of the house children to hold," Kingsley wrote, "there was a stampede of men and women off the verandah, out of the yard, and over the fence, if need be, that was exceedingly comic, but most convincing as to the reality of the terror and horror in which they held the thing."[19]

The slave mother, Iye, did not want the child and was eager to get back to her mistress, who agreed to take her back—without the baby. Her life would be one of shame and isolation from then on. She would be known as "a woman with a past." Kingsley wrote of the mother's sorrowful wailing:

> "Yesterday I was a woman, now I am a horror, a thing all people run from. Yesterday they would eat with me, now they spit on me. Yesterday they would talk to me with a sweet mouth, now they greet me only with curses and execrations. They have smashed my basin, they have torn my clothes," and so on, and so on. There was no complaint against the people for doing these things, only a bitter sense of injury against some superhuman power that had sent this withering curse of twins down on her.[20]

Mary Kingsley said she tried to find out why twins were so abhorred in West African culture but always got the answer that it was "the custom of our fathers." She added her opinion: "that always and only means, 'We don't intend to tell.'"[21]

When she returned from an exploration to Cameroon in October, Kingsley went to see Slessor again and to tell her goodbye. She took a parting gift of "a case of milk and twenty-eight pounds of rice."[22]

"Mary Kingsley has become a canonical figure in the study of colonial discourse," writes Princeton professor Simon Gikandi. She wanted

18. Ibid., 475.

19. Ibid., 476.

20. Ibid., 476–77.

21. Ibid., 477.

22. Birkett, *Mary Kingsley*, quoting a Kingsley letter to Albert Gunther, October 5, 1895, 34.

to be known "as a naturalist and ethnographer rather than a traveler or explorer."[23] However, she is most often described as a traveler and explorer. She was an extraordinary Victorian woman, but in a very different way from Mary Slessor. Kingsley's writing gives an inside look at Slessor's modus operandi, and in her own way she spread admiration for the eccentric Scottish missionary, just as Charles Ovens' letters had already done.

Kingsley went home to England and wrote many letters and articles about West Africa. She became a popular speaker even before her *Travels in West Africa* was published. In 1900, she left England for South Africa to serve as a volunteer nurse during the Boer War. Caring for sick and injured Boer prisoners of war, she contracted typhoid fever and died. Kingsley was buried at sea, as she had requested.

In response to a letter from a Mr. Irvine, Slessor wrote of her admiration for Kingsley and of their friendship. Irvine specifically asked her to address the question of Mary Kingsley being an opponent of Christianity. In many of her writings, Kingsley had roundly criticized most missionaries and their methods.

Mary responded: "Miss Kingsley *adored* the Christ of God, the Savior of the world." She admitted that Kingsley was "sometimes a little unjust toward the churches," but only because she could not unravel "the mystery of pain and suffering," and the "hard things of God *as the creeds represented* him."

> But while she longed for light and yearned for the confidence and freedom which some she loved enjoyed [like Mary Slessor] and which was in great measure denied to her, she clung constantly and pathetically to the fact that God would at least approve the *sincerity* of her desire to live for the highest ends and to be of some use to others. "Light or no light, I shall do ever what my conscience tells me He will approve." That was her attitude, and will any Christians say that God shall have disappointed her?
>
> . . . She sees light now in His light, and she has not lived in vain; so for her past, and I am sure for her present, we may thank God, and follow in her steps of self-sacrifice, for she, of all the women I knew, lived not for herself.[24]

23. Gikandi, *Maps of Englishness*, 153, 143.

24. Livingstone, *Mary Slessor*, quoting MS letter to Mr. Irvine, December 14, 1903, (Zondervan, 1984), 360–61, 363.

Mary's attitude toward Kingsley mirrors her attitude toward other friends who did not share her faith, those outside the mission setting whom she managed to fit into God's plan outside of her own expressed faith and beliefs. Slessor still had a dozen years ahead of her after Kingsley's death—years that would bring new adventures and challenges.

AKPAP

Mary collapsed late in 1895 and was taken to Duke Town to recover. William Anderson had retired six years earlier after serving forty years in Calabar. He had returned from Scotland and planned to stay for the fiftieth anniversary celebration of the mission the following spring. "Daddy" Anderson sat with Mary and held her hand. It had been just two months since Hugh Goldie—long-time pastor of the church at Creek town and the only other living pioneer Calabar missionary—had died at the age of eighty.

Slessor's health improved, but only a few weeks later, he was the sick one. Mary sat with him until he died. It was as if he had come home to die, to be buried beside his wife at Duke Town. Mary wrote, "Dear Daddy Anderson! Calabar seems a strange land to me now. All the friends are strangers to the old order. The Calabar of my girlhood is among the things of the past."[25]

By 1896 Mary realized the people of Ekenge were moving on, typical of an agricultural society as the land was depleted. Many of the old farms were abandoned. Slessor didn't waste much time before deciding to move to the new Okoyong market center at Akpap. The Mission Committee in Calabar had reservations about her move eight miles west to more remote territory, but knowing Mary Slessor and her resolve, the presbytery approved the change. The British had no qualms about allowing her to move the native court. Ekenge was three miles from the Calabar River, while Akpap lay six miles from the Cross River trading center of Ikunetu.

Slessor went ahead with the move, settling her large family in a two-room mud house. She left boys at Ekenge and Ifako to carry on with school. Mary continued to hold court. People came long distances for her to settle their disputes. Other cases were referred to her from Duke Town. Consul Macdonald pretty much left her on her own. He knew she would judge cases fairly and would keep peace in her own way. The Okoyong honored

25. Livingstone, *Mary Slessor*, 153.

her and accepted her decisions willingly.[26] Mary was in Akpap nearly a year before the Foreign Mission Board in Scotland finally approved the building of a shed on the beach at Ikonetu and a house there.[27]

In addition to her own illnesses and the deaths of her two old-timer friends, Slessor was overcome with sorrow in mid-1896, when adopted fourteen-month old Susie died. The tired missionary reported the loss of several more babies before the end of the year.

In the spring of 1897, a smallpox epidemic struck the area. Mary vaccinated as many people as she could, until her supply of vaccine ran out. When a mission engineer ("captain of the smoking canoe") called with supplies and mail, he helped her scrape scabs with a knife from those who had already been vaccinated and use the pus to inoculate others.[28] Slessor heard that the epidemic had hit hard in Ekenge, so she set off to see what she could do. She opened her old house as a hospital, but as people were stricken, those who were still well left the area. There was no one to assist her or to bury the dead. Chief Ekpenyong, whom she had talked out of taking the poison bean eight years earlier, died. When his brother, Chief Edem, who had befriended and protected Mary in her early days in Okoyong territory, camc down with smallpox, she took care of him until he died. She couldn't save his life, but she felt obliged to bury him. She managed to make a coffin and dig a shallow grave. Then, exhausted from her nursing duties, she dragged herself back to Akpap.

Charles Ovens and mission engineer Alexander arrived at the village that morning and found Mary in bed. Ovens was ready to build Mary's new house. Alexander went to Ekenge two days later, hoping to find some building materials there. He found Mary's old house full of corpses and the village abandoned. Biographer Livingstone wrote, "The place was never fit for habitation again, and gradually it was engulfed in bush and vanished from the face of the earth."[29]

Mary's success during these years of transition and turmoil for the peoples of Nigeria continued to lay at least partly in her ability to act as liaison between the people and the British government. And any village

26. See Buchan, *Expendable Mary Slessor*, 155; Christian and Plummer, *Redhead*,105; Livingstone, *Mary Slessor*, 160.

27. Christie, "Annals," 1897.

28. Buchan, *Expendable Mary Slessor*, 156; Christian and Plummer, *Redhead*, 106; Livingstone, *Mary Slessor*, 161.

29. Livingstone, *Mary Slessor*, 162.

where she set up housekeeping gained some prestige from the presence of the white woman. Mary Kingsley went to West Africa with a revolver in her bag and said, "Have your hand on it when things are getting warm." She acknowledged that the weapon might never be needed, "but if you did need it you would need it badly."[30] Mary Slessor carried her Bible. She judged, but she also taught and preached. She was a different sort of British agent.

30. Kingsley, *Travels*, 330.

Mary Slessor wearing engagement ring (1891)

McManus Galleries and Museum, Dundee

Duke Town market (ca. 1889)

McManus Galleries and Museum, Dundee

Creek Town houses (ca. 1889) Note courtyard, lower right

McManus Galleries and Museum, Dundee

King Eyo VII, Creek Town (1888)

McManus Galleries and Museum, Dundee

Mary Slessor with Charles Ovens and John Bishop (ca. 1890)

McManus Galleries and Museum, Dundee

Mary Slessor's household (1890)

Mary Slessor with Chief Edem, Ma Eme Ete and others, Ekenge (ca. 1889)

Slessor with daughters Janie, Mary, Alice, and Maggie, Scotland (1891)

Author's Collection

Old mission church at Akpap (2001)

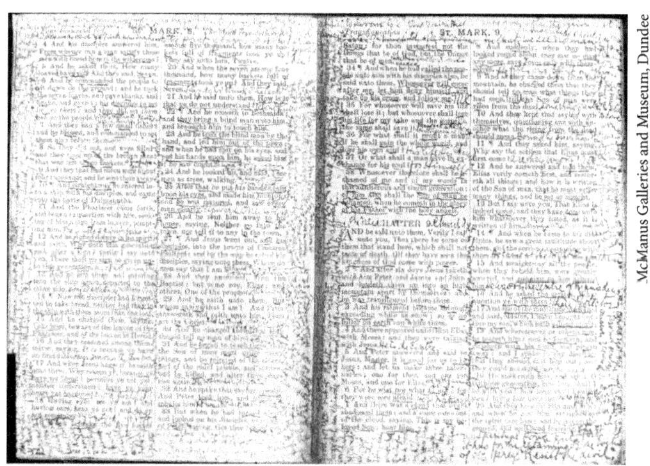

McManus Galleries and Museum, Dundee

One of Slessor's annotated Bibles—Lower right: "Resist the devil."

McManus Galleries and Museum, Dundee

Top: Loading palm oil at Emuramura (ca. 1889)

McManus Galleries and Museum, Dundee

Courthouse at Ikot Obong (ca. 1905)

Author's Collection

Mary Slessor statue at Akpap Presbyterian Church (2001)

Courtesy of Slessor family, Calabar

Daniel McArthur Slessor and Daniel McArthur, Scotland (1907)

McManus Galleries and Museum, Dundee

Mary Slessor and family (1912)

Author's Collection

Students at Hope Waddell Training Institution, Calabar (2001)

Author's Collection

Students at Presbyterian Secondary School, Use Ikot Oku (2001)

Author's Collection

Port of Calabar (2001)

McManus Galleries and Museum, Dundee

Queen Elizabeth II laying a wreath at Slessor's grave (1956)

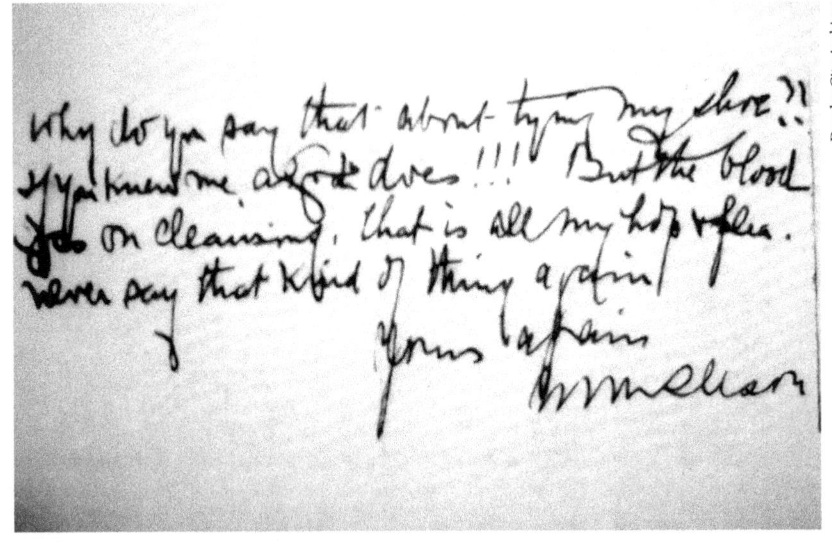

Why do you say that about tying my shoe?? If you knew me as God does!!! But the blood goes on cleansing, that is all my hope & plea. Never say that kind of thing again.

Yours again

M M Slessor

Dundee City Archives

Quote from Slessor letter to Charlotte Crawford, September 6, 1907

Author's Collection

Cross River from Itu near Mary Slessor Hospital

THIS PLAQUE COMMEMORATES
MARY SLESSOR
BORN 1848, DIED 1915
"MOTHER OF ALL THE PEOPLES"
A MISSIONARY AND MAGISTRATE
WHO LIVED IN THE COWGATE
AND WORKED AMONG THE POOR
OF DUNDEE FROM THIS BUILDING
THE WISHART CHURCH.
IN 1876 SHE JOINED THE CHRISTIAN
MISSION IN THE CALABAR REGION
OF SOUTHERN NIGERIA
SHE LABOURED TO SPREAD HER
FAITH AND TO HELP OTHERS.
"LOVE SUFFERETH LONG AND IS KIND"

Author's Collection

Plaque at Dundee honoring Mary Slessor (2000)

Author's Collection

Slessor's great-granddaughters: Inyang Bassey and Emelia Udom (deceased) (2001)

Author's Collection

Dan Slessor's children and grandsons: daughters Mary Slessor Bassey and Olive Slessor Henshaw, sons Kenneth and Alfred Slessor, grandsons Edward R. Slessor and John K. Edet, Calabar (2001)

Author's Collection

Cairn honoring Mary Slessor at Use Ikot Oku, near her house (2001)

Author's Collection

Monument, Slessor holding twins, roundabout at Mary Slessor Blvd., Calabar (2001)

PART FOUR

Queen Mary

1900–1909

11

Bairns

> I came to Akpap on 22nd July and found Miss Slessor well and busy amongst her children. There are six little boys, only two of whom can walk; four little girls and two big ones. Miss Slessor goes out at 6 a.m. to a village about three miles off to hold a school. She comes home at 10, when there is always some one waiting for a palaver with her. In the afternoon she has school in the house here, when a good many young lads come, all very anxious to learn. After tea, she attends to the sick. Every fourth day is market-day, on which she has a lot of visitors. They come to her with all their troubles, big and little, and her word is law. On Sabbath mornings at 6 she goes to the village where she has the school, and holds a short service. Some of the boys who attend the school, go with her to a still more distant place. When she comes home she has two meetings in different villages, and in the evening she goes to some big yard and has a service for children.
>
> —Charles Ovens, 1902[1]

MISSION ORGANIZATIONS TODAY WOULD frown upon adoption of their charges except in extreme circumstances. Mary Slessor's were extreme circumstances. Missionaries saved twins and orphans early in the mission's presence in Calabar, but not many integrated them completely and permanently into their homes and lives. All were "at risk" children and would not have survived without intervention and love. One visitor who admired Mary's devotion to her children wrote, "She had a poor sick boy in her arms all the time, and nursed him while walking up and down directing the girls. He died at 11.30 and she slept with him in her arms

1. *WMM*, December 1902, 294, "A private letter of 16th August."

all night. Next morning he was put in a small milk packing-case, and the children dug a grave and buried it and held a service."[2]

Mary Slessor never married—neither did her sisters, for that matter—but she had many children. Most were rescued or abandoned twins or orphans; some were brought to her doorstep; some she was able to place in native homes as the children grew and thrived, and hearts were changed to acceptance, when people learned the old superstitions about twins were unfounded. Some she farmed out to other missionaries or friends, especially when she left for her few furloughs in Scotland; some she raised as her own.

There are three main sources for information about Mary's bairns, her children. One comes from visitors who rarely failed to remark on her houseful of children. Another comes from Mary herself, as she wrote to friends about her joys and sorrows, her hopes, disappointments and her love for her adopted children. A third source is the writings of adopted son Daniel McArthur Slessor, who had no unkind words for his Ma.

The number of children in Slessor's household varied, but there was never a time, at least after 1882, that she had none; often she had a dozen. Over a period of twenty years, she adopted nine: Janie, Annie, Mary, Susie (who died very young), Alice, Maggie, Dan, Asuquo (William), and Madge White (Whitie). She gave each one an English name, though native names are recorded in some instances.

JANIE (JEAN)

Atim Eso, not only a twin but also the child of a slave, was renamed Janie Annan Slessor and became Mary's first adoptee. Mary wrote in an affidavit for the mission that Janie was born October 12, 1882 at Ikot Amin Abakpa. The baby's mother killed the twin boy at Old Town when he was five weeks old. Mary wrote, "[Janie's] mother died . . . while the child was with me in Scotland, where she was baptized in Wishart Church. Her family never contributed anything other than . . . yams and fowl . . . to her support. Her master Eso [the slave owner] and her father died shortly after our return from Scotland, [in December 1885]."[3]

2. Livingstone, *Mary Slessor*, 182–83.

3. MS affidavit, 1953-6-n, August 10, 1905.

Janie (or Jane, or Jean, as Mary called her when she was older) was a big hit in Scotland during Slessor's furloughs—always popular with the people the missionary addressed at obligatory deputation meetings.

Dan Slessor wrote that when his mother went looking for her girls, "more often than not she would catch Jane with both legs stretched on the wall, a Scottish newspaper over her face; she would be absorbed in reading." Mary admired Janie, Dan wrote, "because she was so deftly keen in reading."[4]

As Janie grew older she became shopper and cook, babysitter, even Bible teacher; and she ran interference for her Ma when people were too demanding, especially when Mary was ill.

On December 21, 1899, Mary's great helper, daughter Janie, was married. Slessor said the groom was "my best scholar," though not high on the social scale ("not quite a free boy," possibly one of Ma Eme Ete's slaves), but he was "a real companion to [Janie] and to my bairns." Mary performed the ceremony herself in Efik and wrote in the marriage register, "Janie Annan took oath before Obon [chief] Okon Ekpo, and Eme Ete, that she will marry Akibo Eyo alone. Akibo also took oath that he will marry Jane alone. They went to the farm with Eme Ete. M.M.S."[5]

Mary wrote of the marriage to Mrs. Symington, who had been her hostess in Scotland more than a year earlier.

> You will be surprised too to hear that Janie is married. She married a school boy who has been in the house for a couple of years.... He ... is very intelligent, and decent looking, and they live (in a cottage I built for them) in the grounds.... I have felt the loss of Jean more than enough, as Annie my next girl, is not very intelligent or quick, but she is willing, and Jean does all the baking and my meals when I am kept outside, and the little ones live with her a deal.... If she had married a free man, she would have had more prestige and wealth, but she would have been away from me, and might not have been able to withstand the temptations of a heathen life in a big man's house. So I am fain to be thankful. She is sobered, and quiet, and dilligent [*sic*] and in every way improved since her marriage. She is young, but all girls of her age are mothers long ago.[6]

4. D. Slessor, "Reminiscences."
5. Livingstone, *Mary Slessor*, 174.
6. MS to Symington, 1958/8380E, March 17, 1900.

Without Janie's constant help, Mary found herself busier than ever. She wrote, "I have only three girls at present [old enough to help] and I have nine babies, and what with the washing and the school and the palavers and the visitors, you may be sure there are no drones in this house."[7] Visitors told of Slessor bathing babies in buckets and bedding them down in boxes or little hammocks slung from the ceiling, where she could rock them when they cried in the night. She even took sick babies to bed with her. When she was frustrated with her houseful, she would repeat to herself, "There was an old woman who lived in a shoe, she had so many children she didn't know what to do" until she regained her composure.

Mary's satisfaction with Janie's marriage could not have lasted long. Her infant son died and her husband deserted her, apparently deciding the twin taboo was true after all. Mary left no record of this turn of events, but Janie returned to Mary Slessor's household in the fall of 1900 and continued where she left off as her Ma's right hand. She carried messages to angry chiefs and went off to retrieve abandoned babies; she even nursed the newest household baby, Dan.[8] Nine years later, Slessor wrote, "Jean is still the House Mother. The doctor has told her she can't marry, and she is fain to keep the kids here."[9]

Slessor wrote of Janie's participation in caring for the babies that kept coming. "A new baby . . . has come today but Jean is always pleased and never thinks a baby is trouble."[10] With Mary's increasing responsibilities and illnesses, she knew her daughter's viewpoint was unrealistic, but she still found it difficult to turn away an infant who needed care.

In 1910 she wrote from her home in Use Ikot Oku, revealing her increasing dependence on her beloved Jean, "I'm hungry and am sending for Jean to get my chop [food] brought here, and as she is going to Nkana [about twenty miles from Use] to open a school, I expect there will be little time for writing as I have only Maggie and Whitie with me!"[11] A year later, she reiterated that Jean was at Nkana, "as I have no boys, and they have been clamorous for a teacher for years. She was once there before, and . . . I'm glad the people asked for her as she is a *very* good, smooth in-

7. Livingstone, *Mary Slessor*, 175.

8. Christian and Plummer, *Redhead*, 115; Livingstone, *Mary Slessor*, 174.

9. MS to CP, December 22, 1910.

10. Ibid., March 3, 1910.

11. Ibid., December 22, 1910.

telligent reader, and will not murder the Scriptures as half, or imperfectly taught boys do."[12]

Mary expected Janie to do her share (perhaps more than her share) of work at home, to keep things operating smoothly by cooking, cleaning, building, and caring for children, while Slessor went about her missionary duties. Mary's diaries of 1911 and 1914 often mention Jean cutting brush, clearing the road, gone to market, cooking, building or mudding (plastering) walls, or collecting stones for cement.[13]

When Mary Slessor died, Janie was there; she would live just three years longer herself.

ANNIE AND MARY

Annie Wilson Slessor was Mary's second adoptee, born near the end of 1886. Slessor wrote: "[She was] brought to me at Creek Town Mission House in a filthy state, by the slaves of Mana-Ibok Okon. Her mother had died from *mbiam* and there was no one to care for her; she was about 4 to 6 months old. . . . She came on 3rd April 1887."[14]

Mary mentions small donations given by Annie's "mistress" and her father, then the affidavit continues with the story of how she asked the mistress to take Annie for a while when the child was older, because she had been stealing. Mary soon had to rescue her again, though. When she learned that the mistress was trying to sell Annie, she threatened to call on the British Consul for help, and Annie was hastily returned to Akpap. She had not been sick, Mary wrote . . . [and "since then nine years ago, I have not allowed her to go to see them, nor does she wish to. This child belongs entirely to the Mission on my demise."[15]

In another document Slessor relates the history of her namesake, Mary Mitchell Slessor, born February 2, 1893 in Okoyong. Her mother was found guilty of unfaithfulness to her first husband by the ordeal of boiling oil. She ran away to Ikoneto[16] and married another man. When little Mary was born her mother died; her father left her at the side of the road beneath a mango tree when she was ten days old. . . . Slessor asked

12. Ibid., January 1, 1912.
13. MS Diaries, 1911 and 1914.
14. MS affidavit, 1953-6-1, August 10, 1905.
15. Ibid.
16. Formerly known as Ikunetu.

around for volunteers to take the baby, but took her into her own home when "they laughed at me and told me to try to make her live."[17]

Sixteen-year-old Mary and twenty-two-year-old Annie both married during 1909, and from this time on Slessor mentions them and their husbands often in her writings. She is happy for them and appreciates their ministries but misses their presence to help with various tasks.

Slessor wrote to *The Women's Missionary Magazine* of Mary's marriage, "So our girlie has gone out to a new life, but David, who is the motor driver on the Government staff, is a Christian lad, and I am pleased to give her to him. . . . Before they left David came and said, "Mother, you won't let us go without prayer," and down he knelt; so we gave them to God, and had a solemn time together."[18]

She wrote to others about Mary's wedding, as well, though mention of Annie's wedding is not found except as an accomplished fact. To her friend Charles Partridge she wrote:

> Mary has been married to the motor driver here, and there has been a very quiet wedding, but it made a deal of work too, to get her off nicely and to clear up after it. She did a deal of the heavy work of the house too before she went. Mudding and building . . . we were kept at it.
>
> Annie was there [at Mary's wedding] with her husband and baby, and they seem to do well and have a decent home; so though I'm short handed—for the babies come all the time—I'm glad to see them settled.
>
> [David] is a steady lad, and his mother has written from Lagos, and his brother who holds evidently a good post, so I am pleased, and it is [Mary's] own choice, though two other men, one Ibibio and one Okoyong man, were waiting for her consent. Don't be sarcastic now over this![19]

She also wrote that she was glad Mary and David did not live in a compound. She considered that "the ugly part of our native life, the publicity of it all."[20]

To her friend Charlotte Crawford, Mission Society worker in Edinburgh, Slessor wrote,

17. MS affidavit, 1953-6-m, August 10, 1905.
18. *WMM*, January 1910.
19. MS to CP, October 15, 1909.
20. MS to CP, December 9, 1909.

> Mary has been down with all her new full blown importance as a Matron and what with Bananas for me, and a water cooler, and biscuits for the bairns—she turned the house upside down before they started for the market. We got a new baby too yest[erday]—from Aro Chuku, and she has had to be admired and handled and petted, and the older one [probably daughter Whitie] did not see the fun of that, and made herself known. . . . As Annie & Mary have both been married this last year and gone to homes of their own, Janie and the young ones are only [avail]able for house and station work.[21]

David was a great help to his mother-in-law during her later years in Africa, especially since he had access to a government vehicle and permission to take Slessor anywhere she wanted to go. She was upset when she received news that he was being transferred . . . and her Mary would be gone. "A mere bairn herself and an infant in arms and noone with her! I'm just knocked over, and not to see her and advise or give a letter to any one," she complained.[22]

Annie's son died before he was a year old. "He was running about, and began to speak," she wrote to Partridge. Slessor's good news was that Mary now had a baby girl. She put in a good word for her daughters' husbands, too. "David has been a good son-in-law, so has Akpa[n] Inyan."[23] By 1913, Annie had a baby girl, and she and Akpan were acting as teachers at Nkana, where Jean had served earlier.

SUSIE AND OTHER LOSSES

Less is known of most of the other adopted Slessor children. No affidavits tell their stories, though their birth years can usually be inferred. Susan was born in April 1895 and lived just fourteen months. She pulled a pot of boiling water on herself and was badly burned. Mary nursed her for two weeks, then carried her to Creek Town, hoping the doctor could help. He couldn't. She returned to Akpap, and Susie died the next day.

Mary was grief-stricken at this loss. She asked missionary Mary Ann Murray to conduct the funeral. "She laid Susie in her coffin dressed in a white pinafore, put a flower in her hand & her own necklace. . . . Mary wrote home, 'My heart aches for my darling. . . . Oh, the empty place and

21. MS to Crawford, November 19, 1909.

22. MS Diary, April 6, 1911. See also MS to CP, April 12, 1911.

23. MS to CP December 11, 1910. Akpan was Annie's husband.

the silence and the vain longing for the sweet voice and the soft caress and the funny ways. Oh, Susie! Susie!'"[24]

Susie's slave-mother, Iye, had also learned to love her remaining twin. She mourned along with Mary. Going against her normal rule of not buying slaves, mainly because it created the wrong impression for those in the community, Mary saved money to buy Iye's freedom. At a cost of ten pounds, she became part of Slessor's household and later acted as an interpreter, when Mary moved the center of her ministry further inland, closer to Iye's birthplace. Iye could not be sold except to cannibal tribes for "chop," Slessor wrote, since twin-mothers were outcasts.[25]

Susie was not the only child Mary wept for. She wrote:

> I had such a lovely boy too, and after he was the length of having four teeth cut, he was taken in a convulsion from his teething while I was lying ill. It nearly broke my heart to lose him feeling that had I been well, he would have probably got over it. I have a nice wee laddie, two months old yesterday, and he is thriving, but I dread letting my heart get set on him for I can't keep a boy and when I am ill, and [when] the young infants are left to the natives, I scarcely fail to lose them.[26]

Slessor's correspondence often told of interruptions and problems. She wrote of being constantly surrounded by children studying their lessons,[27] and another time apologized, "I have a sick baby who will not stop crying if I lay him down. I had two girlies very ill—a remarkable thing for this healthy hungry household. . . . Baby will not be quiet so must stop."[28]

Early in 1909 she wrote to Partridge that Annie and Mary were away and Janie was ill. "So I have been left with the little ones, and I have two babies without Mothers, and they are in my hands night and day."[29] And, "Here is the baby yelling for all she is worth, so I suppose I'll have to go to her."[30] Still later,

24. Christian and Plummer, *Redhead*, 102–3; Livingstone, *Mary Slessor*, 141–42.

25. Christian and Plummer, 103.

26. MS to Symington, March 17, 1900.

27. MS to CP, June 18, 1905.

28. Ibid., May 30, 1908.

29. Ibid., February 17, 1909.

30. Ibid.

> I have two baby girls talking, one lies on my knee asleep now, and a wee ricketty boy whose mother died, and his father works on the road and he has no one to look after him. He has just got over that fearful scab—the Yaws—and has swollen feet and hands often, but with codliver oil and milk he puts on flesh apace.[31]

Entries in her diary of 1911 and 1914 continued to report new babies taken in and the sad news of too many deaths. Were other diaries available, they would no doubt contain more instances of this part of Mary Slessor's work. In February 1911 she wrote, "Baby Mbiabet died and buried in lower garden. Gave so little trouble, and fought so for life. Jaundiced as I never saw a baby. White of eyes quite green for days. Could not remove it."[32] In April, "Me Mbim died this morning, . . . could not take his milk, but tried to when I begged him. Very hard to say Amen." She was quite put out with the baby's father, who appeared drunk a few days later asking for a gift. "Got a smart rap on the knuckles for an answer," she confessed. "I've kept, fed, nursed by night and by day, and kept girls as nurses . . . and now I'm to find a gift. He went off without speaking."[33]

In May, Slessor told of more twins arriving: "One child thrown on the head of the other and all the birth matter on top of that. A filthy mess seeping through the basket. A girl underneath quite dead, tho not cold. Fine well formed children." Then, "Had to nurse babies all day. Twin baby began calling out in simple cries, no sign of what hurts, except the cheeks draw back as if breathing hurt."[34] And, "Had to bury twin baby . . . who died over night. Neither father nor mother have ever asked for her. Poor wee lamb. A fine baby can't tell what was wrong. Grew rigid and cried out constantly like in a fit."[35]

In 1912 Slessor wrote to Charlotte Crawford from her current station.

> We have had the first twins saved here. Fine babies, but what a sulky heathen of a mother. . . . This mother simply *would not* have the children, and after a fortnight of fighting with her night and day, the last one died from sheer starvation. I had no teats or bottles but what the other babies were using, else I might have broken my

31. Ibid., December 9, 1909.
32. MS Diary, Feb. 24, 1911.
33. Ibid., April 20 and 25, 1911.
34. Ibid., May 25, 1911.
35. Ibid., May 26, 1911.

> own resolution never again to take children from their mothers. It is not only bad in principle for all concerned, but I am not able physically for this now.[36]

New babies arrived as late as September 1914, when Slessor reported a "new baby girlie" arrived and a twin boy died and was buried in the yard behind the house. She told in her diary how she sometimes dealt with reluctant parents of twins: "[The father] was unwilling to stay . . . [but] I made him stay [to bury the child], telling him if he went, he must take the child with him. . . . Not one word of thanks to Maggie . . . nor to me. . . . But as sulky as a bear."[37]

Responding to a letter in late 1914 from the editor of *The Record*, when she was nearing the end of her own life, she begged his pardon for "the 'apparent slovenliness' of her letter: 'I've had a fractious, newly vaccinated baby on my knee under the pad, and she does not like it any more than I do.'"[38]

ALICE, MAGGIE, AND WHITIE

If documentation existed for Alice McCrindle and Maggie Cunningham, born about 1894 and 1897, or any of Slessor's later adoptees (Dan, Asuquo, and Whitie), it has been lost. Slessor praised her daughters in her diaries as being hard workers. She recorded her terrible fright when Maggie fell off a ladder. "Could not sleep after fright about Maggie," she wrote. "Got up before daylight, the light of fire wakened Alice and Jean. Then we had a thanksgiving. Maggie all right."[39] And, "Maggie and I managed to wash over the wall in Hall Partition, so as to get Books brought in. She is a brick! . . . Whitie and I between us helped her high up and kept babies."[40]

Mary wrote to Charles Partridge about Alice, eighteen years old, on New Year's Day 1912. "I have two proposals for Alice, of marriage, last month. One from the Bendi interpreter. The other from one of Mr Russell's clerks, a Gold Coast man. Neither are to my mind. The interpreter she will not have. The other she does not yet know of till I see Mr.

36. MS to Crawford, March 23, 1912.
37. MS Diary, September 7, 1914.
38. *Record*, 1915, 58.
39. MS Diary, April 5–7, 1911.
40. Ibid., May 28, 1911.

Russell or Underhill to see about his antecedents. Janie won't hear of it, as Alice would be lost to us if she went to Gold Coast."[41]

Thomas Hart, who visited Slessor at Odoro Ikpe two years later, reported, "While I was there a native clerk asked Miss Slessor for Alice's hand, but the request was turned down. Alice was a princess!"[42] Mary wrote of one marriage proposal, "Carpenter . . . asked that he might have either Jean or Alice for a wife. Knows nothing of what marriage means more than dogs."[43]

DAN AND ASUQUO

If Mary feared she couldn't raise a boy, she changed her mind when Daniel McArthur Slessor (whose African name was Etim) won her heart. His extensive reminiscences, written in 1958, and two letters from ten years earlier, give clear pictures of the family and the loving home Dan recalled so well. Born in late 1900 or early 1901, he accompanied Mary to Scotland in 1907 on her briefest stay, just five months. There he met his namesake, not much older than he, Daniel McArthur. Mary often referred to Dan in her writings to *The Missionary Record* and in personal letters. She wrote of her hope that he would be home from school for holidays, described him as "a good boy, and obedient and cleanly in all his habits and ways,"[44] and later bragged that "Dan had almost the full 100% for all his classes except writing . . . and [the] Principal says his conduct is good."[45] Still later, "Dan does well enough at school. His last report in November was 'Passed Government Inspector with flying colours.' He is quiet and grows apace."[46] Mary busied Dan with "keeping the school," while he himself was home from school four months before she died, when she was so ill she was unable to drag herself from bed.[47]

Dan admitted he was spoiled, and he had an explanation of why this was so.

41. MS to CP, January 1, 1912.
42. Hart to W. P. Livingstone, April 1915.
43. MS Diary, April 24, 1914.
44. MS to CP, December 22, 1910.
45. Ibid., September 3, 1911.
46. Ibid., January 1, 1912.
47. MS Diary, September 21–27, 1914.

> It is true that I was described as Ma's favourite. Indeed I was, and it had to be, because the King of the Okoyongs, Obong Okon Ekpo, implored Ma to nurse me and bring me up for Okoyong. Accordingly, that she paid special and particular care of me was understandable. Besides the fact that Ma had no boy inmates except myself and my half brother goes to support the fact. . . . So careful was she that all Okoyong and in the Ibibio country I came to be regarded and called "Akpan Ma" (meaning Ma's eldest son), and in these parts . . . the eldest son is more like a gem and a jewel than anything else.[48]

Slessor's relationship with her younger adopted son is puzzling. Dan Slessor says his Ma named her only other son William Mactavish Slessor, but Mary always referred to him by his African name, Asuquo, in her letters and diaries. She did not do this for her other children, and Asuquo is not often mentioned in a favorable light. His birth year is uncertain, but it would have been before 1903. He did not accompany Mary and Dan to Scotland in 1907. He was probably put in the care of another missionary or a relative during Slessor's absence. Missionary Beatrice Welsh wrote that as a toddler he "looked with his big innocent eyes a wee angel, and who yet was in constant trouble, chiefly for insisting on sharing the cat's meals."[49]

In December 1909 Mary wrote to Charles Partridge: "Dan and Asoquo [a spelling variant] are gone to the Institute. It would make them such ninnies to be always among girls even if they had good schooling."[50] The next year she wrote, "Asoquo, the little Adam, who would not wear his clothes, is at school there too, but is not at all satisfactory. He is a young tatterdemalion and a regular man of CHOP."[51] Apparently, he was unconcerned with appearance and hygiene but very concerned with food. Four years later Slessor confided in her diary: "Girls have rubbed half the walls of the hall. Boys mudding the new house. Asoquo is not improved as he grows older. None of the makings of a man, or even a worker in

48. D. Slessor, "Reminiscences."

49. Livingstone, *Mary Slessor*, 182.

50. MS to CP, December 9, 1909.

51. Ibid., December 22, 1910.

him."[52] Later that month she wrote, "Asoquo made off from his work. A lazy worthless boy."[53]

Mary would not tolerate disobedience or laziness in her children or others; one can only assume that Asuquo was a disappointment to her because he failed in the characteristics she demanded. However, by this time she did not often mention her adoptees by name in correspondence but simply referred to "my dear children." Also, her remarks of disappointment are recorded only as entries in her private diary and in one letter to her friend Partridge.

Asuquo was included in her requests for prayer for all her children. W. P. Livingstone cites a letter Slessor addressed to Alice at school in Duke Town in 1912. "My Precious Children—I am thinking a lot about you, for you will soon be losing our dear [teacher] Miss Young, and while I am sorry for myself, I am sorrier for you and Calabar. How are you all? And have you been good? And are you all trying to serve and please Jesus your Lord?" She continued with details of family news and closed with, "My heart is hungry to see you and to touch your hands. . . . Greet each other. All we greet you. With much love to Maggie, Dan, Asuquo—I am, in all my prayers, your mother, M. Slessor."[54]

Mary made a special request of Charles Partridge's parents in England:

> "I shall be glad if you give me a share of your prayers, and if you specially pray for my *dear* Children, that they may be saved and be made saviours of others. I feel so frail sometimes nowadays, that I feel as if the work must be left to them and while they are all good and affectionate and obedient there is a lack of spiritual life, and the lack of that passion for the saving of others, that I long for in them, and in myself."[55]

It is notable that in a will written January 28, 1907, Slessor mentioned specifically "Janie Annan Slessor, Mary Mitchell Slessor, and Alice McCrindle Slessor, and Maggie Cunningham Slessor, and Madgie White Slessor and Dan McArthur Slessor. All of whom I have brought up from their very birth, and on whom not a single soul can lay the shadow of a

52. MS Diary Dec. 1, 1914.

53. Ibid., Dec. 15, 1914.

54. Livingstone, *Mary Slessor*, 326–27.

55. MS to Mr. & Mrs. Partridge, Sr., March 10, 1910.

claim."[56] Thus, it is likely that Asuquo did not join Mary's bairns at birth and that he had a remaining family connection, however tenuous.

Few of Slessor's children were a success by the world's (or their culture's) definition, but descendants of Annie and Daniel remember fondly "everybody's mother," but most of all their own mother—and the Slessor household. Dan wrote of his brother and sisters.

> Mary was our best cook and Maggie our best riddle teller. Alice perhaps because of her stammering, was glummy and almost forbidding, but all the same she had a kindly soul. She was always to be found, bible in hand, and in a contemplative mood. Annie was completely illiterate, and she filled time in the kitchen garden behind the house; but a more genial woman there has not been. Whitie, young but quarrelsome; and Asuquo, he spent almost half the day examining birds nests, rat holes and shooting arrows at any passing object, including lizards.[57]

"Ma," Dan wrote, "was the ideal mother; with us she was not the mistress or the missionary worker, she was our mother and the home our family." He wrote of tender care for the children when one was ill, "utterly oblivious of her own frailty and greater and more deserved needs . . . she would gladly and readily forgo her rest or sleep to mount guard over one of her sick children." In telling of his return to school in Duke Town, he wrote,

> Ma would follow our shadow in that cold, chilly early hour at five a.m. shepherding and offering prayers for our safety on the launch and road. She would stand in that early cold wind, her hair fluttering in the breeze, tears rolling down her cheeks, and calling out, "Good bye my son, see you do your lessons well, obey your masters and never be rude or unmannerly. We would bend the far corner, yet alone out in that wild dark and lonely road she would remain, her very soul hungering after us, her thoughts with us, oblivious of her surroundings, her utter defencelessness, but her faith as great as lions and her courage greater than warriors. She would return home, chilled to the bones, weeping and forlorn . . . and nothing could comfort her till she hears from Etubom Macgregor [principal of Hope Waddell Training Institution] that I arrived safely back to school.[58]

56. MS, "My Will."

57. D. Slessor, "Reminiscences."

58. D. Slessor to Hart, November 25, 1948.

"As long as I can nurse a motherless bairn," Mary wrote to Partridge, "or help to keep peace in a home or town; or be a mother to my own bairns, I'm to stick to my post."[59]

"Can I forget?" Dan asks. "No, never. Not even the minutest happenings; each day I let my mind roam over all those places where we lived so happily. A happier family I cannot admit existed."[60]

59. MS to CP, October 15, 1909.

60. D. Slessor to Hart, November 25, 1948.

12

Long Juju

In 1901 slave-dealing with the Ibos (or Aros or Inokons, as they are sometimes called) was suppressed by an armed expedition. . . . The result of this expedition has been to open up a vast country in the interior. . . . The fame of our valued missionary, Miss Slessor, travels far, and for years many of the Inokon chiefs had been in the habit of coming long distances to visit her in her station at Okoyong for advice and guidance. Had she been able to settle in Inokon, it is doubtful whether an armed expedition would have been necessary, and it is at least possible that the suppression of the slave trade would have been achieved by the peaceable means of the gospel.

—The Rev. A. W. Wilkie, 1905[1]

Mary was depressed, sorrow following sorrow. Illness and deaths did not stop with the passing of Goldie and Anderson and her little Susie. She continued to hear reports of the smallpox epidemic from "upcountry" and worried that the people there had not heard the gospel message. It was no secret to colleagues and the Mission Board that Mary wanted to move on to this new territory, but the mission sent no one to help with the overwhelming workload in Okoyong.

It was past time to go home to Scotland. The tired missionary—a veteran of more than twenty years of service—wouldn't hear of leaving, though, sick or not, with nobody to replace her in Akpap. Mission officials were frustrated with Slessor when she refused to leave on furloughs without certain of her children. However, it was the only way to get her to go, even when she seemed at death's door. Mary was relieved when

1. *Record*, 1905, 261.

mission carpenter Charles Ovens volunteered to stay in Akpap during her absence. She farmed out all the children she could, but insisted on taking four of her girls with her: fifteen-year-old Janie, five-year-old Mary, three-year-old Alice and sixteen-month-old Maggie. Once she was convinced she must return to Scotland to convalesce, and mission officials had acquiesced to her demand that she take the children with her, she looked forward to going. When she got home, she just wanted a place to hide, she said, "away from conventionalities and all the paraphernalia of civilization."[2]

Mary and her daughters sailed from Duke Town on March 14, 1898. She neglected to notify anyone she was coming home. Her friends, the McCrindles, received a telegram from Liverpool asking them to meet her at Edinburgh's Waverley Station. Here came Mary—not well—with four children who, except for Janie, found everything new and confusing. Their arrival caused quite a stir. They stayed with the McCrindles in Joppa for a couple of weeks, rented a small place nearby for a while, and finally moved to the Scottish Borders village of Bowden. Nora Adam, Secretary of the women's Zenana Committee, who often found housing for missionaries on furlough, made arrangements for this final move.[3]

When Slessor began to feel better, the usual rounds of speaking engagements began. Wherever she appeared, funds for missions poured in. She still suffered with extreme shyness in these situations, especially when men were in the audience. Two ministers attended a meeting in a Glasgow home. When she began to speak, Mary asked the men to leave. It was pointed out to her that the men would be disappointed not to hear her, so she asked that they sit where she could not see them.[4] This was not the only recorded instance of Mary asking men to either leave or hide. On one occasion, she was so nervous that she ran off the platform. She spoke in Aberdeen at Belmont Street Church, the church she attended as a young girl. She spoke in Stirling, Charles Morrison's hometown. She spoke in various cities and villages, in churches and homes.

Though the money rolled in, Mary Slessor kept complaining that the real need was for more missionaries. She declared, "When Sir Herbert Kitchener, going out to conquer the Soudan required help, thousands of

2. Livingstone, *Mary Slessor*, 164.
3. Livingstone, *Mary Slessor*, 167–68.
4. Christian and Plummer, *Redhead*, 108; Livingstone, *Mary Slessor*, 166.

the brightest of our young men were ready. Where are the soldiers of the Cross? In a recent war in Africa in a region with the same climate and the same malarial swamp as Calabar there were hundreds of officers and men offering their services, and a Royal Prince went out. But the banner of the Cross goes a-begging. Why should the Queen have good soldiers and not the King of Kings?"[5]

When people praised her, Slessor insisted that all the missionaries worked as hard as she did, or harder. She told audiences that she wanted to go "upcountry," to new territory. But she also worried about the Okoyong people back in Calabar. She remained in Scotland less than a year.

Nora Adam accompanied Slessor and her bairns to the ship at Liverpool near the end of 1898. The press heard the famous missionary would be there, so Reuters sent a reporter to interview her. Mary chatted about the customs regarding twins in West Africa and her practice of rescuing babies. She didn't mention the interview to anyone and didn't realize the wide publicity her words would receive in newspapers after she boarded the *Oron* to return to Calabar. Such reports reached a public eager for stories of African experiences and added to Mary's popularity in the homeland.

When Mary returned belated high praise and thanks to her furlough hostess, Mrs. Symington, she wrote that Maggie had grown into "a great fat sturdy girl," a "chatter box" and "a proper Home Ruler." She apologized for not writing sooner:

> I shall never forget all you did for us, and how your care was more like a mother's than to a stranger lodging with you, but you did it for Christ's sake I know, and you know that if we belong to Him, we cannot give a cup of cold water without His seeing and thinking of it. That [time with you] is a more real life to the children than this one, as they are not allowed outside the compound, so . . . when I think of going home again, It is always to that dear village, and to your lives . . . and the memory of that larger world they left.[6]

5. Livingstone, *Mary Slessor*, 167–68.
6. MS to Symington, 17 March 1900.

BACK IN AKPAP

Mary surprised everyone by taking a "personal assistant" with her on the return trip—Annie Macintosh.[7] Mary recruited the young woman herself to help with rescuing, nursing and training children. (Macintosh was not on the Scottish Presbyterian Mission staff.) The relationship turned out to be an unhappy one. Mary wrote to her friend Mrs. Symington:

> You will know that yon woman Mcintosh [*sic*] was not a success. She was like many another, the humdrum life of home was hard, and the romance of the mission field had a glamour. But she found that the duties of a missionary were all the small duties of a home life, in addition to teaching and preaching and healing and guiding; and so she turned tail and fled. She never got up in the morning even on board ship till we were all washed and dressed and breakfast ready—and out here I made her tea and sent it in, and the children were all dressed and running about, so that I had only one more to feed and care and cook for, and that one, a silent, sulky woman whom I was at my wits end to please and keep sweet. It was a happy release for me when she went, and for the bairns too, for I had to whip them to make them go to her, and Maggie, till the day she left, hated to go to her. I have not said as much to any one about her, for you see she has her bread to earn, and I should not like to spoil her chance among the folks who could employ or recommend, but she is a lazy sulky woman.[8]

Of course, this is a one-sided picture. The scorned assistant and missionary Martha Chalmers both aired complaints of their own about Slessor. W. Risk Thomson, serving as secretary of the mission in Calabar, wrote to the Zenana Committee from Duke Town on June 9, 1899, "Both Miss Annie Mackintosh [*sic*] and Miss Chalmers, at different dates, have left Akpap for good." The committee's minutes acknowledged that letters verified that "strained relations existed between Miss Slessor on the one side, and Misses Chalmers and Mackintosh on the other."[9]

The committee sent Mary a letter in June, saying, "From various statements in your recent letters . . . the members of the Zenana Committee have become much concerned as to the state of your health. We fear that your recent visit home has not done you the good that we hoped it

7. Christie, "Roll of Missionaries" in "Annals."

8. Slessor to Symington, March 17, 1900.

9. *UP Church Mission Minutes*, "Minutes of Meeting of 25th July, 1899," /3721, 52.

would."[10] The letter went on to inform Mary that Dr. Cowan was coming to examine her and would send the committee a report. They hoped she would not be irritated with this development, and trusted she would see that it was concern for "your health and your usefulness" that guided their decision.

Martha Chalmers was in Akpap less than four months, then left for Duke Town. She remained in Calabar more than thirty years as a missionary, running the large girls' school in Duke Town. Annie Macintosh sailed for home in September, after only eight months in Calabar, three or four of those months with Mary Slessor. Macintosh traveled home with Dr. and Mrs. Cowan—the same doctor the Zenana Committee had sent to examine Slessor; he was being "invalided" home and died at sea.

BACK AT WORK

Mary complained that her new house, with its corrugated roof, was too hot—she couldn't help but wish for her old mud house with the palm thatch roof. But she worked on alone as a missionary and government agent, all the while either fighting off or succumbing to sickness. E. U. Aye reports that missionary doctor Peter Rattray was often on the go to care for both missionaries and natives. Aye writes, "The ailing Miss Slessor always needed his attention at Akpap."[11]

When the government began to ask Mary for court reports, she fretted over them. She would have agreed with the character in a novel who said reports were "a waste of time, but in accordance with the first principle of colonial government: that at all costs the yawning maw of the registry, the gaping mouths of files, must be fed."[12] Evidence often involved charges of witchcraft, and testimony was long and rambling. She heard the cases in the native language and tried to make sense of them in English for reports. She sat at a small table outside or in the "palaver house" with three chiefs appointed to hear testimony with her. Officers continued to follow Consul Macdonald's habit of letting Mary run her area with minimal interference, since the native peoples recognized her authority—without Maxim guns. She preferred not to use legal pressure, but to convince people of the right decision. "After all, we are foreigners

10. Zenana Committee to MS, June 29, 1899.

11. Aye, *Hope Waddell*, 15.

12. Huxley, *African Poison Murders*, 95.

and they own the country," she said, "so I always try to make the law fit in, while we adjust things between us."[13]

Mary became known to Europeans as queen of the Okoyong.[14] Though she lived alone, she often had visitors—both missionaries and military officers. They frequently found her bareheaded and barefoot, carrying a baby and with children all around, or working on her roof, or hearing court cases. Many were impressed by her, though they could not fully appreciate her circumstances, living as she did as one of her African neighbors. They admired but did not emulate her.

Slessor reported that things were changing in Okoyong territory. She wrote of twins being born but not being discarded, of a father giving a dead child a decent burial. When she called a meeting of the heads of houses in the area, Mary wrote, "I spoke to them not as a white woman, but as a mother. . . . I reasoned about the evils of the old customs from every point of view; the goodness of God in sending the Gospel to them before He sent the Consul; and lastly, and most strongly, about the relation of human life to God's creating, and especially His redeeming, sovereignty."[15]

Mary told the group that parents should take their twins home, that anyone was free to visit the new parents, and that people must not blame the twin births for any trouble that might occur later. The response at the meeting was silence, until "the old chief of the town and district" said, "Ma, what can I say? I have nothing to answer you. You have given your advice and commands, and I can only obey them."[16]

To Europeans, Mary Slessor may have been "white queen of the Okoyong," but to Africans, she was "the white Ma who lives alone," and eventually *eka kpukpru owo*—everybody's mother.

AFRICA, THE WORLD, AND ARO

The new millennium brought many changes throughout the world. The Boxer Rebellion was in full swing in China to rid the country of "foreign devils;" in South Africa, the second Boer War raged on; Australia was proclaimed a Commonwealth. In America, President McKinley was assassinated. In Scotland, the United Presbyterian Church and Free Church

13. Christian and Plummer, *Redhead*, 119.
14. Livingstone, *Mary Slessor of Calabar*, 180.
15. MS in *WMM*, May, 1901, 110.
16. Ibid.

of Scotland combined to become the United Free Church of Scotland, a merger that worried many but did not result in much change for Calabar's missionaries.

Queen Victoria died in January 1901 and Edward VII became king. In Nigeria, the Niger Coast Protectorate became the Protectorate of Southern Nigeria, and Ralph Moor was appointed High Commissioner to succeed Macdonald.

W. Risk Thomson, Hope Waddell's first superintendent, had gone home on furlough a year after the school opened. When he was interviewed for a Dundee newspaper, he revealed his bias regarding Britain's presence in Calabar and the all-too-often superior attitude of British citizens of the era:

> British expeditions have penetrated by various routes into the interior; the clash of the sword and the rattle of the Maxim gun have rent the stillness of the forests, and silenced and subdued the opposing hordes of heathenism; Kings and Chiefs have fled or laid down their arms; and unspeakably barbarous rites have been swept for ever from this fair portion of the earth. This is the pioneer work of civilization, and it is grim, bloody work. . . . I believe that the British nation has a mission to lay hold of as much of Africa as it can take for the purpose of civilizing and elevating its peoples.[17]

He went on to claim that all of Britain's government officials had been "exceedingly kind and considerate to the chiefs and their tribes within our sphere of influence," and he lauded their "great forbearance . . . before taking any active measures to reduce them to proper order." Such claims, of course, would be denied by many of the people who came under the jurisdiction of the new empire's edicts and by historians in years that followed.

The British continued to strengthen their hold in West Africa. They were determined to impose their own brand of civilization on Nigeria and to eliminate practices they considered brutal or superstitious. Author G. I. Jones remarks on the "liberal, evangelizing, and expansionist attitudes [of Britons in general] accompanied by a determination to put an end to the more barbarous and 'obnoxious' customs of these people."[18] British leaders on the scene in Calabar were concerned about frequent

17. *Dundee Advertiser*, April 19, 1897, 3.

18. Jones, *Trading States*, 73.

inter-tribal warfare and stories of human sacrifice and cannibalism. They knew the Aro people dealt in the internal slave trade and monopolized commerce in commodities such as cloth, tobacco, guns and ammunition. The Aro were known, as Jones indicates, for their "effective, if unscrupulous, religious and economic exploitation of the country."[19]

The Aro exploited religion by a shrine to their god, Chukwu (with variant spellings), represented by an oracle known as *Ibinukpabi* or Long Juju.[20] Calabar mission historian Geoffrey Johnston believes the Aro people "marketed [the shrine's] services as they marketed anything else."[21] Aro from settlements along the Cross River advised other groups to take their concerns to Long Juju. If Chukwu demanded a human sacrifice, a person might be killed. Sometimes, the Aro just bundled off the person as one more slave to sell, and put camwood dye in the stream as "blood," proof of death for onlookers.

"Chukwu, the god of the oracle, provided both arbitration and divination. It settled disputes and solved problems which could not be handled by normal means . . . [and] while it was claimed that the deity "ate" those who lost their case, most of them disappeared into the slave markets at Itu or elsewhere."[22]

Johnston points out that the Aro could not have continued this exploitation if all the supplicants or pilgrims disappeared. An interview he had with an Aro man in 1966 indicated that probably half the people went home satisfied with the disposition of their cases.

Nevertheless, lurid descriptions of the Aro and Long Juju continued to circulate. While their domination was primarily economic, rumors persisted and were exaggerated until Consul Moor came to believe it was also political and military. Historian J. C. Anene says the protectorate's administration believed Efik "stories" and that Ralph Moor "built up a case against the Aro" so he could justify his expedition.[23] This was in spite of the fact that the Colonial Office back in Britain thought war was unnecessary. But the stories persisted. According to Christian and Plummer, one

19. Jones, "Who Are the Aro?," 101.

20. "A Juju" in *WMM*, December 1904, 292–93. Rev. William T. Weir wrote of the ambiguity of the word "juju." It could be any object believed to have magical power to protect its owner.

21. Johnston, *Maxim guns*, 34.

22. Ibid.

23. Anene, *Southern Nigeria*, 224–25.

such tale appeared in the Governor's 1899 report. It told of a party of eight hundred people who had gone from near the Niger River to consult the Long Juju. Only 136 of them remained. They were "the most wretched and emaciated body of people I ever saw grouped together," the report said.[24]

Moor was convinced that the only way to pacify (or control) the country and its trade was to destroy Long Juju. Though the Aro had no idea the British government planned to invade them, Moor set forth his aims: "i) to stop slave raiding and the slave trade; ii) to abolish the Juju hierarchy of the Aro tribe; iii) to open the country to civilization; iv) to stimulate legitimate trade; v) to inculcate the use of currency in lieu of slaves . . . and other forms of native currency; vi) to establish eventually a labour market as a substitute for the present system of slavery."[25]

Some time in August 1901, fearing missionaries might be kidnapped, the British ordered all missionaries to return to Duke Town or Creek Town while a military campaign was carried out.

Mary Slessor responded with her usual confidence and candor. She was perfectly fine, she said. No one would harm her, and her people would not fight. She was not happy when a boat arrived with an officer who had orders to escort her back to Duke Town. She had not been there in nearly three years. When she got there, she rejected the offer of a government house, and instead took a room in the European hospital. Upriver chiefs, worried at the turn of events, lost no time coming to Duke Town to ask her advice, hoping for reassurance that the British government's changes would not harm them or their people.

Near the end of 1901, African troops were borrowed from Lagos and Northern Nigeria to assist the British to attack and destroy Long Juju at Arochukwu.[26] Then the forces spread out to disarm other Aro settlements. Villages that failed to surrender at once were burned, while cooperation meant a place was left unharmed.[27] Christie's mission "Annals" reported

24. Christian and Plummer, *Redhead*, 123. With no documentation, it is difficult to verify the source of the report. There was no "Governor" at this time. Ralph Moor was Commissioner of Niger Coast Protectorate from 1897–1899. Livingstone says the prisoners were housed in an Aro village, led away in groups of ten to twenty, all of whom were "either sacrificed or sold into servitude," 192.

25. Anene, *Southern Nigeria*, quoting C.O. 520/10, Moor to Chamberlain, 24 November 1901, Memo of Instructions, 229–30.

26. Afigbo, "Calabar Mission," 99; Arochukwu is also known as Arochuku.

27. Johnston, *Maxim Guns*, quoting A. F. Montanaro to High Commissioner April 5, 1902, CSO 1/4/2, 35.

on March 23, 1902, "The Aro expedition, with complete success, came to an end."[28] Some have placed blame on missionaries for the conquest, but documentation does not support this theory.[29]

Missionary James Luke wrote to *The Women's Missionary Magazine*, expressing both his doubts and a quite different concern of the missionaries:

> If all the stories told of the "Long Juju" are true . . . we have, I think, sufficient means for arriving at the conclusion that the authorities on the spot were justified in taking action. . . . What is sad about this expedition . . . is that nearly all the town names in connection with it are unknown to those of us who thought we had a passable knowledge of Old Calabar. I never heard of the Aros, of Bendi, of Awete, of Aro-Chuku or of Awran. . . . It is somewhat humiliating that after over fifty years' work there as a Mission, the district to the one side of the river . . . should be so little known amongst us. The reason? The old one, lack of money and men. . . . The Aros, or Inokuns, are first cousins to the Ibo tribe, if not Ibo themselves. . . . It has always been held as a principle with us in opening a station in Calabar, to open it on the bank of the river. . . . But as the Inokuns had no large or small towns on the bank of the river [and] kept well inland, we never had a chance of touching them. . . . The fact is, that we as a Mission have been unable to do this work; and the war may, partly at least, be charged to our neglect.[30]

CHANGES

E. U. Aye lists some "painful turns" for the Efik in the new millennium. First, High Commissioner Ralph Moor took up the question of domestic slavery. "He issued 'free papers' to domestic slaves who could testify that they were subjected to continuous neglect or maltreatment by their masters or mistresses. . . . Thus, the Slave Dealing Proclamation No. 9 of 1901 . . . abolished the legal status of slavery and guaranteed freedom to slaves who were born after that year. But the . . . Proclamation was silent about how the servile groups thus free would maintain themselves."[31]

28. Christie, "Annals," March 23, 1902.
29. See the complete discussion in Afigbo, "Calabar Mission," 94–106.
30. *WMM*, February 1902, 55–56.
31. Aye, *Efik People*, 206.

The pronouncement solved one problem but brought another, since slaves had no wherewithal to support themselves. This, of course, would be a problem for slaves freed in other parts of the world, as well.

The second painful turn of events was the 1902 edict that the title of king was abolished. It was decreed that there would be two Chiefs Paramount (*obong*)—one for Creek Town and one for Duke Town. The ruling went on to deal with the election of chiefs and declared that "every 'Obong' or Chief Paramount shall hold office during the pleasure of the High Commissioner." Thus, says Aye, "the idea of the Protectorate Government 'not to interfere unduly in tribal government' and 'the chiefs to continue to rule their own subjects' was virtually thrown to the winds."[32]

1902 was also eventful in other ways after the destruction of Long Juju. In February, missionaries received permission to return to their stations, except for Okoyong. James Luke (who served in Calabar from 1885 to 1894, then spent six years as a missionary in Jamaica, where the climate was deemed easier on missionary health) returned to Calabar. He became superintendent of Hope Waddell Training Institution just as the Aro expedition ended. (And he soon introduced football at the school, as Alexander Cruickshank had already done in Ikot Offiong.) Missionaries also reoccupied the station at Unwana, more than a hundred miles up the Cross River, though troops were still there.

In December, Esien Esien Ukpabio, the first Efik convert and pastor, died. Baptized in 1853 and ordained April 9, 1872 (four years prior to Mary Slessor's arrival in Calabar), Ukpabio was an honored and respected evangelist and minister. He had preached at the Golden Jubilee of Hope Waddell Training Institution in April 1896 and at synod and missionary meetings. When Hugh Goldie died, Ukpabio became pastor at Creek Town. His obituary was published in *The Record*, where he was praised and remembered fondly from his earlier visits to Scotland. He was described as "a faithful and earnest minister."[33]

Ukpabio was one of a considerable number of native teachers, evangelists and pastors in Calabar and its outlying districts. Esuqua Ekanem, for example, was ordained in 1879 and served many years in Ikonetu. Geoffrey Johnston writes, "It is significant . . . that when a question of

32. Ibid., 209–10.

33. *Record*, 1903, 67.

relating to the customs of the country arose in the Presbytery, Ukpabio was sometimes asked to prepare a paper on the subject for guidance of the court. Ekanem, for his part, was a keen student and a reasonably successful translator."[34]

Not many native names are recorded in mission papers, but later writers agree that without the assistance of Nigerian converts, the mission's work would have been more difficult and sometimes impossible. Donald McFarlan wrote of early mission years, "Had it not been for the native agents who were carrying on fully half the work of the mission, the veterans who still remained would have been defeated."[35]

Jamaicans also contributed significantly to the Calabar Mission. Three of the original party of six who landed in 1846 were Jamaicans or Africans from Jamaica. The rest were those who had been serving with the Scottish mission in Jamaica; they encouraged the drive to start a mission in Calabar. In the 1880s two ordained Jamaicans joined Calabar's missionary staff. Between 1902 and 1924 fourteen Jamaican teacher evangelists arrived to serve, two of those for more than thirty years. Calabar's first mission doctor, Archibald Hewan, was from Jamaica, as were a few wives, one carpenter, and at least ten "Assistants and Domestics."[36] "Mammy Fuller" was one of the Jamaican domestics highly regarded by Mary Slessor.

The mission struggled to provide teachers in new areas. By the time of Slessor's arrival in 1876, the younger Samuel Edgerley was conducting courses a minister in Scotland would follow: "a training in both secular and theological subjects."[37] Mary herself sent young boys (or sometimes girls), often from her own household, to outlying villages to teach what they knew of reading and the Bible.

As soon as she could arrange it after the destruction of Long Juju, Mary headed back to Akpap. The "white Ma who lives alone" offered solace and refuge to many. Women, slaves and desperate people sought her aid. Chiefs came miles to seek her advice or to ask her to act as mediator in disagreements. At one point, the chiefs of the Umon people asked Slessor to settle a dispute between themselves and the Okoyong. War seemed imminent. Both sides recognized that this white woman would

34. Ibid., 107.

35. Donald M. McFarlan, *Calabar*, 69.

36. Christie, "Roll of Missionaries, in "Annals."

37. Johnston, *Maxim Guns*, 106.

judge fairly, even though she lived among the Okoyong. They were not disappointed.[38]

The younger Edgerley had sent a teacher to Umon in 1881, but the work ended four months later, when war broke out with Calabar. The old customs persisted in Umon's settlement on an island some sixty miles upriver from Duke Town. James Macgregor, from Hope Waddell Training Institution, told of a trip he took with other missionaries in 1903. Macgregor thought they were the first missionaries allowed to hold worship services in Umon. After worship, the missionary party went to the chief's house, where they saw sixty-seven skulls lined up. The chief said they were from his great-grandfather's days, but Macregor reported that "some of them looked very new and very ghastly, with their teeth still in."[39]

When a murderer was caught in Okoyong territory, the chiefs were determined to put him to death. The culprit shouted a curse, saying his spirit would come back to "spoil" the chiefs unless they took him to "Ma's house" in Akpap. Intimidated, the chiefs sent him to Slessor. She unchained him and sat with him in her house until late in the day; then he was chained again and bedded down in a storeroom to await a boat to carry him to Duke Town for trial. No one knows what Mary and the murderer talked about that day, but during the night he slipped out of his chains. He didn't run away. In the morning Mary found he had hanged himself with his loincloth.[40]

ITINERATING

Slessor continued to nag the mission for help in Akpap so she would be free to explore further up the Cross River and on Enyong Creek. In January 1903 she visited Itu, on the big bend of the Cross River near where Enyong Creek entered it, about 40 miles from Creek Town. She chose sites for a church and school and left two boys and a girl there to teach and hold worship services.[41] A few weeks later she was pleased to find her young "teachers" were having a good response. Itu's chief said he was too old to change, but he had no objection to the younger generation

38. Livingstone, *Mary Slessor*, 171; Buchan, *Expendable Mary Slessor*, 163.

39. *Record*, 1903, 456.

40. Livingstone, *Mary Slessor*, 182–83.

41. Christie, "Annals," 1903.

learning new ways.[42] Mary decided it would be a good home base from which she could explore the creek and its villages.

In April, the mission finally sent Janet Wright, who had already served seven years in Duke Town and Creek Town. Slessor was delighted. Janet knew the language and soon took over the Akpap school and dispensary. Mary wrote, "She is a right sisterly helpmate and a real help and comfort in every way. . . . I don't know how I got on alone. It seems too good to be true."[43] She was reluctant to leave Wright at Akpap alone, though. It was "too isolated," she said. This seems an odd comment, since Slessor had been the lone missionary assigned to work with the Okoyong for nearly fifteen years, except for two furloughs and a couple of brief periods (not more than four months) of temporary help. Slessor hoped she and Janet Wright could live at Itu and explore the Enyong Creek together.[44]

Mary visited Arochukwu with British officer Col. Montanaro in June. Less than a month later, she took two boys back and, with the approval of local chiefs, began a school in the village of Amasu. On the way back to Akpap, a canoe suddenly appeared and rammed the larger craft. It was no accident, the oarsman said: his master wanted him to bring Slessor to his house in the village of Akani Obio. "We turned . . . and glided into such a lake of aquatic plants and flowers as I believe could not be surpassed anywhere. I was simply intoxicated with beauty!" Mary wrote. She went on to tell of meeting the "fine-looking, well-dressed man" at a beach crowded with canoes, many laden with palm oil for trade.

Onoyom told his story. His house had burned down, and he swore that witchcraft had caused it. But something happened to change his way of thinking.

> A Duke Town man told him the Bible way of looking at things, and prayed for and with him. From that time he had had thoughts of God and doubts of his old heathen beliefs; but he never took a step to find out more, till lately his only child died. Then he vowed he would seek God, and though the town people laughed . . . he was determined to go on and be delivered from the slavery and darkness of his doubt. . . . He went to Itu [while Mary was away] and found an old teacher of Creek Town . . . a besotted drunkard. . . . [Onoyom] engaged him to come and read the Bible to him.

42. Livingstone, *Mary Slessor*, 196.
43. Ibid., 198.
44. Ibid., 202.

> . . . And now would I deliver him, and show him what to do. . . . Then I got the drunken teacher's Bible, and read from it all the passages which occurred to me, and tried to show him the way of salvation.[45]

Missionary accountant Thomas Hart wrote to biographer Livingstone about the advice Onoyom received to "go and see the white woman who lived alone and talked God palaver." Mary "led him to Christ," Hart wrote, "and in time about half his following, some hundreds, had been brought in to Christian Worship."[46]

In Akpap Slessor wrote of her continuing concern for Okoyong. "As no ordained minister has ever been resident or available for more than a short visit [to Akpap], no observance of the ordinances of Baptism or the Lord's Supper have been held. . . . We have just kept on sowing the seed of the Word, believing that when God's time comes to gather them into the visible Church there will be some among us ready to participate in the privilege and honour."[47]

Mary was happy when Rev. W. T. Weir of Creek Town traveled to Akpap to conduct the first baptism and communion service ever held in Okoyong territory on August 9, 1903. Seven adults and eleven children were baptized, including Jean, young Dan, and Iye (the slave-mother of Susie).[48] Biographers Christian and Plummer reported that seven of the eleven children were Mary's own.[49]

By October 1903, a house for Mary and Janet was started at Itu. The next month, Slessor spoke at the Calabar Mission Council meeting. She praised Janet, then presented a plan she said came from both of them. Slessor reported that she had no intention of returning to Britain for her furlough. With Itu as her home base, she said, "I propose to ask leave from the station for six months, during which time I should, in a very easy way, try to keep up an informal system of itinerating between Okoyong and Amasu." She described the progress already made, including the church built by the people at Itu that drew as many as three hundred people to worship each week, and the rooms provided at Amasu on Enyong Creek.

45. *Record*, 1903, 455.

46. Hart to Livingstone, June 1915.

47. Livingstone, *Mary Slessor*, 156.

48. Ibid., 501. See also Christie, "Annals," 1903.

49. Christian and Plummer, *Redhead*, 130.

She would, she said, arrange for her own housing, find her own canoe and crew, and her family members would teach in the schools. With three women working together, she argued, they could also manage the Akpap station and "dovetail the details of the work" so that their health would not suffer. Mary made a case for Itu as "a natural and strategic point" in conducting mission work, in reaching Aro and Ibibio peoples.[50]

"Her views," wrote Livingstone, "did not commend themselves to all her colleagues in Calabar."[51] The Mission Council decided that Itu should be developed as a medical center, but they sent the question of itinerating to the Women's Committee in Scotland. Meanwhile, Mary kept moving ahead with plans and projects.

In April 1904, a year after Janet Wright arrived in Akpap, the Mission sent two more women to serve there. Mary was already spending much of her time at Itu, busy carrying out her own—or, as she believed—God's plan. In November, a year after she first addressed the Mission Council, she returned to report on the progress of the work at Itu and in various villages on or near Enyong Creek. The Council agreed to extend her leave of absence for another six months. Five months later, they would extend it for another year.[52]

From then on, Slessor would be on the move. It was not the end of building houses and churches or of setting up other home bases as she took the gospel to new areas. It was not the end of judging legal cases. It was not the end of malaria and other debilitating illnesses. The end was still a long way off.

50. Livingstone, *Mary Slessor*, 206–8.

51. Ibid., 195.

52. Christie, "Annals," 1904–1905.

13

A New Man and New Work

During my long life, I have had intercourse with many distinguished people, chiefly men. Of the women, I place first Mary Slessor, whom you call "the White Queen of Okoyong"! She was a very remarkable woman. I look back on her friendship with reverence—one of the greatest honours that have befallen me—and I had and still have a superstitious feeling that she has been and still is one of my Guardian Angels. (I have been twice seized by cannibals, thrice shipwrecked, etc., etc.,!) This belief exists in spite of my being agnostic (non-knower) and non-religious, though, as we all are, thoroughly imbued with the ethics of Christianity. Excepting Miss Slessor, I thoroughly disapprove of all missionaries!

—Charles Partridge, 1950[1]

MARY, FAMILY IN TOW, made her final move to Itu in July 1904. Dan Slessor recalled the chaos of their departure from Akpap.

Great was the wailing, of men and women. . . . [They came] in large crowds to plead with her not to leave Okoyong. None other would be as suitable, they moaned; but as Okoyong has already embraced the gospel, she must obey the call to go and open new lands and win more souls. . . . It was a most pathetic morning; wailing rent the air, you cannot imagine a whole people stricken and so distressed; swarms of them came from distant villages . . . with all sorts of presents including yams, plantains, goats, chickens, eggs—so plentiful that if all had been accepted there would be no room in the Mission launch, the "Jubilee". . . . At Ikoneto, as the launch moved off for Itu, the great wail went up like a thousand thunders, men and women weeping and staffing, "Our mother and our son are gone." Standing on the upper deck, waving emotionally . . . her

1. CP to Dundee City Library, August 24, 1950.

> thoughts still remained in that Mission House far away up the hill at Akpap. The launch turned the bend, and she collapsed into her arm chair, "Oh my people, my people, my friends."[2]

Before she left Akpap, Slessor went to Duke Town and resigned her position as vice consul for Okoyong, a position she had held for twelve years.[3] Once she made the move, Itu became her official base of operations.[4] Mary's reception was very different from the one Hope Waddell experienced, when he and two other missionaries visited the village in 1851. "They fairly drummed us out of their town," he wrote.[5] Alexander Cruickshank, missionary at Ikot Offiong, had visited Itu at least twice before Mary came, but the chiefs had rejected his offer to begin a work there.[6] As changing British rule and new laws affected and regulated trade and their old social customs more and more, local peoples deemed the presence of a missionary important, especially one as well known and respected as Mary Slessor. Mary was begged to come. Chiefs and villagers wanted her to serve as peacekeeper, arbitrator and judge—as a chief—with or without British approval. Although Itu was her headquarters, Slessor spent much time visiting villages along Enyong Creek. Her arrival at Itu had been by mission motor launch: the smoking canoe. Trips from Itu were by local canoes.

If the people of a village in Itu's environs or along Enyong Creek wanted Mary to come to them, they built a church or school to entice her. According to O. U. Udoh, "several church buildings sprang up within a short time, even in communities Mary never had the opportunity to visit."[7] Calabar mission historian Donald McFarlan reported there were soon congregations at the villages of Okpo, Akani Obio and Asang along Enyong Creek, and there were many requests for teachers and evangelists.[8] Mary herself admitted, "We took charge of the creek stations more by proxy and management than by personal visitation."[9]

2. D. Slessor, "Reminiscences."
3. Christian and Plummer, *Redhead*, 133.
4. Christie, "Annals," July 1904. See also *Record*, 1905, 413.
5. Waddell. *Twenty-nine years*, 465.
6. McFarlan. *Calabar*, 110.
7. Udoh, "Growing Witness," 34.
8. McFarlan, *Calabar*, 115.
9. *Record*, 1905, 414.

Itu, Udoh contends, became a model society with "agriculture, schools, industries, clubs, vocational training, worship, [and] community life. . . . It enhanced the expansion and spread of the Christian witness in the country and raised higher the banner of victory for the Presbyterian Church of Nigeria."[10]

Missionary A. W. Wilkie wrote that the school and churches, in the area and up Enyong Creek, were all built without anyone asking for money from the Foreign Mission Board. This would have been welcome news at home in Scotland, since the church was having financial shortfalls early in the century. The progress at Itu was not due to the efforts of Mary alone, of course. Dr. David Robertson played a big part in the village's ministry and development; he was soon superintending the churches along Enyong Creek, while Mary kept moving into new areas.

A letter Slessor wrote in September 1904 told of being in her "shed" at Amasu, on Enyong Creek. The place was a shambles because of "ants and damp," but boys were making a new wall for her, and she expected to be able to stay in it on her next visit. Meanwhile, British officials made her welcome and housed her when she showed up where they had space available.[11]

On that trip, the Consul arranged to lease the land Mary Slessor was to occupy on behalf of the mission. The chief refused any money, but the Consul insisted. Finally the chief accepted a shilling from Mary herself. "This was merely nominal recognition of the fact that the ground is not mine," Mary wrote, "They [the people] are protected, and I am installed and authorized to build other structures necessary for any teaching work."[12]

Mary was surprised and delighted to meet a young man there who had visited Niger and heard the Gospel. He was "craving for teaching and light," she wrote. The next day, when she got lost on a forest path, she met two men, who helped her get back on track. "Then one asked me if I had come with God's Word. 'What else should I come with?' I replied. 'Oh,' he said, 'we have built a small church and are longing for you to come and teach us, and we will build a house for you to stay in.'" Slessor had to catch

10. Udoh, "Growing witness," 36.

11. *WMM*, December 1904, 295.

12. Ibid.

the Consul's boat, but she planned to return in a month.[13] She expressed her disappointment to Christians back home, though, that there were not more workers: "Thank God for two places in this creek, which during this year have begun services, and are seeking the Lord," she wrote. "The darkness is fleeing before the rising of the Sun of Righteousness, but where are those who are to teach?"[14] When a messenger arrived from Okoyong with news that the women missionaries left and the people now had no "Ma," Mary again bemoaned the lack of workers. "Oh Britain, surfeited with privilege! Tired of Sabbath and Church, would that you could send over to us what you are throwing away!"[15]

EXCITEMENT ON ENYONG CREEK

An event on Enyong Creek expanded Mary's mystique and renown. Two canopied canoes carried Mary and her children up the creek one day to visit a village. Suddenly, a paddler shouted, "*Ma, se Isantim! Se Isantim!*" A hippo—one of Africa's most dangerous animals, known for unprovoked attacks—charged the canoe. Adopted son Dan remembered the attack well, though he was only a small boy. "As is always her custom, she sought for the safety of the children first. . . . Then rising stately, fearless and her hair waving wildly, she grasped the long bamboo pole from the hands of a terrified native. . . . She hit with all her frail strength on the back of the creature, crying "go away, go away. . . . Sit you still, Dan, she is moving away." And sure enough the hippo was making for the farther shore."[16]

The men were afraid the hippo would turn and attack, but it didn't. Mary told the reluctant crew to turn the canoe around to meet the other boat. "Ma with a triumphant smile beaming all over her pleasant face, told Jane and the others her experience with the Hippo. Jane then suggested that the two canoes should travel parallel, so that we could all be together, but Ma said that it would have been better if she had died and we were saved rather than us all drowning at the same time."[17]

When the canoe reached its destination, one of the oarsmen brought Mary a gift of a chicken and some eggs. If it weren't for her, he said, they

13. Ibid.

14. Ibid., 296.

15. Livingstone, *Mary Slessor*, 212.

16. D. Slessor, "Reminiscences." See also Slessor to Hart, November 30, 1948.

17. Ibid.

would all have drowned. But Mary assured him, "It was not my power. God is with us." Mary prayed with him, and he began attending church "and was later baptized and converted," Dan reported. The oarsmen wondered why a wild animal obeyed this woman and compared it to the story of Christ calming the sea. "Her deed," Daniel wrote, "became the sole topic in Okpo for years."[18]

THE NEW MAN

By the end of 1904, Slessor met the new District Commissioner for her area. He was the third significant man named Charles in her life: Charles Partridge.

Mary began 1905 with a letter to Partridge. She thanked him for his gift of a Christmas pudding. Plum Pudding was her weakness, she told him, "and it was always on the table on my birthdays (when I had a home and birthdays)." The only other thing she wished for was someone "who understands" to share it with. She continued, "This is not leap year is it? And I'm over 50 years old!! and probably you have a wife, so there's no manner or shadow of my being immodest. Eh?"[19] (Partridge was single, and remained so all his life, just as his correspondent did. Mary chided him from time to time for not marrying.)

Slessor went on to commend Partridge for his work with the Ibibio-speaking people of his district: "If you can discriminate between fear and stubbornness," she wrote, "you have won half the battle. She believed they were "deceitful as a race," but she added, "I have many true and intelligent friends among them every where, and *so shall you! Trust them* and *have patience*. . . . May the wisdom and tact needed be abundantly given you."[20]

The people continued to bring complaints to Slessor when she moved to Itu. For miles up and down the rivers and creeks, they knew her as a good and fair judge, and as an effective go-between for them in their dealings with British officials. She wrote to Partridge about a problem.

"Here I am already meddling with your affairs. Twenty free men and chiefs came here on Sunday from Ibiaku Itam. I met them, with the Itu Chief yesterday and gave a hearing and sympathy and etc, to their story; and as a result, I found that the nearest way to help them was to send

18. Ibid.

19. MS to CP, January 6, 1905.

20. Ibid.

them to you and ask you to take them under your wing and give them any guidance and help you think best."[21]

Mary related a complicated story of market disputes that led to killings and the refusal to return their chief's body for burial according to custom; then one faction told "tales" to "the White Man" that resulted in a government attack on their village, causing more deaths. The men believed Calabar (the Efik) held unfair power over them. Slessor continued with a request and proposed a solution:

> So, in order to meet their case, *if it commend itself to you*, could you not . . . in order to gain the confidence and obedience of those people, and to make them our allies instead of our enemies, try to put it thus. If you cannot have separate Courts . . . *give the two sections strong Mbiam*, "that if the one side, went with deceit, and told lies on the other, to the White Man, or to Calabar judges, let *Mbiam* treat with them," etc. etc. "If one side or the other knew, or sent, or in any way sought the hurt of the other, or revenge for past palavers," etc. etc. "let *Mbiam* judge between them" etc. etc. . . . What do you think? It is the Conciliation of the peoples in a right and just way, which is my *only* motive, as you know, and by a patient hearing you will *win* them.[22]

Mary's solution—using the native *mbiam* oath—continued to meet with disapproval from fellow missionaries and from many converted Africans, who considered it a remnant of "heathen" customs. But she found the oath useful in settling court cases and did not hesitate to recommend it to the District Commissioner. The people believed it proved guilt or innocence, and it generally did not have the drastic consequences of other ordeals. In at least one instance, though, a man who obviously lied purportedly dropped dead after taking the oath.[23] This served to reinforce belief in *mbiam*'s power. Slessor's rationale may have been the knowledge that cases in the Native Courts (which were mandated by the British but always subservient to British higher courts) were to be judged according to traditional native law and customs when possible. Aside from *mbiam*, though, Mary's own convictions of what constituted justice and God's will affected her court decisions.

21. Ibid., January 17, 1905.

22. Ibid.

23. Livingstone, *Mary Slessor*, 233.

In May, after less than a year in Itu, Slessor received an official invitation to act formally as a British magistrate again. "I am directed by His Excellency the High Commissioner [Walter Egerton] to enquire whether you would accept office as a member of the Itu Native Court with the status of permanent vice-president. His Excellency is desirous of securing the advantage of your experience and intimate knowledge of Native affairs and sympathetic interest in the welfare of the villagers, and understands you would not be averse to place your services at the disposal of the Government."[24]

The letter also indicated that the court should move to Ikot Obong (about five miles from Itu and somewhat closer to District headquarters at Ikot Ekpene). Mary was offered payment of one pound per year, plus forty-seven pounds to be used for mission work. So at the age of fifty-five, Mary Slessor began a new chapter in her life: a roving missionary at a new base of operations, and once again an agent of Her Majesty's government.

It is unclear who signed the invitation to Mary to serve. It may have been Charles Partridge, with whom she was already corresponding and whose aid and advice she frequently sought. Or T. D. Maxwell, who served as an Acting District Commissioner just prior to Partridge's arrival and who continued to serve in the area, may have played a part in the request. A younger man, Maxwell was a favorite of Mary Slessor. She wrote to Partridge early in 1906, "My dear laddie Mr. Maxwell is back, but not in good health I'm sorry to say. He is doing office work, as he is not fit to rough it this term." She said that Maxwell was not really a great administrator, because "He is like myself, too nervous and impatient. But he is a good boy, and a clean, straight clever lad, a lad to *love* and cherish."[25]

THE COURT AT IKOT OBONG

In September 1905, Mary made the five-mile move from Itu to Ikot Obong to facilitate conducting court matters. Before she left, she welcomed the arrival of Dr. and Mrs. Robertson and wrote that she would soon be able to "run up the creek or into Ibibio, just as God may lead" after the move.

24. Jeffreys, "Magistrate," 629.

25. MS to CP, February 24, 1906.

"It is a great relief," she said, "but it brings a sense of loss, too. . . . The Itu people have made us love them dearly."[26]

In December she wrote to Partridge about his pending visit from Ikot Ekpene. She had sent three prisoners on but was holding the paperwork for him. "You had better bring a 'Maxim' [machine gun] and some blunderbusses," she wrote, "for there is no Court House yet."[27] Conditions were unsettled, quarrels still flared up, and too many people were quick to take the law into their own hands.

Mary recounted her happy 1905 Christmas day memory from Ikot Obong.

> What do you think? In this bush place no fewer than eight white men were gathered yesterday to Christmas dinner. My superintending officer, who came to take court money, etc.; an officer from a neighbouring district who walked over with him; the two engineer surveyors in the shed close by; the merchant from the creek; a surveyor from Ekoi, miles beyond Duke Town; and an officer from Calabar—all were here, six of them sleeping in the shed, two walls and a roof open to the world. They were the guests of Messrs. Darly and Smith [British officials], who are both the sons of ministers, one Anglican, and the other Methodist, and I tell you they kept up the tone of the conversation and singing, and not one glass was drunk, and we had all the tender home songs and hymns till eight o'clock, and Jean and the bairns sang an Efik hymn and "This night when I lie down to sleep." In the early morning they sent me a sheet of surveying paper as a Christmas card, and the signatures in the middle. I went along at teatime—five o'clock—and stayed till eight. I think I was the happiest woman in the mission, and it gave a taste of home to the men to have me with them. I was the only Scot, but we all sang "Here's a hand, my trusty frien', for auld lang syne."[28]

"Now, there's a dissipation for the mother of the camp!" Slessor wrote. "They are all off to work to-day, each to his lonely post. May God go with them! They are each 'somebody's bairn,' and life is infinitely harder for them than for the missionary."[29] She worried about the young government men she often called "laddies." They were far from home, usually not

26. *WMM*, January 1906, 19.

27. MS to CP, December 5, 1905.

28. *Record*, 1906, quoting private MS letter of December 26, 1905, 116.

29. Ibid.

by choice, and often without the strong foundation of faith the missionary claimed.

Two months later, Mary reported to Partridge,

> My, but the days do fly! This Court *is* a shop, and not an hour of respite, not even on my way to service on Sundays. And yet, if it weren't I should be sorry, for it is better they come direct to myself, even to ask about their summons . . . than that they went to policemen, or to any other body who might make mischief. But it is a silly people and a trial to patience, and I'm so tired as a rule, that all my good resolutions, made daily, to write a lot at night are put [to] one side at the sight of my sofa and a book.[30]

Slessor continued her letter with news about the changes that were occurring in the district. Roads were being built, making it much easier to travel to Itu. But there were still "lots of guns all over the place," she said.

> One can see now what is being done, and the surveyors are kept at it like navvies. A White foreman has come and they have now a large compound on the top of the hill [near] Ikot Obong, with office, a clerk's house and all. A lovely house and a lovely site. . . .
>
> It is a big responsibility [for Mr. Rosario, road foreman], the having of 600 men without wife or home on the road. . . . Ikot Obong is its old prevaricating lazy self, but—we are comfortably housed. . . . Two rooms of the policemen's houses are up, but we were helping with [roof] mats for the camp, and they paid us well.[31]

Mary reported that she was working on her third "Summons Book" and her second "Evidence Book," part of the record keeping required by the British. She was glad to tell Partridge that court cases from Calabar were declining, as old cases finished up. "I'm glad," she said, "as they rile me." She didn't like the fact that the Efik were still "intercepting the market people" along the rivers and creeks but believed that would soon end.

Slessor's letter of February 24, 1906 is just one of many very long, handwritten letters to Charles Partridge. She told him of other mutual friends or acquaintances—their comings and goings, sickness and deaths; of the first sickly twins being saved at Ikot Obong (who died after only two days); of her concern that she had permission from the Presbytery to continue her work only until April. She settled that concern with her

30. MS to CP, February 24, 1906.

31. Ibid.

follow-up comment: "I'm supposed to go back to Okoyon then I expect, which I shall simply refuse to do." Mary saw no need to return with Janet Wright still serving there. The mission extended Slessor's itinerating work for another year when April rolled around. They may have had little choice in the matter.

THE WORK IN ITU

While Mary traveled to new areas, she also continued to serve in Itu and Ikot Obong. Because the British government had opened a hospital in Duke Town, the local Mission Council decided they could send a physician and establish a hospital and mission station at Itu without expanding the workforce. A bargain! Missionary doctor David Robertson was transferred to Itu from Creek Town when he returned from furlough in September 1905. The students of New College (Edinburgh) pledged funds toward the total estimated cost of one thousand pounds, which included not only a hospital but also a mission building and a motor launch for the area.[32] Friends of Mary Slessor and Dr. Robertson sent funds, too. A Mr. Kemp in Scotland promised a large sum on condition that the hospital be named for Mary Slessor. She wrote to her friend, William Stevenson of the Women's Foreign Missionary Society:

> It is a grand gift, this of Mr. Kemp's, and I'm so glad with and for our people in its bestowal. Then too, Itu is already being justified as the site for such a house of healing, for there are hundreds of men on the river frontage there, making a Railway Embankment. It will be the base of lines for Road and Rail which shall intersect the whole of this Ibibio Country, down and to the Estuary, and across to the Niger. Such things are being rushed before our eyes, things that never entered the wildest dreams of Calabar.[33]

The dream of a railway across the country was premature, but roads continued to be built around Calabar's trading areas near the rivers. In 1913 the bar at the entrance to the harbor at Lagos was removed, but Calabar's importance as a port began to decline. The railway was built to Port Harcourt rather than to Calabar, which lessened Calabar's importance to trade.[34]

32. *Record*, 1905, 262, 413; Christie, "Annals," 1905.
33. MS to Stevenson, February 28, 1906. See also *Record*, 1907, 507.
34. Nair, *Politics and Society*, 258–59.

Slessor expressed her embarrassment to Stevenson about the hospital.

> O if you only kent how small and ashamed I feel at the very thought of such a piece of Christian philanthropy being associated with my poor name you would never speak of my writing about myself or my wanderings, for you feel as if I can never come out of the bush and go among other people with this distinguishing mark on me. Why should I be lifted up above the others who are working better and perhaps far more successfully in God's Sight than I am? And what have I ever been able to do except what God has done Himself and could have done as easily without me. . . . I feel quite a fraud.[35]

Mary was delighted when the first baptisms and communion took place at Itu on February 5, 1906. Dr. Robertson reported that 350 people attended; there were twenty-two baptisms: seventeen women and five men. The Nigerian teacher from Akani Obio, Esien E. Esien, served as elder with missionary doctor Peter Rattray. Rattray preached after communion, *The Record* reported, "followed by a rousing address by Miss Slessor."[36]

MARY AS LITERARY CRITIC

A close friendship developed between Mary Slessor and Charles Partridge. The letters Mary wrote to him were quite different from those she wrote to fellow missionaries or to friends or mission publications at home. The latter dwelt on mission needs, progress (or lack of it), and discussion of spiritual matters. Although her letters to agnostic Charles Partridge occasionally preached to a minor extent, more often they talked of mutual friends, of travel and sickness, of clothes and personal concerns, of books read.

The breadth of Slessor's reading is evident. She liked to read—and not just spiritual tomes. She placed the Bible at the head of the list, but she read whatever else she could get in the way of newspapers and books. At one time, Mary wrote that she had been at a new station seven weeks "without one scrap from the outside—letter or paper [except those lining boxes). . . . If you wish for the names of hotels or boarding-houses in any

35. Ibid.

36. *Record*, 1906, 171.

part of Europe," she wrote, "send to me. I have them all on my tongue's end."[37] She spoke of studying Milton and Dante with an older friend as a young woman in Dundee. "I had a friend," she wrote, "who, much older than myself, nevertheless a very intimate friend and was my first confidant regarding my desire to be a missionary." That friend, Mary wrote, was a bank manager in Dundee, who "used to shew me the beauties of literature."[38]

To the District Commissioner, Mary wrote, "Have you good reading? It is such a good help to keep off nervousness and weariness to have a good book and someone to read with."[39] When he sent her a copy of his book, *The Cross River Natives*, Mary wrote,

> What a fraud you are!! Here you [are] with a record like this of observation and research; and half the letters of the alphabet running after your name, and you speaking as if you were the merest beginner and the most commonplace of mortals in the protectorate!! . . . I don't know whether to praise most your modesty or your industry. Fancy having a piece of work like this over & above doing a DC's work!—and in a new district too. . . . The natives have seldom had an interpreter so absolutely truthful, and free from prejudice.
>
> It is so seldom that one sees anything from this Coast that is not embroidered. . . . I wish you had let yourself go a little though in regard to nature, in vegetation, etc., and colouring, and the mystery or mysticism or whatever you would call it, of the forest. I am sure you have had times when the bush with its myriad voices has called you, and you have not felt her monotonous and tiresome. The spell of it is very strong on me sometimes, then there are the sunrises and sunsets, the face of the river and etc.![40]

37. Livingstone, *Mary Slessor*, 288.

38. MS, Lesson Notes, 1874. In someone other than Slessor's handwriting, this document identifies the friend as William Henderson Duncan. However, Duncan died at the age of 74 in 1928 and would not be old enough to be Mary's "much older" mentor. The name of Alexander Logie is handwritten on the "lessons," and he may have read some previous sermons. However, Slessor mentions that he was already deceased by the time she wrote these messages. Logie may have been the father of minister James Logie of Tay Square United Presbyterian Church, whom Slessor called "the best earthly friend I have." Biographer Livingstone identifies another older "friend and counselor" in Dundee, a Mr. J. H. Smith. I have failed to find further information regarding the bank manager friend.

39. MS to CP, October 3, 1907

40. Ibid., April 12, 1905.

Two years later, Slessor told Partridge that missionary Beatrice Welsh was using his book, and she returned to her own admiration for the work.

> What I have admired both in your book and in all your subsequent writing and talking has been your contempt of all kinds of embroidery. . . . It is so very prevalent in literature and in all public and social life at home. Let me give you good advice, dear boy. Speak the TRUTH, and nothing but the truth in days to come. AND AGAIN do not let your imagination get the upper hand. . . . It is one of God's greatest gifts to men, but unless it is in a world of facts and forces and has to play the game of give and take to the full, it will lead you to be a dreamer of dreams . . . and a D.C . . . must be made of sterner stuff than mystics are fashioned from."[41]

Mary was surprised to learn later that Partridge had written a novel, too.

> Why did you never tell me that you were the Author of "King Edward's Ring?" I found the book at Itu, and it had—that copy—been read so widely that the Covers were torn off and no one now can learn the publisher's name. You are a fine one! To have kept your secret so well! and never to give one a chance of getting the book. Come now, "fess up"! . . . Let me know for I have no way of knowing. . . . After you tell me and I have another reading of it, we shall discuss it.[42]

"You have so much to write about," she said. "Write!!!" Mary encouraged Partridge to write more—with one caveat.

> It will only need a beginning. What has been done, What *may* be done, What should be done in the Protectorate, the native, His habits, Life and Laws, etc.; the Country, its produce, its possibilities, etc., but please leave *religion* out this time, as I don't deem you fit to write on such a wide, and inward subject. . . . Your ideas on that subject are too loose and disjointed and take too little reck of such facts as sin. . . . How do you like that for plain speaking? You are my Friend, so I *dare* do it. However no one who has been in the Protectorate can do better work for it than you can.[43]

41. Ibid., April 17, 1907.
42. Ibid., April 27, 1910.
43. Ibid., October 25, 1907.

Concerning her own writing prospects, Mary said, "I shall maybe write a book when we get to the other side of this world where the wicked cease from troubling and the weary are at rest. Certainly I shall not do so here."[44]

The missionary did not hesitate to pen censorious reviews of novels she found offensive, even if the books were gifts. In 1906 she wrote about Mrs. Humphrey Ward's novel, *Helbeck of Bannisdale.*

> It is not the best of Mrs Wards.[45] She has created a most original, and difficult heroine, and the evolution of her character under such strange and extreme circumstances and environment is interesting, but she can do better work in analysis than this. . . . The very burden of the ritual and the unloveliness of the characters, both Protestant and Catholic, make the whole system something above the level of the African Fetish and its Product. I trust Christ and Christianity will do more for the high spirited, finely strung, independent young woman of today than it did for poor Laura and her noble husband to be, and for the poor "starved soul" of the invalid stepmother.[46]

Mary thanked Partridge for the books he sent but said she was "anxious to renew my girlhood friends of the 'Mill of the Floss', those wholesome, natural sinners bred in our own homeland, who somehow are very dear because of their very faults and frailties."[47]

When Partridge was later transferred to Lagos, Slessor wrote, "Thousands of a population in one locality, does not meet my approval under tropical African conditions, and I do hope your residence is far apart from the madding crowd—tho I dont know what 'madding' means."[48]

Mary also thanked Partridge at various times for other books he sent: "a lovely 'Burns';" a copy of *White Capital and Coloured Labour*, which she greatly admired and passed around to missionary friends;[49] she

44. Ibid., September 21, 1907.

45. Mary Arnold Ward (Mrs. Humphrey Ward) was a popular Victorian novelist.

46. MS to CP, February 24, 1906.

47. Ibid.

48. Ibid., April 27, 1910, referring to Thomas Hardy's novel, *Far From the Madding Crowd.*

49. Olivier, *White Capital.* Originally a 1906 pamphlet, the author declared: "When [a European] really wants to go to Africa for the sake of the natives he becomes a missionary. . . . The European only begins to become obnoxious when he seeks to entrap, constrain, or coerce uncivilized natives into subservience to his personal interest under

mentioned reading more of Mrs. Humphrey Ward's work; newspaperman Richard Whiteing's novel, *No. 5, John St.*; and "some Hawthorne." When Partridge sent a book telling of Shackleton's explorations, Slessor wrote, "Isn't it a wonderful time, South and North poles, and the air so far conquered!" She issued a warning, though: "Surely you will not be so foolish as to try the dirigibles or the aeroplanes. Better cross the Channel by boat, or even by Tube! Eh?"[50]

Another novel Slessor chose for a scathing review was *Fools Rush In*, by Australian author Mary Gaunt. "This novel," Mary wrote, "may suit the tastes of a few who feed on garbage in West Africa. It will disgust the honourable and so defeat its own end."[51]

Mary described one main male character as "a ninny," and said of him, "If that's a West African hero, I give it up." Two women characters came in for Slessor's displeasure, too: One woman "had been a wife for twelve years, and in less than two days after her husband had been murdered before her eyes, she was turning to another man." The other had gone to West Africa to meet her fiancé, and ere two days in that land had gone, she had given her heart once again to another." The missionary in the story met with more disdain. "As for Webley!!!" Mary wrote, "There may be such duffers among missionaries, but they are *not in charge* of Missions or of men's lives."[52]

WRITING HOME

The Women's Missionary Magazine printed one of Slessor's more typical reports for home consumption a few months after her relocation to Ikot Obong. Mission-minded parishioners were eager to hear good news from the mission field, and Mary supplied it whenever she could honestly report progress. She wrote,

> To-day every canoe passing hails us with such kindliness and joy. Only a year ago all this region was as much outside the Church as if it had been a thousand miles away in the interior, now we have a baby girl on board, motherless, belonging to their tribe. I have six boys reading very fairly, and a number coming up in the ear-

the pretext of doing them good," 27.

50. MS to CP, April 30, 1906, June 27, 1907, July 11, 1907, October 15, 1909.

51. MS to CP, June 27, 1907.

52. Ibid.

> lier classes. We have the Sabbath recognised, and I have a room in three separate towns, besides Itu, which is my head-quarters. There we have a congregation of from 250 to 350, many readers, nearly a score of catechumen, and half-a-dozen Sabbath-school teachers.[53]

Slessor also sent a detailed report of reverent worship services held at Amasu and other villages: She spoke of prayers, hymns, the commandments, Scripture reading, sermons, and the Lord's prayer. "How often during these last fourteen days . . . have I mentally written all that my eyes have seen and my ears heard of God's grace and salvation! Rejoice with Him, for He is finding His lost ones there, and being glorified in them!"[54]

More news would follow throughout Slessor's years in Nigeria. Not all news was good—and bad news was not always mentioned.

53. *WMM*, December 1904, 296.

54. *WMM*, June 1905, 124–26.

14

Court and Furlough

The court takes up a great deal of my time, but I do not know how to let any of it go, for it holds such possibilities for good.

—Mary Slessor, 1906[1]

MISSIONARY MINA AMESS VISITED Slessor in Ikot Obong from Akpap in 1906. "One could not be long in her company," she wrote, "without enjoying a right hearty laugh."

> There was no routine with "Ma." One never knew what she would be doing. One hour she might be having a political discussion with a District Commissioner, the next supervising the building of a house, and later on judging native palavers. Late one evening I heard a good deal of talking and also the sound of working. I went in to see what was doing and there was "Ma" making cement and the bairns spreading it on the floor with their hands in candle light. The whole scene at so late an hour was too much for my gravity.[2]

Mary lived in mud-floored houses during her years in Nigeria, but she preferred a cement floor. Not only was it cleaner and more permanent, it was also a barrier to the frequent ant problem. Congo missionary Samuel Lapsley once reported that white ants (termites) crawled up his bedpost in the night and made a hole as big as his hand in his mattress before morning.[3] Black driver ants travel in columns by the thousands and can kill any small animal (or abandoned infant) in a short time. Slessor

1. *WMM*, April 1906, 91.
2. Livingstone, *Mary Slessor*, 236.
3. Phipps, *William Sheppard*, 57.

wrote of getting up in the middle of the night and finding driver ants, "thousands and thousands of them, pouring in on every side, and dropping from the roof. We had two hours' hard work to clear them out."[4]

Biographer Livingstone tells of fellow missionaries teasing Mary about her "richer than usual . . . household gear" when she moved to Ikot Obong. Mary surprised them with her explanation that the trunks were filled with cement. When a woman in Scotland had asked how she learned to make cement, Mary said, "I just stir it like porridge; turn it out, smooth it with a stick, and all the time keep praying, 'Lord, here's the cement, if to Thy glory, set it,' and it has never once gone wrong."[5]

Charles Partridge gave Mary a bicycle about the time she moved to Ikot Obong. At the age of fifty-seven, she wrote, "Fancy, an old woman like me on a cycle!"[6] She was excited that the combination of new roads and her bicycle made it easy to get to villages several miles away. She made good use of it and often mentioned it to Partridge or in letters to Scotland. Mary wrote home, "There are 700 men on the four or five miles between [Ikot Obong] and Itu, living in grass huts by the roadside. They are from every part of the country, and it is such a grand chance to sow the seed and have it carried far and near as they return to their homes!"[7]

Despite Slessor's high spirits about the way things were going, she continued to have frequent bouts of fever. She was unable to attend the opening of the new church in Duke Town in January because she was ill. In February, she wrote, "I had fever right on three or four times a week, all through January, and I have only twice been able to walk to Church this year. But last Saturday I took quite a turn for the better and am now just myself again."[8]

Mary soon enjoyed "a most pleasant visit" from High Commissioner and Lady Egerton. She found Lady Egerton "charming," and she let Commissioner Egerton know that the changes he saw in the district were due to Charles Partridge's good work. "He was speaking on the difference

4. Livingstone, *Mary Slessor*, 271.

5. Ibid., 213.

6. Ibid., 219.

7. *WMM*, June 1906, quoting MS letter of February 28, 1906, 142.

8. MS to CP, February 24, 1906.

in it from his last visit," Slessor wrote. And, "He thinks it is too civilized for me now," a conclusion she no doubt appreciated.[9]

Later in the year, *The Women's Missionary Magazine* published a letter from an enthusiastic Miss Slessor:

> Our Administrator [Partridge] has just come back from Britain after furlough, and has brought with him a phonograph, a magnificent instrument, and a number of grand old hymns—e.g., "Holy, holy, holy!" "Abide with me," &c., and on Sunday night he gave the village a great treat by having this at the service. We also hung a sheet up, and filled the lamp, and gave an exhibition of several Scriptural slides on the screen. It was all done without any forethought, but it proved a great success . . . and I spoke into the "trumpet" the parable of the Prodigal. . . . The audience was simply electrified. That parable has gone on to be reproduced all over the Ibibio towns where our Administrator will be going on his civilizing and governing tours. Is it not grand? It seems like a dream! It has opened up new ideas of means and possibilities for service. A person with means could get the Gospel carried round like that, when he or she could not speak a word of the language. It is so marvelous: every sound reproduced! Even the little halt I made to remember a word came; the people could not keep down their delight and wonder. . . . Oh, it was a red-letter day![10]

JUSTICE?

Court work went on. Mary wrote of a murder committed by a woman.

> She is but a girl, and they have brought her here in preference to tying her up and torturing her to confess whom she wants for a husband, seeing she declares she will never marry this one to whom she has been betrothed from infancy. She has invented several excuses, the chief one being that there is one of wives whom she does not like. God help these poor down-trodden women! The constant cause of palaver and bloodshed here is marriage. . . . It is almost impossible for a European magistrate to hold this horde of people; I wish we had mission stations here and there, to which things could come till they are enlightened a little. What an awful thing heathenism is![11]

9. MS to CP, April 30, 1906.
10. *WMM*, November 1906, 277.
11. *WMM*, January 1906, 20.

A Foreign Mission deputy from Scotland visited Mary Slessor during his stay and later reminisced about her court. "At a little table sits the only woman judge in the British Empire," he wrote. She had some toffee beside her, along with her cup of tea. He described her court routine.

> Behind her sit the chiefs, who form a sort of jury. In front is the dock (a bamboo rail); at one side another rail forms the witness-box. The body of the court is occupied by interested spectators. With voluble language and abundant gesture pleas are made and evidence is given. Then the judge has a word or two with the jury (retiring to a little shed to consult if the case needs more consideration), and a decision is pronounced which may not be always welcome, but which is always recognized as just. And as a rule the decision is accompanied with some sound words of Christian council [*sic*], for this court gives an opportunity to dispense both law [and] gospel.[12]

The deputy, Rev. James Addison, wrote of the informality of the scene. If a car was heard on the newly built road, "jury, prisoner, witnesses, audience, native policeman"—everyone except Mary and European visitors—dashed off to see it. When the commotion died down, they returned to their places and court resumed.

A District Commissioner (D.C.) was president of the Native Court; Mary was vice president. The commissioner often did not know the language of the people, and the clerks who translated could be bribed to interpret in favor of one side or the other. In practice, the D.C. seldom attended court. But when he did, Addison told how the two judges sometimes held different points of view. When a man hacked his wife with a machete, the D.C. considered it simple assault. Mary called it "a cowardly shame" and wanted severe punishment. When a man was arrested for possession of a gun, the D.C. considered it serious and wanted to make an example of him. Mary said just take his gun and let him go—he didn't do anything.[13]

A European eyewitness to the trial for the machete incident wrote about the jury retiring with Judge Slessor to deliberate the case:

> The headman started by laying down as a fundamental principle that they had a perfect right to do whatever they liked with their wives; they could not yield an inch on this, as their women would

12. *Record*, 1915, 172. Report of Rev. James Addison, who visited MS in 1909.
13. Ibid.

> soon become unmanageable! But in deference to the white man's peculiar views, as to the treatment of women, they would go the length of admitting that, perhaps, the husband had gone just a little too far in his use of the matchet. They could not see that the man had done anything to merit a severe sentence, but in view of the prejudices of the white people they sent him to prison for a short term![14]

T. D. Maxwell said the first time he met Mary he saw "a little frail old lady with a lace . . . shawl over her head and shoulders . . . swaying herself in a rocking chair and crooning to a black baby in her arms." He commented on her "very strong Scottish accent" and described later court proceedings. Court was near Slessor's house, he said, "full of litigants, witnesses, and onlookers," and Mary was back in the rocking chair holding another baby.[15]

> Suddenly she jumped up with an angry growl: her shawl fell off, the baby was hurriedly transferred to some one qualified to hold it, and with a few trenchant words she made for the door where a hulking, overdressed native stood. In a moment she seized him by the scruff of the neck, boxed his ears, and hustled him out into the yard, telling him quite explicitly what he might expect if he came back again without her consent. . . . The man was a local monarch of sorts, who had been impudent to her, and she had forbidden him to come near her house again until he had not only apologised but done some prescribed penance. Under the pretext of calling on me he had defied her orders.[16]

Maxwell wrote, "I have had a good deal of experience of Nigerian Courts of various kinds, but have never met one which better deserves to be termed a Court of Justice than that over which she presided . . . and it was essential justice unhampered by legal technicalities."[17]

Biographer Livingstone wrote, "Some of her methods were not of the accepted judicial character. . . . Often, instead of administering the law, she administered justice by giving the prisoner a blow on the side of the head!" Or, he wrote,[18] "She would try a batch of men for an offence, lecture

14. *WMM*, November 1909, 258–59.
15. Livingstone, *Mary Slessor*, 129.
16. Ibid., 130.
17. Jeffreys, "Magistrate," 628–29.
18. Livingstone, *Mary Slessor*, 232–33.

them, and then impose a fine. Finding they had no money she would take them up to the house and give them work to earn the amount, and feed them well."[19] Mary justified this action by saying that she hoped to influence the men in a lasting way.

The authors of *God and One Redhead* wrote, "An administrative officer once saw her flailing a chief of some importance over the head with his own umbrella for telling lies. . . . But the victim of her wrath seldom commanded any public sympathy since she was felt to be just."[20]

M. D. W. Jeffreys, whose career as a British administrative officer began two months after Mary Slessor's death, analyzed some of her cases from archived court records in the missionary's handwriting. He commented that reports often indicated that "both sides took oath [*mbiam*]." He wrote, "It is usual in English practice to take the oath first, and in native practice to take it last, that both parties accept the verdict and bear no ill-will to each other. It seems that this instance is another record of a pagan practice accepted by Mary Slessor, but not permitted by European magistrates."[21]

Even if she "concluded a pagan trial with a pagan ending," in Jeffreys' words, he agreed with T. D. Maxwell that, in at least some of Mary Slessor's cases, "if law was not always administered, at least justice was."[22]

Slessor's methods have come under fire, not whether she administered justice. One twentieth-century author wrote, "A natural meddler with an iron will, the role of magistrate suited her well."[23] Others noted a different aspect of Slessor's role as magistrate. A former Calabar missionary wrote, "Let no one think that the spiritual adviser was lost in the law-giver. I am safe in saying that in no Court of Justice in the world was the Gospel preached so habitually."[24]

Calabar mission historian Geoffrey Johnston quoted the minutes of the Presbytery of Biafra, stating that Slessor's "acting in an official or semi-official capacity is calculated to compromise her position and interfere

19. Ibid., 233–34.

20. Christian and Plummer, *Redhead*, 110.

21. Jeffreys, "Magistrate," 805.

22. Ibid. Jeffreys also pointed out that Mary Slessor was not the only missionary to serve as magistrate in a Native Court in Calabar. Three men were also appointed, though not from the Scottish Presbyterian Mission.

23. Birkett, *Mary Kingsley*, 34.

24. *WMM*, March 1915, 56.

with her usefulness." Johnston states that the presbytery either did not realize what Mary's significance was or did not understand "that being a reforming chief rather than a reforming preacher was a legitimate missionary function."[25]

UDO ANTIA

Mary Slessor first mentioned Udo Antia in a letter to Charles Partridge in February 1906. Partridge was in England at the time, and another would have filled his position during his absence. Antia was convicted and incarcerated at Ikot Ekpene for slave dealing and seizing a boy for debt. He escaped, and when he was recaptured, he was sent to the Native Court at Ikot Obong with additional charges of escape, resisting arrest and disturbing the peace. Mary sentenced him to two more years in prison.[26] Before he was recaptured, road surveyors sent some boys out to ask for use of a shed. Antia made them take the *mbiam* oath and threatened them if they told where he was. After an extended search, during which his house was burned down, he finally turned himself in. Mary wrote about the trial, "His mother came in, and she expecting they would shoot him, hung on to me, lay on me, hugged me for four long hours. I could not get out of her embraces till I was nearly fainting. . . . It was a bad hour for me I tell you, for even Udo Antia is loved by a Mother. What a mighty, what a mysterious thing is mother love! She coveted the chance of dying for him."[27]

A large crowd attended the trial and wanted to see "how the White Man would punish, and to gloat over him," Mary wrote. She thought they were disappointed that she gave the prisoner only a two-year sentence. "His slaves have stolen every thing and run away," Mary told Partridge. "I wish you had been at Udo's trial, if only to study Ibibio character."[28]

Asuquo Udo Antia, a son of Udo Antia and a respected physician and emeritus professor at the University of Ibadan, published a family history in 2002. Dr. Antia asserts that Obong Udo Antia II "was, without any doubt, the most eminent, powerful and influential Obong [chief] of his village and by extension that of Mbiabong Clan in Ibiono Ibom."[29] He

25. Johnston, *Maxim Guns*, 258.

26. Asuquo Udo Antia, *Obong Udo Antia II*, 19–20.

27. DUNLIB, MS to CP, February 24, 1906.

28. Ibid.

29. Antia, *Obong Udo Antia*, ix.

owned a great deal of land, including farms, and had many wives and slaves, a sign of wealth.[30] (Twenty-seven wives or concubines are named in Dr. Antia's work.) One of the titles of Udo Antia II was "a beheader of human being, a title usually conferred on a warrior, or a man of bravery."[31]

When Dr. Antia was growing up, he heard stories about his father's imprisonment. "The alleged and widespread reason for the imprisonment that circulated then and up till now," he writes, "was that he had serious disagreements with Slessor . . . who imprisoned him for daring to describe her as just being another woman like any of his wives and also by calling her unprintable names."[32]

Udo Antia continued to appear in Mary's letters to Partridge, frequently in 1908 and from time to time until the month before she died. In April of 1908, she reported that Udo was back home. Four months later she told of sending a court messenger on an errand, when one of Udo Antia's slaves shot and killed him. To Mary's consternation, the current District Commissioner put Antia in charge of "seven policemen with a corporal" to find the culprit. Slessor complained, "And so these dogs of war were let loose with all Udo boys on these poor villages, with the result that there has been a reign of Terror—every Chief insulted, chained and tied up [and] beaten; women and men hailed into Udo Antia's place and beaten and kept in hunger and fear; the villages plundered clean of every thing, and all the time I had to sit and bear it. knowing that the DC had given the order."[33]

At the end of August, Slessor wrote that the murderer had been recaptured but then escaped "after the manner of his Illustrious Master."[34] The next month she wrote, "Five Chiefs all as mad on revenge, came to the Court on Thursday to take oath on what the 'Raid' [by Udo Antia and his men] had taken from their places, in order to get compensation. Udo is certainly not beloved by his neighbours."[35] In November, the news was,

30. Ibid., 33–38.
31. Ibid., 13.
32. Ibid., 14.
33. MS to CP, 14 August 1908.
34. Ibid., August 29, 1908.
35. Ibid., September 13, 1908.

"Udo Antia has a case against him going on in which I'm sure he lies like a Dragoon."[36]

Udo Antia's biographer son admits that not everybody was glad when his father was released from prison but states that he was "readily reconciled with his subjects." He rebuilt his ruined compound, including a new "residential palace" on donated land, and "his entire surviving households of wives, children, slaves, servants, etc. returned from wherever they had been."[37]

In 1909 Antia complained to Slessor that his "boys" were trying to kill him. She told him to call them into court. She wrote to Partridge that Antia's boys were in revolt, and his wives were scattered. The *obong* was punished for "brutality to a wife with four fine children she has brought up for him."[38] Antia's biographer says the chief's "travails . . . continued for as long as the Scottish Presbyterian Missionaries and the British government were firmly established." Although he continued to suffer "insults" from missionaries and British authorities, Asuquo Antia writes, "he maintained his status as an important, powerful and influential ruler of the people."[39]

Mary was incensed to report in 1911 that the troublemaker was again "the pet of Ikot Okpene[40] under [the new D.C.], who won't hear that his record is bad. . . . Udo is a hero to some White Men, who utterly deny his record. It is most distressing."[41] By December 1912, Udo was back in prison and Slessor wrote, "Their eyes are opened at last, and he gets his deserts, and the land which groaned rests." Antia was out again in 1913 and had gained "power and prestige" by giving the court clerk a wife. Mary's last letter to Charles Partridge (1914) complained that whenever there was a new D.C., Udo "breaks out," and "when he is out of prison, there is not much Peace." She added, "Perhaps one of God's reasons for keeping me here so long, is the keeping of such miserable characters in subjection and silence to a certain extent."[42]

36. Ibid., November 28, 1908.
37. Antia, *Obong Udo Antia*, 22–23.
38. MS to CP, February 17 and May 8, 1909.
39. Antia, *Obong Udo Antia,* 23–24.
40. Variant spelling of Ikot Ekpene.
41. MS to CP, April 12 and September 4, 1911.
42. Ibid., December 26, 1912, August 10, 1913, December 24, 1914.

A Final Furlough

Mary was pleased with the progress she saw up and down the river and creek. Churches and schools were established, and people sought her out to ask for teachers. But episodes of malaria and other maladies continued. She knew she needed to go "home" for a rest, though she later wrote, "I don't know that it is an unmixed pleasure to be at home, without a home. . . . It is certainly a great strain, but I suppose it is because the churches want to hear of God's work, so we must do it as a duty if not as a pleasant privilege."[43]

Mary continued to hold court at Ikot Obong, but she had moved to another house at Use Ikot Oku by December 1906. She had a "cottage" built there and had a site cleared for a "ladies' rest house." The Calabar Mission Council also approved Slessor's offer to build a house at Arochukwu, if the Women's Foreign Mission Committee okayed it; the council also agreed to ask for two more women missionaries to be sent to Calabar.[44] There would be other houses built for Mary in new areas, but Use would become her "retreat" for the rest of her life.

Slessor worried about leaving her girls behind, but finally decided to leave them in Jean's care at Use while she went to Scotland. On this trip she took along six-year-old adopted son Dan. Government officials helped with preparations and travel. A friend, Mr. Gray, helped pack and store things and took her to Duke Town. He even arranged for his sister to meet Mary in Edinburgh. Charles Partridge sent her a warm coat, which came in for a lot of praise during her furlough. Slessor wrote, "And now comes this Cloak, which says 'Here your needs are all met.' It is simply wonderful. . . . It is so good of you and your family circle to care for me like this."[45] A Mr. Middleton, she told Partridge, joined the ship in Lagos and oversaw the admired missionary's care on board the ship and following her arrival at Liverpool.[46]

The trip in the *Orcades* was a special treat for both Mary and Dan. She wrote to Charles Partridge from the steamship that she was feeling stronger and enjoying the voyage. "The breeze has been delightful," she wrote, "and the water so calm and deep green and clear, and the lap, lap

43. MS to Mrs. Black, DUNMG, Nov. 20, 1907.

44. Christie, "Annals," October 16 and December 13, 1906.

45. MS to CP, April 2, 1907.

46. Livingston, *Mary Slessor*, 239.

of the waves is . . . restful to wearied nerves." She worried, though, that the chiefs in his district in Calabar not only missed Partridge but would also be afraid of a new District Commissioner.[47]

When Hope Waddell's J. K. Macgregor and his young wife visited Slessor before they returned to Calabar, he described Mary with admiration. "A slim figure, of middle height, fine eyes full of power, she is no ordinary woman." He and his wife enjoyed sitting with her and listening to her, "for she is most fascinating, and besides being a humorist is a mine of information of mission history and Efik custom.[48]

Mary's June letter to Partridge told him more about the trip home. Her bicycle was missing from the luggage when they reached Liverpool, but Mr. Middleton found it and had it sent on to her. "Mr. Middleton . . . cut himself off from company and fun and everything to keep me company," she wrote. The weather had been beautiful on the trip, but Scotland's weather was terrible. "Winter could not be much worse," she wrote, "and where are the roses and the strawberries and the beauty of the traditional June?" The Prince and Princess of Wales were coming to visit Edinburgh, she informed him. She admitted she wasn't feeling very patriotic but thought that might change when they arrived. Mary wrote of a frightening visit to Edinburgh, too. "After getting somehow to an Electric Car, I nearly shrieked from the pain at my back, just from the fear, but I was more afraid of a carriage, and refused it, as a Judge here [was] caught between two cars and barely escaped with his life. It is an awful country for bustle and movement. It is a splendid country for all that, and the achievements of Man are marvelous."[49]

A July letter thanked the Commissioner "for ordering off all male visitors from the Use house" and asked him to repeat the order before he left England to return to Africa. Later Mary hinted at problems that would cause her to cut her furlough short. She wrote of Rev. Arthur Wilkie going to Use and Ikot Obong and not finding Jean there; "she had gone to Okpo at the request of the Old Chief there for a day." Her letter doesn't make clear what happened except to say, "It *would* be better for them to leave

47. MS to CP, May 20, 1907.

48. Livingston, *Mary Slessor*, 211; MS to CP, June 27, 1907.

49. Ibid., MS to CP.

things alone I think, for Jean has her side of the story, but I am sorely perplexed . . . and cannot sleep at nights because of it."[50]

Slessor even wrote to her D.C. friend about shopping.

> I have been reveling in "frocks and furbelows." It is simply lovely to see the shop windows and to examine and very nearly *envy* the beautiful creations the girls wear, and to look at the "milk and roses" of complection [*sic*], and the beauty and roundness of form they all possess. But of course this is most unbecoming in the senior member of a Presbyterian Mission! and you must keep my weakness a secret. . . . I am trying to take the plainest and cheapest of frocks out with me. Only fancy them telling me that my costume is like a brides rigout!!!! Really, the three junior mission ladies, Misses Peacock, Reid and Amess told me so when we all met the other day in Glasgow, and I confess to feeling ashamed to be in grey and silk when they were so modestly and consistently garbed in Navy Blue, and I could be the mother of the lot!! Well, it is my last shew off, so I may be pardoned.[51]

Mary was pleased that she had recovered from her illness soon after she got home, and "here I am [now] cycling all over the country and behaving like a young lady," she wrote. Partridge's letters to Slessor are lost, but the letter she was answering told of his delay in returning to Calabar due to his own illness. She wrote, "I ought to be preaching to you and telling you 'it serves you right' for you are such an agnostic. & etc., etc., but I am too sorry to indulge in this, and I shall sing the *other side* and remember all your constant and uniform patience and kindness to me, through thick and thin, and shall say that you are just a dear good old man." She continued, "I intend to leave for Calabar by the boat leaving on the 19th [of October]." She had "a hard fight to get away," though, she said, because the Mission Board "were persisting in making me stay all winter 'to get quite strong' on one hand, and on the other 'to go through the Churches telling about Calabar and its needs.' As if I could at my age do the one and gain the other."[52]

The return trip to Calabar was not like the pleasant trip home five months earlier.

50. Ibid., July 11, 1907; October 3, 1907.

51. Ibid., September 21, 1907.

52. Ibid., October 3, 1907.

Mary wrote to her friend Charlotte Crawford from the steamship *Fantee* on November 6. She praised the good weather, the "sea and sky one sheet of blue" and wished she could share it with those at home in Scotland. She had rested and not missed meals, she said.

> But we had dreadful company all the way to our last stoppages. A crowd of men going to the gold mines [in Ghana or Ivory Coast], made a perfect pandemonium of the ship. Night and day, they roared and hurrahed and behaved like Hooligans. Every low music hall song and every vulgar chorus the boys on the street shouted was given here in the middle of the night, and all the day long. The Cap'n got angry in the end, and so did some more of us, specially last Sunday when they roared and danced till 4 o/c a.m. and then did the same till 4 o/c a.m. the next morning. That was their last night, so we all let them go on, but poor fellows they went off in that dreadful [sun], to go up country to a homeless place and a rough life, after a fortnight of drinking and gambling and sleeplessness. One passenger said as they went, "They will all die like dogs up there."[53]

Slessor did have some kind words for the "poor fellows." They were "kind in their own way," she said, "and all came and bade me a kindly goodbye and smilingly agreed to my word of warning advice." She told of one man whose parents were Baptists and who "spoke nicely always about missionaries," but whose behavior had been upsetting. Another "wild lad" had "constituted himself my cavalier and fellow at table, and I think he has been touched to better living at least. He looks so young, and he has a wife and two children, yet he squanders his money and his health like anything," Mary wrote. She was also not impressed with the news that the man's favorite poet was Omar Khayam.[54]

Mary enjoyed her last two nights at sea. They were quiet, but hot. Nearing the end of the journey, Mary revealed, "No one knows I am coming by this boat."[55] It would not surprise those who knew her.

The *Fantee* reached Calabar on November 9, 1907. As soon as she could, Mary headed for Use. She wrote to thank a friend for the gift of a cake when she and Dan departed. It was "a great treat when I came home," she wrote, "and had nothing else to eat for two days, till we got bread at

53. MS to Crawford, November 6, 1907.

54. Ibid.

55. Ibid.

the beach."[56] A letter also found its way into *The Record*, asking that Mary's thanks be passed along for letters and gifts of money that had been sent to her while she was on furlough. She especially thanked those who had taken her and Dan into their homes. "What the Bethany Home must have been to our Lord," she wrote, "no one can better appreciate than the missionary coming home to a strange place homeless."[57]

Before the year ended, Elizabeth McKinney, a new missionary at Creek Town, visited Slessor and reported surprise at Mary's accommodations—the veteran was sleeping on a mattress laid over a sheet of corrugated iron. The newcomer saw Slessor's inventiveness in action. McKinney had to catch a boat early the next morning. Mary, who had no clock, tied a rooster to her bed. It worked.[58]

Mary wrote to Charles Partridge that she was "rudely healthy" and surprised at how easily she could walk up the hill. She was glad to report that the chiefs of the town came the morning after her arrival and "cleaned all the bush and the road before the sun was high." British officials on board the *Fantee* had told Slessor the current District Commissioner expected her to resume court duties. The forward-looking missionary had more than Use and court on her mind, though. "I purpose going up to Ikpe [some twenty-five miles away], to see if I can begin work there," she wrote.[59]

She hurried to go there before starting court work, because the Ikpe people had often come to beg her to visit and to send a teacher. She found that it was a large market town, that a church had already been built, and that the people already understood something about Christianity. No one could read, but she wrote that "they regularly meet for worship and keep the Sabbath." The people gave her plenty of food, "and if all goes well, I shall stay in the vestry of the Church till I build a House, and make that my head quarters when the [new missionary] ladies come."[60]

Making Ikpe headquarters would be a long time in coming. Meanwhile, Mary continued to live at Use. Living conditions there were

56. MS to Mrs. Black, November 20, 1907.

57. *Record*, 1908, 21.

58. Livingstone, *Mary Slessor*, 238.

59. MS to CP, November 23, 1907.

60. MS to CP, December 7, 1907.

still rustic for her household, as they were for others in the community. In 1908 she wrote to Partridge,

> I've done my best here, for I've bought a cow . . . and the cow has been added to the menagerie. She took us all in tow the first week, every night and morning and gave us a run through bush and every thing, till of course we had to let go; and then we had wild excursions all over the bush with an occasional race after her again, till again she took the rope. And thus we played in the moonlight till I was at my wits end and everything was broken to pieces. My hands are wounded still. One night she took the young men of Use for a run and had them well on the road to Ikot Obong, but at length she did arrive dragging four or five of them, and she was kept a prisoner with grass and water in her room. Speak of milking this creature! But she lets me scratch her nose now, and she came home with Jean quite quietly, so I shall try to tame and pet her, and perhaps in the future, we too, may have Fresh Milk, not necessarily out of whiskey bottles, well, well![61]

Whether or not the household ever got their fresh milk is unknown. No further mention was made of the cow, though the story of "Ma Slessor's coo" became well known among the missionaries.[62]

61. MS to CP, September 13, 1908.

62. Livingstone, *Mary Slessor*, 253.

15

Disagreements In and Out of Court

> I know this more and more from all I see and hear, that without the Gospel, the White Man will never keep or rule what he is trying to snatch. The very men you are educating with gun and motor and telegraph will turn you all out & keep Africa for the Africans. Only *Christianity* will give them a motive for loyalty, & good living, & obedience to law.
>
> —Mary Slessor, 1909[1]

THOUGH THINGS WERE CHANGING in Use Ikot Oku, they were not progressing well in settlements outside the village. Slessor wrote, "We have to start early for the services on Sabbath morning, as we go far over the hills, and it is stony land and hard to manage—the cycle is no use then." The sun was high, she said, before they reached the first town, where she was once met with news of a dead child.

> There, sure enough, were the mourning women round the door, and the little grave dug at the door-step. Pushing among the sweating, howling crowd, I asked for the mother; then the wailing ceased. I found her in a dark corner. She had fainted. After a little she recovered, and her first conscious wail was "my boy, my boy!" By-and-by the wee laddie was brought out, just held in his mat. I opened it to see him, and there was the poor emaciated body with swollen head in all the hideousness of disease and dirt, to be hidden from the sight of the people. The grave was far too short, and rather than desecrate the poor wee body, I made them make it longer, and they laid him down to do this just as if he had been a piece of goods; then they laid him in, and threw on the earth less

1. MS to CP, July 7, 1909.

> than foot from the top soil. There was no want of tenderness either, for the women again burst forth with wailing. . . .
>
> As I went from village to village the memory of this scene coloured all my outlook. It led me to take as my subject Revelation xxi.4: no more pain, no more sorrow, no more death; God wiping the tears from all eyes. But even that great assurance could not lift the sadness, the terrible squalor, the utter hopelessness of these crowds of sister-hearts.[2]

News from Use village was better. Mary wrote to Charles Partridge.

> It is a great trial to the native giving up what they gloried in, their Egbo [organization] and its drinkings and orgies and the glory thereof; and all that differentiates a big man from a nobody, and it curtails their liberties as heathens to live as they used to, but it is the usual outcome of the Gospel, and the compensations are evidently sufficient, as there are no inducements other than the moral and spiritual ones. Can you explain why the Gospel should always have this effect, as I never asked any one to be Baptized or to put his house in order. I only gave the Gospel, and over a score of our best young lads and some women are thus working the old sequel.[3]

Mary also wrote of her surprise at church one day when she spotted "a richly painted basin set on a gin case—the only boxes and seats we have as a rule in this country—and heard a coin drop into it." This was the first instance of an offering being received at Use. Slessor said,

> I have never mixed up money with the preaching of the Gospel to the heathen lest they should misunderstand, but I was thinking of breaking the subject to them at the Catechumen class which meets on Saturday evenings. Here they had anticipated me, and though we keep the plate at our place where the Christians sit, and do not put it before the heathen, they have made nearly 20 s. [shillings] already. . . . So you see, though we are poor so far as money goes here, God works out His own way and does His work quietly and without fuss. . . . It is very wonderful, and only explainable on the ground that "the same Spirit works in all," producing the same results in every nationality and type and condition of men.[4]

2. *WMM*, July 1908, 149.
3. MS to CP, August 29, 1908.
4. *Record*, 1909, 119.

Later, Slessor would write of continuing changes at Use. "Our old chief has died," she wrote, "and instead of a week of drinking and flogging, the town was quiet, but for the mourning women, and the Egbo drum for one night." Members of the chief's "house" came to Mary for advice regarding the funeral and agreed that the chief's widow would not be forbidden to come to church. The old custom of seclusion and allowing the widow little to eat and not washing or caring for her hair would not be followed. "So I thank God and take courage," she reported.[5]

Mary did not forget her promise to Ikpe. "Our folks at home are all telling me I must not on any account stay [in Africa] more than two years," Mary wrote to Partridge, "but that is nonsense. I have never got to redeem my promise to Ikpe Ikot Nkon yet." (In her letters to Partridge Slessor often wrote that she had no news in the middle of a long, newsy letter. In this pages-long letter, she wrote, "But this must go as it is without any news, as I have none, but it goes with a very warm heartful of love and good wishes.")[6]

When Mary spoke at a farewell meeting before she left Edinburgh, she told of the continuing need for women to serve in Calabar. She explained that punitive expeditions had caused Africans to distrust European men; they wanted women instead. Too many times, when conditions did not meet with British approval, government officials and forces had simply attacked a town, resulting in deaths, destruction and distrust. Slessor also emphasized her view that "had it not been for the work of the Church, [the British government] could not have done what they have; and they will never hold the country without gospel light."[7]

Mary had expected new female missionaries to arrive for some time to help at Use. That didn't happen for nearly two years. (One new missionary, Annie Turner, did arrive in September 1909 to help Mary at Use. Turner was destined to stay less than a year before malaria felled her and she returned to Scotland.)[8] Slessor continued to write with delight about any progress she saw.

She reported to *The Women's Missionary Magazine* about "our first baptism and our first observance of the Feast of Love" at Ikot Obong on

5. *WMM*, DUNARC, January 1910, n.p.
6. MS to CP, July 7, 1909 and May 8, 1909.
7. *WMM*, November, 1907, 279–80.
8. *WMM*, June 1908, 142.

September 6, 1908. "It was just a day of heaven upon earth, and the crowds outside, as well as the crowd packed within, were as reverent as if it had been a sacrament day in Scotland. The stillness was intense, and all hearts were touched and subdued."[9]

Mary wrote about changes. The missionaries used to "seek for open doors, [but now the people] cry from everywhere to us, and we are fain to take small boys or any one who will go to give the rudiments."[10] She bemoaned the fact that, though the church at home was providing money for extension of mission work, the mission was closing some stations for lack of workers.

To Charlotte Crawford in Scotland, Mary wrote: "The Ikpe people are wondering, I'm sure, what kind of promisers we are. For I don't seem any nearer to keeping my word to them than ever I was." She related the story of an Ikpe woman who had died. The woman told her parents and husband not to grieve for her when she died. "For, she said, 'I have seen Jesus and I want to go to him, and it is He who calls me, and you must learn and come after me, and all the friends who love Him will come and by and bye [*sic*] we shall be happy for ever more.' Etc. etc. This from a flock without a shepherd! They just meet and sing and pray and separate. But the Spirit is there! And He teacheth savingly."[11]

PROTECTING WOMEN

Mary fretted about the status of women almost from the day of her arrival in Calabar. Thirty years later, she was, if anything, more resolute about the need for change. She wrote to Women's Foreign Mission secretary William Stevenson in 1906, "The weak part in our Calabar mission work is the want of any industry or shelter for women. . . . We *must* have something at which a decent Christian woman who wishes to earn her living, can do so apart from native marriage. We must really try *at once* to get something done. . . . Every woman born here can work land, raise stock, and etc.; and we could get land up country for this purpose."[12]

Mary's letter went on to outline some possibilities: the women could do laundry work for the officers "scattered all over the Cross River and Aro

9. Ibid., December 1908, 286.

10. Ibid.

11. MS to Crawford, December 27, 1908.

12. MS to Stevenson, February 28, 1906.

Chuku, and Ibibio districts;" or they could bake or sew. She deplored the fact that the mission had not done more for women already and recommended "new places with inexpensive houses and with girl's schools, and a ministry with a boys industrial school station." She added, "I can give up this very good comfy little house to any one you may send up here, and I shall go farther on, or I shall get up a place farther on inexpensively for any one and stay here. . . . As the Dr. is at [nearby] Itu, there is no risk, and this is healthy high land, well watered every where, so one or two ladies are safe—aye safer, than in Duke or Creek Town."[13]

Slessor addressed the problem from time to time in letters to friends or to mission magazines at home. *The Women's Missionary Magazine* published Mary's concern:

> The kind of advance, which concerns the women of the Church . . . lies in the direction of some development of our work which will make the native woman something more than a cipher in the community; something more than a mere creature to be exploited and degraded by man. According to native law, a girl child, if not betrothed by her guardians to some man, lacks all protection of law. If she be not "a man's wife" she may be insulted or injured with impunity, no punishment except the merest rebuke can be meted to a man. Then, too, as emancipation advances under Britain's administration, something must be done to meet it. Not only must we provide some way of protecting and sheltering women, but in order to this end we must create some industry by which these women may earn their living, and thus become independent of the polygamous marriage and the open insult.[14]

That industry should be, Slessor wrote, "Something not too hard for her strength, something that will sell. Something that will not cost too much for initial expense can be found doubtless, and thus not only the woman be provided for, but the country be benefited."[15]

In May 1908, Mary wrote to friends in Scotland that the Women's Foreign Mission Committee had approved her plan for "a settlement for women and girls," that "two old and valued lady friends in Perth" had

13. Ibid.

14. *WMM*, January 1908, 4.

15. Ibid., 5.

given her one hundred pounds for it, and that houses were "being got ready bit by bit for the girls and the workers in charge."[16]

Toward the end of the year, Mary informed Charlotte Crawford, when she asked about the settlement, "The Deed is in the hands of the two pastors in Calabar. It will emerge some day, I have no doubt, when they get time and we can meet, but during all the year we have been steadily working . . . building new bits of houses and putting additions to this house, so that Europeans may find it suitable; and by planting fruit trees and in various ways working up towards being ready to flit whenever anyone will come to take over."[17]

"Mr. Gray says we can develop the cocoa nut fibre for matting, also basket making in our women's industrial scheme," Mary wrote, "and he will help us."[18] But two more years passed before she wrote to Crawford, saying, "The settlement can not be a fact till we get help. . . . All the extension and talk and money notwithstanding . . . a settlement or anything else must have . . . a permanent and . . . trained staff if it is to be anything. One can't take in and start people and then throw them off when someone goes home."[19] Mary and her girls had finally taken lessons and learned the art of basket-making themselves just four months earlier.[20]

ADMIRATION AND CRITICISM

Although Mary Slessor may have been known in some missionary circles as "that coarse woman,"[21] many people found their way to her door, no matter where she was. This was especially true of the men who represented the British government. Frequent staff changes brought new, mostly young men, who were regaled with stories of the eccentric missionary. The men were from different churches than Mary, or no church at all. They appreciated Slessor's down-home hospitality and her sense of humor. They admired her ease with the native language and her ability to enlighten them on the culture of the area or discuss political problems.

16. MS to "Dear Friends and Fellow Believers," May 30, 1908. See also, Christie, "Annals," October 17, 1907.

17. MS to Crawford, December 27, 1908.

18. MS to CP, November 23, 1907.

19. MS to Crawford, November 19, 1909.

20. *WMM*, July 1909, 147.

21. Buchan, *Expendable Mary Slessor*, 170.

They teased her; she teased back. When they moved on, she wrote to them and to their wives or mothers. They sent her gifts. They sent workmen to assist with house repairs. They became guilty, an unnamed missionary said, of "Mariolatry." Government officials decreed that she could use "any and every conveyance belonging to them in the Colony."[22]

From Slessor's perspective, those in government service did not have it easy. She wrote to William Stevenson,

> Government officers have not a Home life. We [missionaries] have. Their duties are much more multifarious than ours. They have a constant going about, and are exposed to long marches in the roughest surroundings, and are never sure of a day of ordinary routine. . . . Hence they are kept on strain and stress as we never are. Our lives are comparatively quiet, and our ordered methodical routine allows us to have times of rest and to have comforts such as those men never have. Our food is also regular, and as far as is possible is what is best for the climate. . . . These conditions make a government official's life a very strenuous and a very wearing one, and it would be impossible for them to go on very long.
>
> But apart from all this, the motives which lie at the root of a missionary's life are, or ought to be, so far above those which rule any worldly calling, that there must be given some proof of their reality. If they for a worldly calling can do much, we from our loftier standpoint and our higher ideals, should surely do more. If they follow and obey, wherever and whenever duty calls, surely we should far outstrip them, seeing ours is a service of love and gratitude.[23]

Slessor's friend, British official T. D. Maxwell, wrote, "She was young . . . in her enthusiasm, her sympathy, her boundless energy, her never-failing sense of humour, her gift of repartee, her ability always to strike the apt—even the corrosive—epithet. A visit to her was, to use one of her own phrases, 'like a breath o' caller [fresh] air to a weary body.'"[24]

Things did not always go smoothly among the missionaries themselves. Personality clashes were as likely among them as in the general population. Hope Waddell wrote extensively in his journal in 1855 of a

22. Livingston, *Mary Slessor*, 290–91.

23. MS to Stevenson, October 28. 1907.

24. Livingston, *Mary Slessor*, 290.

disagreement with William Anderson. And Anderson confessed that "everything that Mr. Waddell writes annoys me somewhat."[25]

Waddell's proclamation: "We are not fit to be missionaries of Christ to the heathen if we have not sense and grace enough to settle matters of dispute among ourselves when they occur and to endeavour to avoid their recurrence. This is my *ultimatum* so fare ye well."[26]

Another major clash between Alexander Ross—the missionary who met Mary when she arrived in Calabar and who some described as "a young and tempestuous newcomer"—and pioneer missionary William Anderson gave a severe blow to the Calabar Mission. When Acting Consul Easton appointed Duke Ephraim "King Duke Ephraim Eyamba IX" in 1880, there was bitter dissension between the two men. Ross favored the appointment and denounced Anderson for "his support of cruel and unconverted chiefs, and his general toleration of barbarous customs."[27] A. J. Latham wrote that Anderson "realized that the election of a king from the comparatively weak and impoverished Eyamba would be an unsatisfactory solution, [so he] tacitly supported Prince Duke of the powerful Duke section."[28]

The upshot of the matter was that in December 1881 synod deputies from Scotland denounced Anderson's part in the feud, and at the same time decreed that Ross was to leave Calabar and return to Scotland. Ross refused to go. Not only that; he resigned from the church and seceded from the mission. He formed a new independent mission with his followers in Henshaw Town, adjacent to Duke Town, and stayed there until his death three years later.

In spite of the adulation heaped on Mary (she would call it blarney), as her reputation grew and as she got older and sicker, Mary became more cantankerous. Her sharp tongue often inflicted hurt when she held an opinion contrary to someone else's. And sometimes the victims of her tongue were co-laborers who had worked for years in difficult circumstances.

One who felt Mary's sharp criticism was Alexander Cruickshank, who served as a missionary in Calabar from 1881 to 1936. For most of

25. Johnston, *Maxim Guns*, 16.
26. Waddell, "Journal," 10–15.
27. Latham, "Scottish Missionaries," 47–52.
28. Ibid.

those years he was at Ikot Offiong. When he began his service there, he said he would be glad to see fifty people in church. By the time he retired fifty-five years later, he had a congregation of 1,500.[29] He was a methodical teacher (who kept his strong Aberdeen accent), and the people he served loved him. But he thought Mary Slessor's "mud kirks" and "schools taught by the semi-literate" were not the way to minister.[30]

According to one eyewitness report, Slessor gave Cruickshank "a tongue-lashing" at a meeting of all the missionaries. It is doubtful that her outburst was connected with his criticism of her methods; more likely, it concerned some mission policy discussion at that particular meeting. Cruickshank escaped to the verandah. Dr. John Taylor Dean followed, saw him with tears in his eyes, and tried to console him. "Don't take to heart, she's a sick woman," he said. Dr. Cruickshank replied, "It's been a guy lang [very long] sickness."[31]

Mary may not have even realized the distress she caused Cruickshank. She held him in high regard and praised him in letters. A letter to Charlotte Crawford told of a native who wanted Mary to settle a complicated problem. "I told him," she wrote, "to wait for Mr. Cruickshank, who is so gentle in his very rebukes."[32] Later she would write in her diary that Cruickshank was very "kind and gentle with the disciples and the old wives. He is a gem."[33]

Regarding her "mud kirks," Slessor believed it was wrong to introduce European-style churches. According to biographer Livingstone, she was wary of "too much" civilization. She thought people would consider expensive buildings "a foreign thing in which they would worship a foreign God."[34] Mary's little churches placed worshipers in a more normal environment, where she thought they could concentrate on spiritual matters.

Biographers Christian and Plummer wrote of a Mission secretary who visited Mary and was shocked by Mary's response to a disagreement. It "caused her to stalk from the room, refusing to speak to him further. At

29. Gammie, *Cruickshank of Calabar*, 61.
30. Christian and Plummer, *Redhead*, 175.
31. Dean, reported by his widow, Mrs. C. Duff.
32. MS to Crawford, August 3, 1913.
33. MS Diary, April 20, 1914.
34. Livingstone, *Mary Slessor*, 320.

supper-time they took their places in silence. But, when grace had been said, he looked up to find the mischievous old lady sticking out her tongue at him like an unrepentant schoolgirl."[35]

Some colleagues did not want to work with Slessor, not because of her caustic tongue but because of her unpredictable schedule. Meal times were irregular. And they were distressed that she neither boiled her water nor used mosquito nets. Christian and Plummer wrote, "At other mission stations, those who were ill were isolated. . . . Not so in Mary Slessor's abode. Everyone was together—malaria, dysentery and other diseases went from child to child to adult. Mary ignored flies, roaches and rats, while other missionaries tried to be rid of them. And when Janie cooked, she was known to take the chicken from the pot and lay it on the mud floor while she made gravy."[36]

Mary was aware of her own shortcomings. Psalm 141:3's prayer, "Set a watch, O Lord, before my mouth," prompted a marginal note of frustration in her Bible: 'I cannot do it.'"[37] She spoke in her diaries and letters of being irritable or short-tempered. She wrote to Charles Partridge about her impatience and thanked him for "that far too kind letter you sent just at the time I needed it badly to cheer me up!"

> Never mind though all you say in it misses the mark by a long way, for thats not Mary Slessor on the Pedestal you set up! . . . never the less though I can't lay claim to it, I can aspire to be the sort of being it pictures. . . . Still I *can* try, old as I am, and last Court day, I *did* try, and pray too, and I think I *was* more helpful and patient. Wait a bit, when you come back, I *will* try again, if I get the privilege, and perhaps you may then praise.[38]

The cranky missionary didn't hesitate to send irate comments to Partridge about government policies and officials. One time she complained about two carpenters she had for a day's work. Angry when they accomplished little, she wrote, "Have I been a sweet-tempered, sweet-tongued Christian lady today???" She was nice to the carpenters' helpers, she said, "But those———!!!"[39] And later,

35. Christian and Plummer, *Redhead*, 175.

36. Ibid., 110.

37. MS Bible, Psalm 141:3.

38. MS to CP, February 24, 1906.

39. Ibid., March 10, 1910.

> I am not at all in love with either side of our Political District. We have got such an ———! of a man at Itu. I'm glad he was in a separate launch, for there would have been a sparring match, and I'm not physically fit yet for it, but it *will come* if he is long enough there. The average length of the A.D.Cs [Assistant District Commissioner's] time there . . . is about three weeks, and "I am glad." That's from a Hymn refrain, but it is not meant to be irreverent, for it just came to the pen point before I thought.[40]

Mary complained in her diary about her disgust with government insistence that its edicts be followed at once. Young men did not want to do roadwork for the Consul when it caused them to miss school; they argued with their chiefs about it, and Mary, reluctantly, felt compelled to uphold the government's rules. She wrote, "Why does not the White man try to time his work to circumstances? All this last season Itu District has groaned under this oppression. All school boys [are] on consular work."[41]

HARD WORK AND ITS FRUITS

In the spring of 1908 the *Government Gazette* published reports for the previous quarter. Mary Slessor's name was becoming well known throughout the Protectorate.

> It is worthy of special mention to record that in September a number of summonses were issued by the Ikotobong Court, Ikot-Ekpene District, against husbands of twin-bearing women for desertion and non-support, with the result that in every case the husbands agreed to take the women back. . . . It has previously been the custom to turn these poor women out of their homes and leave them to starve, the reason being that according to native belief one of the twins is supposed to be the result of intercourse with the devil. . . . [It is] a sign of the civilizing influence worked through this Court by that admirable lady, Miss Slessor.[42]

Mary confirmed that she had resumed Court work early in 1908. Acting District Commissioner Horace Bedwell had visited her belatedly, and she chided him for not coming sooner. But, she wrote, "We made it all up. The Governor had written asking him to help me in any way he could, which was most kind." She would superintend the court, she said, with

40. Ibid., June 23, 1910.

41. MS Diary, March 29, 1911.

42. *Record*, 1908, 66.

Halliday as Court Clerk, and would keep her "eye on things as best I can," when she was away.[43] By February Slessor was already feeling pressure from the added duties. She wrote to Partridge, "The Court is a great trial to me. It has got into a dirty irregular line of working."[44] "I'm not *too* fit," she added, "though I'm well."

Mary wrote of her exasperation when Halliday sent her a message saying there would be no Court on a scheduled day. Halliday, it seems, had been away with the court books. Slessor took matters into her own hands, a typical Slessor response. She wrote, "When I saw over 200 people! and Jury men from far and near, and this is their busy season, I felt the injustice of it and just held the Court.... And we did a good days work, too."[45]

By the end of March she wrote, "I sat eight hours on Thursday; from 6 o/c till night I was occupied on Friday; and all night I was out at Ikot Obong with a woman in trouble; got home at dawn and was at it yesterday till late; was up at midnight with a twin mother who died . . . leaving her babies with us. I've had a hard morning's work getting the body buried and Jean's room cleaned, where [the woman] lay."[46]

Meanwhile, other news from the mission cheered those serving in Calabar. In August, Goldie Hall (built in honor of Slessor's friend and early Calabar missionary, translator and historian) was dedicated and opened at Hope Waddell Training Institution, with Bedwell participating as Acting Provincial Commissioner. In October a new church was dedicated in Akpap, "built by the people, a good native building," with seating for about three hundred. Likewise, a new church opened at Unwana, far up the Cross River. And by the end of the year, Wellington Church in Glasgow adopted Mary as "their" missionary.[47]

Missionary W. A. J. Gardiner reported an exploratory trip from Unwana to Bende to determine whether or not the Ibo spoken on the Calabar side was the same as that spoken on the Niger side of the territory. He and his companions met with Archdeacons Crowther and Dennis of the Church Mission Society and others to discuss mission work. On their way home, Gardiner reported: "All the way home we were well received

43. MS to CP, January 20, 1908.

44. Ibid., February 15, 1908.

45. Ibid., March 10, 1908.

46. Ibid., March 29, 1908.

47. Christie, "Annals of the Calabar Mission, 1846–1945," 1908.

by the people, and had much kindness shown to us at every turn. The first night homeward we stopped amongst the people who, three years ago, killed and ate Dr. Stewart, whom we knew so well. To us they were kindness itself."[48]

When three representatives from the Foreign Mission Committee arrived on the equivalent of a modern-day mission trip, they visited Mary Slessor. They heard her reminisce about her years with the Calabar Mission and watched her at work in court. They also visited the church at Akani Obio on Enyong Creek. There they met Chief Onoyom and his people. One of the visitors, Mrs. Lindsay from Bathgate, wrote that the chief, who had built the church with his own funds, "seemed a true gentleman in all his ways, and yet it is only four or five years since Miss Slessor led him to the Saviour."[49] The success of the mission seemed even more evident to the deputies when they visited Asang, "where a congregation of at least seven hundred people assembled."

> The sitting accommodation was uncomfortably taken up by the grown-up people, the space in front of the pulpit and all the passages were packed with young folks, and eager faces peered through every window and door. . . . The atmosphere was stifling, but failed to subdue the enthusiasm of the audience. Dr. Robertson has a splendid voice for leading, powerful enough to keep any ordinary congregation together, but these Assang [*sic*] people were too much even for him. They fairly let themselves go, in different times and tunes, and if singing could have lifted a roof, it would have done so that Sunday afternoon. . . . It was difficult to realize that what we saw had taken place within eight years.[50]

HEALTH AND THE BIKE

When one considers the pace *eka kpukpru owo* kept and how little she cared for her own health, it is ironic that she scolded Partridge for working too hard, saying he must "take a lesson from other D.C.s and take a little more care next time, for the way you worked was, to say the least of

48. *Record*, 1908, 168.
49. *WMM*, April 1910, 80–81.
50. Ibid.

it—suicidal."[51] Mary's old D.C. friend had returned to Africa from sick leave, but to Lagos, not Calabar District, to her dismay.

From time to time through 1908, Mary remarked on her good health. There were occasional bad spells, but on the whole it was one of her better years, and she accomplished a great deal. She wrote to friends in Scotland, "Since the rains came I have been ever so much stronger, and for over two months I have been able to take 7, 8 and 10 hours on end on Sundays going round the villages, 6 to 9 meetings on end in various places."[52]

She didn't fail to talk about her bike, either, especially to its donor, Charles Partridge. She wrote, "Do you think for a moment that I shall ever part with it?"[53] And, "I'm fit (so is my Bike, and I love it more than ever)"[54] She told him the women missionaries brought bicycles with them to the station at Ikot Obong, and they all rode together. She vowed, "I would not change [my Bike] with any one, or anything."[55] Eventually the old bicycle gave out, though, and Partridge sent her a new one. "But my dear old Rudge [brand name of old bicycle] is my bosom friend," Mary wrote, "and I'm jealous for the dear Bike that has carried me so long and given me such pleasure and healthful exercise.[56]

In Mary's adopted son Dan Slessor's remembrance, he wrote of pushing Mary on her bicycle up the hill to Ikot Obong to visit the missionaries there. "On the return journey," he wrote, ". . . I would let her go—and down she would fly, her hair flying behind her, a smile lingering on her lips until she came right up to the village, where the sandy plain held her." Slessor would pedal on as far as she could, then lay the bicycle down. Dan would pick it up on his way home, and by the time he arrived, Mary would have tea ready for him. "'Here, boy,' she would say in welcome, 'You must be tired. . . . Oh, you pushed very well and very hard today, Dan. I didn't realize we were climbing a hill. You are really developing nicely, becoming a fine strong lad. May God help you, my lad.'"[57]

51. MS to CP, May 8, 1908.
52. MS to "Dear Friends & Fellow Believers, May 30, 1908.
53. MS to CP, October 25, 1907.
54. Ibid., September 14, 1908.
55. Ibid., October 3, 1908.
56. Ibid., February 3, 1910.
57. D. Slessor, "Reminiscences."

Toward the end of 1908, Mary wrote, "I've had a bit of fever, but so has every one else as the smokes [harmattan] are heavy. I am able to go up hills on my cycle now I never took before, so that tells its own tale. And I came down in the dark twice over from Ikot Obong So!!! I *love* my cycle and could live on it. If only it could take me through bush roads, I should never be at home."[58]

After a sick spell, Mary told Charles Partridge of Dan pushing her on her bicycle. He pushed her up the hills, she said, when she had "not been able to pedal a step . . . [but] I'm quite sure I could pedal all the levels today, I feel so well."[59] At the first hint of improvement in her health, Slessor was inclined to pronounce herself "rudely healthy."

Mary's health took several turns for the worse during 1909. In February, she wrote, "I have just lain down every time I have had a spare bit of time, for the reason that my poor back will not sit up."[60] In April, her report was, "I have been so very feeble and frail, that last week I had almost made up my mind to take a sea trip, and if it was not of sufficient good to encourage me to hoping to be better, I was just to go straight home. But I have rallied again a little, and today the weakness and the pains in my limbs are ever and ever so much better."[61]

In July, Mary wrote of her terrible episode of boils, of her hair falling out, and of spending a whole month in the care of missionary wife Marian Wilkie. She declared herself still "a very shaky bundle of nerves."[62] In October, it was, "I have had a good deal of fever, but not too severe."[63]

Besides her illnesses, Mary's hands had been full with two weddings (Mary and Annie); and sons Dan and Asuquo had gone off to Hope Waddell Training Institution. But work continued, with babies and mothers and court duties.

One of her Scottish visitors wrote that meeting Mary Slessor "outside her mud-walled, palm-thatched house was one of the most memorable of our experiences." They enjoyed her "charming mixture of English, Scotch,

58. MS to CP, November 28, 1908.
59. Ibid., April 12, 1909.
60. Ibid., February 17, 1909.
61. Ibid., May 12, 1909.
62. Ibid., July 7, 1909.
63. Ibid., October 15, 1909.

and Efik," but the writer also expressed concern about Slessor's poor health at the time.[64]

Another visitor, an Irishman who was Secretary of the Qua Iboe Mission, did not mention Mary's health, but wrote, "It [was] a great privilege to meet this veteran pioneer in her own home, a simple two-roomed mud hut. Old in years and aged by service, Miss Slessor has the heart and limbs of a girl. She received us like old friends, and mounting her cycle, accompanied us for several miles, gaily saluting the numerous groups of Aros which we met and passed, in one of the dialects of the Ibo tongue."[65]

Another of the Scottish deputies, Rev. James Adamson, reminisced about his visit to the church at Use. It was "the simplest church in the mission field, and Ma Slessor has helped to build it," he wrote. A chief had a message for the visitors: "Tell them in 'obio makara' (the white man's country) that we thank God and them for sending Ma Slessor to bring us the light. But many of our brothers are in darkness. Will they not send more?"[66]

THE LAST STRAW

Slessor continued to pass on the black man's dismay with the white man to Charles Partridge. The people asked for more white women missionaries like *eka kpukpru owo,* but they did not want more government men. In December 1907 Mary wrote, "The Chiefs here said, the White Man had done a few good things, but had done many bad things to them."[67] Three months later, she reported, "All this last week a procession of Chiefs from everywhere . . . have been here to plead with me to save them from the White Man."[68] In April, it was, "The White Man breaks his own law too often and makes it ridiculous in native eyes."[69]

Mary wrote to "Dear friends & fellow believers" in Scotland: "If only our Church had been ready to go into those places when the Government went in and thus have spared both parties the punitive burnings and fightings which took place, and which the natives do not forget, we might

64. *WMM,* November 1909, 257–58.

65. *Record,* 1910, 19.

66. Ibid., April 1915, 171–72.

67. MS to CP, December 7, 1907.

68. Ibid., March 29, 1908.

69. Ibid., April 15, 1908.

have had just a walkover, instead of being "the White Man" who burned their towns. They don't know any distinction in our work till they know us, and till we live with them, we are just "White Man.'"[70]

In August of 1908 Mary wrote that a new District Commissioner, Mr. Hargrove, had arrived in Ikot Ekpene to govern the district, one who seemed to measure up to Slessor's (and Africans') esteem of Charles Partridge. Hargrove's presence resulted in new "respect for the White Man," Mary wrote.[71] But by 1910, Mary was begging Partridge to return to the district. "Will ye no come back again?" she asked. "[The people] don't want White Man's rule, or his God, but one or two individuals represent to them the best and highest they have known."[72] Later, Mary would tell Partridge about two chiefs who came to Itu while she was staying there, who told her that "Black men had a continuous, consistent Policy, bad though it might be, but the White Man changed constantly."[73]

The disgruntled missionary was fed up with incompetent men—both British and African—and with the lack of help for court work. She wrote to Charlotte Crawford, "'The flesh is weak' and gets weaker in regards to writing as it makes me nervous. . . . I was not at court yesterday and in fact I am wondering if with my weak health and the 'beyond' calling out, I should not leave it altogether." Everyone wanted her to hear their tales of woe, to "recast" a case, to appeal, to give advice.[74]

Late in1909, Mary wrote a long, sad story to Partridge. She told of new road-building supervisors.

> [They] have resented their boys coming to me with any complaint. Later the bigger officers have made it plain that they believe themselves to be the only persons responsible or competent to judge anything for their boys. *I* hold that . . . outside the day's work; or if discipline as administered by an Efik scamp who has picked up a little English . . . [or] given *outside* the work hours and place, the rights of citizenship have been invaded, and every boy has a right to take out a summons and be heard in open Court. This *may*

70. MS to "Dear friends and fellow believers," May 30, 1908.
71. MS to CP, August 29 and November 28, 1908.
72. Ibid., October 16, 1910.
73. Ibid., September 4, 1911.
74. MS to Crawford, November 19, 1909.

> have something to do with developments, but I'm only *supposing* it has.[75]

Mary went on to explain the "developments." Someone brought her a large broken bottle and told her a woman had fallen, cut an artery and bled to death. The woman was from another tribe, and the people were afraid of retaliation. They asked Slessor to intervene on their behalf. She did not think there was a British officer at Ikot Ekpene at the time, so she ordered a court messenger to see the body and take the *mbiam* oath regarding the accident. The men were also to contact the woman's relatives to view the body and bury her. There could be an inquiry later, Mary decreed.

Meanwhile, men from the road department came, saying the woman had been murdered. "I explained that we had done what was necessary," she wrote, "and as the C.M.s [court messengers] had their orders, it would be well that no outsider interfered." She thought that would be the end of the matter. It was not. A chief and boys came to tell her two white men had taken "nine or ten people" to district headquarters and that others in the party "wrecked a lot of property." The people didn't understand. They requested that Mary ask the District Commissioner "what the palaver was." The response to her note stunned her.

> Two large sheets of Rhodomontade [ranting] came back type written, with such an impossible story, and with what I can only call insult to me. I wrote at once . . . "Sir, as I have yet to learn when and where I ever interfered with 'a case being handled by a D C,' as I have also to learn how and when I 'shewed active sympathy' or passive sympathy either for that part, 'with *those people*,' I fail to see the point of this communication, and of course it is impossible for me to serve any longer under your rule, in any form, so I resign all connection with Ikot Obong Court."[76]

Mary received "a *most official* note" from new District Commissioner R. B. Brooks a few days later. He accepted her resignation. "The ludicrous side then dawned on me," she wrote, "and I laughed and despised the height of the man more than ever."

Slessor was somewhat mollified by a letter that came a few weeks later from Provincial Commissioner F. W. Fosbery, which expressed "great regret" and "deep appreciation" that she had resigned and "with a *gentle-*

75. MS to CP, December 9, 1909.

76. Ibid.

man's thanks for service rendered and wishing me all good." She fumed, "So that's the position! And I'm dismissed, and that by utter strangers." But the fact that Mary Slessor no longer worked for the government would not change things much. She was a "social leper" to some British. But the people would still come to her, she wrote, "as they have always come before there were Courts." She added, "Now I have not told a soul but you, so you will respect my confidence and keep it closely in your own heart. Never speak of it. . . . Besides, perhaps it is the only way to bring home to me the fact that I'm growing too old to be trusted with the affairs of a people."[77] Mary Slessor was sixty-one years old.

77. Ibid.

PART FIVE

A Life Spent

1909–1915

16

Faith Matters

It is borne upon me here that "not by might nor by power, but by Thy Spirit" is the only leverage. Man and Mary Slessor are simply nothing. I can get obedience and respect, and gifts and heaps of things, but not one soul can I move to its own salvation. A fine corrective to blarney!

—Mary Slessor, 1914[1]

MARY BEGAN TO CORRESPOND with Charles Partridge's father when the District Commissioner returned to Africa from sick leave in England in 1910. She was delighted to learn that the parents were not only Christians, but "*evangelical* Christians." Slessor wrote:

> When I was a young girl, I entered in Gods Great Grace, on the experience of His Keeping sanctifying power, and excepting for a very little while when Cheyne and Driver were at their worst in their destructive Criticism, that Perfect Peace and faith has never wavered, and if any one may testify as to the reality of His Presence and power, it is surely this unworthy servant. . . . *He* and *His Word* are a living bright reality for sure, and the fact, that I meet my congregation, knowing that it is not me, nor my message, but just that I am in the Hand of the Spirit as the Channel of Communication and that my part is to see that the Channel is open and clean.[2]

Mary went on to say that a Dundee mentor had given her a copy of Boardman's *Higher Life* when she was a girl and asked if she knew about "Sanctification by Faith." She had not heard the term, but after she read it,

1. MS to Livingstone, when asked for a "contribution on some aspect of her work" after she received the Order of St. John medal, *Record*, 1915, 58.

2. MS to CP, Sr., March 10, 1910.

she told him, "It is splendid, but there is nothing *new* to me in it." That, she said, was when she began to search for "all the works on Sanctification, etc. and the Higher Life as it was then called."[3]

LESSONS

An indication of Mary Slessor's faith and practice comes from a notebook that holds two of her handwritten "lessons"—sermons, really. Although Mary partially overcame her extreme shyness at some point, these particular sermons may have been read aloud by someone else. Slessor wrote about the older friend to whom she confided her wish to become a missionary. "When I wrote papers for our Fellowship society," she wrote, "he criticised mine and read them in the meeting, as ladies did not do these things in our stern Presbyterian Church meetings."[4] (Presbyterian minister James Logie later convinced her it was her duty to God to speak when she was doing mission work in Dundee.)

The first "lesson" in Mary's notebook welcomes a new year (probably 1874). "[The Christian] must turn from the past, buckle on his sandals, gird up the loins of his mind, and prepare for renewing his march," she wrote. The Scripture selection was Isaiah 41:10: "Fear thou not for I am with thee." It was an evangelistic sermon in the fullest sense, some thirty-five handwritten pages, filled with Bible references and a call to action. Mary wrote near the end of her message,

> Thank God! For such men and women here and everywhere, who in the face of scorn and persecution dare to be singular, dare to stand firmly and fearlessly for their Master. Their commission is today what it was yesterday. "Go ye into all the world and preach the Gospel to every creature." This command is exceeding broad: you see it is not "look at" but "go into!" the world. Then it is. "*all* the world," not the nice easy places only, but the dark places, the distant places, "all the world." Then "to every creature." To the low as well as the high, the poor as well as the rich, the ignorant as well as the learned, the degraded as well as the refined, to those who will mock as well as to those who will receive us, to those who will hate as well as to those who will love us. In short, "to every Creature"!
>
> Are we not apt to ask sometimes, "Who is sufficient for these things?" How can we break all the tender ties that bind us to home

3. Ibid., January 10, 1911.
4. Ibid.

> and kindred and country? How could we go out into that coldness and darkness and pollution, from which our souls instinctively turn? How can we leave the society of the near and dear, the gifted, the refined, and associate with men and women who are characterized only by that from which we naturally shrink? What saith the Lord? "Fear thou not, for I am with thee." . . . "Lo! I am with you always even to the end of the world."[5]

The eager preacher came close to giving an altar call when she added, "Oh! My friends who are still outside the Court of Israel, still without a Guide and Protector, how can you dare to face the dark, unknown future, all alone. Change and decay are written on everything here, and you cannot expect your life circumstances to be always an exception. Your treasures may be snatched from you in a moment, your life may go down in darkness, in the twinkling of an eye. And then, and then! *What* then?"[6]

The challenge Mary issued in her sermon was one she answered herself by dedicating her life to carrying out the command to "go" and "preach."

The subject of Mary's second lesson was on the importance of the Bible.

> Apart altogether from the fact of inspiration, and viewed as an ordinary work of literature, the Bible is entitled to the name and position of "Book of Books." This is true from whichever side or standpoint we look at it. It is true if we look at its antiquity. Here we find the only clear and definite Knowledge we possess regarding the Creation of the world and the origin of our race. Here we have the loftiest conceptions of man.
>
> Our opinion of the Bible as a book is too narrow and hampered. What is more common than to find Christians poring over Milton to satisfy their love of the magnificent in poetry or keeping company with Shakespeare to gratify their love of the dramatic. Or studying (almost exclusively) the works of Coleridge and Wordsworth for beauty of imagery and expression. Or searching the annals of War for examples of heroism. What need is there of going so far? God has provided in the Bible for all the wants of our nature.

There follow a number of pages of defense of the Bible and extolling its beauty and excellence, then a number of pages about its message

5. MS, Lesson Notes.
6. Ibid.

and the "universality" of its "cure." It ends with an evangelistic call to take a stand. Let us be "filled with the Spirit," she wrote, ". . . [and] from the efforts of a few consecrated, God possessed men and women, the Lord will add even to Wishart Church [in Dundee], multitudes of such as shall be saved." A warning followed the challenge. "But there is another side to the Subject. 'He that believeth not is *condemned already*.' Will anyone here be content to sit still in this position while there is deliverance near? Surely not. Come to Jesus, even now, and you may leave this room Healed, Pardoned, Saved. 'We beseech you in Christ to stand, be ye reconciled to God.'"[7]

In Calabar, Mary declared, "To preach the gospel is our *one* aim in all our work. With every visitor who comes to give compliments, with every curious passer-by who comes to see what the white woman and her house are like, with every company who bring a palaver to settle, with every dose of medicine, we try to send home the message of salvation."[8]

THE BIBLE ACCORDING TO SLESSOR

Mary's love affair with her Bible, her guidebook for life, can be seen in the two remaining copies that are held by McManus Galleries and Museum in Dundee. The devoted Christian penned a running commentary as she read. Obviously not intended for any eyes but her own, she wrote in every margin and between verses: sometimes a single word, sometimes a comment on Calabar; sometimes a retort or warning to the Apostle Paul or Job or some other character in the narrative; sometimes a question; sometimes a challenge to herself. Reading Mary's comments, even without referring to the text and with only a vague notion of what the text says, gives insight into her beliefs. Some excerpts from her Genesis commentary are a good example of this:

7. Ibid.

8. *Record*, 1882, 194.

Creation	Order, utility, beauty. . . . By what means? Nothing here that scientists can dispute.
Temptation and fall	Preposterous. God did not mean death. . . . Innocence lost. . . . Conscience awakened.
Man's sin and the ark	God can grieve. So should his people. . . . No good thing can die. . . . What a trial of faith.
The rainbow and covenant	He has kept His word.
Cursing Canaan	Character alone rules.
Abram in Egypt	Where is your faith now? . . . Poor Sarah! How did she feel?
Sodom	Ah! The fly in the ointment.
Abraham's laughter	Was this unfaith?
God warns Abraham of his plan	God does His revealing with man's receptiveness.
Sarah—wife or sister?	Cowardly weak reply. . . . How lame! . . . Rot! . . . O Sarah!! . . . Africa . . . Calabar fashion.
Rebekah's prayer	Prayer the dynamic. . . .
Isaac's lie	Okoyon every day.
Abimelech and Isaac's oath	Itu mbiam, Calabar history.
Theft of Esau's blessing	Profane! . . . Poor Heart!!
Leah given to Jacob	Had they been drinking? . . . Calabar!
Rachel trades for her husband	Rachel, you are a disgrace.
Rachel steals images	Don't be so sure, Jacob! . . . Mbiam oath.
Angels meet Jacob	Who were they?
Jacob sends others to meet Esau	Cowardly.
Judah and Tamar	Ibibio law. . . . Calabar morality.

Slessor's commentary on Psalm 94, at the start of World War I, is notable. She underlined certain phrases and added her notes: "German war!" "Wilhelm!" "All military Powers." Her judgment regarding the killing of widows, strangers, and the fatherless is, "By armaments & war." Concerning the promised *pit . . . for the wicked,* Mary wrote, "Who delight in war."

Other revealing comments are these: "Am I willing to take scorn for his sake?" (Isaiah 50:6); "Sin kills devotion." (Matthew 24:12); "'Sorry' is not salvation." (Mark 6:26); "Reason wants to see!" (John 20:25); and, "Don't sit and mope." (John 21:19).

Mary did not hesitate to hold conversations with anyone she found in the Bible. In her study of 1 Corinthians, she wrote at the bottom of one page, "How the missionary thanks God for these chapters! Paul is so sane." On the other hand, when the apostle wrote in 1 Timothy 2, *Let the woman learn in silence with all subjection*, Mary retorted, "NO NO Paul!!" At the end of the chapter, she wrote, "A good deal of patronage from Paul, which is not borne out by His Master." At Paul's question in 1 Corinthians 11, *Is it comely that a woman pray unto God uncovered?* Mary responded, "Cheeky a bit." Who knows whether she referred to Paul's words or to women without head coverings. When Paul told of being *pressed out of measure, above strength, insomuch that we despaired even of life*, Mary added, "A missionary!"

RIGHT THINKING?

"We are great Heresy Hunters, we Presbyterians," Mary wrote to Charles Partridge, Sr. (retaining here her common abbreviations when she wrote), "& Mother like most of those old Calvinistic Xtians was afraid of anything like presumption & felt surer of a Xtian who was *very* conscious of sin." Slessor seemed to agree with her mother. She complained about the "noise & fuss & sensation & a craving for something new" everywhere in the church and worried that "the old meditative spirit & the old sense of sin, seems to be sadly lacking." She thought "the unrest in the world" was paralyzing the Church and keeping Christians "from seeing 'Jesus Only.'"[9]

Later, Mary wrote to missionary accountant Thomas Hart, "I am a seceder and voluntary born and bred, and I wonder if it is the government connection which makes the Church seek out academicians and technical workers and be satisfied with them apart from the Evangel?? Education is Good, Culture is Good, and God needs and uses them, and He is worthy of all. But His Work can't be done on the Intellectual plane, and unless we get to the spiritual and sit with Him in the Heavenly places, I fear we will be but barren workers."[10]

Ever mission-minded, Mary expressed interest in the World Missionary Conference held at Edinburgh in 1910 but felt that nothing

9. MS to CP, Sr., January 10, 1911.

10. MS to Hart, May 9, 1912.

"practical" resulted. Her observation: "After all, it is not committees and organisations from without that is to bring the revival, and to send the Gospel to the heathen at home and abroad, but the living spirit of God working from within the heart."[11]

Mary disdained some kinds of preaching. William Abednego Thompson, who went by the name of Bendigo (a corruption of his birth-name), was an illiterate bare-knuckle prizefighter who became a Methodist preacher in his later years. On the platform, he would point to his trophies and say, "See them belts, see them cups, I used to fight for those. But now I fight for Christ."[12] Since bare-knuckle prizefighting was illegal, Bendigo spent time in prison and held a "ticket-of-leave" when he was out on parole.

Slessor wrote to a friend in Dundee,

> I am not a believer in the craze for "ticket-of-leave men" and "converted prize-fighters" to preach to the poor and the outcast. I think the more of real refinement and beauty and education that enter into all Christian work, the more real success and lasting, wide-reaching results of a Christian and elevating nature will follow. Vulgarity and ignorance can never in themselves lay hold on the uneducated classes, or on any class.... There is need for knowledge ... of the Bible as a whole, not merely of the special passages which are adapted for evangelistic services.... I am pained often at home that there is so little of depth, and of God's word, in the speeches and addresses I hear.[13]

In 1912, Slessor wrote to Hart, "I have gone through the Pauline Epistles slowly and thoroughly this year, and oh, how inexpressibly rich they are. Language is strained to its utmost capacity and beyond it, to express the grandeur of this Salvation and Gospel committed to our hands. ... I just feel cheap, and my work and prayers and everything seems to

11. Livingstone, Mary Slessor, 320. There is no record of her response to the Missionary Conference held at Calabar in 1911, but she likely agreed with its aims: to "teach Africans to be African Christians;" deprecating "any method of education which tends to denationalize, and [affirming] the principle of relating all education to the conditions of Native thought and life;" recognizing "that everything in Native Life has religious significance; and retaining and utilizing "everything distinctly African, not inconsistent with the Christian Ethic." (Report of Missionary Conference)

12. Studeny, "Bendigo."

13. Livingstone, *Mary Slessor*, 45.

shrivel alongside the Pattern Book of the King's tracing, and of the service and spirit of Paul his Prisoner, and *utterly* selfless servant."[14]

At another time, Slessor wrote of the "grand pattern" of the communion of the saints, as found in Paul's writings, especially in Ephesians. Again she revealed her sense of humility and sin in her comment, "His gifts to me overwhelm me and make me feel ashamed of my poor halting service and faith."[15]

Charles Partridge's father sent Slessor "papers," which she said were "a great comfort and uplift." She enjoyed the Bible study material and mentioned specifically "The Christian," "Life of Faith" and "The Overcomer." She wrote: "I give away 'The Christian,' and the other papers I take to the English speaking clerks and employees of the Government. But I'm keeping up the 'Life of Faith' for further use in the Classes for Teachers and etc., as well as for my own use personally. It is so good to have unequivocal a Testimony to Divine Truth as the 'Life of Faith' gives. I prize it and 'The Christian' for their uniform faithfulness to the pure Gospel."

Mary remarked on the demise of "The Overcomer": "It upheld some aspects of the Christian Life, but to the rank and file of Christians it was too polemical and too academic in its style. I shall not say too doctrinal, for want of that is the fault and lack of the present day preaching and teaching I think. Doctrine is deprecated, but I'm Scotch, you see, and have had it in my blood to be doctrinal as a foundation for practice."[16]

MINISTRY TO CHRISTIAN FRIENDS

To close friend and confidant Charlotte Crawford, Slessor wrote, "May God get His proper place as He chooses and then all will be well, for He is able to guide His church as ever He was. Only we sometimes make the choosing and the doing our business too much, and then we get trouble."[17]

Not many of Mary Slessor's letters to friends have been preserved. We have some letters to Crawford and those to Charles Partridge, Sr. along with his son's. Several letters to Thomas Hart are found, a few to William

14. MS to Hart, 1912.
15. MS to Crawford, November 6, 1907.
16. MS to CP, Sr., June 7, 1913.
17. MS to Crawford, December 27, 1908.

Stevenson, or others. Excerpts of some letters also appear in *The Record* or *The Women's Missionary Magazine*. Letters Mary sent for publication were less personal and more what one would expect from a missionary's newsletter. Although they pressed for needs and told touching stories, they seldom included her intimate concerns.

Even in personal letters, though, Mary's faith and humble spirit—and her mother's sense of sin—shone through. As the years passed, and people heaped praise on her, the aging missionary continued to insist that she was not worthy of it. She wrote to Crawford in 1913, "What a love of a letter you always write, and this one is simply a "Crowner," only, please spare the butter a wee bit for I'm awfully fond of butter . . . so beware of pandering to the depraved natural tastes of your missionary, to whom self abnegation should be everything in life. . . . Surely no member of His Body is so unworthy of notice as I am!"[18]

Much earlier, Slessor had warned her friend not to think too highly of her missionary friend. "Why do you say that about tying my shoe??" she wrote. "If you knew me as God does!!! But the blood goes on cleansing, that is all my hope and plea. Never say that kind of thing again."[19]

One of Slessor's earliest letters from Calabar is her writing as a counselor. Written to an unknown "Maggie" in her early days with the Calabar Mission, Mary's letter advised:

> I know Maggie dear, that it is not impulse but real love to Jesus that fills you with desire to serve Him among your fellows, and if I have been the means in God's hand of making F. [Foreign] Mission work something more real to you, give Him the glory. . . . If He has work for you here—I mean in Africa—He will fit you for it in His own time and bring it to your hand. Just serve Him *where* you are . . . [and] don't trouble about the *sphere*. If He is to call you to this work, don't wonder if He gives you severe discipline and keeps you long waiting. I have passed through deeper waters and darker valleys, than you are aware of. But down there I learned to *trust him*. I feel Humbled at your opinion of me, for before God I feel that it is so different from true.[20]

Mary then discussed Maggie's concern with a "new" doctrine. "My dear, you are troubling yourself about what every *Free Churchman* knows

18. Ibid., September 11, 1913.
19. Ibid., September 6, 1907.
20. MS to "Maggie," April 17, 1877.

and *believes*. If you have seen any translation of the English Bible into another language, you will see that the original Greek word "hades" is given. Whatever *we like*, we *must* take the Testament as *it is*, and this word signifying a place is there assuredly. . . . "Hades" means simply the "Place of the Dead". Hades, is in my opinion, not the place where the *Spirit* waits, but the place where the *Body* waits for the resurrection morning."

From that point, Slessor's long letter expounds on Psalms, 1 and 2 Peter, and Revelation. She finishes with words to reassure the anxious girl.

> And Maggie, Would He who was the friend of the fallen woman, Who wept at the grave of a friend when a sister's tears were before Him, Who is like us in all our human yearnings and longings, Would He shut you out in the cold? Mr. Smith [a Dundee mission-work friend] tells me of this Heresy you speak of. But God reigneth, not Mr. Short. Poor man! He will soon be in the dust. But the word of the Lord standeth *sure*.[21]

In an 1878 letter to former Dundee co-worker David Stewart, Mary was uncertain about his spiritual beliefs, so she concluded with a plea: "And if I never see you here, will you let it be said, that we shall see each other only as *separated* friends at the great day? Surely not! There is only one Saviour. He is waiting to be gracious *now*. Pleading with *you*. Oh, if you have not yet settled the palaver that lies between you and Him, do so *at once*. Then here, or hereafter, all shall be well."[22]

PRAYER

Mary Slessor considered prayer the foundation for all she did; she believed it was responsible for any success. Before she left Scotland on her final furlough in 1907, she said the mission needed a "host" of men and women in order to "take possession" of any new area "for Christ." The problem with the home church, she declared, was that it didn't pray enough. "If we had a praying people we would have a missionary Church and a victorious Church. The Church will have to set times apart just for praying, and keep on." The need, she said, was for "something more than money and a kneeling prayer of a few minutes twice daily."[23]

21. Ibid. Mr. Short and his supposed heresy are unknown.
22. MS to David Stewart, December 10, 1878.
23. WMM, November 1907, 280.

Mary asked Charles Partridge's father, "Do you think we thank God enough for and use enough the ministry of privilege in intercession? I think not."[24] And she advised the younger Partridge (twenty-four years her junior) to pray, saying it would "unravel lots of things that are tangled. . . . I've *tried it* for as long as you have lived, so *I know*."[25]

When Charlotte Crawford told Mary of an answer to prayer for the salvation of family members, Slessor confessed that she did not see the same answer to her prayers for her own father. "But I *know* my Father and Lord so well," she wrote, "I can leave it with Him for the lower fatherhood."[26]

Mary once wrote, "I do not like that petition in the Prayer Book, *From sudden death, good Lord deliver us*. I never could pray it. It is surely far better to see Him at once without pain of parting or physical debility. . . . Don't talk about the cold hand of death—it is the hand of Christ."[27]

Slessor often asked others to pray for her. In a letter to William Stevenson, secretary of the Women's Foreign Mission Society, she wrote, "I have been thinking much about the Christian's armour, and the shoes have come home to me more than ever before. Just now, I am the feet of the Church, as it were, and I am to go with shoes of peace. What a preparation for the Government that is—to pave the transition roads with Gospel peace! Pray that I may have both patience and tact, and that I may be able to lift the whole question up to a higher than a political plane."[28]

On Christmas day 1910, Slessor wrote to Crawford in Scotland, "I need not say pray for us. I know you will. Pray that all my bairns be *converted*. Born again. More and more I am feeling that nothing short of this is much good."[29] At another time she emphasized that "the grand dynamic is prayer."[30]

24. MS to CP, March 10, 1908.
25. Ibid., MS to CP, August 14, 1908.
26. MS to Crawford, November 19, 1909.
27. Livingstone, Mary Slessor, 324.
28. WMM, January 1906, 20.
29. MS to Crawford, December 25, 1910.
30. Ibid., September 11, 1913.

FAMILY MATTERS

Mary practiced her faith at home with her bairns. It was not just a matter of teaching and preaching outside the home or seeking prayer for herself or the mission or the church in general. Missionary Mina Amess told how Mary "dearly loved" her bairns and reported, "When at prayers with her children, she would sometimes play a tambourine at the singing, and if the bairns were half asleep it struck their curly heads instead of her elbow."[31] She expanded on the difference between Slessor's interaction with her children and with others. "In the morning one would hear evildoers getting hotly lectured for their 'fashions,' but evenings at home were a different story."[32]

Another missionary who visited Slessor described the scene for evening prayers in Mary's household. They sang an Efik hymn Mary had written, the visitor said. Then she quizzed the children on the morning's lesson "and gave them a homely but powerful address." The writer said, "She prayed, and the children bowed down their heads till they rested upon the ground. They next chanted the 'amen,' and half-chanted the Lord's Prayer, and finished with what she called 'one of the new fanciful English hymns.' . . . Then very simply and sweetly she commended us all to the Father's love and care."[33]

The following episode brings to mind the report of Hope Waddell Training Institution principal, J. K. McGregor Slessor's report on Mary's life: "[She said,] 'He has promised that we can take up serpents, why should I be afraid of leopards?' So along the track she walked, praying, 'O God of Daniel, shut their mouths.'"[34]

Adopted son Dan wrote of one time when they were walking several miles to their home after dark:

> On we walked, our light cutting far into the thick darkness around. "Dannie, my son," she said turning to me, "never allow weakness to overpower you. I know that these roads are full of danger, but if I were to admit weakness the sooner I had pack and return to Aberdeen. My God is ever present with me, His strength and power greater than man's . . . [and] if the danger had to come it would

31. Livingstone, Mary Slessor, 236.
32. Ibid., 237.
33. Ibid., 183.
34. Record, 1913, 373.

> come all the same." She was leaning heavily on my shoulders, with her one arm resting on Maggie, suddenly she turned on Maggie. "Child," she said, "you behave as having seen seven ghosts," and she herself burst into a brisk laugh. But there it was, just as we turned the corner, as if the animal had wondered who had dared so care-free to trespass in his domain, there stood a wild animal. . . . Ma, who just a wee while before looked like a sick woman, suddenly stood erect and bending down picked up a fair size of stone, hurled it at the beast and pressed forward herself to the attack. Poor kiddies, we all shouted, panicky, with mingled tears and awe. . . . We all rushed forward, for what we could hardly say. Turning round she rebuked us for attempting to follow. "Go back, you little ones," she screamed, and with bare fists she dashed on; the excited animal instantly made off showing not a little sign of its own fear.[35]

Dan Slessor also wrote of his mother's devotional life after the children were cared for and tucked into bed at night.

> Even at that late hour, she would remain awake on bed, repeating a psalm, a verse or some of her beloved songs. . . . In the moonlight nights, she would remain . . . gazing straight into the moon and calling for God for help, strength, courage and resource. At these moments you can imagine Ma as far away from her surroundings, we used to look upon her then as a Spirit, her eyes steadfastly fixed above, her blue eyes gazing intently, her lips moving gently as she communes with her Heavenly Father. At times, we could not hide our anxiety and fears, often times Jane would think Ma gone; with tears she would approach her, call gently, "Ma, are you here with us?" Slowly and gently she would turn her head, smile affably, and admonish her sternly, "Woman," she would say, "knowest thou not that I commune with my Father?" At that moment the light would return to our eyes, our hearts beat more normally, and we are sure our Ma is still with us.[36]

Late in her life, Mary expressed her fears for her children to Charles Partridge, Sr. "Unrest and doubt and pessimism" seemed to permeate life at home in Britain. "Does it point to our Lord's near approach in the Parousia [second coming of Christ]?" Her feelings? "I think so and I hope so!" she wrote. "My only draw back, is, that I fear my bairns are not *all* ready, and what if we were separated! But they are His, and He surely has

35. D. Slessor to Hart, November 30, 1948.

36. Ibid.

infinitely more interest and love, in and for them than I have, so He will do *all things* well, for us all. He will not throw back the children given Him, in loving trust. A Gentleman of the World would not do that."[37]

A year before she died, Mary wrote in her diary, "*Grand news* from Ikot Ekpene, David & Family to be baptized next month. Marion's sudden and very serious sickness [David and Mary's daughter] has been the means of this. Had just written begging them to come to Christ and bring their babies with them and this is the glorious reply. May it be indeed for ever, and to the glory of God."[38]

MINISTRY TO THE DISTRICT COMMISSIONER

Mary Slessor did not buttonhole people to make life changes, but she did not hesitate to make the gospel plain when she knew a person was not Christian or when she was unsure of their beliefs.

Charles Partridge, the agnostic, was not exempt from Mary's proddings. Her usually pages-long letters sometimes included admonishment to follow God. But she mostly spoke of mutual friends and acquaintances—missionaries, Africans, and other Europeans—and news of all sorts concerning mission work, personal health or experiences, government actions, and changes or discord among African peoples.

On Christmas 1905, Slessor thanked Partridge for his kindness and friendship during his first year in Calabar. She concluded with a restrained "God bless and guide and keep you through all the years on before."[39] Two months later, Mary's conclusion was a bit more emphatic; "I pray God to bless you and to *satisfy* you with *Himself*," she wrote. "*It is a* Grand *Reality* this *personal* relationship through Christ."[40]

By the time she had known and corresponded with Partridge for nearly two years, the missionary felt more at home discussing the matter of his faith in greater detail. She wrote,

> Now don't be angry when I call your attention to a way which I have *proved often* and which it is well worth your while trying. It is an old fact and promise given in the Old Book which professes to be more than a human document. It says "I am the Lord Who

37. MS to CP Sr., June 7, 1913.
38. MS Diary, January 20, 1914.
39. MS to CP, December 25, 1905.
40. Ibid., February 24, 1906.

> Healeth Thee", and centuries later, the "Son of Man" verified the same fact and promise, and has been doing it still every where and at every time, where and when He found a believing heart. *Try it.* I am always asking Him to do this for you and more. This is of course between ourselves, but I'm serious.[41]

Witnessing to her faith and urging it upon others may have been a high priority in her mind, but in practice only about ten percent of Slessor's approximately eighty letters to Charles Partridge recommended or urged a commitment from her favorite District Commissioner. Most letters simply asked God to bless, and to keep, heal, strengthen, or guide him. She seemed to play the wiseacre when she wrote, "May you be kept in health and optimism and in God's Keeping! You renegade!"[42] And though the years rolled on, Slessor did not give up. She wrote to Partridge in 1912: "I often remember you in my prayers, and though you may laugh, *I believe* in it."[43]

In her final letter to Partridge, Mary wrote, "This is Christmas Morning, and I must wish you—out loud with my voice—a very happy Christmas and a very Good New Year. God can carry it all to you and give you all I wish, without any interval for Telegraph or Post, *and He Will.* May 1915 be the best year you have yet known."[44]

It is difficult to separate the question of faith from a life so imbued with it. Still, a study of Mary's belief system and lifestyle offers useful insights and reveals much about her character. There can be no doubt that Mary Slessor's faith was deep and genuine.

41. Ibid., October 25, 1907.
42. Ibid., May 9, 1909.
43. Ibid., December 26, 1912.
44. Ibid., December 25, 1914.

17

Ikpe and Nkana

> Her courage and independence often alarmed her senior colleagues. . . . Miss Slessor became more and more the liaison between [native peoples] and the Government which was coming into being. . . . "Settled" is not a word that ever applied to Miss Slessor.
>
> —R. M. Macdonald, 1964[1]

MARY WAS TIRED. SHE was sick. She was homesick. *The Women's Missionary Magazine* published her thoughts of home.

> The sun is so brilliantly bright that last time I raised my head I felt quite giddy, so I shut my eyes for a bit, and have gone over all your homes, and the lane up to the Tweed, and the road far out that we went for the Sabbath school trip to Sandyknowe, then up the road towards Newtown, past the church and manse, the houses and shops under the railway bridge, and up by the lovely road, round by the Eildons to Bowden, each farmhouse and each garden standing out separately, and it has been such a blink that it has made a feeling like home-sickness. I wish I could get just a fortnight, or even a week-end to realize it, and to grip each hand, and look into each face, and to hear the dear homeland language, and to have an English service with the congregation singing a psalm. . . . Just a wee blink of home and a home Sabbath!
>
> But though the tears are coming at the thought, you are not to think for one moment, that I would take the offer, even though it was given me! A thousand times "No." I feel too grateful to God for His wonderful condescension in letting me have the privilege of ministering to those around me here, who otherwise would have no one to guide their worship or teach them. . . . I tell you, dear

1. Macdonald, "Mary Slessor."

> friends, I would not, for all the weight of responsibility, and the feeling of my unfitness, change places with the happiest and the mightiest on earth.[2]

Groups of young men came occasionally to Use to consult with their admired counselor. When was she coming to Ikpe? They wanted to know. They needed a teacher. When Mary decided it was hopeless to think the Mission would send someone to help her at Use, she began making the long trip (usually lasting a day-and-a-half, most of it by canoe) between the two towns. Once Martha Peacock accompanied her. Another time, Mr. and Mrs. Macgregor went along.

Even before the end of 1909, before she could see her way to open a station at Ikpe, Slessor wrote to Charles Partridge, "I do believe that I am doing Ikpe and Use good, by giving them that which takes away the hunger of the Spirit and gives them a definite 'tangible' Helper and hope and life. So there!!!"[3] A group of Christians were already meeting at Ikpe and a few miles away at Nkana. They had even built a church. Mary told Charlotte Crawford, "They are not well grounded in the faith . . . but they have fruit, and they are in dead earnest and have borne persecution." Several were "soundly converted," she wrote, "and among them are the best human material there is in the place."[4]

By October 1910 Slessor and her entourage had a temporary place to live at Ikpe. They stayed in two rooms at the church. They were "very comfortable, but rather cramped," she wrote; but . . . "a teeming crowd pass and repass all the day long, and on market day it is simply sickening in the heat. The noise and the smells are about enough to turn one over."[5]

"An uproar of fighting" outside interrupted a worship service one day in November. "While I had intended to be engaged in the worship of God," Mary wrote, "I had to take hold of this ticklish case of two languages," an affair that took four hours. The result?

> The two parties who an hour or two previously were at each other's throats, [shook] hands. When I was leaving, amid the cheers and laughter to both sides, the old chief rose and said, "Please, Ma"—holding out both hands for mine, which I most willingly gave him;

2. *WMM*, March 1910, 66–67.
3. MS to CP, October 15, 1909.
4. MS to Crawford, December 25, 1910.
5. MS to CP, December 22, 1910.

> and they rose as one man and caught my fingers Aro fashion and twirled them with their salaams. So if I lost the orthodox service, perhaps it was meant, so that some who are not yet willing to listen to the Gospel may be won to do so.[6]

Slessor was not happy with the "low-lying" land she was given for the Ikpe house, but she loved the palm trees and watching the monkeys play.[7] She confessed that the people were not all "desirous of the gospel." She wrote, "They want and have my help in other ways, and the security and safety of having me there, and they want their children to learn English in order to compete with the other tribes who are going in for government service. . . . But it can be the means to an end, and by this open door, we can get in the gospel wedge, which *alone* can help or lift up any people."[8]

Mary wrote to Crawford at the end of the year, when she returned to Use, about how busy she was with humdrum chores and commented, echoing David Livingstone's opinion, "Not much evangel there? Eh? Well! It is all for His Dear sake, as I am His, and all my work is His."[9]

She had promised to divide her time between Use and Ikpe, as well as trying to meet the needs of the other villages that sought her help. "The [District Commissioner] has said he will help me to make a cycling road to Nkana from Ikpe," she wrote, "so that I may be better able to take it on."[10] She explained to the folks back home, "I came here to make a home [at Use] for the bairns at Christmas, and also to see my dear people . . . [and] to get more building material. . . . [Ikpe] is far up, and very isolated, and visitors will need accommodation."[11]

Mary spoke highly of the chiefs and people of Ikpe for their help in building her house there. The shell, at least, was nearly finished by Christmas. "How these people have worked!" she exclaimed.

> Never did I have such material for building provided before, not one single inferior stick in the lot, and there are loads of stuff left over for out houses. We have got a hill about seven minutes from the Market Place, away from the dirt and noise, and we have a spring of good water inside the grounds. We will land at the upper

6. *Record*, 1911, 169, quoting MS letter of November 7, 1910.
7. Livingstone, *Mary Slessor*, 268.
8. MS to Crawford, December 25 and 28, 1910.
9. MS to CP, December 28, 1910.
10. Ibid., December 25, 1910.
11. *WMM*, March 1911, 66, quoting MS letter of December 1910.

> beach. It is always free from mud, that road, but is a bit farther on the river. I don't know whether I can get anyone to take over Use. . . . A new person could hardly take up this town, they are so heathenish, so brutish even, a novice would find it more than he could hold onto; besides, he would never get to know things under the surface. And then there is a Church and a hungry clamourous people at [nearby] Nkana, and ever so many other places want supply. So I must get the roads cleaned and use my cycle among them till the spade work is done, when some one can take it up.[12]

The house itself was the largest and most expensive she had ever built (so large that she needed a hundred more sheets of iron than she expected),[13] but Slessor reasoned, "It is far out of the way, so every comfort that can minimize the loneliness and conserve the health . . . is good." When someone else finally came to serve at Ikpe, and when visitors came, it would be "more cozy and homelike for them," Slessor wrote. Again she praised the workers and workmanship, and marveled that it had been accomplished in two weeks, once the work began.

Slessor and her family had spent much time living in less than ideal accommodations—small mud houses and cramped quarters. But as she looked forward to receiving visitors at Ikpe and to the day she could hand the station over to someone else, Mary insisted, "It would be wrong to insist on mud-huts for a nervous or aesthetic person."[14]

On Christmas Eve 1910, Slessor and her children left Ikpe at 6:30 a.m., traveled all night in a canoe and reached Use just before 6:00 a.m. Christmas morning. Daughters Mary, Alice, and son-in-law David gave the family a warm reception. They "heard the canoe boys singing and the drums" and met them as they reached the beach.

"I have done the thing now," she wrote to *The Women's Missionary Magazine*, "and am committed to it. The site is cleared for the Ikpe Mission House, and the first fifty sheets of corrugated iron have gone up. I am in the dark on many points, but my mind is in perfect peace, that God will work and carry it through, for the Pillar leads."[15]

12. MS to CP, December 22, 1910.
13. *WMM*, March 1911, 66, quoting MS letter of December 1910.
14. Livingstone, *Mary Slessor*, 321.
15. *WMM*, January 1911.

HEALTH

Mary's health continued to be a problem. She wrote to Partridge In February 1910, "I still have this gouty Calabar swelling and can't hold the pen. My thumb is so sore."[16] The following month she wrote of the recurrence of boils on her head and neck. She had been "quite blind" for some time, but was improved to the point that she expected to be back on her bicycle "in a couple of days."[17]

In mid-May, Slessor suffered the vomiting episode that landed her in the Mary Slessor Hospital at Itu, where Dr. and Mrs. Robertson nursed her. She owed her life to them, she said, but she was going home to Use in two more days, "so I can have Sabbath with my people." An unexpected benefit from this illness was that Provincial Commissioner Bedwell ordered repairs to Mary's house at Use, plus installation of a "spout" to carry rainwater to a water tank the Mission had sent earlier. The improvements would make it easier on the children, she said, because they carried the water. She also knew rainwater was less likely to be contaminated. Mary's final shot to Partridge was, "I have a filter in mind, so don't preach!"[18] These words came from the woman who earlier exclaimed, "Filters weren't created; they were an afterthought."[19]

Mary praised the new doctor at Itu. William Hitchcock arrived in April 1911. He was "most kind," she wrote, and "his fame is spreading every day," though she thought he was being "nearly killed by hospital work."[20] She told Partridge that Hitchcock was "a man of culture, of fine caliber, and one of the most excellent and enthusiastic Surgeons and Physicians I have ever met." Besides that, Mary was impressed that Hitchcock was familiar with the name of Charles Partridge and his home in England.[21]

The good doctor prohibited Slessor from attending church in June; he told her she should not think she was well enough to do anything. Mary confessed in her diary that she went anyway. She was "feeling able," she wrote, "so took the privilege of preaching the blessed Gospel."[22] A week

16. MS to CP, February 3, 1910.
17. MS to CP, March 3, 1910.
18. Ibid., June 23, 1910. See also *Record* 1911, 168.
19. Livingstone, *Mary Slessor*, 236.
20. MS Diary, April 15, June 7, 1911.
21. MS to CP, September 4, 1911.
22. MS Diary, June 21, 23, 1911.

later, things were not good. "Dr. sent me back to bed with more stringent rule than ever. Dare not rise. Have to eat meat. Sent a big Fowl up late evening with directions as to cooking, etc. Very stern." The next day, "Dr. again examined very carefully, better pleased, but very stringent rule. Lie full length and *perfect rest*. Changed medicine. . . . What a deal of trouble he takes." On July 4, Hitchcock sent another chicken, and the next day, Mary wrote, "Of course *to the Dr. my health is the only thing*, but I can't get rest for body while my mind is torn about things. *He is vexed and I am vexed at vexing him*."[23]

For his part, Dr. Hitchcock knew Mary's diet was poor, and when she demanded to know why he sent a chicken, he retorted, "Because it could not come by itself." He did not approve of her excursions from Use to Ikpe when she was ill. "I only stopped her," the doctor said, "by threatening to close all work at Itu and follow her. This was effectual, and since then she has been amenable. She has been really very ill—it is her heart, and I am obliged to see her every day." He expanded on his concern: "She has only a native house—the floor is of beaten earth, the walls of clay, the windows are bits of absent wall. . . . I am glad she is improving, but she is so frightfully headstrong."[24] Fortunately for Mary, Dr. Hitchcock had a will as strong as hers.

Hitchcock wrote to his mother about the well-known missionary. "Often her wit flashes out and splendid discernment shows itself. She is quite a small woman—fair hair, clear complexion, exceedingly vivacious, an excellent conversationalist. . . . But what a fine woman she is, with a magnificent brain."[25]

In September, Slessor wrote to Partridge about having to rebuild her Use house. She believed it caused the "overstrain" of her heart, anemia and fevers. "I'm forbidden my cycle . . . and I'm MAD over it," she wrote, "but [the doctor] says it is only for a time."[26] During that period of weakness, Slessor wrote that she "had to do things in a silly soft sort of way. . . . The service in Church seemed unreal almost," she wrote, "when sitting on a table all the time, and school work never seemed thorough when done on a sofa." Her people at Use came to her own verandah, she confessed, so

23. Ibid,, June 30, July 1, 4, 5, 1911.

24. Christian and Plummer, *Redhead*, 174.

25. Ibid..

26. MS to CP, September 4, 1911.

she would not have to walk to meetings.[27] Before the end of the year, Mary was feeling "very much better." She didn't know whether to attribute this to the doctor's ministrations or to her vomiting that "cleared up" the "bile," but she felt better than she had for two months, "and the appetite which was gone so long is splendid."[28]

Earlier in this year of heart trouble, fevers, and other illnesses, Slessor made one of her puzzling statements about her health in a letter from Use to Charles Partridge: "I was on the roof all day yesterday and today have been vomiting Bile, so am sitting quiet, for I've not slept the last two nights, and the Ikpe Fatigue is not gone yet. But I'm very, very fit."[29] In the same letter, she asked her friend a question she had asked a few years before. When would his next book be published? Mary advised him to write about the land and the people but warned him again not to "meddle with Christianity. You've no experience there." Then she assured him that her "halo" was getting grayer, "but no boils live this year on my head." And her children, she added, "often ask if Mr. Partridge is never coming back. SO DO I!"

A QUESTION OF ATTITUDES

Mary's attitude toward other faiths was what one might expect from an evangelical protestant of her era (and in later years, in many instances). In 1903 Roman Catholic mission work began in Calabar. She said that year, "If we do not look ahead, the Roman Catholics will be hemming us in and leaving us far behind. Their school is full on my old site at Old Town, and the sisters have opened a large sewing-class right in Duke Town."[30]

She added, "The thought that all that is holiest in the Church, should have been shed to create an opening for that corrupt body makes me ill. . . . Oh, if I were able to go or send even a few of my bairns just to take hold. The country is far from being at rest, but if the Roman Catholics can go so can I. . . . There is a great future for Nigeria; if only I were young again and had money!"[31] In spite of such pronouncements, Slessor had

27. MS to Crawford, March 23, 1912.

28. MS Diary, December 23, 1911.

29. MS to CP, 12 April 1911.

30. *Record*, 1903, 455.

31. Livingstone, *Mary Slessor*, 196.

a habit of fitting folks who differed with her theologically into what she considered God's scheme of things.

In 1905, Slessor reported in a more moderate tone to *The Record*. "It is time we were bestirring ourselves to choose a site or sites for the taking hold of these hordes of people, else the Roman Catholics will be before us, or any one the government may find willing to guide and teach the natives. And justly, too, as we have no right by reason of our past history to keep out those who, but for us, would take the word of life to these peoples."[32] In a burst of ecumenism, Mary also declared that the Mission should keep "an open door for Protestant gospel truth without our ever incurring the blame of transgressing the principle of Christian comity."[33]

She had no trouble separating the Roman Catholic Church from individuals who belonged to it. She wrote to Charles Partridge during her 1907 furlough that a certain woman sent several invitations for Mary to visit. "I shall try to run down there," she wrote. "They are RCs [Roman Catholics] but he is a good man, and has ever been kind to me, and if they don't mind being of a different faith, I am sure I don't, for they and we have one and the same master and saviour."[34] Besides, Mary said, she wanted to pay them back for all their kindness.

"I am sure that her own Church never had a more loyal adherent," British officer T. D. Maxwell wrote about Slessor, "but her outlook on this life—and the next—was never narrow. Her religion was above religions—certainly above religious differences. I have often heard her speak of the faiths and rituals of others, but never without the deepest interest and sympathy."[35]

Mary's ambivalence toward others was also evident in her relationship with native peoples. One missionary told biographer Livingstone that Slessor did not allow a native to sit in her presence. They were to keep a "respectful distance" except when she was nursing them, and she did not shake hands with them. When asked why, Mary's reported comment was, "I live alone." This is in contrast to her frequent close contact with babies and children, the endless arrival of those who needed and received her care,

32. *Record*, 1905, 414, 416.

33. Ibid.

34. MS to CP, October 3, 1907.

35. Livingstone, *Mary Slessor*, 290.

especially in such instances as when she slept with a dead boy in her arms all night[36] and her own report that she "willingly gave" her hands at Ikpe.[37]

Missionaries had little contact with their Muslim neighbors, who were a small minority in southeastern Nigeria. Rev. John Taylor Dean wrote in 1899 that the government had brought a contingent of Hausa soldiers to Calabar, "along with their priests," several years earlier and that Muslim traders soon followed. They had advantages, Dean wrote, because they were a "closely allied race," they lived among the people with a similar lifestyle, and they understood "the natives' way of thinking." The main drawback to their gaining converts, he believed, would be their "opposition to the liquor trade,"[38] (which, of course, the Mission shared). Mary Slessor would have an interesting meeting with at least one Muslim in 1909.

One of the big events of that year had been the marriage of daughter Mary. David was a "young well-educated Anglican" from Lagos, who served as an officer's car driver in the Engineering and Road Department. Young son Dan was fascinated with the new "motor car" and its driver. So was daughter Mary. The couple had a civil marriage before the District Commissioner, then a church wedding performed on October 15 by Alexander Cruickshank, who, Mary wrote, "has been just like a father to us all."[39] Biographer Livingstone wrote of a breakfast at the wedding, cooked by Jean and the bride. The table was decorated with heather from Scotland, and "an aged Mohammedan in white robes and turban, a friend of David's family," sat at the head of the table. "A number of his co-religionists had come to the district, and some even attended 'Ma's' services," according to Livingstone. "This particular man greatly admired [Slessor]." He said, "Only God can make you such a mother and helper to everybody" . . . and on leaving he had taken her hand and bent over and kissed it, and with tears in his eyes invoked a blessing on her. Few expressions of respect from white men had touched her more, though she was half-afraid her feeling was scarcely orthodox."[40]

36. Ibid., 181–83.

37. *Record*, 1911, 169, quoting MS letter of November 7, 1910.

38. *Record*, 1899, 117–19.

39. MS to "My Dear Friend, October 15, 1909.

40. Livingstone, *Mary Slessor*, 258.

The Muslim told Mary, "I knew David's mother before he was born, and I praise God he was led here for a wife."[41]

TOO OLD TO JUDGE?

The fact that Mary was no longer officially a judge did not mean people stopped coming to her to settle questions, just as she had predicted. Assistant District Commissioner E. M. Falk had reason to feel her wrath. She wrote to him from Use on September 1, 1910 in response to one of his rulings:

> I speak what I *know*. I *know Akpap* and know it is a sacred grove and that you meddled with some of the yams at its verge. You have not disproved my statements and cannot. They . . . have never refused for twenty years under any proclamation of mine to clean roads, but have done it without asking when they knew of *my coming* or of the white officers who ever visited them. They are law abiding citizens, whom *I know* to be such for *two decades* back, and as Sir Ralph Moor put them under my charge at first, I do not apologize for receiving them and hearing them. Thanking you for the reply which I did not solicit. I am "*Not*" your obedient servant.[42]

Falk immediately shot a complaint to his superior, District Commissioner R. B. Brooks.

> In view of the lady's age I make no comment on [her letter]. On the other hand I should be glad if you would forward it to the H.P.C. [High Provincial Commissioner] together with this, to point out the extreme difficulty involved in negotiating with her, which is frequently necessary. The facts of this particular matter are simple. I recently visited Akpap, a town on the left bank of the Cross River, and called upon the people to clear the bush path leading into the interior. I camped on a farm clearing close to the town. There were no complaints beyond that the people strongly objected to the idea of clearing the path. However they promised to do so. I left Akpap on the 29th. On Sept. 1st a deputation from the Akpap people came to see me at Itu. They brought a letter from Miss Slessor stating that I had violated a sacred grove at Akpap. I requested the deputation to state any complaint they might have in the presence of two disinterested interpreters and a European Officer. They stated repeatedly that they objected to clear the road and that they had

41. Ibid. See also MS to "My Dear friend" October 16, 1909.

42. MS to Falk, September 1, 1910.

> no other complaint whatsoever. I wrote to Miss Slessor explaining matters and added that it was vexatious for me to receive communications from her showing that she credited information received from Natives which was discreditable to me. I also pointed out to her that her assistance would be most valuable if she would explain to natives coming to see her the object and value of roads, resthouses etc.[43]

Brooks, in turn, wrote to Provincial Commissioner Horace Bedwell. He attached the correspondence between Falk and Slessor and wrote:

> 1. I beg to point out the extreme difficulty of giving any orders to natives who have, and have had any dealings directly or indirectly with Miss Slessor.
>
> 2. It appears that the Natives consider her to be a Court of appeal through which the orders of the Political officer may be evaded; in this case they have misled her by obvious mis-statements.
>
> 3. In the attached letter from Miss Slessor I would venture to point out that AKPAP is the name of a town and also of a society. . . . There is nothing sacred in "AKPAP", but they probably have a grove or Arkai which is the meeting and drinking place of the society, but cannot be classed as sacred. . . .
>
> 4. Regarding the yams alleged to have been "meddled with", these can have no sacred significance, as sacred yams are unknown in the country, though at the "New Yam" season the worthless parts of old yams are offered to their departed ancestors.
>
> 5. For the most part the Groves or Arkai being merely Societies, Groves are of a non-sacred Character.
>
> 6. Will you kindly advise me.[44]

Bedwell sent word back to Brooks that A. D. C. Falk should not "communicate with that lady where it is possible to avoid it." Instead, he must work through the District Commissioner. "All officers concerned," he wrote, "will recognize the necessity of making large allowance for Miss Slessor's unique position and will use all tact they are capable of in dealing with her." Brooks was to forward any complaints Slessor made directly to Bedwell's office. He made a pointed comment: "It must be remembered

43. Falk to Brooks, September 1, 1910.

44. Brooks to Bedwell, September 5, 1910.

that Miss Slessor is becoming an old lady and says and writes many things that on reflection she would withdraw, and she must not, officially speaking, be taken too seriously in this respect."[45]

Bedwell's attitude would be typical of Britons who, not knowing the beliefs and practices of the people, did not recognize or acknowledge the role of "sacred yams" to Africans. Besides, one could not rely on an accurate and complete translation by "disinterested interpreters," who knew quite well what their British employers wanted (or did not want) to hear.

Mary continued to criticize British government men as she saw fit. She wrote in her 1911 diary of a man whom she held in high esteem being held on a trivial charge. "What a pity," she wrote, "there is not some consecutive government cognisance of the citizens who are real assets to the country. . . . What idiots these government officials are sometimes!!"[46] Another diary entry indicated she "had to write a resume of [a certain] case. . . . Sorry to meddle, but government officials are iniquitous sometimes in their methods or want of method and heart."[47]

The following year Slessor wrote unhappily to Partridge that "Falk the German who strained the loyalty of the villagers his last term" was due to return. "Pity Me!!," she begged. She was afraid that if things didn't "better themselves," she would be obliged to remain at Ikpe, staying as far from Falk as possible.[48]

BACK AND FORTH

Government roads, built with the aid of conscripted Nigerians, crisscrossed the land as the new century progressed. Those roads undoubtedly helped Mary Slessor and others push ahead with mission work. In 1910 she was writing of expanding the work at Nkana. She had sent Jean there as a teacher with her Bible and ABC cards. The completion of roads was not all good, however. Mary wrote to Partridge before Christmas,

> I have heard from Mary's husband at Ikot Obon Camp that my room window [at Use] has been broken. [Someone from] Use ran up and told him, but I don't know whether the house is robbed. If it is, it is the first time I have had that experience in all my life among

45. Bedwell to Brooks, September 12, 1910.
46. MS Diary, April 22, 1911.
47. Ibid., May 5.
48. MS to CP, September 4, 1912.

> black folks. That Government Road is a pest House. All sorts of scoundrels from everywhere skulk on it, and nothing is safe. I have sent down Annie's husband, who is up here with me, to see, and to tell [people at] Use to live there till I come back.[49]

Back and forth Slessor went, from Use to Ikpe to Use. The trip up to Ikpe was good on March 15, 1911.

> A splendid passage, boys paddled wonderfully. Water risen a boot bit, current fearfully strong in the narrows. Canoe well packed, boys obliging, only stopped once to eat . . . and they boiled my kettle, and Jean gave me such a lovely cup of tea. . . . Reached Ikpe at 4 o/c. Ran onto a tree, which was covered. Three boys thrown into the water. Paddled back against such a swirling current & got into the canoe. Milk spilt, all thrown over, but noone pitched into the water. . . . Reached helpers, many at beach. Crowds of boys to carry up the stuff. Four head chiefs came to meet us on beach road, never did so before. Was it the smallpox & the little help they got? They never came down the road before. Egbo out all night, screaming, drumming like mad men till daylight. All drunk.[50]

Slessor spent two weeks in Ikpe that trip and was happy to tell of the family's first night in their new house on March 17, 1911. A "terrific wind storm" inaugurated their move. "Shook the house, rattled the iron on roof flapping at gable. One ridge iron lifted one side, & such a rush of rain came in, flinging my dress from a pole where it hung." She lauded the comfortable upstairs room, though. Its "air & light & a timber floor," Mary wrote, made it "just a palace."[51] The following nights also brought severe wind, rain and thunderstorms.

Succeeding days, punctuated with frequent storms, saw much activity at Ikpe. District Commissioner Rising and a doctor vaccinated "200 people at least" against smallpox (which was rampant in the district) during a visit, until they ran out of vaccine. Perhaps because of that visit, Mary received a gift of "paper, cement for my stair slabs, and etc., [and they] are to loan me a filter, as they think the water bad."[52] Meanwhile, Slessor's girls had been carrying sand and pebbles to make cement for the new house. Before the end of March, she said she hoped to "begin

49. Ibid., December 22, 1910.

50. MS Diary, March 15, 1911.

51. Ibid., March 18.

52. Ibid., March 24.

cementing" the next day. The next day, the entry was, "Carrying sand for floor. . . . Alice carrying, Janie digging, and myself leveling floor and laying sand." She wanted to get as much cementing done as possible for the floors of the new house while she was at Ikpe.[53]

On April 10, Slessor made the return trip to Use. She recorded in her diary,

> Current fearfully strong. Dared not paddle among the fallen trees. Got down [to Use] by 5.30. pm., the quickest trip down I've made. Met the trees fallen everywhere. . . . My front window blown half way out of wall and room flooded. Every mat stripped off verandah, & the water broke the mud, which in its fall broke many things. Don't know where & how to begin . . . Iron sheets blown out of verandah to a distance. Mud wreck on all sides. Picture of Forth Bridge & [daughter] Mary's photo spoiled and broken from a fall of sand from the wall.[54]

Slessor wrote to Charlotte Crawford of the high winds of that "tornado season." At Use, she wrote, "we are situated high up and get the full sweep of it since the government Road took away the high trees, so the damage done in our village and Church and my house was very considerable." She went on to tell how "the people insisted on making almost a new house instead of patching it."[55] She wrote in her diary on April 25, "Have laid out a lot of money on this repairing, but think it is economy."[56] So, after months of building at Ikpe, the tired missionary began to rebuild at Use.

Stories circulated of Slessor building, roofing, making cement floors, and repairing. Son Dan Slessor accompanied groups to the home site at Use while their first house was being built, when he was a young boy. He spoke of grass with "edges as sharp as blades," of biting flies, snakes, monkeys, and deer.

Dan wrote of his mother.

> No matter how slack times appeared to be, but Ma would think of something to do—from house building to house thatching, putting a wee bit of putty to a leak in the roof; mending a shaky window, getting mud for a broken wall, hoeing and raking the yard even to going round and pruning trees and shrubs. . . . Even when

53. Ibid., April 7.
54. Ibid., April 10 and 11.
55. MS to Crawford, 23 March 1912.
56. MS Diary, April 25, 1911.

> stricken with fever, she would at least give instructions or sit with a shawl round her shoulders and a rug over her worn legs to watch the work done. . . . She would never leave any work half done. There have been times when working on a wall or thatching, that lanterns have been brought out, but the work must be completed.[57]

In 1948 Dan wrote about his *Ma* to Thomas Hart, who was not only a friend to Mary Slessor but also one of his teachers.

> We had no need for carpenters, masons, etc. Between us we worked as carpenters and mason, builder and designers, as and if required. She would go under the roof and point out where to nail and I would be on top with a hammer and nails and nail the zinc home; all the time she would keep saying "that's the ticket my boy" as each nail went home. There is nothing she had not done, mud making for the mud walls, none of the elders could boast to be a better builder, nor could they think of tying the wattle any stronger than she did. . . . Ma could not tolerate a slow worker, she rather would prefer you stood off than waste her time in a slow progress. She so often took down what [others] had done, to ensure it was properly done [rather than accept volunteer help and worry] that that very portion will soon give way and all her other labours come to naught.[58]

A week after her return to Use in April 1911, Mary wrote of a near disaster, "First thing on sweeping this morning after a sleepless night, was to find the white ants [termites] in millions in the Drawers. God was good to shew me so soon. Very little damage done, but one hour longer & everything would have been destroyed. . . . Whole day airing clothes & cleaning drawers & house, salting holes, etc. Mercifully a sunny day, so the smell of the ants gone down, but can't get them out of frame, which is indented with holes."[59]

Mary was no stranger to hunger. She lived like an African, and when food (or money) was in short supply, she and her family suffered. In April, May and June 1911, she and her family faced that situation again at Use. She wrote in her diary of the poor market, of yams being scarce and expensive, of having "not a penny to buy food with." She sent ink, machine

57. D. Slessor, "Reminiscences."

58. D. Slessor to Hart, November 30, 1948.

59. MS Diary, April 18, 1911.

oil, thread, and other small items to market with the girls to buy food. One day she wrote, "Our food is done. Girls very good over it."[60]

Finally, in November 1911 after an absence of seven months, Dr. Hitchcock allowed Mary to return to Ikpe. There, she wrote, she was "out of the clutches of the dearest and cleverest and most autocratic Mission doctor that ever lived."[61] After she had been there five weeks, a letter intimated her sense of isolation. "I am feeling as if it were a long time since I heard of the world, and yet, I love it (the solitude) and feel so grateful to God for giving me once more the opportunity of telling the gospel story. The House has stood empty the whole long wet season, and it is marvelous how little it has suffered. . . . When these poor solitary shepherdless chiefs from this wilderness came down pleading for the help which seemed impossible, I *could not* let go, and God has sent me back."[62]

The fact that there was no regular mail service to Ikpe heightened her feeling of isolation, but Mary wrote about how much she appreciated the people, who carried her up the hill to church. With that assistance, she was able to "take both services and the Sabbath school twice every Sabbath and the school twice every day."[63]

Rev. J. K. Macgregor attended a Presbyterian Session meeting in Itu and found that Chief Onoyom Iya was a member of the Session—the chief who earlier "went to Miss Slessor, and was shown the way of life by her." Macgregor gave a surprising report: there had been no church members on Enyong Creek in 1906, but by 1911 there were eight self-supporting churches with 891 members on their rolls.[64] At least part of the advance can be laid at the feet of a determined Mary Slessor.

60. MS Diary, April 3, 4, 20 and 22, May 25 and 28, June 26, 1911.

61. Livingstone, *Mary Slessor*, 273.

62. MS to Crawford, December 14, 1911.

63. Ibid.

64. *Record*, 1911, 261.

18

Rest and Honor

> Few women, or men, have served God and man better than Miss Slessor has. Giving up everything, she has, to her surprise, discovered that the path of sacrifice (of which she never thinks) is the path of fame (for which she does not care). Living in the wilds of Africa, where white people are few, she finds that the eyes of many in her own country and the world over are turned on her.
>
> —J. K. Macgregor, 1913[1]

On New Years Day 1912, Mary wrote one of her long letters to Charles Partridge. She told him he wouldn't recognize Ikpe. The chiefs were "more sober, and less quarrelsome," than when Partridge worked in the district, she said, "and the market does not now have bigger or more frequent brawls than that of Itu or Ntan." The people were farming and selling produce, and the town had been cleaned up, much of it moved to higher ground on the beach road, "out of yon pit of black mud." To her regret, the chiefs still were not interested in the Gospel, but they allowed their people to attend her school and worship services. A minor court had opened about five miles away, she wrote, "and all the Chiefs round are members," which had "a very steadying effect" in the District. People came to Slessor from all the surrounding villages (and some from far away), not only with their "palavers and sickness" but also as friends, or out of curiosity, and to ask her advice. It made her heart ache, she confessed, that she could not provide the teachers they wanted.[2]

Concerning "yon pit of black mud," the Mission decided to send two women missionaries to Ikpe if it received a satisfactory medical report

1. *Record*, 1913, 372.
2. MS to CP, January 1, 1912.

on the site. Slessor's esteemed Dr. Hitchcock visited her there in mid-December 1911. "He was afraid about me, and came to see!" Mary wrote. She may not have been aware of the other reason for his visit.

The doctor's report was not good. "The Creek overflowed its banks for four hundred paces on one side and thirty on the other, and the surroundings of the house [were] muddy and damp."[3] Based on the information the doctor provided, the Mission Council banned Ikpe as a station.[4] Mary did not take kindly to this judgment. She had no intention of abandoning her station. In fact, she happily told Partridge of the arrival of a set of stairs that District Commissioner Brooks had just sent from his headquarters at Ikot Ekpene, twenty miles away. He visited Slessor while Dr. Hitchcock was there and was disturbed that she had to climb a ladder to get to her bedroom.

Mary wrote, "The ladder was a real trial to me and not very safe," so she was delighted when Brooks sent her a ready-made staircase. She hoped a carpenter would come soon to install the gift. This was the same Mr. Brooks who had written of the difficulty of getting along with the cranky missionary. Once he met her, though, he was won over. He told her he would send chickens at court price, would take care of her mail, and that she "was to go and occupy the Rest House which is on high land at four or five miles distance" any time she wished. Mary thought Brooks' change of heart may have had something to do with her son-in-law, David, who was his driver and "a great favourite" of Brooks. Or, she wrote, "I am mean enough, or you may call it presumptuous and egotistical enough, to sometimes connect it with a recent tour made by an old D.C. of mine [Partridge], who is now at the top of the tree and who never forgets me."[5]

A CARRIAGE AND OTHER GIFTS

One important piece of news in Mary's New Year's letter told of writing home for a carriage of some sort. The doctor had again forbidden her to ride her bicycle because of her heart condition ("though I'm quite sure I've got over that bit of overstrain, and my heart is as good as ever it was," she assured Partridge). In the carriage she imagined, Mary said she could carry her lunch "and a baby or two inside with me," and it would take

3. Livingstone, *Mary Slessor*, 278.
4. Christie, "Annals," January 1912.
5. MS to CP, January 1, 1912.

just two boys to push it.[6] She didn't like being carried in a hammock. She wrote, "I feel a brute, it seems so selfish to be lying there, while four boys sweat like beasts of burden. To push a little carriage is like skilled labour and no degradation."[7]

"Dan is my hammock," Mary told villagers. Son Dan wrote of helping his mother cross streams. "[Usually] all she needs is for me to go by her side and she would lean on me and wade over." But he carried her at times, too.

> Being of frail body and failing health Ma was not heavy at all to carry, and the villagers used to marvel just how a lad of my age could do it. But I think it was not my little strength . . . but the inspiration in the task and Ma's own faith in the undertaking. She would have been the last soul on earth to belabour anybody, least of all a young lad, but it was all a matter of faith and courage. If it becomes impossible for me to carry her, she would strongly refuse being carried by any of the villagers, no matter how treacherous the brook. Rather she would order all the men to get away, then with her dress tied firmly round her waist, she would walk over with the aid of a stick, but always with Dan nearby in case.[8]

Mary sent her request for a catalog of carriages to her friend, Nora Adam. When the women of Wellington Street Church in Glasgow learned of Mary's need, instead of sending a catalog, they sent the gift of a Cape cart,[9] a carriage that could be pushed by two boys or girls.

When her new means of transportation arrived, Slessor's resolve to stay in Africa strengthened again. She wasn't going home, she wrote. The Cape cart would enable her to cover a lot of territory, and she couldn't resist the opportunity to continue her ministry. The postponed furlough would never happen.

Mary was comforted and encouraged by letters and gifts from home. In August 1912 she wrote to a Mrs. Jamie to thank her for a box she had just received, which included a gift of perfume. "Not one in a thousand at

6. Ibid.

7. Livingstone, *Mary Slessor*, 279.

8. Daniel Slessor, "Reminiscences."

9. MS described a box on wheels. The Cape cart was referred to variously by her as a carriage, a buggy, a rickshaw or a wheel-chair. Biographer Livingstone described it as a basket-chair (*MarySlessor*, 280). It was larger than a modern wheelchair, since she could carry babies and small packages inside. Some Cape carts were larger, pulled by horses or mules, or motorized. (Cadillac even produced one.)

home thinks of the weary hot missionary, with throbbing heat outside and inside, and throbbing head to match, which will not listen to anything," she wrote. "It is so good and so wonderful to get a letter and a parcel from any one who remembers that a missionary is not made of cast iron and that sublimary things are still a very real necessity to her." Mary recalled the washing she got

before church as a child, the bit of perfume on gloves and handkerchief, and the peppermint for sermon time. Her girls had been treated the same, she wrote, except there was no peppermint. She was afraid, Mary confessed, "they thought much more of their perfume than of the sermon." She added, "The first thing I found them telling Annie—our married girl in Town, was "to smell," and she, sniffing, was telling them she had been smelling all the forenoon, and each had to be smelt in turn except Jean, at the church door. You see we are very human and not goody goody at all, though we're the minister's family!!"[10]

Another long letter to Mrs. Jamie from Use Ikot Oku refers to perfume in another package: Customs didn't find all the perfume that time, "and I was dishonest enough not to enlighten them," Mary wrote. "I just lay low . . . [until] in a burst of shame and repentance on seeing their leniency, I sent word of the other two bottles."[11]

When Mary spoke of gifts from home, she remarked that they came with "real Scottish love . . . full of pathos and prayer; the dear love inspired in our strong rugged Scots character by the Holy Ghost and moulded by our beloved Presbyterianism of the olden time."[12] Biographer Livingstone reported that Slessor always sent something from her gift boxes to "Mammy Fuller" in Duke Town. Fuller, a Jamaican who arrived in Calabar in 1858 as a domestic servant, had been there fifty-five years. She was, Mary wrote, "perhaps the best-loved woman in Duke Town. . . . So we all love to share anything with her, and she especially loves a cup of tea."[13]

Charles Partridge rarely failed to send Mary a plum pudding at Christmas, a gift she always looked forward to. Her thank-you letter said the pudding and his Christmas card "have been a great joy to me." It was the first she had heard from him in months, though, and she expressed

10. MS to Mrs. Jamie, ACC6825/15, August 24, 1912.

11. Ibid., August 19, 1913.

12. Livingstone, *Mary Slessor*, 175.

13. Ibid., 312.

her disappointment. "I have been very sore about your long and complete silence," she wrote, "and have often wondered if I had hurt or offended you in any way. I have not many real friends on the Coast. I think I can nearly count them on the fingers of one hand. And when one of these withdraws his countenance, my heart is sorely troubled. There are not so many of this kind that I can afford to lose one."[14]

THE TRIP OF A LIFETIME

Slessor carried on for a while with her new Cape cart, but as her health continued to decline, she realized she needed a furlough to regain her strength. She described herself as "a spluttering candle," and admitted, "I'm lame and feeble and foolish." Her reluctance to leave her work came from the knowledge that there would be no missionary serving Use, Ikpe and their surroundings if she left. A Miss Cook of the Foreign Mission Committee offered to pay all expenses for Mary and daughter Janie to vacation on Grand Canary Island, but Slessor was reluctant to accept such a gift. Other missionaries prodded her to go. She realized she could not afford it herself, so when a box of warm clothes arrived from Scotland, Mary felt God was giving his blessing to the trip. She decided it was her duty to take care of herself as God's servant. The pair sailed from Calabar on October 7, 1912.

Housed at Hotel Santa Catalina on Grand Canary Island, Mary wrote, "I have been carried over at everybody's expense but my own. . . . Everybody up to the hotel servants here have had as Great care of me, as if I were somebody." She was appalled by the expense, she said, but was excited by this "first [vacation] trip in all my life." Slessor wrote to Charlotte Crawford that when the trip began she thought maybe she should keep going all the way home for a three-month furlough. "But the first bit of coolness . . . I got a bad throat and am coughing . . . so that was out of the question." She hoped that Grand Canary would suffice for a furlough. Besides, Mary wrote, "The sunshine and the breezes and the blue expanse of ocean, the gardens, and the atmosphere of love make it like a visit to Paradise."[15]

The Women's Missionary Magazine printed part of a letter Slessor wrote en route back to Calabar in November. The vacation was, she said,

14. MS to CP, December 26, 1912.
15. MS to Crawford, October 27, 1912.

"worth waiting a lifetime for . . . [and] it will ever be a dream of beauty and joy. . . . Thank God with me for all the goodness and tender mercy He has made to pass before me during these last two months." Mary was "greatly benefited," the article said, by her brief vacation. It ended with words of hope: "God grant that in health and strength for many years to come she may be spared to help the people for whom she has lived, and to whom she has brought the Word of Life."[16]

AN IMPORTANT VISITOR

Frederick J. D. Lugard was appointed governor of the Protectorates of Northern and Southern Nigeria in December 1912. (When the Protectorates of Northern and Southern Nigeria were combined to become The Colony and Protectorate of Nigeria effective January 1, 1914, he was named governor-general). Major Edward Lugard wrote in his journal of his famous brother's visit to Calabar. He described their days there: their approach and arrival, the reception, the people, mission work—and Mary Slessor.

> We crossed the Bar in the early morning and steamed up the great Cross River . . . and then up the Calabar River. . . . A tremendous reception awaited the Governor—all shipping was dressed with flags, and the native Chiefs' great canoes came out to salute the Governor in a way that they said had never been done before. I counted some 40 great canoes—many with 30 to 40 paddlers in each—making a brave show and cutting through the water at a great pace.[17]

Major Lugard wrote about the people they met and revealed a typical European attitude of superiority, as well as ignorance of the culture of southeastern Nigeria.

> This parade of native Chiefs was the most wonderfully comic sight I have ever seen in Africa! The very antithesis of the dignified Mohammedan Emirs of Northern Nigeria in their flowing robes with their medieval civilization. Here, on this pagan, cannibal, gin-ridden Coast, is a very different type. . . . One young man was got up in immaculate Bond Street kit but with a tinsel crown on his head! Chiefs in tinsel crowns and Chiefs in top hats—black top

16. *WMM*, January 1913, 372.

17. Lugard, "Journal Jottings," 48–49, Dec. 1912.

> hats, green top hats, and top hats of every colour!—with any fancy garments below—European garments or native garments—or half and half. But the *piece de resistance* was a Chief got up in a kit as a fancy *admiral*, but with a tinsel crown and *labelled* "Chief of Calabar"! It was a *wonderful* sight!—the like of which I have never seen in any part of Africa before!
>
> Then F. [Frederick] was introduced to the Europeans—a great number of officials and traders and missionaries—the latter a *particularly* fine lot here . . . numbering amongst them Miss Slessor, the heroine of the Coast, a woman of 64, who for 37 [36] years has led a life of self-abnegation and heroic devotion to the uplifting of these savages that commands the *enthusiastic* admiration of *all.* But of her more anon. Then we motored up to Government House . . . situated on a charming site some 200 feet above the river. . . . En route F. was greeted by a parade of some 1600 Mission School children—one of whom read an Address, while a tiny girl . . . presented him with a bouquet.[18]

Lugard spent four days in Calabar. Visits, conferences, receptions, and dinner parties filled his days. His brother's first impression was that the Europeans in Calabar appeared to be "such a happy family—seemed to get on so well together—officials and missionaries and traders." (This, of course, was not always true.) The major praised both Scottish Presbyterian and Roman Catholic missionaries and their work.

> The Scotch Missions are the best I have ever seen. . . . [Missionaries Arthur Wilkie at Duke Town and James Macgregor at Hope Waddell Training Institution] and their wives were quite charming—and *very* Scotch. The R.C. Mission under a very delightful and popular Priest . . . with 2 or 3 more Priests (French and Irish)—and the girls school under the three R.C. Sisters (two such fragile, gentle souls), all seemed to be doing splendid work. . . . To me there was an infinite pathos in these lives of devotion. But their work is mild, and they live in comparative comfort, by comparison with that of Miss Slessor. . . . This devoted woman, a woman of great force of character and personality—of great mental and physical power—has become, by reason of the great influence she has achieved over the natives of this part of the country, a great political factor of much value to the Administration. She is, or was, a Judge in a

18. Ibid.

> Native Court, and the reputation of "the good white Ma who lives alone" is a power for good over a wide stretch of country.[19]

Edward Lugard was so taken with Slessor's story and reputation that he sent a request to Secretary of State Harcourt[20] on behalf of his brother asking for the king's "bestowal of some recognition of her great service." He emphasized that the request was confidential and "must not be repeated until the reward appears."

> [There have been] long years of *not* quiet, but fierce, devotion—for they say she is a tornado!—unrecognized and without hope of, or desire for, recognition—in these blatant days of self-advertisement. Her great work has been combating witchcraft and the awful custom of murder of twins (universal in this part of the country), and she has established twin villages and farms, and always has some little black urchins about her. But she has not feared to go under fire to separate warring tribes—and has herself broken trade monopolies—and been a dominant factor in the land! She is a wild woman of the bush—hatless and stocking-less—she donned both for F's arrival. F. was introduced and shook hands and told her he was proud to do so—but she disappeared into the bush next morning, and, to my great disappointment, I got no opportunity of being introduced.[21]

REPORTING

When Slessor was asked for an article about her life, she wrote,

> When one gets into the sixth decade one is on the wrong side of the line, and the pace does not slacken on the mission field, it needs husbanding of odd moments to get the tale put in at all. If I were sitting down in Edinburgh and a kindred spirit asked me questions, I might recall the dear fellow-labourers and the days in Calabar when it wasn't a picnic. White and black, there were giants in those days . . . but to sit down and conjure it all up and then write it out, makes me feel faint. One cannot do much amidst schoolboys

19. Ibid.

20. Lewis Harcourt was Secretary of State for the Colonies from 1910 to 1915. Port Harcourt was named for him, and he was present when Slessor received her award.

21. Lugard, "Journal Jottings," Dec. 1912 , 51–52.

> and visitors, and sick folks and a household, and through the long sleepless nights which are now my portion.[22]

Mary wrote to Charlotte Crawford, at the urging of her friend Nora Adam, what she hoped would pass for a dreaded report. She began her letter saying, "The very word 'Report' dries up anything at once and makes me stand quite foolishly wondering how it can be done. I'm afraid my mind is not a trained or methodical machine, it only works as it chooses, and then I have not an elaborate system or method of work. It is just any and every thing as it comes. Of course the school and church services are the same always, but they don't fill up the time, and the other things are not classifyable."[23]

At the end of the fourteen-page missive, she remarked, "For all I have written I don't seem to have told you any thing of any consequence. But as I said, I don't know how to write a Report. If you can pick out any thing that will suit you, I shall be glad, though I much doubt it."

A growing number of people were studying for church membership at Ikpe, but most of them, Slessor said, "saw no hope of full membership in view, as the wives betrothed to them by their parents were either not willing to become Christians and go into Christian marriage, or their parents were not favourable to their giving up girls thus betrothed to them, telling them they must stick to their bargain, church or no church." Mary was also worried that "unworthy women and men may make Church membership a mere excuse for breaking Home ties and giving licence to vice. So I am not in a hurry to give in to the lads or to blame the chiefs and parents, even if it keep the Communion Roll low in numbers."[24] She also wanted church readers "to be as perfect as possible, as the half taught are the down drag and the big danger of these infant congregations, and I shall insist on the Reading of God's Word, with miles less of exhortation than they are accustomed to from the native itinerant."[25]

Meanwhile, Mary was concerned with family matters as well as physical problems. Daughters Alice and Maggie were enrolled at Edgerley Memorial School in Duke Town, in the care of missionary teacher Agnes Siddons Young. Slessor thought highly of Young, who had been in Calabar

22. *Record*, 1915, 59, quoting MS letter of 1914.

23. MS to Crawford, March 23, 1912.

24. Ibid.

25. Ibid.

less than two years. When Agnes wrote that she was returning to Scotland to be married, Mary wrote, "I'm a nasty grudgy mean thing! I'm telling it to myself often and often, for I'm *not* glad you are going. I won't pretend to be. I have felt as if I had somebody all of my very own since you came to Calabar, and yet I feel as [if] I have been cheated and disappointed, because it has been all past longing and hoping to have you in my own place with me for a long spell." Slessor was convinced Agnes would never return to Calabar. "If you could only have spent a week at Ikpe and seen this big town and seen the beauty of our Creek and ——! Bah!!" she wrote. "I'm not feeling well today . . . and the mental atmosphere is wet and gloomy." She went on to express congratulations and blessings on the young teacher, and concluded with "When the journey is over (if not sooner) we shall spend a long eternity in perfect friendship.[26]

Mary's letter expressed a mother's concern, telling Young she hoped the children would be home for a visit soon. "I'm wearied to see them," the tired Ma wrote of her bairns.

In an April 1913 letter to Nora Adam, she included news of an accident the previous month. "A pellet of mud from the motor wheel struck me on the eyeball," she wrote, "but God brought me up again." That misfortune at Ikpe resulted in a serious case of erysipelas of her face, head and eye and put her "just at the valley [of death]." Slessor's letter also bemoaned the fact that her newly repaired glasses had broken again. "You might tell the man that if they won't hold," she quipped, "he might put in a new pair of eyeholes [and] a new face on the old hooks."[27]

In a June update on her eye injury and infection, Mary wrote: "I have not yet got rid of that trouble over my eye. It is so distressing sometimes, though not acutely painful, and so devoid of sensation, that I [thought] sure the movings are worms, and the slight flesh swelling moves about, but yesterday Dr. Parkinson said just what Dr. McKay said at first, that it is the nerves not yet recovered from the erysipelas. Maybe it is so, but its horridly like living things moving about."[28]

Mary mentioned her "small accident" in several letters. Livingstone wrote that Mary was taken by government car from Ikpe to Use after the accident and that she was blind for two weeks. She "suffered acute pain

26. MS to Young, February 24, 1913.

27. MS to Adam, April 21, 1913.

28. MS to McMinn, June 6, 1913.

and heavy fever; but very shame at being ill after so fine a holiday [to Grand Canary] made her get up . . . and she was soon in the midst of her work at Ikpe as if nothing had happened."[29]

Slessor wrote of one 1913 episode of malaria, "Jean says I crawled to bed, perhaps I did, I don't know, but that was one such fever for length and strength as I have not had for years, and it was the first of a few, and my spleen got up again, and I have not known such utter weakness for years. *Three weeks off duty*! And unable to speak or eat or sleep. . . . Mr. McGregor writes, 'God does so much of His work here by bodies half dead but alive in Christ.'"[30]

When Mary was invited to the opening of the new church at Akpap, she wrote, "If I'm on my one end, head upmost, I shall be there."[31] She had not been to Akpap for eight years. She was eager to see "her people," and they were excited at her coming. In June 1913 most of Mary's children went with her to the celebration. "These will be an object lesson [to the people]," she wrote, "and I hope there will be an ingathering and an awakening all over."[32] Having her children there meant a great deal to Mary. "If only Dan and Asuquo had been here we should have been an unbroken family."[33]

Not only did Slessor attend, she also preached a half hour to the four hundred Okoyong who attended the service.[34] "There were as many people outside as were crammed inside the church," she reported, "and everything went off splendidly." She herself was a big draw for the occasion. Even Ma Eme, Mary's "dear old friend and almost sister," visited her, and they talked over old times. To former missionary colleague Janet Wright, back in Edinburgh, she wrote, "I had only one disappointment, so many seemed interested only in me, with no concern for the things of God."[35] Part of that disappointment stemmed from the fact that Ma Eme was still making sacrifices to all the old gods.

29. Livingstone, *Mary Slessor*, 286.

30. MS to Adam, April 21, 1913.

31. MS to McMinn, June 6, 1913.

32. MS to CP, Sr., June 7, 1913.

33. *WMM*, March 1915, 76–77, quoting MS letter of January 25, 1914.

34. Buchan, *Expendable Mary Slessor*, 231.

35. Ibid., 232.

HONOR

The Women's Missionary Magazine published one of many reports of an important event in Mary Slessor's later life.

> The Grand Priory of the Order of the Hospital of St. John of Jerusalem in England was dissolved at the same time as the monasteries [which occurred from 1535 to 1540 under Henry VIII], but was reconstituted in 1827, and was granted a Royal Charter in 1888. The Badge of the Order is a Maltese Cross of white enamel, with a lion and unicorn in alternate angles. King George V. is the Sovereign Head and Patron of the British Order; H.R.H. The Duke of Connaught is the Grand Prior.
>
> Of this ancient and honourable Order, whose present work is entirely devoted to the relief of the sick and suffering, Miss M. M. Slessor, our veteran missionary in Calabar, has been enrolled an Honorary Associate. It is a unique honour to a missionary, but none could have better deserved such recognition.[36]

(The honor was also the only kind of government recognition available to a woman commoner in Britain at the time.) The magazine report continued, "We all unite in offering to Miss Slessor hearty congratulations on receiving this decoration, and we pray that she may be long spared not only to wear the badge of the Order, but to continue that work for the relief of suffering . . . to which she has already given so nobly thirty-six years of her life."[37]

Mary herself had much to say about the embarrassment, the ceremony, the hullabaloo that resulted. To Martha Peacock, who was home on furlough, she wrote,

> Word [came] to come down to receive a mark of honour, which I am ashamed to accept, and though I had known of it for some months, it would never have passed my lips to anyone. I felt so very unworthy. But they would not send it. I had to go for it and was promised that it would be only a few *old old* friends in the Mission House. . . . As it turned out, it was a big thing in the Goldie Hall, Mr Bedwell making the speech and presentation. All the white people who could possibly get from duty were there, those who could not, officers and bankers, etc., came to the house with congratulations. All the nurses, all the Orange Grove school teachers & wives &

36. J. Johnston, "Mary M. Slessor," 4; also e-mail correspondence from Pamela Willis, Curator of the Order of St. John Museum, November 20, 2002.

37. *WMM*, August 1913.

> officers were there. . . . Mr McG[regor] opened with prayer, made a speech of which I heard not a word, then the other thing [the presentation], and with all the ladies either in tears or swallowing hard. It was almost impossible for me to get a word out, but I *did* want to bring in my Master and Lord. Mrs. McG excelled herself in entertaining, and the school was decorated and a tea provided to which all the Europeans and the Creek Town elders were [invited]. . . . Dear Mammy Fuller was there. It ought to have been on her breast, not on mine.[38]

Mary wrote to Charles Partridge, "They would not hear of sending [the medal] up quietly to me, but told me a few old friends would. meet in the Mission House at the Institute. And behold, they made quite a public thing of it. Mr. and Mrs. Bedwell and Mr and Mrs Harcourt were there, and altogether it was quite imposing. . . . I never felt more unworthy, or more small in my own respect than when I was singled out from others who are, and have been working with far better results than mine." She added her appreciation for Partridge's influence in the district, too, saying the foundation he laid made conditions in Calabar more stable.[39]

To Mrs. Jamie in Scotland, Mary repeated her assertion that she "never meant anyone to know" about the award and that "they simply would not send it up surreptitiously." She was "ashamed by the fuss they made and the kind things they said." The honor, Mary wrote, was "an expression of the worth of the work of the Mission with which I have the honour and privilege to serve. O to be worthy in some sense or measure of this 'well done' of the King of Kings."[40]

Back home, notices were effusive. A columnist for *British Weekly* wrote,

> Of that Protectorate [Southern Nigeria] the real founders are the missionaries; and Mary Slessor is now receiving from the British Government some of the tribute due. . . . "An uncrowned queen"? Yes, by deep, pitiful love and service; by strenuous oversight and teaching and homely toil; by intimate knowledge of a people's ways and language such as a scholar might covet; by the "dash" and coolness that win through dangers and mesmerise the barbarian; by the fixed purpose that has become life itself and cannot cease. By all these Mary Slessor, to those who personally know her, stands a

38. MS to Peacock, August 3, 1913.
39. MS to CP, August 13, 1913.
40. MS to Mrs. Jamie, MS6825/15, August 19, 1913.

> genius among women because she has "consecrated" a good Scots head and a vigorous Scots will to the redemption of a people with an absolute contempt for convention and the un-needful. There have been days of criticism; but I expect they are over. They ought to be. When she stands up—unwillingly—to speak of her work, the effect cannot be rendered in any words at my command. The remembrance of a meeting in Aberdeen, during her last furlough, will never leave me. The steady control of the face, the calm intensity of the words, few, yet out of a storehouse and charged with all the force of human need, human desire to meet that need. She told three little stories. A fourth, and some of us would have sobbed aloud. The air was tense with spiritual drama like that of the early Christian days.[41]

Slessor did not waste time enjoying the prestige her award brought. She hurried back to Ikpe. In one of her long I-have-no-news letters to Crawford, she wrote of being transported in a government car as far as the road went. From the end of the road, Mary's girls walked the remaining ten miles, but the government arranged for a hammock and carriers for Slessor on one side of the creek and boys for her Cape cart on the other. She pointed out that the carriers were often British prisoners, and "they never try to run away." She thought it was good for them, as they got "a walk," though they had to carry something. Her girls appreciated it, because they were relieved of carrying things.

Mary said Annie and her husband were on their way to Ikpe, too—walking all thc way from Use. They planned to stay with daughter Mary "at the middle of the journey, for a day or two to rest their limbs and then tackle the last twenty-four miles when rested." Annie's husband was to take over the work at Nkana, five miles away, where Jean had been teaching. Slessor explained that Annie could not travel by canoe and sleep by the road with her seven-week-old baby girl in the rainy weather.[42]

"Well, 'oor kirk' [in Use] was opened at last on Christmas Day [1913]," Mary wrote to the church in Glasgow about the new church.

> Mr. Cruickshank came over on Christmas Eve, and stayed all night at Ikot Obon, and then Miss Peacock, Miss Couper, and he came here. . . . The church was crowded outside and inside, and all quietly but neatly dressed, children and all. Mr. Cruickshank was at his best—he is always that among bairns. . . . The service was hearty

41. Watson, "Mary Mitchell Slessor, August, 1913.

42. MS to Crawford, September 11, 1913.

> and reverent. . . . When the visitors left, our own people held a praise meeting, the women in the house square, and the men on our quiet road, walking up and down like a Salvation Army march, waving occasionally a silk handkerchief.[43]

"The two ladies from Ikot Obon stayed the whole day with me," Slessor wrote, "so it was an unforgettable Christmas."[44]

Mary wrote to Women's Foreign Mission Secretary William Stevenson in February 1914 from Ikpe. She was back "up in the bush," she said, "determined to have another 'try' at some of the big towns which bitterly oppose the entrance of the Gospel, though they are eager for Education for their boys." She refused to open schools without also opening a church. She settled into the government rest house at Odoro Ikpe. She happened to meet a chief she already knew, which made it easier to debate each other.[45]

> At first it was that God's Word would spoil their town and make them all die, then one excuse and another that kept them from receiving teaching, then the truth was blurted out: "You will be letting twins and twin-mothers into our midst to kill us." . . . I told them, when I had them laughing at their own bogeys and fears, to show me the town I had spoiled, going over all the places I've been in, and all of which they know very well . . . and then, when we had threshed out everything . . . the old chief, laughing, said, "Ma, take them all! . . . You young men go and build a House of God, and let everything be done she wants."[46]

Mary assured the chief that God was in no rush for a house. They could talk about a house later, when it wasn't farm season and when they saw that she was teaching the truth. The aging missionary was exhilarated by the hope that "these 'other sheep' are likely to become His flock and His people!" She urged the recipients of her long letter, "Oh, pray hard, all of you Christians, constantly and definitely for those four large towns round here, that now the door is opened some one may be sent to take possession in the 'Name that is above every Name.'"

Slessor began to teach with her usual ABC cards. "I did not dose them with theology," she wrote, "but pointed out the Rubber and Cocoa the

43. *WMM*, April 1914, 93, quoting MS report from Use.

44. *WMM*, March 1915, 76, quoting MS letter to Glasgow January 25, 1914.

45. MS to Stevenson, February 20 and 24, 1914.

46. *WMM*, March 1915, 66–69, quoting MS letter to Glasgow February 12, 1914.

Government had planted all over the grounds." (Cadbury sent a representative to Calabar in 1908 to investigate the possibility of growing cacao there.)[47] The world was moving on . . . and they would need education, she told them. They saw the point, Slessor wrote, "and their sullenness gave way, and they began to ask questions and to chat, till before the end of the week we were chums, and they came every spare hour to get a lesson."[48]

Mary worried about what the District Commissioner would think of her taking over the rest house for more than an overnight stay. "I dared not let [people] think that an officer would be other than delighted with their capitulation," she wrote, when they said she should stay in the rest house until her own place could be built, "so I agreed, and made my confession to the D.C. later on by letter."[49] (In another letter, Mary wrote, "What will the D.C. say? When he finds four women in his place, he will think it is time to draw the line.")[50]

The rest house was no hotel. The Slessor family was "gypsying by the roadside in a mud-house without doors and innocent of windows other than holes in the wall," Mary wrote. She had only Martha Peacock's borrowed cot and her Cape cart for furniture. Other than that, they had little other than the provisions they had carried along. It was kept clean by prisoners, who acted as servants, so she and the family were "in clover." They considered themselves "royally housed" and "the happiest of mortals."[51]

Slessor described the first Sunday worship at Odoro Ikpe as strange and mixed up. It was "unsatisfying to a Coven of order and beauty and the regular ways of the sanctuary," she wrote. "Women were away at their farm, men traveling, girls dancing and singing at a play. But one chief sent a chair, and boys and young men came to the meeting, and later they went into town and met in front of a chief's house. We had a meeting, unconventional," Mary wrote, "but I think not ineffectual." She described the pleasant Odoro Ikpe location. "The road all round and up to the top of the hill is full of beautiful white smooth stones. They are very hard to walk upon, but so clean and homelike, It is just like the sea shore at home, only what should be the sea is a vast expanse . . . of bush held just now

47. MS to CP, April 15, 1908.

48. MS to Stevenson, February 20, 1914.

49. Ibid.

50. MS to "My Dear Chummies," DUNMG, n.d.

51. *WMM*, March 15, 66–69, quoting MS letter to Glasgow February 12, 1914.

nearly all the time in the grey blue grip of the Harmattan Haze. Away on the horizon lies woodland and several tribelets, with the creek valley between. It is the widest outlook I have seen in Calabar."[52]

The road ended at Odoro Ikpe then, mainly because the hill was so steep. "If the Presbytery wants height," she wrote, height which they did not have at Ikpe, "they can have it here in full measure!" Mary thought back to Ikpe and wondered "by what means God will lift off the embargo Dr. Hitchcock put on this large town! It is very pitifully sad," she wrote. "The house is always in wonderfully good order! I am surprised each time at the mud house being so, after such long absences and no fires ever put on."

Ever the dreamer, Slessor came forth with a new plan "born from a fever experience" to cover more territory easily. "One of my fever nights" she wrote, "was taken up with an experience which does not leave me, and which I believe is a suggestion of God to me." She envisioned a car with a missionary driver and mission houses at both Odoro Ikpe and near Ikot Obong. The car could stop at all the villages, and eight or ten workers could visit and return in the car to a station in one day. Next best, she wrote, would be a motorcycle "to take the missionary to the various places without killing himself and sleeping by the roadside." She even suggested that individual members of the churches in Glasgow or Edinburgh could take this on as a financial project, as "a fitting Thank Offering for special mercies received by them."[53]

Roads were already prepared, Slessor wrote.

> Between this station [Use] and Ikpe, there is fifty miles of motor road being kept in repair constantly by Government. Bridges and everything are there. Other roads and heaps of places branch off in three or four directions. New roads are being made to the new coal-fields. This takes us through villages and market towns, not merely crawling up by muddy creek sides, where only a fisherman or a beach house is ever to be seen. I have the great privilege of asking for a run in this car along this road at any time, and in two hours I can do what takes me two days to do in the canoe.[54]

52. MS to Stevenson, February 20, 1914.

53. Ibid.

54. *WMM*, March 1915, 72, quoting MS report of January 25, 1914.

With her health in a precarious state, Mary may have had in mind more than just the beauty of nature when she wrote to Crawford in May 1914.

> I must send a wee wordie of love and tell you to look up and know that . . . the sky grows the more comforting and the more genial and the more glorious as it sets. The morning is magnificent in its dawn and power, the noontide potent in its glory and splendour, but it is in the westering that the fret is soothed and the nerves quietened and the Home Life realised, and in the golden glow, ere He hushes His own to rest in the hour of Holiest, closest, intensest cementings of spirit bonds, "so he giveth His beloved sleep," not necessarily the sleep of death. His promises and revealings are like Himself just equal to our ability to use and appropriate them.[55]

Slessor's diary was no exception to the common practice of recording intimate problems, questions and concerns. She recounted hum-drum daily chores—house repairs, destruction by ants [termites], weather, marketing, disputes, and infirmities; but she also included expressions of faith and praise, in addition to the more prosaic or more dramatic events she related to friends in letters. Mary's 1914 diary reported very frequent bouts of illness—often the debilitating "fever," diarrhea or hemorrhage. She continued to itinerate between her main stations at Use and Ikpe, and she also served a number of other villages. Mary often mentioned the villages and people of Ndot and Ibom in her diary. In July 1914, the "Annals" duly noted that Slessor had built another house, this time at Odoro Ikpe.

Mary was happy with her children around her. When people in Scotland prodded her to come home or fretted about her health or loneliness, she wrote, "I am just surrounded with love. . . . I wake up in the early dusk of the dawn and call [the children], and before I can see to take my Bible, the hot cup of tea is there, and a kiddie to kiss me 'Good-morning' and ask, 'Ma, did you sleep?'"[56]

55. MS to Crawford, May 2, 1914.

56. Livingstone, *Mary Slessor*, 279.

PART SIX

A Legacy

1915 and later

19

Endings

Oyo! Eka mi akpa o! Ma mi akpa o! *My mother is dead! This* wail of the sorrowing has been raised. . . . Ma Slessor is dead. Ma, who knew all about them, their troubles and their trials, is dead. Ma, who as a chief once said to her, is "our father and our mother," is dead. The world is a very empty place, for there is none who understood so well as she.

—Rev. J. K. Macgregor, 1915[1]

MISSIONARY ACCOUNTANT THOMAS HART visited Mary Slessor at Odoro Ikpe the last week in July 1914. He found her "camping out" in the native-style Government Rest House while her own house was being finished. "It was a great experience to sit and listen to Ma's tales of the old killing days, when she was the Peacemaker and the Mother of the people," he wrote. "To get a recountal of her experiences, the plan was to wait until she began herself and listen."[2]

Mary considered a furlough as her health continued to decline. She decided she couldn't leave until someone else arrived to take her place. "If I am able to hold out," she explained, "it does a little to fill the gap; but oh, for a score of young women who would work even for a year, and let a weary body or two get a rest!" She credited the prayers of friends at home with her ability to keep going. "I get down till the weakness seems beyond revival, and get fever," she wrote, "and then 'Jehovah Rophi' [God cures] seems to come as a dear message, and I get up and begin work and go on again in a fashion at which I myself wonder.[3]

1. *Record*, 1915, 107.
2. Hart, "Visiting," July 20–27, 1914.
3. *WMM*, March 1915, 79, quoting MS letter of August 1914.

Slessor continued to beg for women to come to Calabar. She also kept abreast of what was going on back in Britain. At home, militant suffragettes broke windows in their quest for the vote—and spent time in jail. She said coming to Calabar to serve would be better for them than throwing rocks through windows.[4]

WAR COMES TO CALABAR

Britain declared war on Germany on August 4, 1914, following the assassination of Franz Ferdinand of Austria and the subsequent German invasion of Belgium. The reverberations spread rapidly. In Calabar there were rumors of an expected attack by the Cameroon-based German gunboat *Panther*.[5]

The rumor of attack turned out to be false, but Dan Slessor reported that troops were stationed everywhere with artillery, and everyone was nervous. A steam launch returning to Duke Town at night with no lights or signals received an unexpected greeting. According to Dan,

> All of a sudden the army battery fired a warning flare. To the crew this was nice indeed because it illuminated the river and gave them some light . . . [but] at that moment shots hit the vessel from small arms stationed on the Hope Waddell and Treasury ridges. Frightened and not knowing what this sort of reception meant the poor crew plunged into the river and abandoned ship. The ignorant soldiers therefore took the vessel as enemy craft because it defied signals to stop, and the light artillery opened up. . . . Boarding parties immediately left the Marine Beach, with guns pointed, only to find an empty drifting vessel and men in the water shouting for help. . . .
>
> Meanwhile up at Hope Waddell it was hell let loose. The boys were mustered under the command of the Headmaster . . . [and were] marched out. . . . It was decided to let the boys squat in singles on the grass. . . . But [the headmaster] used the wrong expression; he said, "Boys scatter" (meaning or intending that they should not cluster together) and the boys scattered, scrambling into every nook and cleft, and pandemonium was let loose. Some fled into near by farms, bush, etc. and the Missionaries with their wives were left stranded on the lawns! Our Jamaican teachers . . . each had packed his immediate belongings and with wife and children

4. Livingstone, *Mary Slessor*, 322.
5. Christie, "Annals," August 4, 1914.

> made for the nearest safety. . . . You can imagine the various tales that were told the next day as the boys returned in singles or pairs from their hiding places!![6]

The Foreign Mission Secretary's letters to Calabar chronicled the problems that arose as a result of the war. On August 10 he predicted that passenger fares and freight rates would increase. The Elder Dempster line had retracted its sailing schedules, so missionaries could not count on sailing as planned. On August 19 word came that food shipments had been banned, a restriction that was lifted two weeks later.

There were two letters on September 11, one informing Dr. Hitchcock that shipment of "a very large number of drugs has been prohibited," but they were trying to get a special permit. The other expressed the hope that Calabar would not be bombed, noting that it was headquarters for Britain's military forces for Cameroon. The Secretary wrote, "I am afraid you will find it very difficult to apply your minds to your work, but I hope the unrest will soon disappear, and that all your work will continue to prosper."[7]

On December 7 the secretary wrote, "I am sorry the outgoing Missionaries met with so much delay between Lagos and Calabar. I am afraid as long as the war lasts it would be useless protesting against the poor arrangements made by the Elder Dempster Line. We must be thankful that a weekly steamer is run at all."[8]

Thomas Hart recalled that during his July visit to Slessor, she had asked about "any special news in the Reuters telegrams." He told her about the assassination of the Arch-Duke and -Duchess of Austria. When Mary wrote to him in September, she said, "Little did we think when we sat there that the spilling of a drop of blue blood—with the Jesuitical microbe in it too—would send all Europe into bloodshed."[9]

Mary wrote in December that there was "rather hot fighting going on . . . all round our boundaries."

> We have taken the Capital of Cameroons and some five locomotives and two aeroplanes—they say those have been over Calabar unknown to us—and [the Germans] had the railway laid up to 140

6. D. Slessor, "Reminiscences."
7. FMB to Hitchcock, September, 1914.
8. Ibid., December 7, 1914.
9. Hart, "Visiting," July 20–27, 1914.

> miles of ltu . . . and [the British] have not a single gun at Itu. But Our Father was watching over us and the railway is cut and several Germans taken prisoner, and a steamer has taken all their women who were left behind. That fact of leaving their women is a compliment to Britain I think. . . . There are other companies about, only it is hard to find out where in the dense forests that surround us.[10]

The worried missionary confessed to Charles Partridge: "When the first serious *reverses* in Flanders and France came, it shook me so, I thought it was a shock, and for long was so ill, that . . . they carried me [from Odoro Ikpe] to Ikpe, and then brought me here [to Use]." Three months later she was still ill. "But [if] I can hold out till March, and things are not worse at home, I shall probably then take a trip to Scotland, or at least to Canary." After thanking him for his usual Christmas gift of plum puddings and telling him of the great tea party the family had with everyone "jumping about like Crazy things," Slessor went on to describe her feelings of melancholy: "The depression caused by the death of two old friends . . . and *YOUR DEFECTION* [having received no letters from him] has taken a very great part of the rest of life away and made me feel that I do not care very much whether I get over this long illness or not." She was worried, she wrote, "you had let me drop out of your regard and memory, and it pained me exceedingly. Specially since this terrible trouble of German Hatred and *jealousy* has come to involve our Empire and threaten our Home life with unspeakable gloom." But Partridge's letter was better for her, she said, than the medicine she had to take "to help the old machine to run on." She destroyed his letters. "I have to clear out my desk," she wrote, "as one never knows how soon an attack may pick me off, and I don't want to leave anything of personalities lying about for prying eyes."[11]

With the war always on her mind, Mary wrote to Crawford, "There will be few merry Christmasses in Europe this year." In the same letter she told her friend that she had a "big boil" on her side, so bad that she couldn't stand clothing to touch it.[12]

Slessor had already written to Nora Adam (vice-president of the Women's Foreign Mission Committee, in charge of Mary's financial affairs, and one of her confidants): "If I can hold out till winter is over, and if the European situation is any easier, and passage money reduced a bit,

10. MS to Crawford, Dec 24, 1914.
11. MS to CP, December 24, 1914.
12. MS to Crawford, December 24, 1914.

I think it quite necessary for my recovery and for my fellow-workers to take a change and get fresh food and air, so that I may be of some use still to the people who have so few to teach and care for them, and of whose ways and language and palavers it takes a new person so long to get to know."[13]

In a December letter to Adam, Slessor repeated her intention to go home on furlough, saying, "As the weeks pass I grow more and more convinced that it is a precarious hold I have on this life." When winter weather passed in Scotland, and if Wilhelm behaved himself, and if she was spared and able for the voyage, she would follow through with her plans.[14] Almost every letter Mary wrote in the waning months of 1914 contained some variation of "What if I go home in March?" Dan Slessor wrote that he was to accompany his Ma on that furlough. It was already in the plan. Mary wrote a flurry of long letters between Christmas Eve and the end of the year, almost as if she needed to get them done before she was gone for good.

Not all of Mary's Christmas letter to Partridge was sad. She told him he would not recognize Use any more.

> We . . . have a neat Church fenced in and all cleaned, and a big common for the boys of the school and town to play Football. . . . Nice houses, flower gardens, wide paths in the village. The houses built up the hills both sides of the road, and the bush all cleared. The doors of the houses painted, windows and seats in front of the Common, the Church with its small belfry. Everything is beautiful, and they have cleared my Cycle road for a new school, so as to let me have less fatigue. We have a small burying ground now, and it tells its own tale of civilized life.[15]

Thomas Hart visited Mary again on December 27. He preached at Use that Sunday evening, with Dan interpreting, and wondered if it might be Slessor's last Sunday at a worship service.[16] But that was not to be. Mary would keep going as long as she could, even though everyone knew she must be close to her final "home-going."

On December 30 Slessor wrote to a boy and his little sister in Scotland. She thanked them for their gift of money and told how she planned to

13. *Record*, 1915, 106, quoting MS letter to Adam, November 1914.

14. *WMM*, March 1915, 52, quoting MS letter to Adam, December 22, 1914.

15. MS to CP, December 24, 1914.

16. Hart, "Visiting," July 20–27, 1914.

spend it: she would buy two hymnals to use as prizes for schoolgirls. About the war she wrote, "We are not free from the dreadful sorrow which hangs over the European countries." She told of a German found in the forest far up the river and of African soldiers who discovered fifty more Germans. She repeated the tale of rails being laid too close for comfort and the two airplanes. Slessor expressed her astonishment: "Fancy aeroplanes Here! In the heart of an African Jungle??"[17]

Dan Slessor wrote of going home to Use for the holiday season. He found Mary changed.

> Her bonnie face took quite a different hue, the veins stood out clearly on her face and arms; her eyes were sunken and the knuckles all over her hands showed out like rough uncut stones. Her blue eyes had lost their lustre and without her false teeth her jaws hanged down leaving a little projecting mouth.
>
> She had known I was arriving that afternoon and so she sat out on the door step, with legs crossed, staring down the drive. . . . I saw Ma and burst into tears, she was very pale and very ill, but she refused to see the doctor. No, she would say, it is not a matter for the doctor. I am an old woman now, my task is over and I must go to my Maker.[18]

Mary lay muttering as she suffered from malaria and dysentery. Often the family gathered around her, "hopeless, helpless and in tears." When Janie asked permission for all her children to stay with her through the night, the failing missionary refused. "Dan will be enough for me, thank you; you Jane will disturb me, and Alice will give me the jumps, and she would smile and look up bringing a cheer to all. Feeding became difficult; all she could take was barley soup, water and fruits, and all three were in abundance. The villagers came in with bags of oranges and bowls of eggs, chickens and anything that was thought worth while."[19]

When it was time for Dan to return to school, he was reluctant to go. Janie suggested he stay at Use, but Mary wouldn't hear of it. His education must not suffer, she decreed. So he returned to Hope Waddell Training Institution the first week in January.

On Sunday, January 3, 1915, Mary wrote to Nora Adam what may have been her last letter. The ailing missionary still worried about the war,

17. MS to Master Ian and Mrs. Crummey, December 30, 1914.

18. D. Slessor, "Reminiscences."

19. Ibid.

and that may have influenced her sermon that day. "For the first time I have definitely told my people the lines on which we look at prophecy regarding the last times, and it has been a solemn day," she wrote. Her texts were taken from Exodus, 1 Peter, 1 Timothy and Romans 13, "giving our duties as citizens and Christians, and Christ's discourse on Mount Olivet regarding the last days . . . leaving the Holy Ghost to draw the lesson of God's hand in all world history."[20] In spite of that somber note, Mary added a note about her little granddaughter. "Annie's wee girlie is the sweetest pet, and imitates everything and everybody," she wrote. "She runs about in church, and will point to me during the service and call to me. Yet I *can't* say, don't bring her. There should be room in our Father's House even for the babies."[21]

A Pioneer Dies

On Friday, January 8, Mary had visitors at Use and seemed well; the next day she was down with fever; she was better on Sunday and conducted church services again—determined, as usual, to fulfill her duties to God as she saw them. *The Record* reported, "On Monday [Mary] was suffering acutely from diarrhea and vomiting. Miss Peacock went down to Use [from Ikot Obong], and Dr. Robertson went up from Itu. By the use of ice . . . and by medicines, he was able to give her much relief. . . . By Tuesday afternoon she seemed better, but during the night Miss Peacock saw a change and sent for Dr. Robertson. . . . He went immediately, arriving shortly after 3 a.m. [Wednesday, January 13], but at 2.45 she had passed away."[22]

At some time during the evening of January 12, bystanders heard Mary's whispered prayer asking for release: "*O Abasi, sana mi yok*:" O God, let me go.[23]

Martha Peacock was with Mary when she died, along with daughters Janie, Annie, Maggie, Alice and Whitie. "There was no great struggle at the end," Peacock wrote, "just a gradual diminishing of the forces of nature, and *Ma Akamba* ('the Great Mother') entered into the presence of the King." What followed was something Peacock would never forget. "When

20. *Record*, 1915, 106.
21. *WMM*, March 1915, 52.
22. *Record*, 1915, 105.
23. Livingstone, *Mary Slessor*, 377, quoting Peacock.

the people in the town heard the girls weeping, they came to the house. . . . Men, women, and children mourned with a great lamentation."[24]

A story persists in Nigeria that the bite of a rabid dog caused Mary Slessor's death. Eyewitness reports do not support this theory, but family members and others believe a dog bite may have at least contributed to her death. Mary made no mention of a dog bite in her diary, which contained entries up to a month before she died.

As soon as word was received of Mary's death, a launch was sent from Duke Town up the river to Itu, where Mary's body was carried from Use. Meanwhile, Alexander Cruickshank traveled about ten miles from Ikot Offiong to Itu and held a service in Efik. Dr. Robertson held a service in English. The launch left Itu at 5:30 p.m. and reached Duke Town at midnight.[25]

Dan Slessor learned of his Ma's death Wednesday morning, when the school principal called him to his apartment.

> Etubom, as we used reverently to call him was seated on the divan, his cheek in the cup of his hands. He looked up to me, took me between his long legs, gazed straight into my eyes, and after a few moments he told me of the dreadful news. . . . My thoughts were scattered. Use Ikot Oku—how would it be home to me any more? . . . Then suddenly as it was unexpected, I burst out in a torrent of tears. Rev. Macgregor was unmoved; yes, Dan, he said, weep it out here.[26]

When his weeping ended, Mrs. McGregor comforted Dan with scones and tarts before he was sent back to his dormitory. "For the first time, I felt a loneliness which the grave alone can compare," he wrote. "Then I knew I was alone in the world, with nowhere to go, and no one to care." He decided that courage was his only option.

On Thursday morning the coffin was draped with the Union Jack and decorated with a cross made of frangipani blossoms. Those who came to the beach for the mile-and-a-half procession to the cemetery included government officials, traders, missionaries and students from

24. *Record*, 1915, 105.

25. Ibid.

26. D. Slessor, "Reminiscences."

Hope Waddell Training Institution. Others joined along the way.[27] Dan described the funeral.

> I was escorted to Marine Beach. At the foreshore were the High Commissioner, senior British Officials all in uniform, the Officer Commanding 3rd Battalion of the Nigeria Regiment, Members of Leading Mercantile Houses, leading Heads of Ruling Houses in Calabar . . . and surrounding areas, while the Band of the Regiment played the "Dead March in Saul," [the funeral march in Handel's oratorio, *Saul*] very slow and very reverently.
>
> All flags at Government Buildings and Offices were lowered to half mast. The ensign at the Marine Beach was brought down, the Union Jack at the mast head was lowered to half as the "Snipe" [the steamer carrying Mary's body to Duke Town] slowly came in to moor. As soon as the launch was made fast, four British Non-Commissioned Officers of the Battalion marched briskly forward and went into the boat while four others stood on the jetty.
>
> Carefully and with great dignity the mahogany coffin . . . was raised from the launch. . . . The band struck the National Anthem, officers with drawn swords formed an arch under which the distinguished coffin passed. Marine ratings in starch white were brought to attention . . .
>
> [and] the coffin moved slowly cemetery-ward. First went the High Commissioner, his breast bristling with decorations (which took my attention), representing the Government, then followed the Mission as Chief Mourners, then the other high ranking British Officials, other denominations, mercantile houses, Ruling Houses and the rest. The troops along the route all came to attention as the draped coffin passed.[28]

Those at the funeral were impressed with the silence of the crowd, in contrast to the wailing at Use when *eka kpukpru owo* died. Rev. Wilkie wrote, "The silence was a far greater sign of their great respect than the usual loud wailing of a native crowd. Only those who know them can understand what restraint this required."[29]

Dan Slessor wrote about the huge crowd at the cemetery and the young people who climbed trees to get a view of Mary's coffin: "It was

27. *Record*, 1915, 105. See also *WMM*, March 1915, 62–63.

28. D. Slessor, "Reminiscences."

29. *WMM*, March 1915, 62.

an honour befitting a monarch, which indeed she was in the kingdom of Christ."[30]

Missionaries Wilkie and Rankin led a brief memorial service and African Christians led the mourners in two hymns: "When the Day of Toil is Done" and "Asleep in Jesus." Missionary teachers lowered the coffin into the grave.[31] "And that," wrote Dan Slessor, "brought to its mortal end . . . the illustrious life of a great explorer, adventurer, pioneer Missionary, who laid down her life for Christ and Africa."[32]

The *Government Gazette* announced the death: "It is with the deepest regret that His Excellency the Governor-General has to announce the death . . . of Miss Mary Mitchell Slessor, Honorary Associate of the Order of the Hospital of St. John of Jerusalem in England. . . . She has died, as she herself wished, on the scene of her labours, but her memory will live long in the hearts of her friends, Native and European, in Nigeria."[33]

30. D. Slessor, "Reminiscences."
31. *WMM*, March 1915, 62–63.
32. D. Slessor, "Reminiscences."
33. *Record*, 1915, 174.

20

Remembrance

> We salute the Christian missionaries for the great sacrifices they have made in this Region. . . . Were Mary Slessor to rise from her rude and silent grave to attend our independence day celebrations on 1st October, 1960; were she to revisit the scene of her life's adventures as it is today; were that great Scottish Missionary, who toiled, died and was buried in Calabar, to see that even the mothers of triplets are receiving bounties from Government, when in her days mothers of twins were ostracised, she would feel that her sacrifices had not been in vain. And she might say with Saint Paul: "I have fought a good fight. I have finished the course."
>
> —Editorial, *Eastern Nigeria*, 1960[1]

FRIENDS AND ACQUAINTANCES STRUGGLED with Slessor's loss and tried to analyze her charismatic appeal. William Stevenson, Secretary of the Women's Foreign Mission Committee praised her intellectual ability, insight into character, statesmanlike grasp of affairs, heroic spirit, her devotion and self-sacrifice, and her overflowing of love.[2] Hope Waddell Training Institution principal Rev. J. K. Macgregor attributed Mary's popularity to her sympathetic nature combined with her love of Christ. "Her standards for us were high," he wrote, "and she insisted, to official and trader and missionary, on our high calling and our great responsibility. As she spoke, all things seemed possible, and as we left her, we braced ourselves for new endeavour." Conversations with her were "rich in allusion, witty, [and] full of keen insight into men and affairs," he wrote. He noted,

1. *Eastern Nigeria*, 62–64.
2. *Record*, 1915, 107.

too, that "to the end, the cry of a child roused the mother-heart in her," as one might expect from *eka kpukpru owo*.[3]

Jessie Hogg, former missionary to Calabar, wrote after Mary Slessor's death: "Strange tales of the marvelous white Ma, all carrying the fragrance of a Saviour's name, have made a way for the Gospel. . . . If we pay heed to all the hands stretched out in these regions beyond, it will one day become a highway of God."[4]

A thirteen-foot high cross of Scottish granite was erected to mark Mary's grave. The inscription reads:

In Loving memory
of Mary Mitchell Slessor

Born at Aberdeen, Scotland 2nd December 1848
Died at Use, Calabar, Nigeria 13th January 1915

For thirty-eight years a heroic and devoted missionary
Chiefly among the up-river tribes of this land

"The people that walked in darkness
have seen a great light."
"They that turn many to righteousness
shall shine as the stars for ever and ever."[5]

As effusive praise continued, her friend Charles Ovens remarked, "She was nae jist a' that holy!" and "It'll take more than that [granite cross] to hold doon our Mary!"[6]

At Use, a more modest monument stands near the site where Slessor's house stood: a simple granite marker with a plaque that reads, "This cairn marks the site of the house of Miss Mary Slessor, Pioneer Scottish missionary, who died here on 13th January 1915."

Five months after Mary's death, the Women's Foreign Mission Committee decided to build a Mary Slessor House for women and girls. A month later they appointed Agnes Arnot the "Miss Slessor Memorial Missionary," and by December Arnot had opened the home at Ikot Obong.

3. Ibid., 107–8.
4. *WMM*, March 1915, 53.
5. Isaiah 9:2 and Daniel 12:3.
6. Buchan, *Expendable Mary Slessor*, 243.

In addition to Arnot, three other women—Martha Peacock, Beatrice Welsh and Mina Amess—followed in the steps of Slessor by developing and serving mission outstations for years.[7]

YEARS BRING MORE HONORS

Before the end of 1915, the first biography of Mary Mitchell Slessor appeared, written by W. P. Livingstone, editor of *The Record*. (It went through many printings and is still available.) Fifteen years later, after laudatory writings had simmered down some, J. Du Plessis, author of a number of books and articles on missions and travel in Africa, gave Mary a backhanded compliment when he wrote, "Her habits of life and methods of work were unconventional in the extreme, and cannot be recommended as models for general imitation." He then recited the eccentricities (to Europeans) for which she was known—no hat, no shoes, no mosquito net, no filtered water, no regular schedule, eating native food—and concluded, "This catalogue of reprehensible practices denotes clearly that Mary Slessor was a law unto herself, and is not to be judged by the standards which apply to common humanity."[8]

A memorial fund to honor Slessor resulted in a permanent display in Dundee's museum of two ten-feet high by three-feet wide stained glass panels, dubbed the Mary Slessor Memorial Window. Unveiled September 28, 1923 at Albert Institute (now McManus Galleries and Museum), the panels depict events of Mary's life. Among those in attendance were J. K. Macgregor from Hope Waddell Training Institution W. P. Livingstone, Slessor's first biographer. A Mary Slessor Corner was dedicated in the museum thirty years later. Donors of items for the corner included retired Agnes Arnot and Mary's long-time correspondent, Charles Partridge.[9] A detailed newspaper report of the dedication ceremony asked, "What would

7. Agnes Siddons Young heard Slessor speak and volunteered to serve in Calabar. After teaching at the girls' school in Duke Town from 1911 to 1913, she resigned to marry the Rev. David Arnot in Scotland. When her husband died, she returned to Calabar as the Mary Slessor Memorial Missionary. See Buchan, *Expendable Mary Slessor*, 223, 244 and Christie, "Annals."

8. Du Plessis, *Evangelisation of Pagan Africa*, 154.

9. Boyd, *Mary Slessor Memorial*, 14–16; Charles Partridge donated Mary's letters to the City of Dundee in 1950 and provided the phonograph and wax cylinder recordings of Slessor reading the story of the prodigal son (recorded in 1906).

Mary Slessor say were she here today?" The article answered itself: She would want her work honored by providing funds for it to continue.[10]

In the late 1940s retired missionary accountant Thomas Hart made contact with Daniel Slessor, who had become an officer in Nigeria's civil service. Dan was happily surprised by the contact and reported on his family (seven children at the time, with another yet to be born). He wrote of family visits to the cemetery to see the granite cross and of his daughter Mary's whispered, "Pappa, it is my name!" In school, the children were taught about Mary Slessor's life, and when they did their history homework, Dan wrote, they turned to the life of their grandmother first.[11]

Early in 1949, Dan wrote to Hart again. He was glad his notes and reminiscences were considered important enough to appear in a Scottish paper. He believed Hart's efforts would immortalize his Ma's name. She was, her son wrote, "one of Scotland's most outstanding women in the field of pioneer christianisation in what was then known and *was* darkest Africa." He hoped the Colonial Office would take note, too, "for it was the work and lives of such as Ma that Pax Britannica found its feet in these remote parts."[12]

The announcement that Queen Elizabeth II would lay a wreath at Mary Slessor's grave on March 8, 1956 resulted in weeks of planning and preparation. A new entrance to the cemetery and a terrace were made, and steps were built at the base of the cross to make it easier for the queen to place a wreath. Hope Waddell's Carpentry and Engineering Departments were kept busy, and Duke Town women cleaned up the cemetery. Boy Scouts and Girl Guides arrived from all over the Calabar district, some even from the leper colony at Itu.

Rev. John Beattie, then principal of Hope Waddell Training Institution, described dancers, men in raffia (Ekpe) costumes, women dressed in bright colors, the Scouts and Guides, the spectacle of the queen and Duke of Edinburgh arriving, the queen laying the wreath, speeches and presentations, a living tableau in a roadside booth depicting Hope Waddell presenting the first Bible to the Chiefs of Calabar in 1846, and the small talk of the queen and duke before they departed. Canon and Mrs. Oriaku of the Anglican Church in Calabar stood beside Beattie and

10. *Dundee Courier*, September 12, 1953.

11. D. Slessor to Hart, November 25, 1948.

12. Ibid., January 15, 1949.

his wife. Beattie remembered how the queen made everyone feel they were on holy ground at the cemetery. But he was equally impressed by Canon Oriaku, who said as they awaited the queen's arrival, "I have been thinking that we have put such a great labour into our preparations for the Queen, but how poor have been our efforts for the coming of the King of Kings."[13]

A LAUNDRY LIST OF NAME-DROPPERS

Mary Slessor's name and work continues to be honored. Some examples include the following:

In 1930 Elder Dempster Lines—the line that provided transportation for missionaries and others to Calabar from Liverpool—christened one of their eight Explorer Class merchant ships *Mary Slessor*.

The *Dundee Courier* reported on the opening of Mary Slessor Memorial Chapel in Wishart Church on Mary's birthday, December 2, 1960. Furnishings were donated by her old employer, Baxter Brothers and by the Flaxspinners' & Manufacturers' Association.[14] (Wishart Church later fell on hard times and combined with other churches; the chapel was moved to Steeple Church, Dundee in 1978.)

On January 28, 1968, bombs destroyed the Mary Slessor Hospital at Itu. It was rebuilt and taken over by the government after the Civil War. Conditions were less than ideal, including bad road conditions as one approached the hospital, as of the early 2000s. An article in *This Day* newspaper (Lagos) commented on a visit of forty teenagers to the hospital. "If the kids had any regrets," the reporter wrote, "they were the deplorable state of the State roads and the appaling [*sic*] state of the historical Mary Slessor Hospital. They all expressed deep sympathy for the patients they saw there in deep pains and in a state of hopelessness; even as they applauded the doctors who choose to remain there attending to the patients against all odds."[15] The author heard in 2001 that the government wanted to return the hospital to the church but the church could not afford to operate it. However, the Presbyterian Church of Nigeria did accept its

13. Beattie, "Royal Day in Calabar," 3.

14. *Dundee Courier*, December 1960.

15. U. Essien, "Kids Who Tapped Their Roots," September 25, 2000.

return in December 2005; its operation continues under management of the church's Medical Board.[16]

Mary Slessor appeared on Scotland's Clydesdale Bank ten-pound note in 1997. She was the first woman to be pictured on the face of Scottish currency. The reverse side shows a map of Calabar and Mary standing with African children, as depicted in one of the Mary Slessor Memorial Window stained glass panels at McManus Galleries and Museum in Dundee.

The Medical School (a teaching hospital) at University of Calabar named its journal *The Mary Slessor Journal of Medicine*. In an editorial, Professor G. Chuks Ejezie said the decision to name the journal for Slessor was an easy one. He wrote, "Perhaps no other name commands more respect and love than hers in this part of the world."[17]

In 2000, Cross River State named Mary Slessor one of Calabar's one hundred millennium persons. Her name is inscribed with the others on a plaque in Millennium Park in Calabar. Presbyterian Women's Guilds in Nigeria continue to dramatize events from Slessor's life, especially her confrontation with the hippopotamus. Roads, schools, and buildings carry Mary's name in Scotland, Nigeria, and in other countries. (She would be surprised to also find herself honored on the Church of England's annual Calendar of Common Worship for January 11.) There are several statues of Mary Slessor cradling a twin in each arm in southeastern Nigeria.

The Mary Slessor Foundation is a registered Scottish Charity founded by Dr. Lawrie Mitchell (and his wife, Eme, who is a granddaughter of Slessor's friend, Ma Eme Ete). The Foundation focuses on humanitarian projects (skills training, agriculture, and medical care) in Akpap, Okoyong, Cross River State. In that way the Foundation aims "to continue the work of Mary Slessor in order to increase the local economy and raise self esteem among the villagers" and is about "helping the people of Calabar district to help themselves."[18]

16. Benebo Fubara-Manuel, Principal Clerk, Presbyterian Church of Nigeria, e-mail message to the author, October 8, 2007.

17. Ejezie, "Editorial."

18. Mary Slessor Foundation.

ASSESSMENTS

Was Mary Slessor, as Dr. Carrie Pemberton asks, an "Imperialist Mother" or a "Liberating Sister"?[19] The answer is: both, to some degree. As Andrew Walls, founder of the Centre for the Study of Christianity in the Non Western World at University of Edinburgh, writes, "Missionaries had a double identity. They were representative Christians trying (and in the process demonstrating all the elements of human fallenness and all the limitations of human vision and foresight) to do Christian things, things that were specifically, characteristically Christian. . . . But they were also representative Westerners, shaped by Western history and conditions and values, and Western social networks and intellectual discourse."[20]

Brian Stanley, director of the Henry Martyn Centre at Cambridge University, emphasizes that it is an illusion to think that missionaries could "propagate a culture-free gospel which could be absorbed painlessly by the non-Christian cultures that received them."[21]

Mary Slessor was not free from the cultural attitudes of her colleagues. She, along with many other missionaries, advocated what she considered best in British culture (though one wonders today why such things as ironing were deemed so important). On the other hand, she was critical of the arrogance, cruelty, or ignorance exhibited at times by colonial officers. In her position as a judge, she showed greater understanding of local laws and customs than her British counterparts in government. She considered herself—and was—a go-between during the difficult years of economic and social upheaval that came with western imperialism.

Few would disagree with the statement that "missionaries in Nigeria did not always question the theory that Christianity, commerce, and civilization would work together for the great benefit of Africans."[22] Others have accused missionaries of being covert agents of imperialism and merchants, as pointed out in Ogbu Kalu's *History of Christianity in West Africa*.[23]

It is true that missionaries encouraged the other two "C"s, but the goal of most missionaries was to fulfill the biblical command to go and preach

19. Pemberton, Carrie, "Mary Slessor."

20. Walls, *Missionary Movement*, xviii.

21. Stanley, *Bible and the Flag*, 170.

22. Ajayi, *Christian Missions in Nigeria*, 57

23. Kalu, *History of Christianity*, 7, quoting A. E. Ayandele.

the gospel. Mary Slessor, just as David Livingstone had done, accepted the prevalent view that developing trade and promoting "civilization" were the means of ending cruel practices. She also saw it as the means of freeing women from oppressive conditions. Like other missionaries, Slessor disapproved of the morals of many white traders, especially those who came to Nigeria with guns and gin. And, though she benefited from the military presence, she did not hesitate to condemn any in authority who dealt cruelly and unjustly with Africans.

Missionary Robert Macdonald wrote in 1964, "Nothing would have grieved her more than that she should be remembered primarily for her services to the Government, or as an agent of British Colonial development."[24] He was certain, and the evidence bears it out, that Slessor was driven by her deep faith, her love for Jesus Christ and for the people she met. Sharing that message was her highest aim.

Yes, Africa was Mary Slessor's country, and its people were her "children." Why else did they call her everybody's mother? The people asked for—and received—help in settling disagreements, in dealing with new laws and rulers. They expected—and received—wise counsel as well as harsh criticism and discipline (and preaching) from this white Ma. Most critics of missionaries exclude condemnation of Mary Slessor, recognizing the contributions she made during her years in Nigeria, and applauding her "preferential option for the poor that is more often advocated than practiced."[25]

Regardless of Slessor's somewhat mixed role as an imperial mother, there are no doubts about her status as a liberating sister. Her concern furthered the cause of freedom for women. In 1976, a hundred years after Slessor's arrival in Calabar, a Church of Scotland Overseas Council pamphlet stated, "Something . . . endures of her work—to be seen not just in the congregations of faithful African Christians or in the schools and hospitals and training centres—but wherever in the lower reaches of the Cross River and the Enyong Creek an African woman earns her own living and feels herself to be a free and independent person in her own right, or the mother of twins and her husband together bring up their twins, or

24. Macdonald, "Mary Slessor," 1964.

25. Isichei, *History of Christianity*, 79, 176.

the quarrelsome settle their arguments in a court of law rather than with knives."[26]

Mgbeke Okore attributes the fact that the Presbyterian Church in Nigeria was the first missionary-founded church in Nigeria to allow ordination of women to "The Slessor Legacy."[27] Historian J. C. Anene acknowledges that mission motivation was "moral regeneration" and that "a study of the early and often hazardous travels of the Scottish missionaries in the Upper Cross river reveals nothing but self-sacrifice, discomfort, and often death." He recommends the life of Mary Slessor as an example of how missionaries faced a tremendous task, and though he condemns their failure to recognize the difference between terrible evils and innocent cultural heritage and practices, he commends their accomplishments.[28]

Chief E. U. Aye, a former principal of Hope Waddell Training Institution writes,

> "Whatever may have been the weakness of the Efik people who invited the Mission, or the faults of those they invited, something has been achieved which should make both parties feel proud of the past and hold no regrets for the future."[29]

A REAL FAMILY AND A GROWING MYSTIQUE

The *Record* reported the situation of Mary's adopted children soon after her death. Janie, Whitie, and Annie, along with a baby, were at Annie's house at Use Ikot Oku, but mission land (presumably Mary's house) would be available there for their use. (It is unclear whether or not this happened or for how long the land was available for the daughters' use.) Alice and Maggie were at Ikot Obong with Martha Peacock and were scheduled to remain in school at Duke Town. Dan would remain at Hope Waddell, and Mary was in Lagos with her husband.[30]

In later years, little is known of what happened to most of Mary's bairns. Janie died in an influenza epidemic in 1918 at the age of thirty-six. Asuquo ran off to sea during World War I. Only descendants of Dan and Annie can be located today. Annie's granddaughter, Inyang Bassey, lives

26. "Mary Slessor of Calabar," COS Overseas Council, 1.
27. Okore, "Slessor Legacy," 240.
28. Anene, *Southern Nigeria*, 325–26.
29. Aye, *Old Calabar*, 134.
30. *Record*, 1915, 105–8.

in Calabar with her husband, retired Rev. Canon Anderson A. Bassey. Annie's great grandson, Francis Udom, who studied marine engineering in Scotland, lives in Aberdeen with his family. Daniel Slessor died in Calabar on March 27, 1970. His children and grandchildren live in Calabar and Lagos.

Dan Slessor once told of being interviewed for a job promotion. When an African member of the committee questioned why he had not changed his name back to his African name, Dan was angry. European board members explained this was "not a case of one of the old-day traders 'bestowing' his name to an old 'cook or steward.'" He considered it an honor to carry his Ma's name.[31] Dan's children point out in the twenty-first century that they are adopted into Mary Slessor's family just as Christians are adopted into God's family.

In August 1995, "a group made up of elites of Use Ikot Oku of Ibiono Local Government Area of Akwa Ibom State of Nigeria" visited the Slessor family home in Calabar. Dan's children report: "The reason they gave was, 'to show remorse for their hostile attitude towards Ma Mary Slessor, while she was on Missionary work at Use Ikot Oku.'" The group believed that Slessor "was prompted to curse their land, which became barren and unproductive from that time." Four of Daniel Slessor's children accepted the invitation to travel to Use for a meeting of reconciliation: daughters Mary and Barbara, and sons Kenneth and Alfred. At a meeting in an Use primary school, "and in an effort to reverse Ma's curse, a message from Deuteronomy 28:1–14, by one of Ma's great grandsons, Rev. John K. Edet, was read by [his mother] Ms. Mary Slessor Bassey. This was followed by a prayer for forgiveness." In return the Slessor family was presented with a Bible in appreciation.[32]

It is difficult to believe that Mary Slessor cursed the land of the village she was always eager to get back to, and the ones she called her people, but not at all hard to imagine her preaching on Deuteronomy 28, which deals with both the blessing and the curse Moses said God would bring upon Israel, depending on whether or not the people obeyed his laws and teachings.

Television documentaries have presented the life of the well-known missionary (including one by biographer James Buchan), but a distorted

31. D. Slessor to Dundee Museum Curator, May 27, 1954.

32. Granddaughter Olive Slessor Henshaw provided Slessor family information regarding the meeting to the author on November 21, 2005.

representation of the missionary's life was shown in a play presented in Lagos in December 2000, "Mary Slessor Resurrects in *Amana-Mba*." A reviewer of the play describes Slessor as an "untiring, vibrant Catholic Sister," and reference is made to "Mary Slessor and her nuns."[33] A more realistic presentation of Slessor's life is offered in Mike Gibbs's 2003 musical, "Mother of All the Peoples." Repeat performances to full houses in several of Scotland's cities have been well received and serve to acquaint a new generation with the story of Slessor's life.

IMPACT

In November 2007, Aberdeen—Mary Slessor's birthplace—unveiled a sculpture in her honor. Continuing expressions of recognition pay homage to a woman of selfless faith and Christian service.

Slessor had a hand in starting many little churches and schools. She left the development and maintenance of those institutions to the missionaries who followed her.

She was at times painfully shy, but more often headstrong and recklessly bold; thus, stories have been told repeatedly of a woman with an eccentric but powerful personality; with more knowledge of the people, their languages and their culture than that of other Britons, including missionaries; and with an unshakable faith in Jesus Christ.

M. O. Ogarepke, author of *Historical Perspective of the Presbyterian Church of Nigeria*, commented on Slessor's ability to pacify men who exhibited a "war-like attitude," describing Mary as "a slip of a woman who brought down the mighty with the word of God."[34]

"She was different and people celebrate that difference," Professor Ogbu Kalu says of Mary Slessor and her legacy. Her vision was "much broader and activist than her compatriots could imagine." She represented "the social activist component of early evangelicalism" and was among those missionaries who "rejected the social and spatial boundaries" the mission adhered to for years.[35]

Slessor was changed by her years in Africa, as she learned to appreciate and love people there; likewise, many Africans were changed by encounters and relationships with the plucky pioneer as she lived among

33. Agbodo, review of "Mary Slessor Resurrects."

34. Ogarekpe, *Historical Perspective*, 21.

35. Ogbu Kalu, e-mail to the author, February 25, 2002.

them—preaching, teaching, mediating, judging. Regardless of changes, she was determined to be true to God's call on her life. She did not let poverty or her youth keep her from serving God. She did not let opposition or illness keep her from serving God. She did not allow an unhappy home situation or the fact that she was a woman keep her from serving God. And when honors came her way, she did not let the world distract her from serving God.

The missionary zeal of Mary Slessor saved many twins and orphans from death, led to improvements in conditions for women, introduced Nigerians to peace with God, and resulted in admirers around the world: during her lifetime, in the decades that followed, and in the twenty-first century.

Epilogue

African Mission to Liverpool[1]

HE DIED PENNILESS IN Liverpool on July 12, 1964. There was no big funeral procession. But to some he was the "African Saint of Merseyside."

George Daniel was an errand boy for missionary Arthur Wilkie in Calabar. He became acquainted with Mary Slessor about 1904 and followed her to Itu to help with the mission. He may have been one of the boys she sent out to villages to teach what they knew of ABCs, reading, and the Bible.

Some time after Slessor's death in 1915 (perhaps several years later) young George Daniel set sail for Liverpool. Slessor had warned him that Britons were not much interested in the Bible or Christian living, but he thought surely he would find many others in that far land like the woman he so admired—his "holy mother."

Liverpool, Daniel found, was not paradise. According to his biographer, the youth was "shocked . . . by the cheeky children, the quarrelling, swearing, racism, and general licentiousness compared to Itu." He was so disillusioned after a time that he bought a gun and planned to return to Calabar and "shoot all missionaries, black and white." He swore he would show Nigerian chiefs his notebook "in which I had written down all the insults I had received from the 'Christian people' in the 'holy country.'"

1. I am indebted to Professor Ogbu Kalu (Henry Winters Professor of World Christianity and Missions at McCormick Theological Seminary, Chicago and former Professor of History at University of Nigeria, Nsukka) for alerting me to the story of George Daniels Ekarte.

But in 1922 he returned to faith. "A great light came into my heart," he reported. He threw his gun and notebook into the River Mersey.[2]

From that time, the young man began to hold Christian services, sometimes on street corners (for which he was arrested and thrown into jail, where he continued to preach and sing hymns), at other times in private homes or Gospel Halls. At some point he changed his name from Daniel to Daniels and added the surname Ekarte.

By 1930 he appealed to the Church of Scotland Foreign Mission Committee for financial aid to set up a mission center in Liverpool. Liverpool's *Daily Post* recorded the opening ceremonies of the African Churches Mission on July 7, 1931 with Daniels Ekarte as its pastor. Until his death, G. Daniels Ekarte served as a missionary to Liverpool.

Ekarte preached, taught, and spent his life helping the poor of the city: blacks who were racially discriminated against, foreign seamen, the homeless, the destitute, the hungry. The mission often acted as a private aid organization, helping with medical and legal fees, emergency rent, and housing. It received little support from government or other agencies. Ekarte's reputation led to referrals of the needy from the police, the immigration office, and other charitable agencies, especially during the depression years of the 1930s and during and after World War II.

The African Churches Mission provided Sunday worship and evangelistic services, Sunday School for children, secondary school classes, Boy Scout and Girl Guide groups, a Mothers' Union, a reading room, and a billiards room. Free meals were served. In addition, Ekarte corresponded with government officials and others, either seeking financial aid for the mission or protesting the treatment of the poor and the lot of non-European seamen, especially Africans.

The policies of the Elder Dempster shipping line angered Pastor Daniels. He believed shippers were in collusion with the government and the National Maritime Board to treat foreign seamen unfairly; he argued that the "National Union of Seamen was hostile to Black seamen." The men were paid a pittance, had their passports confiscated while they were in the country, and were forbidden to seek a change in employment, even to a different shipping company. In 1941 he wrote in support of seamen, "For the past 18 years I have been endeavouring to preach the Gospel of Christ to my countrymen in Liverpool. I have been telling them that

2. Sherwood, *Pastor Daniels Ekarte*, 25. Except as noted, quotes and most other information come from Sherwood's brief, well-documented work.

in spite of what the race has suffered and is still suffering, they should not hate but love their enemies. In face of this callous attitude of the Shipping Company the Gospel of Christ would sound sheer mockery to my countrymen."[3]

Ekarte constantly sought funding for the African Churches Mission; he was accused of being a "vigorous beggar." An anonymous donor gave him money to buy the building the mission occupied, so he no longer lived under threat of eviction. Still, with little income the condition of the property declined through the years.

Visitors arrived at the Mission often, not only government inspectors but also well-known figures from America, including Joe Louis and Paul Robeson, as well as from Africa. Jomo Kenyatta, Hastings Banda, and Kwame Nkrumah, the first prime ministers of Kenya, Malawi, and Ghana, stayed at the Mission. Dr. Nnamdi Azikiwe, who became Governor-General of Nigeria, led delegations to the mission in 1942 and 1943.

Ekarte did not attend the Pan-African Congress that met in Manchester in 1945, but those who did applauded his work. This important gathering provided impetus for the growing push for independence of African peoples colonized under British rule. One resolution of the conference urged support for the African Churches Mission and other African groups in England and their "vital social work."

During World War II, thousands of American servicemen passed through or were stationed in Britain. In Liverpool, "brown babies" resulted from liaisons between black American men and white English women. In June 1945, Pastor Daniels petitioned the government (to no avail) to open a home "to accommodate 40 to 50" illegitimate children of black American, African, and West Indian men. The government denied his request.

Ekarte took some children in anyway. By 1947 eight children lived at the African Churches Mission. The mission supported twenty-five others in foster homes and had a waiting list of well over one hundred. News of the mission traveled to Australia and to America. "Reverend Ekarte was the children's adopted father in every way except legally," an article reported. "He is loved by the children in the Liverpool nursery . . . [and] white women are matrons who look after the children." The grim ending

3. Lane, *Merchant Seamen's War*, 162.

of the article was: "The African Churches Mission has been struggling along on very limited finances."

The newsletter of The League of Coloured People reported in 1942 that Pastor Daniels, though influential, had both financial difficulties and the problem of "justifying his work to the local authorities." In 1947 a government inspector reported "a group of children living happily in slum conditions." A 1949 report spoke of broken windows and other deficiencies.

On May 31, 1949 the Home Office gave Ekarte a 28-day notice of closure, even though there was no hint of child neglect. Just eleven days after the notice was issued, police arrived at 7:30 a.m., locked Ekarte in his office, and forcefully removed the remaining children. An official of the Home Office visited the pastor and reported he was "distressed at the loss and indignant at manhandling by the police. He was not allowed to visit the children, though the white Mrs. Morris could do so." Racial discrimination continued.

From the early 1940s to the early 50s, the Mission ran a small café, The Cocoa Rooms, in a converted pub near the docks.[4] This provided a little income, besides meeting the needs of seamen and dockers. The mission also held a monthly "jumble sale" and sold homemade toffee and candied apples. Free breakfasts were still provided to children at least through 1953, and in 1955 Ekarte still held worship services, but most of the former work of the Mission had gone by the wayside. When an attack of vandalism further damaged the decaying mission building only two rooms could be salvaged.

The African Churches Mission building was condemned and demolished in 1964, and Pastor Daniels was moved to a city apartment, where he died a few weeks later.

One young girl spoke in awe of Daniels Ekarte: "He might be God come to try and make the world a better place." Her mother said, "We had every respect for this very kind gentleman."

Both Daniels Ekarte and Mary Slessor had their faults and critics. Both lived among the people they served, exhibiting worthwhile traits. In addition to preaching the gospel, they were advocates for the voiceless and the powerless. Ekarte could look back to Slessor as his inspiration. From her he learned to model the Christian life and to seek justice for

4. The area was razed and redeveloped in 1954.

those in need. Part of Slessor's epitaph may well apply to this little-known missionary, too: "They that turn many to righteousness shall shine as the stars for ever and ever."[5]

5. Daniel 12:3.

Acknowledgements

LISTING ALL WHO HAVE contributed to the formation of this work is a daunting task, one that not only raises the fear of omitting someone but also revives pleasant memories of help received. To all I mention, my deepest thanks. To any I have forgotten, please accept my apology and jog my memory. Any errors the reader may find in the text are my own.

Professor Andrew Walls, missions historian and founder of Centre for the Study of Christianity in the Non-Western World, offered persistent encouragement through these years as well as gentle suggestions that corrected my misunderstandings or ignorance. Professor Ogbu Kalu, McCormick Theological Seminary, not only alerted me to the story of G. Daniels Ekarte but also gave me invaluable insights on Mary Slessor and the Calabar Mission. Rev. Jock Stein, publisher and former minister of Wishart Church, which Mary Slessor attended as a young woman, granted assistance and encouragement beyond all expectations.

Staff members of Dundee's McManus Galleries and Museum, past and present, including Eileen Murison, Fiona Sinclair, and others were most helpful. The museum holds two of Slessor's Bible and two diaries, as well as other materials. David Kett and his staff at Dundee Central Library, Local Studies Department, were equally helpful. The library has placed Mary Slessor's letters to Charles Partridge and other materials on the internet, making them available for study and publication, in great part due to volunteer transcriptions by Ruth Riding and Leslie Mackenzie. Iain Flett and staff at Dundee City Archives also opened their files to me. Church of Scotland has given permission to use any of their materials, many of which are archived at National Library of Scotland. Special Collections staff at the library provided materials to me, both at North Reading Room and via mail and e-mail. Clydesdale Bank kindly permitted use of their ten-pound note: the face of the bill shows Mary Slessor; the reverse shows a map of the Calabar Mission area where she served.

From Nigeria, help has come from the children and grandchildren of Daniel McArthur Slessor in the way of hospitality, photographs, information, and friendship. The same is true of Inyang Bassey and Emilia Udom (now deceased), granddaughters of Annie Slessor, and great grandson Francis Udom. Chief Efiong U. Aye, and Chief Okon O. Awatt, retired principals of Hope Waddell Training Institution, each met with me and shared information and insights. K'ufre-Mfon and Kokomma Ekerete offered friendship, hospitality, and assistance in many ways through the years, including help with travel in Nigeria, translation questions, and the listing of Cross River State's millennium persons. Professor Offiong Abia, University of Calabar, guided and accompanied us during our visit in 2001.

Other libraries that have aided my work include: New College Library, University of Edinburgh, which holds the handwritten "Annals" of the mission; University of Edinburgh Library, Department of Special Collections; Andrew Walls Centre for the Study of Christianity in the Non-Western World Library, Edinburgh (with special thanks to Margaret Acton, former staff member); Bodleian Library of Commonwealth and African Studies, Rhodes House, University of Oxford; University of Auckland Archives; Yale Divinity School Library; Public Record Office, London; Charleston County Public Library, South Carolina, especially interlibrary loan staffs, main library and Otranto branch; Presbyterian Church of Canada Archives; and Topsham Museum, Devon.

Thanks are due also to the interest or advice of the following individuals:

Rev. Richard Fee, General Director, Presbyterian Church of Canada, former missionary to Nigeria; Rev. Geoffrey Johnston, former missionary physician to Nigeria with Presbyterian Church of Canada, author of *Of God and Maxim Guns*; Arlene Onuoha, with Presbyterian Church of Nigeria since 1978; Dr. Christian Gardner-Thorpe, consultant neurologist, editor of *Journal of Medical Biography*; Dr. Rosalind I. J. Hackett, University of Tennessee, author of *Religion in Calabar*; Dr. Carrie Pemberton, Executive Officer of CHASTE (Churches Alert to Sex Trafficking Across Europe); Dr. William Knox, University of St Andrews, author of *The Lives of Scottish Women*; Dr. Cathy DiDomenico, University of Abertay; Dr. Rudy & Shirley Nelson, producers of video *Precarious Peace: God and Guatemala*; Rev. Ezekiel Ette, Northwest Nazarene University; Victor Oladokun, Managing Producer, Christian Broadcasting Network; Marcia Whitney-Schenck, former publisher of *Christianity and the Arts*; and friends who served as readers.

Finally, I owe a debt of special gratitude to daughters Alison Edwards and Lani Hardage-Vergeer for many hours of faithful (and critical) editing; thanks to daughters Valerie Dearborn, Karen Schmitt, and Jessica Davis for encouragement; and special thanks to my husband, Owen Hardage, who kept telling me I could do it.

Author's Notes

W. P. Livingstone published *Mary Slessor of Calabar* just months after Mary Slessor died, and many reprints followed. (My own copy, the seventh edition, was published a year after her death.) Livingstone was editor of the Presbyterian monthly mission publication. He had access to all that was written by and about Mary Slessor, as well as the opportunity to interview missionaries and others who had connections with and recollections of her.[1] Unfortunately, Livingstone's records were lost during World War II, as noted in chapter one. While his book has no documentation and no index, it is a valuable resource and is one to which I have often referred.

Carol Christian and Gladys Plummer wrote *God and One Redhead* in 1970. Both women lived in Nigeria and spent considerable time in the Calabar region in the 1940s. They were able to do some on-site research a quarter-century after Slessor's death. James Buchan, a former Grampian Television executive, wrote *The Expendable Mary Slessor* in 1980, after having produced a program about her life for independent television fifteen years earlier. These books neither repeat factual errors of somc other biographies nor invent their own. Both were long out of print, but with new print-on-demand technology, they and others are available again.

When other sources were not found, I have reported some episodes from the three biographies mentioned above, especially from Livingstone. There are a number of other Slessor biographies, most of which draw from Livingstone's account; some are written for children; some make questionable assumptions or conclusions (with no documentation).

Other works that were especially helpful to my study include Geoffrey Johnston's *Of God and Maxim Guns* and the handwritten "Annals of The

1. *WMM*, March 1915, 80. A paragraph informed readers that the editor of *The Record* (W. P. Livingstone) was writing a biography of Slessor and sought "letters, photographs, and other material," as well as "impressions, recollections, and anecdotes" for the work.

Calabar Mission, 1846–1945: A Skeleton for the Historian," compiled by W. M. Christie, Calabar missionary from 1913 to 1945.

Mary Slessor–Everybody's Mother follows the subject's life chronologically for the most part, but there are four topical chapters, identified by titles in parentheses, on subjects that begged for more complete treatment. I quote extensively from Slessor's own writings and from articles about her and her era, as well as modern references from the United Kingdom and Nigeria. This well-documented work contains some information not found in other Slessor biographies.

Numerous spelling variations exist for names of people, places and other words in southeastern Nigeria. Some spellings changed within Mary Slessor's lifetime. Some changes came about as speakers of English became better able to comprehend speakers of various local languages. Others may have developed with time, just as English continues to change through the years.

I have used the writer's spellings in quoted matter. When not quoting, I have used modern spellings. Thus, among many other possible examples, Okoyon (or Akayon) became Okoyong, obon became obong, Ikorofiong became Ikot Offiong, Ikorana became Ikot Ana, Ikot Okpene became Ikot Ekpene, and Egbo became Ekpe or Ekpo.

Direct quotes have not been modified except for obvious spelling errors, though in many cases they have been edited for length. The author trusts the editing has done no harm to the original intent of those quoted. Except in a few instances, Slessor quotes have been changed into American standard English. Her original letters and notes are filled with abbreviations, such as "Xtn" for "Christian", "cd" for "could", "govt" for "government", etc. No dialogue has been invented, even in cases where one can be fairly certain of what was said.

Mary Slessor and Mission Chronology Highlights

1846 Scottish Mission established at Calabar by Secession Church;
Hope Masterson Waddell, founder

1847 Secession and Relief churches unite as United Presbyterian Church;
Hugh and Jane Goldie arrive at Calabar from Jamaica

1848 MS born in Aberdeen December 2;
Goldie publishes *Shorter Catechism* in English and Efik

1849 William and Louisa Anderson arrive at Calabar from Jamaica;
Hope Waddell publishes *A Vocabulary of the Efik Language*

1850 MS brother Robert Slessor born in Aberdeen;
Kings and Chiefs of Creek Town and Duke Town prohibit killing anyone except for crime

1851 King Eyo II of Creek Town agrees to abolish killing of twins;
King Archibong of Duke Town refuses

1852 First twins rescued at Old Town and Creek Town

1853 Esien Esien Ukpabio, first convert, baptized at Creek Town;
Idung Ikang baptized at Old Town

1854 Massacre of slaves at Old Town after death of chief

1855 MS sister Susan Slessor born in Aberdeen;
British ship "Antelope" destroys Old Town

1857 Slessor family moves to Dundee;
MS brother John born

1858 Hope Waddell retires to Dublin;
Presbytery of the Bight of Biafra formed

1859 MS becomes a Christian and starts work in mill

1862 MS sister Janie Slessor born in Dundee;
Goldie publishes Efik dictionary and New Testament

1864 Samuel A. J. Crowther appointed the first African Anglican bishop

1870 MS works at Queen Street Mission;
father and brother Robert die at Dundee

1872 Esien Esien Ukpabio ordained

1873 MS brother John Slessor dies in New Zealand;
Goldie publishes Efik Old Testament

1874 MS volunteers for mission work at news of David Livingstone's death

1876 MS receives training in Edinburgh, arrives at Calabar, serves at Duke Town (Atakpa);
Conference of West African Missionaries at Gabon; Victoria proclaimed empress of India

1879 MS furlough June 1879 to October 1880, moves mother and sisters to Downfield, Dundee;
Asuqua Ekanem ordained at Ikunetu

1880 MS returns to Calabar, moves to Old Town (Obutong)

1881 Alexander Ross and William Anderson feud at the mission, Foreign Mission Board ousts Ross

1882 MS visits Ibaka, intervenes on behalf of slave girls; adopts Janie;
Louisa Anderson dies

1883 MS furlough, baby Janie with her, May 1883 to Nov. 1885, moves mother and sister to Devon

1884 British Protectorate Treaty with Calabar kings and chiefs

1885 MS dispute with mission board, begins to serve at Creek Town (Obio Oko);
MS sister Susan dies in Edinburgh; mother dies in Topsham Dec. 31

1886 MS sister Janie dies in Topsham;
Women missionaries serve under Zenana Committee

1887 MS adopts Annie;
Queen Victoria celebrates Golden Jubilee

1888 MS moves to Ekenge (Okoyong)

1889 Mission carpenter Charles Ovens arrives at Calabar, assists MS with house at Ekenge;
MS adopts Alice and Maggie;
William Anderson retires

1890 MS meets Charles Morrison, becomes engaged;
uses services of Ekpe drummer

1891 MS furlough, January 1891 to March 1892;
Claude Macdonald named Consul General of Oil Rivers Protectorate at Calabar

1892 Mission Board denies marriage;
MS returns to Ekenge, appointed vice consul by Claude Macdonald
Charles Morrison invalided home;
King Eyo Honesty VII dies at Creek Town

1894 MS calls for armed forces help at Ekenge;
Charles Morrison resigns from mission, moves to North Carolina, dies ca. 1895

1895 Mary Kingsley visits MS at Ekenge in April & October;
MS moves with Okoyong from Ekenge to Akpap;
Hope Waddell Training Institution (HWTI) established March 8;
Anderson and Goldie die in Calabar, Waddell dies in Dublin

1898 MS furlough with four adopted girls, March 1898 to January 1899

1900 MS adopts orphan Daniel and later adopts Asuquo;
United Presbyterian and Free Church of Scotland become United Free Church

1901 Missionaries ordered out of Cross River for British expedition against Aro;

British destroy Long Juju at Arochukwu;
Queen Victoria dies, Edward VII crowned

1902 MS first visit to Enyong Creek; Ukpabio dies at Creek Town

1903 MS visits Arochuku district, proposes itineration on Enyong Creek in lieu of furlough;
Roman Catholic work begins in Calabar;
first communion at Akpap after 15 years with Okoyong

1904 MS moves to Itu after resigning from court duties, meets Charles Partridge;
Mission grants leave to work six months on Enyong Creek;
Old Calabar becomes Calabar by government order

1905 Mission Council extends MS leave of absence from Akpap one year;
MS resumes court duties as a magistrate, moves to Ikot Obong is called eka kpukpru owo;
Mary Slessor Hospital opens at Itu

1906 Partridge records MS voice at Use Ikot Oku, gives her a bicycle;
Mission approves MS work on Enyong Creek as "permanent"

1907 MS furlough with son Dan, May to October 1907, moves to Use Ikot Oku;
Women's Committee approves MS proposal to build settlement for women and girls

1908 MS uses mbiam in court; Wellington Church in Glasgow adopts MS as "their missionary"

1909 MS resigns from court, receives new bicycle from Partridge;
Women's Industrial Training Centre opens

1910 MS builds house at Ikpe, itinerates from 1910–1913 between Use and Ikpe;
King Edward VII dies, George V crowned

1911 Dr. John William Hitchcock arrives at Calabar, serves in Itu

1912 MS visits Ikot Ekpene, takes health trip two months to Grand Canary in lieu of furlough

1913 Frederick Lugard visits Calabar, meets MS;
MS awarded cross of Order of the Hospital of St. John of Jerusalem

1914 MS builds house at Odoro Ikpe, World War I begins;
Northern and Southern Nigeria become Colony and Protectorate of Nigeria

1915 MS dies January 13 at Use Ikot Oku; MS Home for Women and Girls established

1918 Worldwide influenza epidemic, MS daughter Janie Slessor dies

1956 Queen Elizabeth II visits Calabar, lays wreath at MS grave

1980 Women's Guild builds Mary Slessor Hostel, Calabar

1982 Ordination of first woman minister in Nigeria, Mgbeke George Okore

1994 Presbyterian Theological College opens at Itu;
renamed Esien Ukpabio Theological College, Itu in 1996

2000 MS named one of Calabar's 100 millennium persons

Appendix

A. MARY SLESSOR'S FAMILY—SCOTLAND

Robert Slessor (father)	b. 12 Dec. 1815, Old Machar, Aberdeen d. 6 Eliza St., Dundee, 16 Sep.,1870
Mary Mitchell Slessor (mother)	b. 1821, Old Meldrum, Aberdeen, d. 31 Dec 1885, Topsham, Exeter
Robert Slessor and Mary Mitchell	m. 16 May 1840, Old Machar, Aberdeen
Mary Mitchell Slessor	b. 2 Dec. 1848, Gilcomston, Aberdeen d. 13 Jan. 1915, Use Ikot Oku, Nigeria
(William) Robert Slessor	b. 1850, Old Machar, Aberdeen, d. 6 Eliza St., Dundee, 16 Apr.1870
Susan Slessor	b. 3 Mar. 1855, Old Machar, Aberdeen d. Feb. (?) 1885, Edinburgh
John Paterson Slessor	b. 18 Nov. 1857, Dundee d. ca. 1875, New Zealand
Jane Ann Slessor	b. 24 Feb. 1862, Dundee d. 5 Mar. 1886, Topsham, Exeter

B. MARY SLESSOR'S ADOPTED CHILDREN—NIGERIA

Janie Annan (Jean–nee Atim Eso) Slessor	b. 12 Oct. 1882, d. 1918 smallpox epidemic
Annie Wilson Slessor	b. ca. Nov.-Dec. 1886
Mary Mitchell Slessor	b. 2 Feb. 1893
Alice MCCrindle Slessor	b. ca.1894
Susan (Susie) Slessor	b. Apr. 1895, d. age 14 months
Maggie Cunningham Slessor	b. ca. 1897
Daniel Henryson Macarthur Slessor	b. ca. 1900 d. 27 Mar. 1970 at Calabar
Madge White (Whitie) Slessor	b. 1902? (last adopted, older than Asuquo)
William Mactavish (Asuquo) Slessor	b. 1903?

C. SLESSOR FURLOUGHS

22 June 1879 to 4 October 1880	15 months
14 April 1883 to 4 December 1885	32 months
December 1890 to 19 March 1892	15 months
14 March 1898 to 2 January 1899	10 months
18 May 1907 to 9 November 1907	5 months
7 October to 2 December 1912	2 months (Grand Canary Islands)

D. SOME CALABAR MISSION WORKERS

1846–1858	Hope Masterton Waddell (d. Dublin—1895)
1849–1858	Jessie Simpson Waddell (d. Dublin—1894)
1846–1865	George Buchanan Waddell (rescued slave, d. Creek Town—1870)
1846–1857	Samuel Edgerley (d. Duke Town—1857)
1846–1865	Mrs. Edgerley (wife of Samuel, d. Creek Town—1874)
1847–1891	Jane Johnstone Goldie (d. Creek Town—1891)
1847–1895	Hugh Goldie (d. Creek Town—1895)
1849–1881	Euphemia Miller Sutherland (d. Duke Town—1881)
1849–1882	Louisa Peterswald Anderson (d. Duke Town—1882)
1849–1889 and 1895	William Anderson (d. Duke Town—1895)
1854–1896	Mary Willis Edgerley (daughter of Samuel, d. 1907)
1855–1864	Archibald Hewan (medical missionary, d. London—1883)
1856–1883	Samuel Howell Edgerley (son of Samuel, d. Duke Town—1883)
1875–1881	Alexander Ross (seceded 1881, d. Duke Town—1884)
1876–1915	Mary Mitchell Slessor
1881–1936	Alexander Cruickshank (d. Aberdeen—1937)
1884–1897	Jessie Forrest Hogg (d. Edinburgh—1940)
1885–1894 and 1902–1907	James Luke (d. Monkseat—4 Nov. 1939)
1887–1893	John Bishop (printer, d. Creek Town—1893)
1889–1903	Charles Ovens (carpenter, d. Portobello—16 Oct. 1919)

1890–1892	William Rae (medical missionary, d. Emuramura—1892)
1890–1892	Charles Watt Morrison (teacher, d. North Carolina—ca.1895)
1891–1893	Elizabeth Jane Hutton (married William Marwick)
1892–1894 and 1898–1900	William Marwick (d. Edinburgh—1940)
1896–1899	Samuel Donaldson Cowan (medical missionary, d. at sea—1899)
1896–1906	Janet Wright (married Peter Rattray)
1898–1906	Peter Rattray (medical missionary, d. Edinburgh—1932)
1899–1899	Annie Macintosh (assistant—January to September only)
1899–1932	Martha M. Chalmers
1900–1916	David Robertson (medical missionary, d. Aberdeen—1933)
1901–1918	Arthur West Wilkie
1902–1903 and 1911–1916	Beatrice Welsh
1903–1930	Martha Peacock (d. Glasgow—1930)
1903–1943	James Kerr Macgregor (d. Calabar 1943)
1905–1930 and 1933–1938	Mina Amess
1911–1912 and 1913–1915	Thomas Hart (accountant)
1911–1919	John William Hitchcock (medical missionary, d. Itu—19 Jan. 1919)
1911–1913 and 1915–1948	Agnes Siddons Young Arnot

Abbreviations

COS	Church of Scotland
CP	Charles Partridge
CSCNWW	Centre for the Study of Christianity in the Non Western World Library, Edinburgh
DUNARC	City Archives, Dundee
DUNLIB	City of Dundee, Local Studies Department, Central Library
DUNMG	McManus Galleries and Museum, Dundee
FMB	Foreign Mission Board
MS	Mary Slessor
NEWCOL	New College Library–University of Edinburgh
NLS-COS	National Library of Scotland, Edinburgh (Church of Scotland)
Record	The name of monthly missions publication changed through the years: *Missionary Record of the United Secession Church; United Presbyterian Missionary Record; The Missionary Record of the United Presbyterian Church; The Missionary Record of the United Free Church of Scotland; The Missionary Record; The Record of the Home and Foreign Mission Work*
RHOD	Bodleian Library of Commonwealth and African Studies, Rhodes House, University of Oxford
SLES	Slessor family, Nigeria
WMM	*The Women's Missionary Magazine*
UED	University of Edinburgh Library, Department of Special Collections
YALE	Day Missions Library, Yale Divinity School

Bibliography

Achebe, Chinua. *Morning Yet on Creation Day*. London: Heinemann Educational Books, 1975.

Afigbo, A. E. "The Calabar Mission and the Aro Expedition of 1901–1902." *Journal of Religion in Africa* 5, no. 2 (1973), 94–106.

Agbodo, Okiemute. Review of "Mary Slessor Resurrects in *Amana-Mba*. ThisDayOnline .com, November 16, 2004. No pages. Accessed February 26, 2008. Online: http:// tinyurl.com/34kfwn.

Ajayi, Jacob F. Ade. "The Sudan Party." in "Henry Martyn Lecture III: Crowther and Trade on the Niger." No pages. Accessed February 28, 2008. Online: http:// www.martynmission.cam.ac.uk/Cajay3b.htm.

Ajayi, J. F. Ade. *Tradition and Change in Africa: The Essays of J. F. Ade Ajayi*, edited by Toyin Falola. Trenton, New Jersey and Asmara, Eritrea: Africa World Press, Inc., 2000.

———. *Christian Missions in Nigeria 1841–1891: The Making of a New Elite*. Evanston, IL: Northwestern University Press, 1969.

Akak, Eyo Okon. *Efiks of Old Calabar*. Calabar: Akak & Sons, 1983.

Amaury Talbot, D[orothy]. *Woman's Mysteries of a Primitive People: The Ibibios of Southern Nigeria*. London: Cassell, 1915.

Amaury Talbot, P[ercy]. *In the Shadow of the Bush*. London: William Heinemann, 1912.

———. *Life in Southern Nigeria: The Magic, Beliefs and Customs of the Ibibio Tribe*. London: Frank Cass, 1923.

Anene, J. C. *Southern Nigeria in Transition, 1885–1906*. London: Cambridge University Press, 1966.

Anene, Joseph C. and Godfrey Brown, eds. *Africa in the Nineteenth and Twentieth Centuries: A Handbook for Teachers and Students*. Lagos: Thomas Nelson & Sons and University of Ibadan, 1966.

Antia, Asuquo Udo. *Obong Udo Antia II of Ikot Aba: His Households and Times in Ibiono Ibom*. Ibadan, Nigeria: University of Ibadan, 2002.

Astrachan, Anthony. "Atrocities and Massacres Feared in Nigerian Civil War." *International Herald Tribune*. February 1, 1968, 3.

Ayandele, E. A. *The Missionary Impact on Modern Nigeria, 1842–1914*. New York: Humanities Press, Longman Group, 1966.

Aye, Efiong U. *The Efik People*. Calabar, Nigeria: Glad Tidings Press, 2000.

———. "Foundations of Presbyterianism among the Calabar clans." In *A Century and a Half of Presbyterian Witness, 1846–1996*, edited by Ogbu U. Kalu. Lagos: Ida-Ivory Press, 1996.

———. *Old Calabar through the Centuries*. Calabar. Nigeria: Hope Waddell Press, 1967.

———. *Hope Waddell Training Institution: Life and Work (1894–1978)*. Calabar, Nigeria: Paico, 1986.

Bibliography

Barber, E. L. "An address by E. L. Barber at the Old Settlers Reunion in Troy Township, Indiana, September 3, 1881." In *History of Whitley and Noble Counties* 1, edited by Weston Goodspeed and Charles Blanchard, 226–34. Chicago: F. A. Battey, 1882.

Beaton, Beverly A. "Agnes Gollan—Modern Pioneer." *Presbyterian Record* (Canada) (October 1960). [PCCARC]

Beattie, John. "The Royal Day in Calabar." *World wide News of the Missions of the Church of Scotland* (March 1956). [NEWCOL]

Beatts, John. "Dundee Life in Days Gone By." A facsimile of sections of *The Municipal History of the Royal Burgh of Dundee*. Dundee: Winter, Duncan and Co., 1878.

Beaver, R. Pierce. "Pioneer Single Women Missionaries." *Occasional Bulletin* 4, no.12 (September 30, 1953). New York: Missionary Research Library.

Bedwell, Horace. *See* Edward M. Falk.

Beeton, Isabella. *The Book of Household Management*. No pages. Accessed February 28, 2008. Online: http://tinyurl.com/2894ng. (Originally London: S. O. Beeton, 1861)

Bendigo. *See* Richard Studeny.

Benge, Janet and Geoff Benge. *Mary Slessor: Forward into Calabar*. Seattle: YWAM Publishing, 1999.

Bennett, Alan. *A Working Life: Child Labour Through the 19th Century*. Poole, Dorset: Waterfront Publications, 1991.

"The Berlin Conference: The General Act of Feb. 26, 1885." No pages. Accessed February 28, 2008. Online: http://tinyurl.com/3dzgzq.

Birkett, Dea. *Mary Kingsley, Imperial Adventuress*. London: Macmillan Academic and Professional, 1992.

"Black and White in Britain: Racist Ideas." No pages. Accessed February 28, 2008. Online: http://tinyurl.com/2rrzg4.

Blackburn, Helen. "Baxter's Half-Time School." In *Baxter's of Dundee*, 61–72, edited by A. J. Cooke. Dundee: University of Dundee, 1980.

Blunt, Alison, and Gillian Rose, eds. *Writing Women and Space*. New York and London: The Guildford Press, 1994.

Bowers, Joyce M. "Roles of Married Women Missionaries: A Case Study." *International Bulletin of Missionary Research* (January 1984) 4–7.

Bowie, Fiona et al., eds. *Women and Missions: Past and Present: Anthropological and Historical Perceptions*. Oxford: Berg Publishing, 1993.

Boyce, Rubert W. *Mosquito or Man? The Conquest of the Tropical World*, 3rd ed. London: John Murray, 1910.

Boyd, J. D. *The Mary Slessor Memorial Window*. Dundee: Harley & Cox, 1953. [DUNMG]

Brian O'Brien, pseud. *See* Albert H. Young-O'Brien.

Brantlinger, Patrick. *Rule of Darkness: British Literature and Imperialism, 1830–1914*. Ithaca and London: Cornell University Press, 1988.

Brooks, R. B. *See* Edward M. Falk.

Brown, Gordon. "The Economics of Hope." Address delivered to the General Assembly of the Church of Scotland, May 10, 1999. No pages. Accessed November 9, 2000. Online: http://www.j2000scot.org/news/007brown.html. (No longer available.)

Bruce-Chwatt, L.J. and J. M. Bruce-Chwatt. "Malaria and yellow fever." In *Health in Tropical Africa During the Colonial Period*, 48–51, edited by E. E. Sabben-Clare et al. Oxford: Clarendon Press, 1980.

Buchan, James. *The Expendable Mary Slessor*. Edinburgh: The Saint Andrews Press, 1980.

Cairns, John. "Melancholy Interlude." *Devon Life* 20 (December 1984) 26–27. [TOPMUS]

Callaway, Helen. *Gender, Culture and Empire: European Woman in Colonial Nigeria*. Urbana and Chicago: University of Illinois Press, 1987.

Campbell, Olwen. *Mary Kingsley, A Victorian in the Jungle*. London: Methuen, 1957.

Christian, Carol, and Gladys Plummer. *God and One Redhead*. London: Hodder & Stoughton, 1970.

Christie, W. M., comp. "Annals of The Calabar Mission, 1846–1945: A Skeleton for the Historian" Unpublished handwritten record. n.d. (ca. 1946) [NEWCOL]

Clough, Raymond Gore. *Oil River Traders*. London: C. Hurst, 1972.

Comaroff, Jean and John Comaroff. *Of Revelation and Revolution: Christianity, Colonialism, and Consciousness in South Africa*. Chicago and London: The University of Chicago Press, 1991.

———. *Of Revelation and Revolution: The Dialectics of Modernity on a South African Frontier*. Chicago and London: The University of Chicago Press, 1997.

"Commemoration of Mary Slessor Fifty Years After Her Death: Notes for Use of Teachers & Preachers." Aberdeen: University of Aberdeen, 1965. [CSCNWW]

Conference of West African Protestant Missionaries Held at Gaboon, February 1876. Calabar: Hope Waddell Press, 1876.

Cook, G. C. "Doctor David Livingstone FRS (1813–1873): 'the fever' and other medical problems of mid-nineteenth century Africa." *Journal of Medical Biography* 2 (1994), 33–43.

Cooke, A. J., ed. *Baxter's of Dundee*. Dundee: University of Dundee, 1980.

Costello, Sean and Tom Johnston, eds. "Mary Slessor." In *Famous Last Words: Two Centuries of Obituaries from The Scotsman*. Edinburgh: Mercat Press, 1996, 50–53.

The Courier. "The City by Glen and Sea: Dundee," 16–17, n.d. (after 1960) [DUNLIB]

Cracknell, Kenneth. *Justice, Courtesy and Love, Theologians and Missionaries Encountering World Religions, 1846–1914*. London: Epworth Press, 1995.

Crawley, Alfred Ernest. "Oath, Introductory and Primitive." In *Encyclopedia of Religion and Ethics*. Vol. 9. New York: Scribner's Sons, 1919, 430–34.

Cromarty, Deas, pseud. *See* Elizabeth Sophia Watson.

Cunningham, Joanne. "Hippo Horror!" *Diver* (September1996). No pages. Accessed February 28, 2008. Online: http://tinyurl.com/34uhy7.

Daniel, W. Harrison. "Patterns in Mission Preaching in the United Presbyterian Church of Scotland Mission to Calabar, 1846–1895." *Scottish Institute of Missionary Studies* 8–9, (1992–1993) 29–47.

Dean, John Taylor. Information regarding MS provided by Mrs. C. Duff, 1993. [DUNMG]

Dickens, Charles. *Dombey and Son*. In *Oxford Illustrated Dickens*, Oxford: Oxford University Press, 1991 edition.

Di Domenico, Catherine D., and Stephanie McDermott. "Mary Slessor's Letters: Images and Reflections." *The Nigerian Field*, 65 (2000) 115–28.

Dike, Onwunka. *Trade and Politics in the Niger Delta, 1830–1885*. First published by Oxford University Press, 1956. Reprint, Westport, CT: Greenwood Press, 1981.

Dowkontt, George D. *Murdered Millions*, New York: The Medical Missionary Record, 1894.

Drury, Paul. "The Great and the Good." *Life and Work Magazine* (January 2001). Edinburgh: Church of Scotland. An interview with Francis Udom, great-grandson of Mary Slessor.

Duff, Mrs. C. *See* John Taylor Dean.

Duke, Donald, Governor of Cross River State, Nigeria. Letter of Appreciation in honor of Mary Slessor, January 2000. [SLES]

"Dundee Women." City Centre Trail, Dundee, n.d. (ca. 1999). [DUNLIB]

Du Plessis, J. *The Evangelisation of Pagan Africa*. Cape Town: J. C. Juta, 1929.

Eastern Nigeria Ministry of Information. "Social Progress." In *Eastern Nigeria*. Enugu: Independence ed.(1960) 62–64.

Ejezie, G. Chuks, ed. *Mary Slessor Journal of Medicine* 1, no. 1, April 1998. Courtesy of Dr. Ejezie, July 23, 2003.

Ekechi, F. K. "Colonialism and Christianity in West Africa: The Igbo Case, 1900–1915." *Journal of African History* 12, no.1 (1971) 103–15.

Ekeh, Peter P., ed. "The Contents and Character of British Colonial Treaties of 1884 and 1894 with the Itsekiri of Nigeria's Western Niger Delta." Urhobo Historical Society. No pages. Accessed February 28, 2008. Online: http://tinyurl.com/yqut83.

Ema, A. J. Udo. "The Ekpe Society." *Nigeria Magazine*, no.16 (1958) 314.

Eme, Nwachuku. "From Heathenism to Christianity." Typescript (March 1958). [DUNLIB]

Enock, Esther E. *The Missionary Heroine of Calabar: A Story of Mary Slessor*. Fort Washington, PA: Christian Literature Crusade, 1937.

Enugwu-Agidi Progressive Union USA. Quoting G. A. Odenigwe from "the new Structure of Local Government in the East Central State." No pages. Accessed February 28, 2008. Online: http://www.enugwu-agidi.org/ea_history_admin.html.

Essien, Okon E. *Ibibio Names*. Ibadan, Nigeria: Daystar Press, 1986.

———. *A Grammar of the Ibibio Language*, Ibadan: University Press, 1990.

Essien, Ufot. "Kids Who Tapped Their Roots." AllAfrica.com. No pages. Accessed January 27, 2004. Online: http://allafrica.com/stories/200009250232.html. (Requires subsctiption.)

Falk, Edward M. "Falk Papers," Falk/Slessor/Brooks/Bedwell letters (September 1–12, 1910) MSS Afr. s. 1000 (1) Falk, f. 4, 5, 7, 8. Bodleian Library. [RHOD]

Felter, Henry Wickes and John Uri Lloyd, eds. *King's American Dispensatory* (by Dr. John King, 1898). "Physostigma" (Calabar Bean). No pages. Accessed February 28, 2008. Online: http://tinyurl.com/35yc2a.

Forde, Daryll, ed. *Efik Traders of Old Calabar*. New York: Oxford University Press, 1956.

Foreign Mission Board, letters to missionaries, MS7654–7959,1874–1915. [FMB, NLS-COS]

"Francis Learns About Mary." *Evening Telegraph and Post*, Dundee (April 10, 2001).

Fraser, Donald. "The Master Missionary: A Study of David Livingstone's Life and Influence." *The Missionary Record* 13 (1913), 109–21.

Friesen, J. Stanley. *Missionary Responses to Tribal Religions at Edinburgh, 1910*. New York: Peter Lang, 1996.

Fry, Michael. *The Scottish Empire*. East Linton: Tuckwell Press, 2001.

Gailey, Harry A. *The Road to Aba: A Study of British Administrative Policy in Eastern Nigeria*. New York: New York University Press, 1970.

Gammie, Alexander. *Cruickshank of Calabar*. London: Pickering & Inglis, n.d., (ca. 1940).

Gikandi, Simon. *The Maps of Englishness: Writing Identity in the Culture of Colonialism*. New York: Columbia University Press, 1996.

Goldie, Hugh. *Calabar and its Mission*. Edinburgh: Oliphant, Anderson & Ferrier, 1890.

———. *Dictionary of the Efik Language*. Ridgewood, NJ: The Gregg Press, 1964. Reprint of 1886 edition.

———. *Memoir of King Eyo VII. of Old Calabar: A Christian King in Africa.* Old Calabar: United Presbyterian Mission Press, 1894.

Gray, Richard. *Black Christians & White Missionaries.* New Haven and London: Yale University Press, 1990.

Greenlee, James G. and Charles M. Johnston. *Good Citizens: British Missionaries and Imperial States, 1870–1918.* Montreal: McGill-Queens University Press, 1999.

Grieve, Mrs. M. "Calabar Bean." In *Botanical.com: A Modern Herbal.* No pages. Accessed February 28, 2008. Online: http://tinyurl.com/25w36h.

Hackett, Rosalind I. J. *Religion in Calabar: The Religious Life and History of a Nigerian Town.* New York: Mouton de Gruyter, 1989.

Hargreaves, John D. *Aberdeenshire to Africa, Northeast Scots and British Overseas Expansion.* Aberdeen: Aberdeen University Press, 1981.

Harlan, Louis and Raymond Smock, eds. *The Booker T. Washington Papers.* Urbana: University of Illinois Press. Vol. 9 (1906-1908), 1980, 626. Accessed February 28, 2008. Online: http://tinyurl.com/36zqqf.

Hart, Thomas. Correspondence with W. P. Livingstone, 1915. [NEWCOL]

———. "Visiting Mary Slessor at Odoro Ikpe, July 1914." Box 52.5.4. [NEWCOL]

Hastings, Adrian. *The Church in Africa, 1450–1950.* Oxford: Clarendon Press, 1994.

Hewat, Elizabeth G. K. *Vision and Achievement 1796–1956: A History of the Foreign Missions of the Churches United in the Church of Scotland.* Edinburgh: Thomas Nelson & Sons, 1960.

Hiebert, Paul G. "Missions and Anthropology: A Love/Hate Relationship." *Missiology* 6, no. 2 (April 1978) 165–80.

"Hiram Maxim." In "Education on the Internet & Teaching History Online." No pages. Accessed February 28, 2008. Online: http://www.spartacus.schoolnet.co.uk/FWWmaxim.htm.

Hobsbawm, E. J. *The Age of Empire, 1875–1914.* New York: Pantheon Books, 1987.

Hogg, Jessie F. *The Story of the Calabar Mission.* Edinburgh and London: Oliphant, Anderson & Ferrier, 1902.

Hogg, William Richey. "The Rise of Protestant Missionary Concern, 1517–1914." In *The Theology of the Christian Mission,* edited by Gerald H. Anderson, 95–111. London: SCM Press Ltd., 1961.

Hollett, David. *The Conquest of the Niger by Land and Sea.* Abergavenny, Gwent: P. M. Heaton Publishing, 1995.

Holman, Arthur R. Note regarding Mary Slessor memorial at graves of her mother and sister (1959). [TOPMUS]

Howard, Cecil. *Mary Kingsley.* London: Hutchinson of London, 1957.

Hudson, J. Harrison, et al. *Let the Fires Burn: A Study of R. M. McCheyne, Robert Annan, and Mary Slessor.* Dundee: Handsel Publications, 1978.

Hutchinson, Thomas J. *Impressions of West Africa.* London: Longman, Brown, Green, Longmans, & Roberts, 1858. Reprint, London: Frank Cass, 1970.

Hutton, Elizabeth. *See* Elizabeth Marwick.

Huxley, Elspeth. *The African Poison Murders.* New York: Viking, 1988 (Harper & Brothers, 1940).

Ibiam, Francis. "Winning Nigeria with the Gospel." *Presbyterian Record* (Canada) (May 1958). [PCCARC]

Ikwe Nche Research Organization. "Committee on Genocide," 30–39. Accessed February 28, 2008. Online: http://tinyurl.com/3brm6s.

Isichei, Elizabeth. *A History of Christianity in Africa*, Grand Rapids, MI: Wm. B. Eerdmans Publishing Co., 1995.

Iwe, N. S. S. *Christianity: Culture and Colonialism in Africa*. Port Harcourt: College of Education, 1979.

Jeffreys, M. D. W. "Mary Slessor—Magistrate." *The West African Review* 21 (June 1950) 628–29; (July 1950) 802–5.

———. *Old Calabar and Notes on the Ibibio Language*. Calabar: H.W.T.I. Press, 1935.

———. "Witchcraft in Calabar Province," *African Studies* 25 (1966) 95–100.

"John Pounds" (Ragged Schools). in "Teaching History Online." No pages. Accessed February 28, 2008. Online: http://tinyurl.com/3bkaa8.

Johnson, E. H. "Letter from Lagos." *Presbyterian Record* (Canada) (ca.1956), 16–17, 31. [PCCARC]

Johnston, Alex. *The Life and Letters of Sir Harry Johnston*. London: Jonathan Cape / New York: Jonathan Cape and Harrison Smith, 1929.

Johnston, G. Deane. "An Accepted Invitation to Africa." *Presbyterian Record* (Canada) (1954). [PCCARC]

Johnston, Geoffrey. *Of God and Maxim Guns: Presbyterianism in Nigeria, 1846–1966*. Ontario: Wilfred Laurier University Press, SR 8, 1988.

Johnston, Harry H. *The Story of My Life*. Indianapolis: Bobbs-Merrill Co., 1923.

Johnston, James. "Mary M. Slessor, the 'Uncrowned Queen' of Old Calabar." Glasgow: Scottish Temperance League, 1914. [DUNARC]

Jones, G. I. *The Trading States of the Oil Rivers: A Study of Political Development in Eastern Nigeria*. London: International African, 1964.

———. "Who Are the Aro?" *Nigerian Field* (July 1939) 100–103.

"Ju-ju Curse Broken Now, Eme Reports." *Presbyterian Record* (Canada) (October 1960). [PCCARC]

Kalu, Ogbu U., ed. *A Century and Half of Presbyterian Witness in Nigeria, 1846–1996*. Lagos: Ida-Ivory Press, 1996.

———, ed. *The History of Christianity in West Africa*. New York: Longman Group, 1980.

———. "The Peter Pan Syndrome: Aid and Selfhood of the Church in Africa." *Missiology* 3, no. 1 (January 1975) 15–29.

Kapuscinski, Ryszard. *The Shadow of the Sun*. New York: Alfred A. Knopf, 2001.

Kingsley, Mary. "The Development of Dodos." *National Review* (March 1896) 66–79.

———. "The Liquor Traffic with West Africa," *Fortnightly Review* (April 1898) 537–60.

———. *Travels in West Aftrica*, London: Macmillan, 1897. Reprinted with an introduction by Elizabeth Claridge by Boston: Beacon Press. Page references are to the 5th ed., 1988.

———. *West African Studies*, New York: Barnes & Noble, third ed., 1964. First published by Macmillan in 1899.

Kirby, Jon P. "Popular Problem-solving and Inculturation in Dagbon, Ghana." In *Life and Death Matters: The Practice of Inculturation in Africa*, edited by Anthony J. Gittins. Nettetal: Steyler Verlag, 2000.

Klein, Herbert S. *The Atlantic Slave Trade*. Cambridge: Cambridge University Press, 1999.

Knox, William. *Lives of Scottish Women: Women and Scottish Society, 1800–1980*. Edinburgh: Edinburgh University Press, 2006.

———. "Mary Slessor: Naïve Imperialist?" Address at Scottish Women's History Network conference, University of Strathclyde, May 25, 2002.

Kulp, Philip M., ed. *Women Missionaries in Cultural Change: Studies in Third World Societies* No. 40. Williamsburg, VA: College of William and Mary, 1987.

Kunhiyop, Samuel Waje. "Poverty: Good News for Africa." *Africa Journal of Theology* 20, no.1, 2001.

"Lack of Interest is Hurting Missions." *Globe and Mail*, Toronto (May 2, 1960). [PCCARC]

Lane, Tony. *The Merchant Seamen's War*. Manchester and New York: Manchester University Press, 1990.

Langridge, Neil. "Charles Partridge." No pages. Accessed February 28, 2008. Online: http://www.stowmarket-history.co.uk/charles_partridge.htm.

Lartey, Emmanuel, et al., eds. *The Church and Healing, Echoes from Africa*. Frankfurt am Main: Peter Lang, 1994.

Latham, A. J. H. *Old Calabar, 1600–1891*. Oxford: Clarendon Press, 1973.

———. "Scottish Missionaries & Imperialism at Calabar." *Nigeria Magazine*, no.132–33 (1950) 47–55.

Lenman, Bruce, et al. *Dundee, Its Textile Industry, 1850–1914*. Dundee: Abertay Historical Society, 1969.

Livingstone, David. *A Popular Account of Dr. Livingstone's Expedition to the Zambesi and Its Tributaties, and of the Discovery of the Lakes Shirwa & Nyassa, 1858–1864*. London: John Murray, 1865. No pages. Accessed February 28, 2008. Online: http://tinyurl.com/yvwfno.

———. "Lecture II," December 5, 1857. In *Livingstone's Cambridge Lectures*, edited by William Monk. London: Bell & Daldy, 1858.

Livingstone, W. P. *Mary Slessor of Calabar, Pioneer Missionary*, 7th ed. London: Hodder & Stoughton, 1916. (Also Grand Rapids: Zondervan,1984, 359–64.)

Lowe, John. *Medical Missions: Their Place and Power*, 5th ed. New York: Fleming H. Revell, 1894.

Lugard, Edward. "Journal Jottings," December 9–13, 1912, MSS Brit. Emp. s. 72. [RHOD]

Luke, James. *Pioneering in Mary Slessor Country*. London: The Epworth Press, 1929.

Macarthur, Daniel E. Letter to Daniel M. Slessor, April 12, 1954. [SLES]

Macdonald, W. M. "Mary Slessor—Pioneer Missionary," ca. 1964. [DUNLIB]

Mackenzie, Catherine. *Mary Slessor, Servant to the Slave*. Ross-shire, Scotland: Christian Focus Publications, 2001.

Macrae, Norman C. *The Book of the First Sixty Years, 1895–1955: Hope Waddell Training Institution*. Calabar: Hope Waddell Press, 1956.

Marwick, Elizabeth Hutton. Diaries,1891–1893, Gen. 768. [UED]

Marwick, William. *William and Louisa Anderson*. Edinburgh: Andrew Elliot, 1897.

Mary Slessor Foundation. No pages. Accessed February 28, 2008. Online: http://www.maryslessor.org/index.html; http://www.maryslessor.org/Our_Aims/our_aims.html.

"Mary Slessor of Calabar." Edinburgh: Church of Scotland Overseas Council, 1978. [DUNLIB]

"Mary Slessor of Dundee." *Dundee Courier*, ca.1961. [DUNLIB]

"Mary Slessor's voice heard again." *Dundee Courier*, August 11, 1953. [DUNLIB]

Maxwell, Ian. "Civilisation or Christianity: The Scottish Debate on Mission Methods, 1750–1835." North Atlantic Missiology Project, Position Paper no. 12. Cambridge: University of Cambridge, Centre for Advanced Religious and Theological Studies, 1996.

Mbiti, John S. *African Religions and Philosophy*, 2nd ed. Oxford: Heinemann, International, 1990.

———. *The Crisis of Mission in Africa*. Mukono, Uganda: Uganda Church Press, 1971.

McEwen, Cheryl. "'The Mother of all the Peoples': geographical knowledge and the empowering of Mary Slessor." In *Geography and Imperialism*. M. Bell, et al, eds. Manchester: Manchester University Press, 1995, 125–50.

McFarlan, Donald M. *Calabar: The Church of Scotland Mission, 1846–1946*. London: Thomas Nelson & Sons, 1946.

———. Correspondence with Asibong A.Okon, 1969. [NEWCOL]

McIntosh, Hamish. *Robert Laws, Servant of Africa*. Carberry, Scotland: The Handsel Press, 1993.

Meek, C. K. *Law and Authority in a Nigerian Tribe, A Study in Indirect Rule*. New York: Barnes & Noble, 1937.

Miller, Basil. *Mary Slessor, Heroine of Calabar*. Minneapolis, MN: Bethany House Publishers, 1946.

Milsome, J. R. "Missionary Extraordinary." *The West African Review* 32, no. 401
(1961) 77–79.

Miskell, Louise, et al., eds. *Victorian Dundee: Image and Realities*. East Linton, Scotland: Tuckwell Press, 2000.

The Missionary Record of the United Presbyterian Church, 1877–1915. (Named successively: *United Presbyterian Missionary Record, The Missionary Record of the United Presbyterian Church, Missionary Record of the United Free Church of Scotland, The Record of the Home and Foreign Mission Work*.) [NLS-COS]

Missionary Record of the United Secession Church, 1846. [CSCNWW]

Moorhouse, Geoffrey. *The Missionaries*. Philadelphia: J. P. Lippincott Co., 1973.

Morrison, William. "Medical Work in the Congo." *The Missionary* (April 1906), 178–80.

Mullen, Robert. "Starved to Death." In *Poems by the People*, edited by The People's Journal. Edinburgh: John Menzies, 1849, 5–6.

Nair, Kannan K. *Politics and Society in South Eastern Nigeria 1841–1906, A Study of
Power, Diplomacy and Commerce in Old Calabar*. London: Frank Cass, 1972.

Nasimiyu-Wasike, Anne. "Is Mutuality Possible? An African Response." *Missiology* 29, no. 1, (January 2001).

Nicolson, I. F. *The Administration of Nigeria, 1900–1960: Men, Methods, and Myths*. Oxford: Clarendon Press, 1969.

Offiong, Daniel A. "Conflict Resolution Among the Ibibio of Nigeria." *Journal of Anthropological Research* 53 (1997) 423–41.

———. "The Functions of the Ekpo of the Ibibio of Nigeria." *African Studies Review* 27 (1984a) 72–92.

Ogarepke, M. O. *Historical Perspective of the Presbyterian Church of Nigeria*. Calabar: Masterclass Press, 1996.

Ogilvy, Graham, ed. *Dundee: A Voyage of Discovery*. Edinburgh: Mainstream, 1999.

———. "Dundee: Most Drunken City in the Empire." *The Scotsman*'s "Scotland on Sunday" (2000). No pages. Accessed January 26 2004. Online: http://www.egroups.com/docvault/dundee-history/Dundee_Booze.gif. (Requires subscription.)

Okore, Mgbeke. "The Slessor Legacy: The Voices of Presbyterian Womenfolk." In *Century and a Half of Presbyterian Witness in Nigeria, 1846–1996*, edited by Ogbu Kalu. Lagos: Ida-Ivory Press, 1996.

Okoronkwo, Mazi.Ngozi.Ukwu. "History of the Aros." No pages. Accessed February 28, 2008. Online: http://www.aro-okigbo.com/history_of_the_aros.htm.

Oku, Ekei Essien. *The Kings & Chiefs of Old Calabar (1785–1925)*. Calabar: Glad Tidings Press, 1989.

Oliver, Roland. *Sir Harry Johnstone and the Scramble for Africa*. London: Chatto and Windus, 1957.

Oliver, Caroline. *Western Women in Colonial Africa*. Westport, CT: Greenwood Press, 1982.

Olivier, Sydney. *White Capital and Coloured Labour*. New York: Russell & Russell, 1971. Reprint of London: National Labour Press, 1910.

"Ordeals." *New Advent, Catholic Encyclopedia* New York: Robert Appleton, 1911. Online edition by K. Knight, 2003. No pages. Accessed February 28, 2008. Online: http://www.newadvent.org/cathen/11276b.htm.

Pakenham, Thomas. *The Scramble for Africa, 1876–1912*. New York: Random House, 1991.

Partridge, Charles. *Cross River Natives*. London: Kraus, 1973. Reprint of London: Hutchinson, 1905.

———. Letters from MS. 1905–1914. No pages. Accessed February 28, 2008. Online: http://www.dundeecity.gov.uk/centlib/slessor/letters.htm [DUNLIB]

———. Letter to Chief Librarian, Dundee City Library, August 24, 1950. No pages. Accessed February 28, 2008. Online: http://www.dundeecity.gov.uk/centlib/slessor/letintro.htm. [DUNLIB]

Pemberton, Carrie. "Mary Slessor, Imperialist Mother or Liberating Sister: in post-Colonial Perspective/ or the problem of history and the superfluity of the generosity of God." Paper presented at Cambridge University, 1998. (Courtesy of the author, 2003)

Peterkin, Thomas. "Spirits Above and Spirits Below." In *Dundee, A Voyage of Discovery*, edited by Graham Ogilvy. Edinburgh: Mainstream, 1999.

Peterson, Derek. "Rhetoric of the Word: Bible Translation and Mau Mau in Colonial Central Kenya." In *Missions, Nationalism, and the End of Empire*, edited by Brian Stanley. Grand Rapids and Cambridge: William B. Eerdmans, 2003.

Phipps, William E. *William Sheppard: Congo's African American Livingstone*. Louisville, Kentucky: Geneva Press, 2002.

Porter, Andrew. "'Cultural Imperialism' and Missionary Enterprise." In North Atlantic Missiology Project, Position Paper no. 7. Cambridge: University of Cambridge, Centre for Advanced Religious and Theological Studies, 1996.

———. *The Imperial Horizons of British Protestant Missions, 1880–1914*. (Studies in the History of Christian Missions.) Grand Rapids: Wm. B. Eerdmans, 2003.

Powers, Jessica. "Converting a Savage Mind: Conversion and Civilization," (January 20, 2002) quoting Charles Dickens, "The Niger Expedition." In *The Works of Charles Dickens* 18, *Miscellaneous Papers, Plays and Poems* (New York: Bigelow, Brown and Co., 1920), 56; No Pages. Accessed February 28, 2008. Online: http://tinyurl.com/2tcjv4.

Proctor, J. H. "Serving God and the Empire: Mary Slessor in South-Eastern Nigeria, 1876–1915." *Journal of Religion in Africa* 30, 2000, 46–61.

Record. See *Missionary Record*.

Report of the Centenary Conference on the Protestant Missions of the World held in Exeter Hall (June 9th–19th), London, edited by James Johnston. London: Fleming H. Revell, 1888.

Report of the Missionary Conference : held at Calabar, November, 1911. Calabar: Book Depot, Hope-Wadell Training Institution, 1913.

Ritchie, Ian. "African Theology and Social Change: An Anthropological Approach." Ph.D. diss., McGill University, 1993.

Robertson, Elizabeth. *Mary Slessor, the Barefoot Missionary*. Edinburgh: NMS Publishing, 2001.

Robertson, J. G. "Carlyle: *Sartor Resartus* [1836]." In *The Cambridge History of English and American Literature*. Vol. 13, 1913. No pages. Accessed February 28, 2008. Online: http://tinyurl.com/2yfuwe.

Rochemont, Joan. "In Mary Slessor's Footsteps." *Presbyterian Record* (Canada) (October 1955). [PCCARC]

Ross, Andrew. *David Livingstone: Mission and Empire*, London and New York: Hambledon and London, 2002.

———. "The African Experience: Scientific Racism, Social Darwinism, and the Churches," Position Paper no. 64. Cambridge: University of Cambridge, Centre for Advanced Religious and Theological Studies, 1998.

Rowbotham, Judith. "This is No Romantic Story: Reporting the Work of British Female Missionaries, c. 1850–1910," Position Paper no. 4. Cambridge: University of Cambridge, Centre for Advanced Religious and Theological Studies, 1996.

Sanneh, Lamin. "A Resurgent Church in a Troubled Continent: Review Essay of Bengt Sundkler's *History of the Church in Africa*." *International Bulletin of Missionary Research* 25, no. 3 (July 2001), 113–18.

Shaw, Carol P. "Mary Slessor." In *Famous Scots*, Glasgow: Harper Collins, 1995, 198–99.

Simmons, D. "An Ethnographic Sketch." In *Efik Traders of Old* Calabar, edited by Daryll Forde. New York: Oxford University Press, 1956.

Slessor, Annie descendants. Interview by Jeanette Hardage, Calabar, April 2001. [SLES]

Slessor, Daniel descendants. Interview by Jeanette Hardage, Calabar, April 2001. [SLES]

Slessor, Daniel Henryson McArthur. Letter to Curator, Museums and Fine Arts Galleries, Albert Institute, Dundee, May 27, 1954. [DUNMG]

Slessor, Daniel. Letters to Thomas Hart, 1948–1949. [NEWCOL]

———. "Reminiscences of Miss Mary Slessor." 1958/8380E, June 1958. [DUNLIB]

Slessor, Mary Mitchell. Affidavits regarding adopted children. [DUNMG]

———. Bibles (2) with handwritten commentaries in margins. [DUNMG]

———. Diaries 1911 and 1914. [DUNMG]

———. Lessons, handwritten. ca. 1874. [DUNMG]

———. Letter to Edward Falk, September 1, 1910. Edward M. Falk Papers, MSS Afr. S. 1000, f. 7. [RHOD]

———. Letters to Thomas Hart and Annie McMinn, 1912–1913. [DUNMG; NEWCOL]

———. Letters to Charles Partridge [CP] and Charles Partridge, Sr., 1905–1914. No pages. Accessed February 28, 2008. Online: http://tinyurl.com/2tpypc. [DUNLIB]

———. Letters to Martha Peacock and William Stevenson, 1906–1912. [DUNARC]

———. Letter to Agnes Siddons Young (Arnot), February 24, 1913. [UED]

———. Miscellaneous personal letters, 1872, 1905–1914. [DUNMG; DUNARC]

———. "My Will." [[DUNMG]

———. "The Prodigal Son in Efik." No pages. Accessed February 28, 2008. Online: http://tinyurl.com/29tu3l. [DUNLIB]

Smith, W. J., ed. *A History of Dundee*. Dundee: David Winter & Son, 1973. Reprint of 1873 edition.

Springhall, John. *Decolonization Since 1945: The Collapse of European Overseas Empires.* Houndmills, Hampshire and New York: Palgrave, 2001.

Stanley, Brian. *The Bible and the Flag: Protestant missions and British imperialism in the nineteenth and twentieth centuries.* Leicester: Apollos, 1990.

———. "Mission and Enlightenment: A Re-evaluation," North Atlantic Missiology Project, Position Paper no. 11. Cambridge: University of Cambridge, Centre for Advanced Religious and Theological Studies, 1996.

———, ed. *Missions, Nationalism, and the End of Empire.* Grand Rapids and Cambridge: William B. Eerdmans, 2003.

Stevenson, William. Letter to Martha Peacock, 19 January 1915, MS7959, 286-287. [NLS-COS]

Stewart, Robert. *Old Calabar: A Brief and Homely Memoir of Rev. Thomas Wells Campbell, Missionary and Minister.* Paisley, Scotland: J & R Parlane, 1884.

Strobel, Margaret. *European Women and the Second British Empire.* Bloomington and Indianapolis: Indiana University Press, 1991.

Studeny, Richard. "Bendigo and the Forest Tavern." No pages. Accessed February 28, 2008. Online: http://tinyurl.com/372o4m

Sundkler, Bengt and Christopher Steed. *A History of the Church in Africa.* Cambridge: Cambridge University Press, 2000.

Syme, Ronald. *Nigerian Pioneer: The Story of Mary Slessor.* New York: William Morrow, 1964.

Tayler, Jeffrey. "The Magistrates of Creektown." *Atlantic Monthly* (November 5, 1997). No pages. Accessed February 26, 2008. Online: http://www.theatlantic.com/unbound/abroad/jt971105.htm.

Taylor, Allan. "On Hippos." No pages. Accessed February 28, 2008. Online: http://tinyurl.com/2t8b93.

Taylor, W. H. "Mary Slessor (1848–1915), Pedagogue Extraordinary." *Scottish Education Review* 25, no. 2 (1993), 109–122.

Taylor, William H. *Mission to Educate: A History of the Educational Work of the Scottish Presbyterian Mission in East Nigeria, 1846–1960.* Leiden: E. J. Brill, 1996.

Thomas, Rolla. "Malarial Fever." In *Thomas' Eclectic Practice of Medicine* (Cincinatti, Ohio: Eclectic Medical Institute, 1907). No pages. Accessed February 28, 2008. Online: http://tinyurl.com/3c6jwm.

Thompson, Eileen J. "Prominent Nigerians Visit Canada." *Presbyterian Record* (Canada) (November 1956). [PCCARC]

Thorp, Ellen. *Ladder of Bones.* London: Jonathan Cape, 1956.

Topsham Congregational Church. Notes from church records, including "Mary Slessor" from Barbara Entwistle, president, Topsham Museum, October 2001. [TOPMUS]

Udoh, O. U. "Growing witness among the Ibibio." In *A Century and a Half of Presbyterian Witness, 1846–1996*, 28–49, edited by Ogbu U. Kalu. Lagos: Ida-Ivory Press, 1996.

Uka, E. M. *Missionaries Go Home?* Berne: Peter Lang, 1989.

United Free Church of Scotland. *Women's Foreign Mission, Minutes of Annual Conference of 1915*, DEP 298/148. [NLS-COS]

United Presbyterian Church, Calabar, 25 native members. Letter to The Marquis of Salisbury, H. M. Secretary of State for Foreign Affairs, FO 84/1557, October 16, 1879, 379–80. [PROLON]

United Presbyterian Church Foreign Mission Minutes, etc. "Minutes of Meeting of 25th July, 1899." [CSCNWW]

Waddel, Agnes. *Memorials of Mrs. Sutherland*, Paisley, Scotland: J. & R. Parlane, 1883.

Waddell, Hope Masterton. "Journal," 1855–1856, MS7743. [NLS-COS]

———. *Twenty-nine Years in the West Indies and Central Africa, 1829–1858*. London: T. Nelson & Sons, 1863.

———. *Vocabulary of the Efik or Old Calabar Language: with Prayers and Lessons*. Leipzig: Zentralantiquariat Der Deutschen Demokratischen Republik, 1972. Reprint of Edinburgh: Grant and Taylor, 1849.

Walls, Andrew F. *The Cross-Cultural Process in Christian History*. New York: Orbis Books, 2002.

———. "'The Heavy Artillery of the Missionary': The Domestic Importance of the Nineteenth-Century Medical Missionary." In *The Church and Healing*. Studies in Church History 19, edited by W. J. Sheils, 287–97. Oxford: Basil Blackwell for The Ecclesiastical History Society, 1982.

———. *The Missionary Movement in Christian History*. New York: Orbis, 1996.

———. "The Significance of Christianity in Africa." Friends of St. Colm's Public Lecture, 1989.

Watson, Elizabeth Sophia [Deas Cromarty, pseud.]. "Mary Mitchell Slessor." *British Weekly* (August 1913). [DUNARC]

Watson, Norman. "Emerging from Obscurity: How Dundee Women Have Made Their Mark." In *Dundee: A Voyage of Discovery*, edited by Graham Ogilvy. Edinburgh: Mainstream, 1999.

Wellman, Sam. *Mary Slessor, Queen of Calabar*. Urichsville, OH: Barbour Publishing, 1998.

Whatley, Christopher A., ed. *The Remaking of Juteopolis: Dundee circa 1891–1991*. Dundee: Abertay Historical Society, 1992.

Whatley, Christopher, et al. *The Life and Times of Dundee*. Edinburgh: John Donald, 1993.

Wilkinson, Wendy. "Housing and Health." In *Baxter's of Dundee*, edited by A. J. Cooke. Dundee: University of Dundee, 1980.

Wishart Church and John O'Groats Public House, photo. No pages. Accessed February 28, 2008. Online: http://tinyurl.com/2fg7k2. [DUNLIB]

Withrington, Donald J. *Going to School*. Scotland's Past in Action Series. Edinburgh: National Museums of Scotland, 1997.

The Women's Missionary Magazine, 1901–1916. [CSCNWW]

Woodward, Kenneth, et al. "The Changing Face of the Church." *Newsweek* (April 16, 2001) 46–52.

World Health Organization. "Global Malaria Programme." No pages. Accessed February 28, 2008. Online: http://www.who.int/malaria/.

Wright, David F., et al., general eds. *Dictionary of Scottish Church History & Theology*. Downers Grove, IL: InterVarsity Press, 1993.

Young-O'Brien, Albert H. [Brian O'Brien, pseud.]. *She had a Magic: The Story of Mary Slessor*. New York: E. P. Dutton, 1959.

Zenana Committee. Letter to Mary Slessor, June 29, 1899, MS7671. [NLS-COS]

www.ingramcontent.com/pod-product-compliance
Lightning Source LLC
LaVergne TN
LVHW020527100826
845148LV00010B/1368